Southern Living®

2022 Annual Recipes

DEVILED EGGS
(PAGE 90)

SKILLET RHUBARB-
STRAWBERRY CRISP
WITH SALTED-ALMOND
STREUSEL (PAGE 54)

HEIRLOOM TOMATO-
CRACKER SALAD
(PAGE 106)

CHOCOLATE-PEANUT
BUTTER ICEBOX PIE
(PAGE 182)

BAKED BRIE WITH
POMEGRANATE AND
PISTACHIOS (PAGE 286)

FIELD PEA PASTA
(PAGE 186)

It's Good to Be Gathering Again

Dear Friends,

After a couple of very challenging years, it seems things have finally begun to feel normal again. We're cooking for and gathering with friends and family, going to church potlucks, and celebrating the holidays and special occasions in person instead of over Zoom calls. We're shaking hands and hugging again.

The book you're holding contains every wonderful recipe that graced the pages of *Southern Living* magazine in 2022. Throughout the year, our editors researched the latest trends in the food world, highlighted great restaurants and dishes to try, and celebrated up-and-coming chefs and home cooks bringing the best food our beloved region has to offer. And of course, we're always mindful of the classic favorite dishes of our Southern cooking tradition. As we've done for more than 55 years, our Test Kitchen pros carefully tested and fine-tuned every recipe, so you can be sure every time you step into the kitchen, you'll get great results. If a recipe appears on the pages of *Southern Living,* you can be sure it's worth making and sharing.

Our mission is to inspire and guide our readers to cook together, eat together, and create memories surrounding food. Our "Suppertime" recipes provide busy cooks with simple but delicious family-pleasing meals. "Healthy in a Hurry" recipes are for those days when you're craving fresh food fast. And "Bounty" celebrates the best produce the season has to offer.

We're excited to present our year to you, and we know you'll love having this collection of *Southern Living* recipes at your fingertips, ready and waiting to share the next time you gather with loved ones–whether that's around the kitchen table on a busy weeknight or at a festive celebration.

Lisa Cericola
Deputy Food Editor
Southern Living magazine

Contents

Top-Rated Recipes

We cook, we taste, we refine, we rate—and at the end of each year, our Test Kitchen shares the highest-rated recipes from each issue exclusively with *Southern Living Annual Recipes* readers

January–February

- Fresh Strawberry Truffles (page 15) These sweet treats taste just as good as the store-bought ones (if not better!) and can be whipped up in just 20 minutes. The basic recipe can be modified in many ways to suit your sweet tooth.
- Creamed-Corn Grits (page 22) Every Southern cook has their own recipe for grits, most likely handed down for generations. This one stands out because of its ability to reheat over and over and still maintain its great taste and texture. Make a big batch and serve it throughout the week!
- Chicken-Parmesan Meatballs (page 35) The secret to success in this recipe is using a mixture of white and dark meat—all white meat tends to be too dry. Your family will never know it's not ground beef.
- Cinnamon Swirl Puff Pastry Muffins (page 39) Sugar and spice, and everything nice! These tasty little bites call for only six simple ingredients—including store-bought

CREAMED CORN GRITS

puff pastry sheets. Keep them on hand for a quick breakfast or a lunchbox treat.
- Winter Greens Pesto (page 42) We used kale, collards, and beet greens in this version, but you can use any of your favorite leafy greens and get the same great-tasting result. Serve over pasta, mix into hummus or guacamole, or use as a marinade for chicken or seafood. The possibilities are endless!

March

- Asparagus Ribbon Crostini (page 47) Celebrate spring with this simple and healthy dish. It makes an impressive appetizer, colorful potluck staple, or side dish.
- Sesame Shrimp Stir-Fry (page 57) Your family will ask for seconds of this simple shrimp dish, and it's ready in just 20 minutes. We like to serve it over rice, but it's also great over pasta or all on its own.
- Green Chile-Chicken Soup (page 59) This delicious dish combines a few of our favorite things. The flavorful mix of traditional chicken soup ingredients, enchilada sauce, and green chiles just can't be beat. Make a big batch and freeze for a super-quick weeknight meal when you're short on time.
- Shepherd's Pie with Scalloped Potatoes and Pesto (page 60) Ditch the traditional mashed-potatoes version of the shepherd's pie and give this recipe a try! The potatoes bake to crispy perfection, and the pesto packs in lots of extra flavor.

April

- Caramelized Vidalia Onion Pasta with Herbed Breadcrumbs (page 69) We usually pair garlic with pasta, but we gave sweet Vidalia onions a try here—and wow! The flavors are unbelievable.
- Lovely 'Rita (page 71) Grapefruit juice, rosemary, and blanco tequila are the stars of the show in this refreshing spin on the classic margarita. Cheers!
- Sausage-Pimiento Cheese Pasta Rollups (page 85) We recommend using chicken sausage in this recipe. It has less fat with no sacrifice to the creaminess of the sauce. Serve it as an appetizer or a main dish.
- Cast-Iron Potato Kugel (page 89) This savory casserole is traditionally served for Passover. Made from potatoes, eggs, and onions, it's also great for brunch any time of year.
- Spicy Fried Deviled Eggs (page 92) If you think you've found the perfect deviled egg recipe, think again! We topped ours with spicy creole seasoning, but if heat isn't for you, simply skip this step. Be prepared to be amazed!

May

- Mint Julep Sweet Tea (page 101) We took two Southern staples and combined them into one refreshing cocktail. You can skip the bourbon if you'd like—the nonalcoholic version is just as delicious.
- Cajun-Style Potato Salad (page 103) We took this potato salad to the next level by adding some Cajun spice, bacon, bell peppers, dill pickles, and a few more surprise ingredients. You'll definitely want to give it a try.

BANANA
PUDDING
CHEESECAKE
BARS

- Chocolate Icebox Cake (page 112) Toasted almonds and a dusting of cocoa make for a beautiful presentation of this classic cake. It's definitely worthy of a special occasion.
- Banana Pudding Cheesecake Bars (page 115) A splash of banana liqueur adds a tropical punch and elevates these bars from classic banana pudding to something extra special.
- Oven-Baked Omelet (page 121) When company is coming, look to this recipe for your new go-to breakfast or brunch. Unlike some breakfast casseroles that need to be made in advance, this updated classic is on the table in less than an hour.

June–July

- Grilled Green Tomatoes with Jalapeño-Honey Vinaigrette (page 133) With dozens of new tomato recipes to choose from, it was hard picking our favorite, but the jalapeño-honey vinaigrette in this recipe put it over the top. It's great served with farm-fresh tomatoes, but it can also be used on a traditional salad or as a marinade for chicken or fish.
- Lemon-Dill Chicken Skillet (page 154) The secret to perfection in this dish is using chicken thighs. The potatoes absorb the drippings, and the end result is absolutely delicious!

- Chipotle Chicken Tacos (page 155) Take Taco Tuesday to a new level with this simple Instant Pot recipe. If you don't have a multicooker, simply grab a rotisserie chicken, mix the ingredients together, and cook on your stovetop.
- Pasta with Pancetta, Artichokes, and Roasted Red Peppers (page 156) Add grilled chicken, steak, or shrimp to this sensational summer salad to take it from side dish to main dish! We love using marinated artichokes rather than plain—it adds so much flavor to an otherwise simple dish.
- Biscuit-Bowl Biscuits (page 163) One of our favorite biscuit recipes of all time. It's been handed down for generations, calls for only three simple ingredients, and takes just 35 minutes from start to finish. You have to try it to believe it!

August

- Roasted Tomato Quiche (page 167) Whether it's breakfast, brunch, lunch, or dinner, this quiche recipe fills the bill! Be sure to remove the tomato seeds for the best results.
- Blackberry-Buttermilk Sherbet (page 170) It takes a bit of time to make a frozen dessert from scratch instead of picking up a pint at the grocery store, but it's definitely worth the effort. Spend a few minutes to prep the ingredients, then let the freezer do the rest of the work! We love fresh blackberries in this simple recipe, but you can use fresh raspberries or strawberries if you prefer.
- Blackened Shrimp Rice Bowl (page 180) All the fresh flavors of the summer season combine in one versatile, beautiful, and hearty dish. You can make it your own by serving over rice, quinoa, or romaine lettuce.
- Crispy Fried Pickle Spears (page 183) Simply irresistible! These crispy, crunchy treats will be your new go-to appetizer. They pair perfectly with simple ranch dressing.

September

- Deep-Dish Loaded Hash Brown Casserole (page 197) Your house will fill with the comforting aroma of this casserole baking in the oven. You won't need to call everyone to the breakfast table—they'll come running!
- Golden Delicious Sticky Buns (page 210) The name gives away our secret ingredient! You'll want to make a double batch because they'll disappear quickly.
- Beef Fajitas (page 216) Give Taco Tuesday a more sophisticated spin and serve fajitas this week! You can use beef as we did here, substitute with chicken or shrimp, or leave the meat out altogether and go vegetarian.
- Broccoli-Parmesan Soup with Grilled Cheese Croutons (page 223) We updated our classic version of broccoli soup with a little Italian flair. Give it a try when soup season rolls around.
- Chocolate Chip-Pumpkin Muffins (page 229) Celebrate the arrival of fall with this big-batch recipe. They freeze well and are great to have on hand for the holidays.
- Vegetarian Skillet Chili (page 228) It takes just 30 minutes and one pan to whip up this speedy and delicious chili recipe. We like to top it off with fresh avocado and lime. Yum!

BEEF FAJITAS

SWEET AND TANGY ROASTED PUMPKIN SALAD

October

- Sweet and Tangy Roasted Pumpkin Salad (page 237) An unlikely coupling, but pumpkin and mixed greens blend so perfectly in this amazing dish. The beautiful colors will brighten your fall dinner table.
- Deep-Dish Ham Pot Pie (page 245) We love taking classic recipes and giving them a modern twist—this is hands down one of our favorites. Give it a try this holiday season, and feel free to put your own creative spin on it!
- Crispy Chicken with Sweet Potato Fries and Green Beans (page 252) This is a great weeknight go-to recipe. You only need 15 minutes prep time and a sheet pan, and your oven does the work.
- Apple Dumplings with Bourbon-Caramel Sauce (page 253) These decadent little treats are as impressive-looking as they are delicious. Make an extra batch of the bourbon-caramel sauce to keep on hand to serve over ice cream or a slice of apple pie.
- Skillet Baked Almond-and-Banana Oatmeal (page 249) Your whole family will love this hearty, nutrient-packed breakfast. You'll never want "ordinary" oatmeal again!

November

- Brussels Sprout Spoon Bread (page 257) What a great way to trick your picky eaters into eating their vegetables! You can add your favorite mix of greens if you're not a fan of Brussels sprouts and get the same great result.
- Sweet Potato Cobbler (page 266) Give your traditional sweet potato pie a break this holiday season and serve this cobbler instead. We love to serve it warm with a dollop of vanilla ice cream.
- Perfect Make-Ahead Macaroni and Cheese (page 272) You can make this crowd pleaser the day before and it still will turn out perfect. We guarantee rave reviews!
- Cheesy Mushroom-Spinach Mini Frittatas (page 281) Start your day off right with these protein-packed little muffins. They freeze well, so you can make a big batch and enjoy them all season long.
- Spiced Glazed Pecans (page 283) After you try this recipe, you'll never use plain pecans again! Keep them on hand during the holidays for topping your pies and cakes, or wrap them up to give as gifts.

SWEET POTATO COBBLER

December

- Baked Brie with Pomegranate and Pistachios (page 286) Sure to be the star of your next get-together, this colorful and hearty appetizer is best served with freshly toasted baguette slices.
- Glazed Spiral-Cut Ham (page 292) We've picked three of our favorite flavor-packed glazes to go along with this holiday ham. Find your favorite and follow the simple steps for preparation, and your holiday meal planning will be complete.
- Spiraled Sweet Potato Gratin (page 297) It takes a bit of time to put together this show-stopper, but we guarantee it'll be worth the extra effort.
- Millionaire Candies (page 310) These little candies are worthy of their name. They call for only five ingredients and 25 minutes of prep time and can be kept fresh for 2 weeks. Wrap up a few in clear bags and festive ribbon for those last-minute gifts.
- Gingered Toddy (page 326) This festive cocktail is ready in just 5 minutes—perfect for the holidays, game days, or any day in between!
- Ivy's Favorite Pound Cake (page 328) This recipe has a few secret ingredients that takes basic pound cake to a whole new level! We also included a mini-loaf variation. Wrap up a mini loaf in a tea towel for a gift any time of the year!

January–February

How Sweet!

Same old chocolate-dipped strawberries? Not this year

MIX IT UP
One batch of this recipe can be split in half to make two different flavors of truffles.

Fresh Strawberry Truffles

ACTIVE 20 MIN. - TOTAL 20 MIN., PLUS 1 HOUR, 30 MIN. CHILLING

MAKES 24

- 3   medium fresh strawberries, trimmed
- 2⅓ cups (14 oz.) white chocolate chips (from 2 [11-oz.] pkg.)
- 1   Tbsp. heavy whipping cream
- 1   tsp. grated lemon zest (from 1 lemon)
- ¼   tsp. kosher salt
      Red liquid food coloring (optional)
- 2   Tbsp. pink sanding sugar
- 2   Tbsp. white sanding sugar

1. Place strawberries in a food processor or blender; process until smooth, stopping to scrape down sides as needed, about 30 seconds. Pour through a fine mesh strainer into a small bowl, pressing pulp with the back of a spoon to release all juices; discard pulp. Measure ¼ cup strawberry puree.

2. Combine white chocolate chips, whipping cream, and ¼ cup strawberry puree in a medium-size heatproof bowl. Microwave on HIGH in 15-second intervals, stirring after each interval, until melted (mixture will be thick), about 45 to 60 seconds total. Stir in lemon zest and salt until well combined. Stir in food coloring, if desired. Cover with plastic wrap, and refrigerate until firm, about 1½ to 2 hours.

3. Stir together pink and white sanding sugars in a shallow dish. Scoop chilled white chocolate mixture into 24 portions using the large side of a melon baller or a small (about 1¼-inch diameter) cookie scoop. Working with 1 portion at a time and using hands, roll each portion into a ball, and place in sugar mixture, tossing gently to coat fully. Place on a parchment paper-lined baking sheet. Serve immediately, or store in an airtight container in refrigerator up to 1 week or in freezer up to 2 months. Let chilled truffles stand at room temperature 30 minutes before serving. If frozen, thaw truffles in refrigerator overnight.

Tipsy Strawberry Truffles

Prepare recipe as directed, substituting 1 Tbsp. **brandy** and ¼ tsp. **vanilla extract** for zest and substituting ¼ cup finely chopped (using food processor) **freeze-dried strawberries** (from 1 [0.8-oz.] pkg.) for sanding sugars in Step 3.

Strawberry-Coconut Truffles

Prepare recipe as directed, substituting 1 tsp. **coconut extract** for zest in Step 2 and 1¼ cups finely chopped **sweetened flaked coconut** for sanding sugars in Step 3.

Creamy Strawberry-Vanilla Bean Truffles

Prepare recipe as directed, substituting 2 tsp. **vanilla bean paste** for zest in Step 2. Scoop and roll chilled white chocolate mixture into balls as directed in Step 3. Microwave 1 (11-oz.) pkg. **white chocolate chips** in a medium heatproof bowl on HIGH in 30-second intervals, stirring after each interval, until melted, about 1 minute total. Reserve 2 Tbsp. melted white chocolate in a bowl. Using a fork, dip truffles, 1 at a time, in remaining melted white chocolate until fully coated, allowing excess to drip off. Place truffles on a parchment paper-lined baking sheet. Stir **red liquid food coloring** into reserved 2 Tbsp. melted white chocolate until desired color is reached. Using a fork, drizzle pink chocolate mixture over the dipped truffles. (Or transfer pink chocolate mixture to a small zip-top plastic freezer bag, cut a small hole in corner of bag, and pipe over dipped truffles.) Let truffles stand at room temperature until chocolate sets, about 15 minutes.

Rising and Shining

In Charlotte, North Carolina, Subrina and Greg Collier have transformed the local dining scene and manifested a vision that uplifts Black chefs beyond the city limits

SUBRINA AND GREG COLLIER move as a unit—always have. About a decade of business partnership, marriage, triumph, loss, and trial and error has created something in them that resembles a well-tended garden that's free of weeds and has plenty of space to grow. They are companion plants thriving next to one another and seeding the next generation.

Their lauded Charlotte, North Carolina, restaurant, Leah & Louise, named after Greg's late sister and grandmother respectively, opened in 2020. The "modern juke joint" pays homage to the South and the ingredients that make up the Black culinary canon through dishes such as the Mud Island (blackened catfish served with smoked catfish stew, pickled field peas, and rice grits).

At Leah & Louise, the Colliers have cultivated a place that celebrates Black culture and their place in it. They also mentor young talent like Courtney Evans, the 22-year-old co-head chef who joined the opening team. "They are beacons," says Evans, who had never worked in a Black-owned restaurant before Leah & Louise, much less a kitchen with Black women at the center. "That connection was beyond words."

As one of the six founding members of Soul Food Sessions, a 2016 pop-up series that highlighted the talents of Black chefs, Greg embraced the notion that representation matters. In 2018, the vision grew and Soul Food Sessions hit the road, eventually landing in New York City at the James Beard House in 2019. Greg's dish, hoecakes with catfish rillettes, showed how he cooks and what he loves without the confines of the soul food stereotype.

"Creating our space and bringing it to the James Beard House was huge," says Subrina, who soon began embracing other opportunities like the James Beard Women's Entrepreneurial Leadership program, which inspired her to continue using her voice to shape the environment she wanted to see.

By this time, a slew of appearances at food festivals had emboldened Subrina to act on a new vision. "The older I became in this industry, the more I understood that everybody has a space," she says. "So I created one that everybody can participate in, but it's rooted in Black foodways."

In October 2021, after they'd spent a tough but successful inaugural year operating Leah & Louise, the first BayHaven Food & Wine Festival descended upon the Queen City honoring Black culinary experts. People came from all over the country to attend cooking and cocktail demos, tasting tents, and ticketed dinners.

Chef Keith Rhodes of Catch Restaurant in Wilmington, North Carolina, was a participant at BayHaven, and he called the experience mind-blowing. "Greg and Subrina have always been passionate about the culture. It's been deeply important to them to be able to reflect the contributions of Black food and hospitality and to do it in a way that says, 'This is who we are, and this is where we are from.' There's much respect for that idea, but even more for making it all manifest." —Keia Mastrianni

Arthur Lou Tart

Vibrant in flavor and color, this dessert is a modern play off the oatmeal cookies and Tang that Greg's late granny Arthur Louise Prewitt would give him as a snack. Top the tart with whatever fruit is in season, or serve it as is.

ACTIVE 35 MIN. · TOTAL 2 HOURS, 20 MIN., PLUS 6 HOURS CHILLING AND 2 HOURS, 20 MIN. COOLING

SERVES 8

OATMEAL PIECRUST
- 1 cup plus 2 Tbsp. oat flour
- ¾ cup plus 2 Tbsp. all-purpose flour, plus more for work surface and hands
- 2 Tbsp. light brown sugar
- 1 tsp. kosher salt
- ½ cup cold unsalted butter, cubed
- ¼ cup vegetable shortening
- 3 Tbsp. cold water

ORANGE CUSTARD
- 6 large egg yolks
- 3 large eggs
- 1½ cups heavy whipping cream
- ¾ cup granulated sugar
- ½ cup plus 1 Tbsp. orange powdered drink mix (such as Tang)
- ½ tsp. kosher salt

SWISS GINGER MERINGUE
- 3 large egg whites
- ¾ tsp. cream of tartar
- 1 Tbsp. cornstarch
- 1½ tsp. ground ginger
- Pinch of kosher salt
- ½ cup granulated sugar
- ¼ cup light corn syrup

ADDITIONAL INGREDIENT
- Sliced seasonal fruit (optional)

1. Prepare the Oatmeal Piecrust: Stir together oat and all-purpose flours, brown sugar, and salt in a large bowl. Using a pastry cutter, cut cubed butter and shortening into flour mixture until it resembles coarse meal (pea-size bits with a few larger bits of fat are okay).

Drizzle in cold water 1 tablespoon at a time, stirring until dough begins to form large clumps. Transfer to a floured work surface. Dough should come together easily and should not feel overly sticky. Using floured hands, fold dough until it's combined (there should be no dry bits visible) and fats are speckled throughout. Shape into a ball; flatten into a 1-inch-thick disk using your hands. Wrap tightly in plastic wrap. Chill until firm, at least 2 hours or up to 5 days.

2. Preheat oven to 375°F. Unwrap dough and roll into a 13-inch round on a lightly floured work surface. Transfer to an 11-inch tart pan, pressing into bottom and up sides of pan. Coat a piece of parchment paper with cooking spray; place, greased side down, on crust. Fill with pie weights. Bake 20 minutes. Remove from oven. Carefully remove parchment and pie weights. Return to oven; bake in preheated oven until crust is set, about 10 minutes. Remove from oven. Cool completely, about 1 hour.

3. While Oatmeal Piecrust bakes, prepare the Orange Custard: Whisk together egg yolks, eggs, whipping cream, granulated sugar, drink mix, and salt in a large bowl until well combined. Let mixture stand until room temperature, about 1 hour, 30 minutes.

4. Fill a large baking pan with water to a depth of 1 inch. Place on bottom oven rack. Preheat oven to 300°F. Pour Orange Custard into cooled Oatmeal Piecrust. Bake until center of filling is set, 45 to 55 minutes. Turn oven off; let tart cool in oven with oven door ajar 20 minutes. Transfer to a wire rack; cool to room temperature, 1 hour. Chill, uncovered, until cold, about 4 hours or up to overnight (12 hours).

5. Prepare the Swiss Ginger Meringue: Beat egg whites with a stand mixer fitted with a whisk attachment on medium-high speed until frothy, about 1 minute. Add cream of tartar; beat 1 minute. Beat in cornstarch, ground ginger, and salt until soft peaks form, about 2 minutes. Turn mixer off.

6. Cook sugar and corn syrup in a small saucepan over high, stirring occasionally, until a thermometer registers 240°F, 3 to 4 minutes. Reduce mixer speed to low, and slowly drizzle about 2 tablespoons syrup mixture into egg white mixture. (If you add too much syrup at once, the whites will scramble.) Slowly drizzle in remaining syrup mixture. Increase mixer speed to medium-high, and beat until meringue is stiff and glossy, about 6 minutes. Spread meringue evenly on top of cooled tart. Using a kitchen torch, lightly toast meringue. If desired, garnish with sliced seasonal fruit. Serve immediately, or store, covered, in refrigerator up to 1 week.

Classic Comfort Dishes

Yes, indeed, it takes a lot of work to make sure that the food never looks skimpy or runs out at a Southern funeral. Cookbook author and *Southern Living* Contributing Editor Sheri Castle shares some of her favorite recipes designed for versatility and ease

I AM ONLY 45 YEARS OLD and live in New York–permanently, with no plans to move back home to Tennessee. But I'm putting it here in writing for my children to find on the internet someday that when I die, I'd like for my funeral to be in the South. I know it's possible to stage the weeping and rending of garments many miles from home. My dad died right before Christmas two years ago while visiting my sister in South Carolina, and we bought his body a Delta Air Lines plane ticket back to Memphis. It wasn't even that expensive. Ship me.

Southern funerals are miracles. They are actually just a step or two below a wedding–except that the reception lasts three or four days, you cry more, and you pull the whole thing together in less than a week. Part of the success of a funeral depends on your community showing up. After my father's service, we expected to welcome people back at the house but hadn't determined what was for lunch. A few neighbors brought platters of cold cuts, a cousin replated leftover side dishes, some sort of buttered cheese puffs materialized, and dozens of people ate all afternoon, loaves-and-fishes style. Which brings me to one of the most beautiful, important lessons I learned about Southern funerals: There's always a logistics operator behind the scenes.

Ours was Aunt Patti. She drove from Little Rock to my mother's house in Memphis, all while we were still in another state, to take down the Christmas tree, make all the beds, and clean the bathrooms. She then spent the days surrounding the service coordinating food deliveries, washing glasses and dessert plates, and–I'm not sure, but I think–running a taxi service for people who stayed too late drinking in my mom's living room. See? A logistics operator. Every funeral has one, and the best part is that they will volunteer. You, the family, don't even have to ask.

Another lesson I learned: As with weddings, there will be a guest book for people to sign at the church or funeral home. I always thought these were dumb. And I still believe this about weddings; I mean, you know who was invited, right? But anyone can–and will–show up at a Southern funeral, including your third-grade teacher (mine did), and you'll never remember them all. My dad used to meet a group of his high school buddies for breakfast at Chick-fil-A twice a week. Once, less than a year before he died, he had a dizzy spell, and a couple of the servers there (who, at that point, were very familiar with the old-man coffee club) stayed with my dad until my mother could pick him up. The day after his funeral, my mom was flipping through the guest book and saw two unfamiliar names signed in a loopy cursive. "His friends from Chick-fil-A!" and a smiley face were written next to them.

I can't tell you what to do for the service. What I can tell you is that friends you haven't seen in 25 years will show up, it will be more comforting than you can imagine, the food will never run out, and it will be a fantastic celebration of a person you loved. I hope someone remembers to fly me down for mine.

Bloody Mary Poached Shrimp

Many a Southern host understands that a big bowl of marinated shrimp can be the centerpiece of a buffet at any gathering. Guests appreciate seeing something they recognize and know they like, but they don't mind it having an unexpected twist, which is why I've made this recipe for years.

ACTIVE 40 MIN. - TOTAL 40 MIN., PLUS 8 HOURS CHILLING

SERVES 8

- 1   (32-oz.) bottle Bloody Mary mix, divided
- 2½ lb. medium peeled, deveined raw shrimp, tails optional
- 4   cups ice
- ½   cup cocktail sauce
- ⅓   cup (2⅔ oz.) vodka
- ⅓   cup olive oil
- ⅓   cup fresh lemon juice (from 2 lemons)
- 1   Tbsp. hot sauce (such as Tabasco)
- 1   Tbsp. Worcestershire sauce
- 1   tsp. celery seeds
- 1   tsp. black pepper
- 1   cup thinly sliced celery (from about 2 celery stalks)
- 1   cup thinly vertically sliced sweet onion (from 1 small onion)
   Garnishes: celery leaves, lemon slices, lime slices, pickled okra, dilly beans, and/or pitted green olives

1. Place 1 cup water and 3 cups of the Bloody Mary mix in a large saucepan; bring to a boil over high. Remove from heat. Add shrimp; cover and let stand until shrimp are barely opaque in centers, about 8 minutes. Immediately stir ice into shrimp mixture to stop cooking; let stand until shrimp are cool, about 5 minutes. Drain shrimp, and pat dry.
2. Stir together cocktail sauce, vodka, oil, lemon juice, hot sauce, Worcestershire, celery seeds, pepper, and remaining 1 cup Bloody Mary mix in a large bowl or a large heavy-duty zip-top plastic freezer bag.
3. Stir shrimp, sliced celery, and onion into cocktail sauce mixture. Cover (or seal bag), and place in refrigerator to marinate at least 8 hours or, preferably, up to 24 hours.
4. Transfer shrimp mixture to a large serving bowl. Top with desired garnishes, and serve immediately. (The dish can be made in advance. Store, covered, in refrigerator up to 3 days.)

CREAMED-CORN
GRITS (PAGE 22)

BLT PAIN PERDU
CASSEROLE
(PAGE 22)

Creamed-Corn Grits

(Photo, page 20)

We can rest assured that someone (several someones, most likely) will bring over buckets and boxes of fried chicken and platters of ham biscuits, but there's always a need for more sides. The addition of old-fashioned creamed sweet corn, what our moms and aunties might have called "fried corn," to a pot of comforting grits ensures that this recipe will go with any meal, from brunch all the way through the dinner hour. The grits tolerate reheating multiple times, an asset whenever a cousin needs to replate a few leftover side dishes.

ACTIVE 50 MIN. - TOTAL 1 HOUR

SERVES 8

4	ears fresh corn, shucked
2	cups whole milk
1½	tsp. kosher salt
1	tsp. granulated sugar
½	tsp. black pepper
1	cup stone-ground grits
2	oz. cream cheese, at room temperature
3	scallions
2	Tbsp. unsalted butter, softened
3	Tbsp. heavy whipping cream
1	Tbsp. melted unsalted butter

1. Cut kernels from corn cobs; set kernels aside. Scrape cobs using a spoon or the back of a knife to release the milky liquid. Place scraped cobs and milky liquid, whole milk, and 2 cups water in a large saucepan; bring just to a boil over medium-high. Remove from heat; cover and let stand 10 minutes. Remove and discard cobs.
2. Stir salt, sugar, and pepper into milk mixture in saucepan; bring to a simmer over medium-high. Whisk in grits. Reduce heat to low; gently simmer, whisking occasionally, until grits are tender and thick, 20 to 25 minutes, whisking more often as they thicken and adding a little hot tap water as needed if grits get too thick before they are tender. Remove from heat; stir in cream cheese until melted. Cover to keep warm, and set aside.
3. Thinly slice scallions, separating white and light green parts from dark green parts; set aside. Melt softened butter in a large skillet over medium-high until it foams. Stir in reserved corn kernels and the whipping cream; cook, slowly stirring mixture, until corn is tender-crisp and liquid begins to

thicken, about 3 minutes. Stir in white and light green scallion parts; cook, stirring often, until corn is tender and creamy, about 2 minutes.
4. Stir corn kernel mixture into hot grits. Drizzle with melted butter, and sprinkle with dark green scallion parts before serving.

BLT Pain Perdu Casserole

(Photo, page 21)

To my way of thinking, a funeral spread has to include at least one casserole. Better yet, two: one for the visitation buffet table and another for the family to have at home. This version delivers the flavors of a BLT sandwich in the form of a savory bread pudding that can feed several people. Because this dish tastes best slightly warm instead of piping hot, it tolerates being assembled in one spot and perhaps baked and served in another. It holds its form for a few hours, and individual portions reheat well—traits appreciated by an ad hoc hospitality committee working behind the scenes.

ACTIVE 40 MIN. - TOTAL 1 HOUR, 30 MIN., PLUS 8 HOURS CHILLING

SERVES 10

12	oz. crusty dense white bread (such as a French loaf), sliced ¾ inch thick
7	medium (about 2 lb. total) beefsteak tomatoes, cored and cut into ½-inch slices
1	lb. bacon, chopped, cooked until crisp, and drained
½	cup loosely packed fresh basil leaves, thinly sliced
12	oz. Gruyère cheese, shredded (about 3 cups), divided
8	large eggs
1½	cups half-and-half
2	Tbsp. tomato paste
2½	tsp. kosher salt
2	tsp. granulated garlic
2	tsp. mustard powder
2	tsp. paprika
1½	tsp. black pepper
1	tsp. grated nutmeg
½	tsp. cayenne pepper
3	Tbsp. mayonnaise
3	Tbsp. fresh lemon juice (from 1 lemon)
2	tsp. whole-grain mustard
½	tsp. granulated sugar
5	oz. arugula

1. Generously coat a 13- x 9-inch baking dish with cooking spray. Cover bottom of dish with half of the bread slices. Top with half of the tomato slices. Sprinkle evenly with cooked bacon and fresh basil. Sprinkle evenly with half (about 1½ cups) of the cheese. Top with remaining bread slices and tomato slices in 1 layer, overlapping edges of bread and tomatoes as needed to fit.
2. Process eggs, half-and-half, tomato paste, salt, granulated garlic, mustard powder, paprika, black pepper, nutmeg, and cayenne in a blender until smooth, about 20 seconds. (Alternatively, place mixture in a large bowl, and process with an immersion blender until smooth.) Pour egg mixture slowly and evenly over bread mixture in baking dish, letting it seep down into the layers. Cover tightly with plastic wrap. Refrigerate at least 8 hours or up to 24 hours, unwrapping dish twice and firmly pressing down on mixture with the back of a large spoon to help bread absorb liquid.
3. Preheat oven to 350°F. Unwrap baking dish; sprinkle evenly with remaining (about 1½ cups) cheese. Bake until casserole is deep golden and just set (a knife inserted into center should come out moist but not wet), 45 to 50 minutes. Cool until barely warm, about 20 minutes.
4. Meanwhile, whisk together mayonnaise, lemon juice, mustard, and sugar in a large bowl until smooth. Chill until ready to serve.
5. Add arugula to mayonnaise mixture; toss until lightly coated. Serve alongside or on top of pain perdu.

Warm Cheese Box Bites

This old-school favorite has made the rounds in family recipe collections and community cookbooks for decades. These bite-size morsels combine the comfort of warm cheese toast with the elegance of tiny cheese soufflés. When they are made ahead and stashed in the freezer, you can pull out as many as needed.

ACTIVE 25 MIN. - TOTAL 35 MIN., PLUS 30 MIN. CHILLING

SERVES 15

4	oz. extra-sharp Cheddar cheese, finely shredded (about 1 cup)
¼	cup unsalted butter, softened
¼	cup mayonnaise
1½	tsp. cornstarch

WARM CHEESE
BOX BITES

1 tsp. hot sauce (such as Tabasco)
1 tsp. Worcestershire sauce
½ tsp. kosher salt
¼ tsp. dry mustard
¼ tsp. paprika
3 large egg whites, at room temperature
⅛ tsp. cream of tartar
5 (1½-oz.) thick-cut, firm white sandwich bread slices

1. Stir together cheese, butter, mayonnaise, cornstarch, hot sauce, Worcestershire, salt, mustard, and paprika in a large bowl until creamy and combined.

2. Beat egg whites and cream of tartar in a medium bowl with an electric mixer on high speed until stiff peaks form (1 minute, 30 seconds to 2 minutes). Gently fold egg white mixture into cheese mixture in 4 additions, being careful not to overmix to avoid deflating egg whites; mixture should remain light and airy. Refrigerate, uncovered, until ready to use.

3. Trim crusts from bread slices. Cut slices in half crosswise; cut each half into thirds to make a total of 30 pieces.

4. Spread cheese mixture evenly over tops and sides of bread pieces. Arrange on a baking sheet coated with cooking spray. Chill, uncovered, until firm, 30 minutes to 1 hour. (To store in freezer, freeze on baking sheet until firm, 30 minutes to 1 hour. Then transfer to a heavy-duty zip-top plastic freezer bag, and freeze up to 3 months. Do not thaw before baking.)

5. While bread pieces chill, preheat oven to 375°F. Bake chilled bread pieces until golden brown and slightly puffed, 10 to 12 minutes. Serve warm.

Crazy for Cabbage

Don't be fooled by its humble looks. Cabbage is a nutritional powerhouse—a good source of vitamins C and K, among other benefits. Now that it's in season, the versatile veggie is extra sweet and crunchy

Tangy Rainbow Slaw

This slaw is great paired with any protein or tucked into a sandwich.
ACTIVE 20 MIN. · TOTAL 25 MIN.
SERVES 8

Whisk together ¼ cup each **unseasoned rice vinegar, olive oil,** and **lime juice**; 3 Tbsp. **granulated sugar**; 1 tsp. **toasted sesame oil**; 1½ tsp. **kosher salt**; and ¼ tsp. **crushed red pepper** in a large bowl. Stir in 3 cups each thinly sliced **green cabbage** and **red cabbage**, 2 cups thinly sliced **Honeycrisp apple,** 1 cup each **matchstick carrots** and thinly sliced **yellow bell pepper,** and ½ cup thinly sliced **scallions** until thoroughly coated. Stir in ⅓ cup chopped **fresh cilantro,** and top with ¼ cup coarsely chopped **roasted lightly salted peanuts** just before serving.

The Best Way to Core Cabbage: Using a sharp chef's knife, split the cabbage in half and then into quarters. Cut off and discard the core/ stem section from each piece. Finally, slice each quarter as desired.

The Icing on the Cake

Six fantastic frosting recipes and decorating techniques that will turn
a boxed cake mix into a dessert fit for celebrating

Confetti Cake with Vanilla-Sour Cream Frosting

(Photo, page 26)

Dress up your favorite confetti cake mix with an icing that's pleasantly tangy, thanks to the addition of sour cream. Salted butter also makes a difference here to balance out the sweetness of the cake.

ACTIVE 30 MIN. - TOTAL 1 HOUR, 20 MIN.,
PLUS 55 MIN. COOLING AND 30 MIN. CHILLING

SERVES 12

- 1 (15¼-oz.) pkg. confetti cake mix (plus ingredients listed on box for preparing cake)
  Baking spray with flour
- 1½ cups butter, softened
- 4½ cups unsifted powdered sugar
- ½ cup sour cream
- 1 tsp. vanilla extract
- ¼ cup rainbow candy sprinkles, plus more for garnish

1. Preheat oven to 350°F. Prepare cake mix according to package directions. Divide batter evenly among 3 (6-inch) round cake pans coated with baking spray.
2. Bake in preheated oven until a wooden pick inserted in centers of cakes comes out clean, 20 to 23 minutes. Cool in pans 10 minutes. Invert cakes onto wire racks; cool completely, about 45 minutes.
3. Beat softened butter in a large bowl with an electric mixer on medium speed until smooth, about 2 minutes. With mixer on low speed, gradually add powdered sugar, sour cream, and vanilla extract. Beat until fluffy, stopping occasionally to scrape down sides of bowl, about 3 minutes. (You will have about 5 cups frosting.) Set aside about 1 cup of the frosting in a separate bowl, and fold in candy sprinkles.
4. Place a cake plate on a stand or a lazy Susan. Put 1 cake layer on plate; spread 1 cup plain frosting over top, smoothing top using a bench scraper or an offset spatula. Repeat with remaining 2 cake layers and 2 cups of the frosting. Using a bench scraper or large offset spatula, spread a thin layer of frosting (about ½ cup) over sides of cake. Chill until frosting has firmed and set, about 30 minutes.
5. Spread a thicker layer of reserved sprinkle frosting on sides of cake, smoothing as you go. Spoon any remaining frosting into a piping bag fitted with a medium round tip. Pipe dollops around top edge of cake. Garnish with additional sprinkles in center of cake.

Devil's Food Cake with Salted Peanut Butter Frosting and Ganache

(Photo, page 27)

Our Test Kitchen called this salty-sweet peanut butter frosting "out of this world." Not only is it lick-the-spatula delicious, but it also spreads easily and smoothly, which makes decorating a breeze. Top it off with drips of chocolate ganache. If you're in a pinch, you can substitute jarred hot fudge, but the homemade version is worth a few extra minutes.

ACTIVE 25 MIN. - TOTAL 1 HOUR, 20 MIN.,
PLUS 70 MIN. COOLING AND 30 MIN. CHILLING

SERVES 12

- 1 (15¼-oz.) pkg. devil's food cake mix (plus ingredients listed on box for preparing cake)
  Baking spray with flour
- 1 cup butter, softened
- 1 cup creamy peanut butter
- 3 cups unsifted powdered sugar
- 1 tsp. vanilla extract
- ¾ cup heavy whipping cream, divided
- 1 cup semisweet chocolate chips
  Chopped salted roasted peanuts

1. Preheat oven to 350°F. Prepare cake mix according to package directions. Divide batter evenly between 2 (9-inch) round cake pans coated with baking spray.
2. Bake in preheated oven until a wooden pick inserted in centers of cakes comes out clean, about 22 minutes. Cool in pans 10 minutes. Invert cakes onto wire racks; cool completely, about 45 minutes.
3. Beat softened butter and peanut butter with a stand mixer fitted with a paddle attachment on medium speed until smooth, about 2 minutes. Reduce mixer speed to low; gradually add powdered sugar, vanilla extract, and ¼ cup of the cream. Beat on medium-high speed until fluffy, about 3 minutes. (You will have about 4 cups frosting.)
4. Spread 1½ cups frosting in a smooth layer over top of 1 cake layer using a large offset spatula. Top with remaining cake layer, and spread 1½ cups frosting in a smooth layer over top, spreading some of the frosting on top layer in a thin layer around sides of whole cake. Chill until frosting has firmed and set, about 30 minutes. Spread remaining frosting (about 1 cup) over sides of whole cake, smoothing as you go.
5. Microwave remaining ½ cup cream in a small microwave-safe bowl on HIGH until steaming, about 1 minute. Stir in chocolate chips until mixture is smooth. Cool 15 minutes.
6. Slowly pour about half of the chocolate mixture over the top of the cake. Spoon more of the mixture around top edge, allowing it to drip down sides, and then spoon any remaining chocolate mixture onto center of cake. If needed, use the spoon to nudge the icing down the sides of the cake. Smooth the top with an offset spatula, and sprinkle with peanuts.

How to Frost a Smooth-Sided Cake

1. Put a cake plate on a stand. Place 1 cake layer on plate, and spread plain frosting on top. Repeat with 2 other cake layers. Use a bench scraper or large offset spatula to spread a thin layer of plain frosting (about ½ cup) on sides of cake, rotating the stand as you work. Chill 30 minutes.

2. Using an offset spatula, spread a thick layer (about 1 cup) of reserved sprinkle frosting on the sides, rotating the cake as you work to make the sides as smooth as possible. Wipe off excess frosting from the spatula as you go. Fix cracks by spreading a little more sprinkle frosting. Smooth the sides with the spatula, if needed.

3. To make the top edge of the cake look smooth and straight, spread excess icing toward the center. Then smooth the top with the spatula.

CONFETTI CAKE WITH
VANILLA-SOUR CREAM
FROSTING (PAGE 25)

DEVIL'S FOOD CAKE
WITH SALTED PEANUT
BUTTER FROSTING AND
GANACHE (PAGE 25)

How to Create an Icing Drip

1. Make sure the drip icing is cool but not cold. Slowly pour about half of it over the top of the cake.

2. Spoon more icing around top edge of cake so that it drips down. Spoon remaining icing onto center of cake.

3. If needed, use the spoon to nudge the icing down the sides of the cake. Use an offset spatula to smooth the top.

WHITE CAKE WITH
BERRY-SWISS MERINGUE
BUTTERCREAM
FROSTING (PAGE 32)

How to Frost a Rose Cake

1. Frost the layers, sides, and top of the cake as directed, using about 3¾ cups frosting. Place remaining frosting (about 3¾ cups) into a piping bag (or large zip-top bag with a corner snipped off) fitted with a Wilton 127D petal tip. Hold the bag so the tip is straight up and down, with the pointed end facing up. Starting at the center of the top of the cake, pipe a small cone-like shape.

2. Pipe small arching lines around the center cone. Lengthen the arching lines as you work your way toward the top edge of the cake.

3. To frost the rest of the cake, make 2-inch arches with the pointed end of the tip facing up, working your way

around the sides of the cake from the top to the bottom to finish the "rose."

How to Make Perfect Petals

1. Starting along outer edge of cake layer, pipe a 1-inch circular dollop of frosting onto cake. Drag piping bag in toward center of cake while squeezing to create a 1½-inch teardrop shape out of frosting.

2. Repeat, making 7 more petals around edge. Drag an offset spatula through the center of each teardrop toward the center of the cake, creating a petal-like appearance.

3. Using spatula, smooth the frosting in middle of top cake layer (where petals meet in the center), spreading into a circle to create the center of the flower.

How to Frost a Ruffle Cake

1. Using an offset spatula, spread a thin, smooth layer of frosting over the entire cake. Starting with the outer edge of the top layer, press spatula down while spinning cake, making a spiral. Remove cake plate with cake, and chill until frosting is firm and set, about 30 minutes.
2. Place remaining frosting in a piping bag fitted with a Wilton 104 petal tip.

Hold the bag with the pointed end of the tip facing up. Starting at the top of 1 side of the cake, turn cake while piping a ring, gently moving the piping bag up and down slightly to create a ruffled effect.

3. Repeat process a bit lower on cake, overlapping each previous ring slightly until you reach the bottom of the cake.

RED VELVET CAKE WITH WHITE CHOCOLATE-CREAM CHEESE FROSTING (PAGE 33)

LEMON CAKE WITH LEMON-THYME FROSTING (PAGE 33)

How to Make Smooth Ombré Stripes

1. Spread 1 cup undyed frosting in a smooth layer over the top of 1 cake layer. Repeat with remaining 2 cake layers and 2 cups of the undyed frosting. Using a bench scraper or large offset spatula, spread a thin layer of undyed frosting over sides of cake. Chill 30 minutes.

2. Starting at the base of cake, pipe the darker frosting in a ring all the way around cake. Leaving space above the dark line, pipe a ring of the lighter frosting all the way around the cake. Repeat again with the undyed frosting. (Alternatively, leave less space between the rings to make more stripes.)

3. Using a bench scraper or large offset spatula, drag the flat edge around the sides of the cake to smooth and press the rings together, creating an ombré effect.

White Cake with Berry-Swiss Meringue Buttercream Frosting

(Photo, page 28)

There's not a drop of food coloring in this pretty pink dessert. The freeze-dried raspberries (available at Target, Whole Foods Market, and other retailers) add a nice rosy hue and a bit of tang to offset the richness of the buttercream. If the frosting separates a little as you are making it, pop it in the refrigerator for 15 minutes. Then continue to beat again.

ACTIVE 1 HOUR, 10 MIN. - TOTAL 1 HOUR, 25 MIN., PLUS 55 MIN. COOLING

SERVES 12

- 1 (15¼-oz.) pkg. white cake mix (plus ingredients listed on box for preparing cake)
  Baking spray with flour
- 1½ cups freeze-dried raspberries (about 1 oz.)
- 8 large egg whites, at room temperature
- ½ tsp. cream of tartar
- ¼ tsp. kosher salt
- 1¾ cups plus 2 Tbsp. granulated sugar, divided
- 3 cups (1½ lb.) unsalted butter, softened and cut into 1-Tbsp. pats
- 2 tsp. vanilla extract

1. Preheat oven to 350°F. Prepare cake mix according to package directions. Divide batter evenly among 3 (8-inch) round cake pans coated with baking spray.
2. Bake in preheated oven until a wooden pick inserted in centers of cakes comes out clean, about 20 minutes. Cool in pans 10 minutes. Invert cakes onto wire racks; cool completely, about 45 minutes.
3. Process raspberries in a food processor until a fine powder forms, about 1 minute. Sift raspberry powder through a fine mesh strainer; discard any unsifted pieces and seeds. Set powder aside.
4. Beat egg whites, cream of tartar, and kosher salt with a stand mixer fitted with a whisk attachment on medium speed until soft peaks form, about 5 minutes, gradually adding ¼ cup plus 2 tablespoons of the sugar.
5. Bring ½ cup water and remaining 1½ cups sugar to a boil in a medium saucepan over medium-high. Cook, undisturbed, until mixture reaches 230°F to 240°F (soft-ball stage), about 5 minutes. With mixer on medium speed, gradually add hot sugar mixture

to egg white mixture. Increase speed to medium-high, and continue beating until meringue is room temperature, about 10 minutes. Remove whisk attachment from mixer; fit mixer with a paddle attachment. With mixer on medium speed, gradually add softened butter to meringue, 1 tablespoon at a time, beating until butter is combined and mixture is smooth. (If mixture begins to look broken, continue beating until it comes back together.) Beat in vanilla and raspberry powder until combined. Increase mixer speed to high; beat until just fluffy, about 1 minute, stopping to scrape down sides if needed. (You will have about 7½ cups frosting.)
6. Place a cake plate on a lazy Susan or stand. Put 1 cake layer on plate, and spread top with 1 cup frosting. Repeat with remaining 2 cake layers and 2 cups of the frosting. Using a large offset spatula, spread a thin layer of frosting (about ¾ cup) over sides and top of entire cake. Spoon remaining frosting (about 3¾ cups) into a piping bag fitted with a Wilton 127D petal tip. Hold piping bag so pointed (thin) tip is angled upward. Pipe a small cone-like shape in center of top of cake to create a rosebud. Pipe small arching lines around cone, slightly lifting and dropping your wrist as you pipe and lengthening arches as you work toward outside edges of cake, to create rose petals. Starting at top of cake, pipe 2-inch arches around sides of cake, working your way toward the bottom and overlapping arches slightly, to create petals around cake.

Yellow Cake with Malted Chocolate Buttercream

(Photo, page 29)

One of the most nostalgic combinations is yellow cake with chocolate frosting. This version, which has a touch of malted milk powder in the buttercream, will bring back sweet memories. It makes enough to cover the cake completely. If you frost it using the flower design and leave the sides bare, you will have leftover buttercream, which can be stored in the freezer for your next baking project.

ACTIVE 30 MIN. - TOTAL 50 MIN., PLUS 55 MIN. COOLING

SERVES 12

- 1 (15¼-oz.) pkg. yellow cake mix (plus ingredients listed on box for preparing cake)

  Baking spray with flour
- 1½ cups semisweet chocolate chips
- 1½ cups butter, softened
- 3 cups unsifted powdered sugar
- ⅓ cup malted milk powder
- ¼ cup heavy whipping cream
- 1 tsp. vanilla extract

1. Preheat oven to 350°F. Prepare yellow cake mix according to package directions. Divide batter evenly among 3 (6-inch) round cake pans coated with baking spray.
2. Bake in preheated oven until a wooden pick inserted in centers of cakes comes out clean, 20 to 23 minutes. Cool in pans 10 minutes. Invert cakes onto wire racks; cool completely, about 45 minutes.
3. Microwave chocolate chips in a microwave-safe bowl on HIGH until melted, about 90 seconds, stopping to stir every 30 seconds. Let cool 10 minutes.
4. Beat butter in a stand mixer fitted with a paddle attachment on medium speed until smooth, about 2 minutes. With mixer on low speed, gradually add powdered sugar, malted milk powder, and cream, beating until just combined. Add melted chocolate and vanilla extract; beat on medium-high speed until fluffy, about 3 minutes. (You will have about 5 cups frosting.)
5. Spoon frosting into a large piping bag, and snip a ½-inch tip off bag. Create frosting flower petals on top side of 1 cake layer: Starting along outer edge of top of cake layer, pipe a 1-inch circular dollop of frosting onto cake; drag piping bag in toward center of cake while squeezing to create a 1½-inch teardrop shape. Repeat process 7 more times, working around top edge of cake. Drag a small offset spatula lengthwise through center of each frosting teardrop from outer circle toward center of cake, creating a petal-like appearance. (Dip spatula in warm water and wipe dry before dragging through each frosting teardrop.) Repeat process using remaining 2 cake layers. Carefully stack frosted layers.
6. Using offset spatula, smooth the frosting in middle of top cake layer (where petals meet in the center), spreading into a circle to create the center of the flower design.

Red Velvet Cake with White Chocolate-Cream Cheese Frosting

(Photo, page 30)

This classic Southern cake calls for a rich cream cheese frosting, and our recipe delivers with extra sweetness from white chocolate. Even if you skip the ruffled design, our Test Kitchen says this dessert will steal the show. Keep the frosting cool because it can soften and melt.

ACTIVE 50 MIN. - TOTAL 1 HOUR, 45 MIN., PLUS 55 MIN. COOLING AND 30 MIN. CHILLING

SERVES 12

- 2 (15¼-oz.) pkg. red velvet cake mix (plus ingredients listed on box for preparing cake)
- Baking spray with flour
- 2 cups unsalted butter, softened
- 2 (8-oz.) pkg. cream cheese, softened
- 10 cups unsifted powdered sugar
- 10 oz. white chocolate, melted and cooled slightly
- 2 tsp. vanilla extract

1. Preheat oven to 350°F. Prepare cake mixes according to package directions. Divide batter evenly among 3 (9-inch) round cake pans coated with baking spray.
2. Bake in preheated oven until a wooden pick inserted in centers of cakes comes out clean, about 25 minutes. Cool in pans 10 minutes. Invert cakes onto wire racks; cool completely, about 45 minutes.
3. Beat softened butter and cream cheese with a stand mixer fitted with a paddle attachment on medium speed until smooth, about 2 minutes. With mixer on low speed, gradually add powdered sugar, white chocolate, and vanilla. Increase speed to medium–high; beat until fluffy, about 2 minutes. (You will have about 10 cups frosting.)
4. Place a cake plate on a lazy Susan or stand. Put 1 cake layer on plate; spread top with 1¼ cups frosting. Repeat with remaining 2 cake layers and 2½ cups of the frosting. Using a large offset spatula, spread a thin layer of frosting (about 1 cup) over sides of entire cake. Using an offset spatula or the back of a teaspoon, gently press into outer edge of frosting on top cake layer. Spin cake to create a spiral pattern in frosting, moving to center of cake. Remove cake plate with cake from lazy Susan, and chill until frosting is firm and set, about 30 minutes.

5. Place remaining frosting (about 5¼ cups) in a piping bag fitted with a Wilton 104 petal tip; set aside.
6. Return cake plate with cake to lazy Susan. Hold piping bag with pointed (thin) end of the tip facing straight up. Starting at the top of 1 side of the cake, turn it while piping a ring around it, gently moving the piping bag up and down slightly to create a ruffled effect. Pipe another ruffled ring a bit lower on cake, overlapping first ring slightly. Repeat process around cake, making each ring a little lower and overlapping slightly, until you reach the bottom.

Lemon Cake with Lemon-Thyme Frosting

(Photo, page 31)

A frosting that's infused with fresh herbs sounds fancy, but it's just as easy as making a cup of tea. Heat up the heavy cream, and then let the thyme sprigs steep. Fresh rosemary would also pair nicely with this lemony cake.

ACTIVE 45 MIN. - TOTAL 2 HOURS, 45 MIN., PLUS 55 MIN. COOLING

SERVES 12

- 2 (15¼-oz.) pkg. lemon cake mix (plus ingredients listed on box for preparing cake)
- Baking spray with flour
- ⅓ cup heavy whipping cream
- ¼ oz. fresh thyme sprigs (about 1 handful)
- 2 cups (1 lb.) unsalted butter
- 1 (2-lb.) pkg. powdered sugar
- ¼ cup fresh lemon juice (from 1 large lemon)
- Yellow food coloring gel
- White sugar pearl sprinkles

1. Preheat oven to 350°F. Prepare cake mixes according to package directions. Divide batter evenly among 3 (9-inch) round cake pans coated with baking spray.
2. Bake in preheated oven until a wooden pick inserted in centers of cakes comes out clean, about 25 minutes. Cool in pans 10 minutes. Invert cakes onto wire racks; cool completely, about 45 minutes.
3. Heat cream in a small saucepan over medium until just simmering. Add thyme sprigs, pressing down using a spoon to submerge. Remove from heat; cover and let stand until cream has cooled, about 1 hour. Remove and discard sprigs. Set aside cream.

4. Beat butter in bowl of a stand mixer fitted with a paddle attachment on medium speed until smooth, about 2 minutes. With mixer on low speed, gradually add powdered sugar, lemon juice, and infused cream. Increase speed to medium–high, and beat until fluffy, about 3 minutes. (You will have about 7 cups frosting.)
5. Measure 1¼ cups frosting into each of 2 small bowls. (Reserve remaining undyed frosting in mixer bowl.) Add 4 drops food coloring to 1 small bowl of frosting, and stir to combine. Add 2 drops food coloring to remaining small bowl of frosting; stir to combine. Spoon ⅔ cup each of dark yellow frosting, light yellow frosting, and undyed frosting into 3 separate piping bags. Snip a 1-inch tip off of each bag. Spoon remaining dark and light yellow frostings (about ½ cup each) and ½ cup undyed frosting into 3 separate piping bags fitted with different star tips (such as Wilton 21, 32, and 2D). Set aside all piping bags.
6. Place a cake plate on a lazy Susan or stand. Put 1 cake layer on plate; spread 1 cup undyed frosting in a smooth layer over the top. Repeat with remaining 2 cake layers and 2 cups of the undyed frosting. Using a bench scraper or a large offset spatula, spread remaining undyed frosting (about ⅓ cup) in a thin layer over sides of cake. Remove cake plate with cake from lazy Susan. Chill until frosting sets and firms up, about 30 minutes.
7. Return cake plate with cake to lazy Susan. Using the dark yellow frosting in the piping bag with the snipped tip, start at the base of the cake, and turn cake while piping a straight line, creating a ring of frosting around the cake. Leaving space above the dark yellow line, repeat the piping process using light yellow frosting. Repeat with undyed frosting. (Alternatively, leave less space between the rings and repeat series of dark yellow, light yellow, and undyed lines to make more stripes.) Turn cake while dragging the straight edge of a bench scraper (or a large offset spatula) around side of cake (holding scraper at a 30-degree angle toward cake), smoothing and pressing the frosting lines together to create blended stripes of frosting around cake.
8. Using the reserved dark yellow, light yellow, and undyed frosting in piping bags with star tips, pipe small rosettes and flowers on top of cake. Garnish with sugar pearl sprinkles.

Old Bird, New Tricks

There's nothing boring about these fresh takes on chicken dinners

Creamy Chicken Sausage-and-Kale Soup

ACTIVE 20 MIN. - TOTAL 35 MIN.

SERVES 4

- 3 Tbsp. unsalted butter
- 1 medium-size yellow onion, chopped (about 1½ cups)
- 3 medium-size garlic cloves, chopped (2 Tbsp.)
- 3 Tbsp. all-purpose flour
- 4 cups lower-sodium chicken broth
- 2 medium Yukon Gold potatoes, peeled and cut into ¾-inch pieces (about 2 cups)
- 12 oz. smoked chicken sausage, sliced diagonally into ½-inch pieces
- 1 small bunch Lacinato kale, stemmed and roughly chopped (about 3 cups)
- 1 cup loosely packed matchstick-cut carrots
- 1½ tsp. kosher salt
- ½ tsp. black pepper, plus more for topping
  Pinch of ground nutmeg
- ½ cup heavy whipping cream
  Shredded Swiss cheese
  Hot sauce (such as Cholula)

1. Melt butter in a Dutch oven over medium. Add onion; cook, stirring often, until softened, 6 to 8 minutes. Add garlic; cook, stirring constantly, until fragrant, about 30 seconds. Add flour; cook, stirring constantly, until just beginning to brown, about 1 minute. Gradually add broth, stirring constantly.
2. Add potatoes to broth mixture; bring to a simmer over medium–high. Reduce heat to medium–low. Cover and cook, stirring occasionally, until almost tender, about 15 minutes. Stir in sausage, kale, carrots, salt, black pepper, and nutmeg. Cover and cook, stirring occasionally, until kale, carrots, and potatoes are tender and soup is heated through, 5 to 10 minutes. Remove from heat. Stir in cream.
3. Top bowls of soup with Swiss cheese, hot sauce, and black pepper.

Chicken-Parmesan Meatballs

ACTIVE 25 MIN. - TOTAL 35 MIN.

SERVES 4

- 2 large eggs, beaten
- 1 lb. ground chicken (white and dark meat)
- 2 oz. thinly sliced prosciutto, finely chopped
- 1 cup panko breadcrumbs
- ¼ cup chopped fresh basil, plus basil leaves for garnish
- ¾ tsp. kosher salt
- ½ tsp. black pepper
- ½ tsp. crushed red pepper
- 2 medium garlic cloves, grated
- 2 oz. Parmesan cheese, grated with a Microplane grater (about 1¼ cups), divided
- 2 Tbsp. olive oil
- ⅓ cup dry red wine
- 1 (24-oz.) jar marinara sauce
- 6 oz. low-moisture part-skim mozzarella cheese, shredded (about 1½ cups)

  Garlic bread, cooked spaghetti, or zucchini "noodles," for serving

1. Combine eggs, chicken, prosciutto, panko, chopped basil, salt, black pepper, crushed red pepper, garlic, and half of the Parmesan in a large bowl. Gently mix with your hands to thoroughly combine, taking care not to overmix. Shape into 12 (1¾-inch) balls.

2. Preheat oven to 450°F. Heat olive oil in a large skillet over medium-high. Cook meatballs in a single layer, turning occasionally, until browned on all sides, 8 to 12 minutes. Transfer to a plate. Reduce heat to medium. Add wine to skillet; cook, scraping bottom of skillet to release browned bits, until reduced to about 2 tablespoons, 1 to 2 minutes. Stir in marinara sauce. Arrange meatballs in skillet in a single layer; turn to coat in sauce. Sprinkle with mozzarella cheese and remaining half Parmesan.

3. Transfer skillet to preheated oven; bake until mozzarella cheese is melted and beginning to brown and internal temperature of meatballs registers 165°F, 10 to 14 minutes. Garnish with basil leaves. Serve with garlic bread, cooked spaghetti, or zucchini "noodles."

THE RIGHT MIX

Be sure to purchase ground chicken that is a mix of white and dark meat; all-white meat is too lean and will dry out. Ground turkey works well in this recipe, too (also use a combo of white and dark meat).

Sesame-Crusted Chicken Breasts with Sugar Snap Pea Salad

ACTIVE 25 MIN. - TOTAL 55 MIN., PLUS 2 HOURS CHILLING

SERVES 4

- 2 medium navel oranges
- ¼ cup light brown sugar
- 3 Tbsp. hoisin sauce
- 1½ Tbsp. toasted sesame oil
- 1 Tbsp. grated fresh ginger
- ¼ cup, plus 1 Tbsp. low-sodium soy sauce, divided
- 2 small red jalapeño chiles, thinly sliced crosswise (about ¼ cup), divided
- 4 (about 9 oz. each) boneless, skinless chicken breasts
- 1 cup mixed white and black sesame seeds
- 1 large egg
- 12 oz. fresh sugar snap peas, trimmed, thinly sliced lengthwise (about 4 cups)

1. Grate 1 navel orange to yield about 1 teaspoon zest, and set aside. Using a sharp knife, cut along curve of each orange to remove peel and pith. Cut oranges into segments, and transfer to a large bowl. Cover and chill until ready to use or up to 8 hours. Squeeze orange scraps into a small bowl to yield about 2 tablespoons juice; set aside.

2. Whisk together brown sugar, hoisin sauce, sesame oil, ginger, ¼ cup of the soy sauce, 2 tablespoons of the jalapeños, and reserved 1 teaspoon orange zest and 2 tablespoons orange juice in a small bowl. Reserve ⅓ cup of the marinade for dressing salad; cover and chill. Combine chicken breasts and remaining about ½ cup marinade in a large zip-top plastic bag; seal and toss to coat the chicken. Chill at least 2 hours or up to 6 hours, turning chicken occasionally.

3. Preheat oven to 400°F. Line a baking sheet with aluminum foil; lightly coat foil with cooking spray. Place mixed sesame seeds in a medium shallow bowl. Whisk together egg and remaining 1 tablespoon soy sauce in a separate shallow bowl. Remove chicken from marinade; discard marinade. Working with 1 chicken breast at a time, dip in egg mixture and then in sesame seeds, turning until completely coated. Transfer to prepared baking sheet. Bake chicken until a meat thermometer inserted in thickest portion registers 155°F, about 25 minutes. Let rest for 5 minutes (internal temperature will continue to increase to 165°F).

4. While chicken bakes, toss together orange segments, sugar snap peas, remaining sliced jalapeños, and reserved ⅓ cup dressing in a large bowl. Serve chicken with salad.

PREP POINTER
The marinade is also the salad dressing. Set aside ⅓ cup for the dressing to avoid cross contamination.

Chipotle-Maple Chicken Thighs with Candied Acorn Squash

ACTIVE 15 MIN. - TOTAL 45 MIN.

SERVES 4

- 1 medium acorn squash, seeded, cut into 1-inch-thick half-moons
- 2½ Tbsp. olive oil, divided
- 2¾ tsp. kosher salt, divided
- 1½ tsp. chipotle chile powder, divided
- 1¼ tsp. black pepper, divided
- 1 tsp. ground cumin, divided
- 8 (6-oz.) bone-in, skin-on chicken thighs
- 2 Tbsp. adobo sauce (from 1 [7-oz.] can chipotle chiles in adobo sauce)
- 1 tsp. apple cider vinegar
- ¼ tsp. dry mustard
- 5 Tbsp. pure maple syrup, divided
- ¼ cup pomegranate arils (optional)
  Fresh cilantro leaves, for garnish

1. Preheat oven to 450°F with oven rack about 9 inches from heating element.
2. Toss together squash, 1½ tablespoons of the olive oil, 1 teaspoon of the salt, ¾ teaspoon of the chile powder, and ½ teaspoon each of the black pepper and cumin on a large rimmed baking sheet lined with aluminum foil. Arrange in a single layer. Rub chicken with remaining 1 tablespoon oil. Sprinkle with 1½ teaspoons of the salt, ½ teaspoon of the black pepper, and remaining ¾ teaspoon chile powder and ½ teaspoon cumin; nestle on baking sheet with squash in one layer. Bake in preheated oven until squash is tender and a meat thermometer inserted in thickest portion of chicken registers 165°F, about 25 minutes.

3. Meanwhile, stir together adobo sauce, vinegar, dry mustard, 3 tablespoons of the maple syrup, and remaining ¼ teaspoon each salt and black pepper in a microwavable bowl. Microwave on HIGH until slightly thickened, about 1½ minutes. Set aside.
4. When chicken and squash are finished baking, increase oven temperature to broil and remove baking sheet from oven. Brush top of squash with remaining 2 tablespoons maple syrup. Brush skin of chicken generously with adobo mixture. Return to preheated oven. Broil until chicken and squash are glazed and beginning to char in spots, about 2 minutes. Transfer to a serving platter. Sprinkle with pomegranate arils (if using), and garnish with cilantro.

Kentucky Hot Brown-Stuffed Chicken

ACTIVE 20 MIN. - TOTAL 40 MIN.

SERVES 4

- 4 center-cut bacon slices, cut crosswise in thirds (12 pieces)
- 2 Tbsp. panko breadcrumbs
- 1 oz. Parmesan cheese, shredded (about ¼ cup), divided
- 1 (5.2-oz.) pkg. garlic-and-herb spreadable cheese (such as Boursin), softened
- ¼ cup chopped fresh chives
- ¼ cup chopped fresh flat-leaf parsley, plus more for garnish
- 1½ tsp. kosher salt, divided
- ¾ tsp. black pepper, divided
- ½ tsp. paprika
- 4 (about 9 oz. each) boneless, skinless chicken breasts
- 1 Tbsp. olive oil
- 1 large plum tomato, cored, halved lengthwise, and cut into ¼-inch-thick half-moons

1. Preheat oven to 400°F. Cook bacon in a large skillet over medium-high, turning occasionally, until crisp, about 5 minutes. Transfer bacon to a plate lined with a paper towel; set aside. Transfer ½ tablespoon bacon drippings into a small bowl. Stir panko and 1 tablespoon of the Parmesan into skillet. Set aside.

2. While bacon cooks, stir together spreadable cheese, chives, parsley, ¼ teaspoon of the salt, ¼ teaspoon of the pepper, the paprika, and remaining 3 tablespoons Parmesan in a medium bowl to make ¾ cup (or 12 tablespoons) cheese mixture. Set aside.

3. Working with 1 chicken breast at a time, make 7 or 8 crosswise slits (spaced ½ inch apart) into the top of each breast, leaving about ¼ inch attached along the bottom of the breast. Place prepared chicken breast on a rimmed baking sheet lined with aluminum foil.

4. Rub chicken with olive oil. Sprinkle all over, including inside slits, with remaining 1¼ teaspoons salt and ½ teaspoon pepper. Stuff 1 bacon piece into each of 3 slits of each chicken breast. Stuff remaining 4 or 5 slits of each chicken breast evenly with spreadable cheese mixture (about 2½ teaspoons each). Press plum tomato slices evenly into cheese-filled slits (it's okay if not every cheese-filled slit gets a tomato slice). Sprinkle with panko mixture.

5. Bake in preheated oven until chicken is cooked through to 165°F and panko mixture is light golden brown, about 20 minutes. Garnish with parsley.

Sugar and Spice

You only need six ingredients to make these flaky, aromatic puff pastry "muffins"

Cinnamon Swirl
Puff Pastry Muffins

ACTIVE 25 MIN. - TOTAL 1 HOUR, 15 MIN.
MAKES 12

1 cup granulated sugar

1½ Tbsp. ground cinnamon

3 frozen puff pastry sheets
(from 2 [17.3-oz.] pkg.),
thawed

Flour for work surface

¼ cup butter, softened

1 large egg

1. Preheat oven to 350°F. Coat a 12-cup muffin pan with cooking spray; set aside. Stir together sugar and cinnamon in a small bowl; set aside.

2. Roll 1 of the puff pastry sheets into an 11- x 15-inch rectangle on a lightly floured work surface. Brush rectangle evenly with butter. Sprinkle evenly with 3 tablespoons of the sugar mixture. Starting at longer side, roll rectangle into a tight log; pinching along seam to seal. Cut log lengthwise into quarters to form 4 long layered strands (they don't have to be perfect). Wrap each quarter into a spiral shape, tucking outer end underneath. Place each spiral into prepared muffin pan. Repeat entire process with remaining 2 puff pastry sheets. Chill pan in refrigerator for 10 minutes.

3. Whisk together egg and 1 tablespoon water in a bowl until frothy. Brush muffin tops with egg wash.

4. Bake in preheated oven until muffins are puffed and browned, about 30 minutes. Cover with aluminum foil after 20 minutes to prevent overbrowning. Cool in pan 10 minutes. Remove muffins from pan, and roll in remaining sugar mixture.

DON'T SWEAT THE SWIRL
Cutting the rolled puff pastry into quarters can be a little messy, but don't worry—even if they are uneven, you'll get a beautiful spiral.

A Creole Classic

Daube, considered to be one of New Orleans' "endangered dishes," is made for cold days and cozy nights

WHEN THE WEATHER has a nip in the air, my thoughts turn to braised roasts and rich, dense stews. For years, I'd made a variation of my mother's beef stew, and then one year in New Orleans, the late Chef Leah Chase introduced me to the Creole daube (pronounced "dohb").

With a major in French, I certainly knew the word and was even familiar with the version that I had savored in Parisian bistros–where the windows were steamy from the outside chill. I had also splurged on an antique copper daubière, the oval pot that takes its name from this stew, which is often cooked in it. But Mrs. Chase's take on daube was a revelation for me: It had the same hearty appearance but with a *je ne sais quoi* that was New Orleans through and through.

Later research suggested that the distinctive Crescent City version of daube, which uses different cuts of meat and spices from the classic French one, is a bit of the city's history in a stewpot. Some food historians have written that the New Orleans variant is a conjoining of the French and Italian (specifically Sicilian) threads that run deep in the city's culinary past. Indeed, New Orleans food expert Dale Curry says that daube is a pot roast cooked in the spaghetti sauce that's known there as "red gravy." That theory holds weight, as it explains how and why the dish contains the region's flavoring "trinity" of onion, bell pepper, and celery as well as cloves and tomato paste.

In New Orleans, daube usually turns up around the year-end holidays, but it's perfect anytime something filling and soul-warming is needed on the table. This beef stew, which Curry describes as one of the city's "endangered dishes," is doubly delightful because, as I would later learn, with the addition of gelatin, it can be transformed into daube glacé–a glorious, terrine-like appetizer that's sliced cold and served with crackers. –Jessica B. Harris

Creole Daube

ACTIVE 50 MIN. - TOTAL 1 HOUR, PLUS 3 HOURS, 15 MIN. BRAISING

SERVES 6

- 3 thick-cut hickory-smoked bacon slices, coarsely chopped
- 1 (3½-lb.) boneless chuck roast, trimmed
- 1 Tbsp. kosher salt
- 1 tsp. black pepper
- 2 small yellow onions, chopped (2¼ cups)
- 1 small green bell pepper, chopped (1 cup)
- 1 large celery stalk, chopped (½ cup)
- 3 Tbsp. tomato paste (from 1 [6-oz.] can)
- 2½ Tbsp. finely chopped garlic (from 8 garlic cloves)
- 1 cup dry red wine
- 2 cups beef stock
- 5 (5-inch) fresh thyme sprigs
- 3 fresh bay leaves
- ⅛ tsp. ground cloves
- 5 small carrots, sliced on an angle into 2-inch pieces (2 cups)
- 2 medium turnips, peeled and cut into 1-inch pieces (3 cups)

1. Preheat oven to 325°F. Cook bacon in a large Dutch oven over medium, stirring occasionally, until it's browned and fat has rendered, about 8 minutes. Transfer bacon to a plate, and reserve drippings in skillet.

2. Sprinkle roast with kosher salt and black pepper. Increase heat to medium-high. Add roast to Dutch oven, and sear until browned on 2 sides, about 12 minutes, carefully flipping halfway through. Transfer to a plate.

3. Reduce heat to medium. Add onions, bell pepper, and celery to Dutch oven; cook, stirring often and scraping up browned bits from bottom of Dutch oven, until onions soften, about 6 minutes. Add tomato paste and garlic; cook, stirring constantly, until tomato paste turns a shade darker, about 2 minutes. Add wine, and bring to a simmer over medium. Simmer, stirring occasionally, until it's slightly thickened and some of the alcohol burns off, about 3 minutes. Stir in stock, thyme sprigs, bay leaves, and cloves. Nestle roast and bacon back into Dutch oven along with any juices that have accumulated; bring to a simmer over medium, and then remove from heat.

4. Cover and transfer to preheated oven, and braise 2 hours. Remove from oven; uncover and stir in carrots and turnips. Cover and return to oven; braise until meat and vegetables are tender, about 1 hour, 15 minutes. Remove from oven, and let rest 15 minutes. Transfer roast to a work surface, and shred into large pieces. Skim off fat from broth, and discard. Remove and discard thyme sprigs and bay leaves. Return shredded beef to Dutch oven, and then serve.

Nail It with Cloves

Cloves get their name from their nail-like appearance ("*Clavus*" means "nail" in Latin). When dried, these small flower buds produce a sweetly pungent spice that has long been a secret ingredient, like the clove-studded onion that has traditionally added an extra layer of flavor to many a French stock.

Whole and ground cloves are readily available, and just about everyone has some lurking at the back of their cabinet. However, as with any spices, they will lose their pungency over time. Buy small amounts, and use them rapidly before their kick is gone.

Pesto with a Punch

Liven up recipes with a good-for-you sauce made with seasonal greens

Winter Greens Pesto

ACTIVE 15 MIN. · TOTAL 15 MIN.

MAKES 1½ CUPS (24 SERVINGS)

- 8 oz. fresh mixed winter greens (such as kale, collards, and beet greens), stemmed and coarsely chopped (7 cups)
- ⅓ cup toasted walnuts, chopped
- 1 large garlic clove, smashed
- ¾ cup extra-virgin olive oil
- 1 oz. Parmesan cheese, grated (about ¼ cup)
- 1½ tsp. honey
- 1 tsp. grated lemon zest plus 1 Tbsp. fresh juice (from 1 lemon)
- ¾ tsp. kosher salt

1. Place 2 quarts water in a large saucepan, and bring to a boil over high. Add winter greens; cook, stirring often, until bright green and slightly wilted, about 1 minute. Drain in a colander, and rinse under cold water. Squeeze firmly to remove as much liquid as possible over sink, and transfer to a food processor.

2. Add walnuts and garlic to greens in food processor, and pulse until finely chopped, about 8 pulses, stopping to scrape down sides as needed. Add olive oil, Parmesan, honey, lemon zest, lemon juice, and salt; process until well blended, about 20 seconds. Transfer to an airtight container. Press plastic wrap directly onto surface of pesto, and cover with lid. Chill up to 3 days.

CALORIES: **81** – CARBS: **1 G** – FAT: **8 G**

Tasty Ways to Use It

1.
Swirl into creamy dips, like hummus or guacamole.

2.
Spread on the inside of a grilled cheese sandwich before cooking.

3.
Brush over grilled meat or seafood kebabs. Serve extra pesto on the side.

Pop Star

When cravings hit, get creative with your popcorn game

Stovetop Bacon Popcorn

ACTIVE 20 MIN. · TOTAL 20 MIN.

SERVES 4

- 8 bacon slices
- ⅓ cup popcorn kernels
- ½ tsp. fine sea salt

1. Heat a large nonstick skillet over medium. Cook bacon slices in 2 batches, flipping occasionally, until browned and crisp, about 8 minutes. Transfer bacon to a plate lined with a paper towel to drain, and pour bacon drippings from skillet into a small heatproof bowl. Crumble bacon, and set aside.
2. Add 3 tablespoons of the bacon drippings into a 6-quart pot fitted with a lid; heat over medium. Add 2 popcorn kernels. Cover and shake saucepan until kernels pop, 5 to 6 minutes. Add remaining kernels; cover and shake constantly until kernels stop popping, about 2 minutes. Remove from heat.
3. Immediately add salt, crumbled bacon, and desired toppings to pot while popcorn is still hot; stir to coat. Serve immediately.

Make Your Own Mix

Four sweet and savory ingredient combos

Maple and Glazed Pecans
Add 1 Tbsp. **pure maple syrup,** ¼ tsp. **ground cinnamon,** and ½ cup chopped **glazed pecans** after bacon in Step 3.

Smoky Chile-Garlic
Add 1 tsp. **ground cumin,** 1 tsp. **chile powder,** ½ tsp. **smoked paprika,** and ¼ tsp. **garlic powder** after bacon in Step 3.

Jalapeño-Parmesan
Add 1 thinly sliced seeded **jalapeño chile** to the skillet with the bacon halfway through the cooking process in Step 1. Sprinkle popcorn with 3 Tbsp. grated **Parmesan cheese.**

Ranch and Chive
Add 3 Tbsp. **ranch dressing mix** (from a 1-oz. envelope) and 2 Tbsp. thinly sliced **fresh chives** after bacon in Step 3.

COOKING SCHOOL

HOW TO CARE FOR A WOODEN CUTTING BOARD

1.
CLEAN

Wipe board with a damp cloth. Sprinkle evenly with kosher salt. Scrub with the cut side of a lemon until board is clean. Repeat on other side. Wipe away excess salt with a dishcloth.

2.
OIL

When the board is dry, use a clean dishcloth or paper towel to rub food-grade mineral oil evenly over the surface. Repeat on other side. Set aside for a few hours for the oil to soak in.

3.
BUFF

Use a clean dishcloth or paper towel to wipe off any excess oil before using.

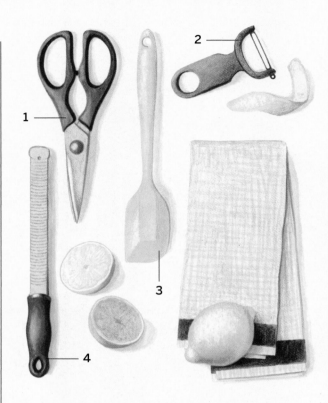

Essential Kitchen Tools
Gadgets that save time and energy

1. KITCHEN SHEARS
This handy pair allows you to cut raw bacon, break down whole poultry, slice a pizza, snip fresh herbs and flowers, and chop canned ingredients right in the container—the list goes on and on.

2. Y PEELER
Hands down, this double-bladed tool is the safest and simplest way to remove skins and peels. It's also good for shaving chocolate and hard cheese into shards and making "noodles" out of wide vegetables, like squash.

3. SILICONE SPATULA
Unlike a wooden spoon (another essential), this type of spatula is dishwasher-safe and gentle on nonstick cookware. It can withstand high temperatures, scrape every trace of batter from a bowl, and even frost a cake.

4. RASP GRATER
Most commonly known by the brand name Microplane, this long metal tool has razor-sharp holes for grating garlic and ginger and making fine, fluffy piles of citrus zest, chocolate, spices, and hard cheeses.

WE'RE LOVING THESE PANTRY FAVORITES

Two Test Kitchen picks

"Alecia's Tomato Chutney is great on grilled meats as well as sandwiches. I also like to swirl it in mayonnaise with chopped fresh lemon thyme and a squeeze of lemon juice for an easy, tasty dipping sauce." $7; aleciaschutney.com

Karen Schroeder-Rankin
Test Kitchen Professional

"Sauce Queen Honey Hot Sauce is honey that is blended with peppers (not infused and strained) for a chunky texture and lots of heat. Try it in salad dressings, cocktails, or marinades. Or drizzle on cornbread or fried chicken." $16; saucequeen.com

Jasmine Smith
Test Kitchen Professional

March

We're All Spears

Whether you choose green or white asparagus, it's a welcome sign of spring.
Here, three delicious ways to enjoy it

ASPARAGUS WITH EGGS
AND PROSCIUTTO

Asparagus with Eggs and Prosciutto

ACTIVE 15 MIN. - TOTAL 15 MIN.
SERVES 4

Cook 1 lb. **asparagus** (trimmed) in salted boiling water until tender-crisp, 2 to 3 minutes for thinner spears or 4 to 5 minutes for thicker spears. Transfer to a bowl of **ice water**; let stand 1 minute. Drain. Whisk together 1½ Tbsp. **apple cider vinegar**, 1 tsp. **Dijon mustard**, and ½ tsp. **maple syrup**. Gradually whisk in 3 Tbsp. **olive oil** until smooth. Whisk in 2 Tbsp. minced **shallot**. Arrange asparagus on a platter. Top with 2 oz. torn **prosciutto** and 4 **soft-cooked eggs** (peeled and halved). Drizzle with dressing; sprinkle with **flaky sea salt**, **black pepper**, and **fresh basil leaves**.

Creamy Asparagus Soup

ACTIVE 25 MIN. - TOTAL 30 MIN.
SERVES 4

Trim 2 lb. **asparagus**; cut into 2-inch pieces. Set aside 1 cup asparagus tips. Heat 1 tsp. **olive oil** in a Dutch oven over medium-high. Add reserved tips; cook, stirring occasionally, 2 to 3 minutes. Transfer to a plate. Reduce heat to medium. Add 2 thinly sliced **leeks** (white and light green parts only) and 2 Tbsp. **olive oil** to Dutch oven. Cook, stirring occasionally, until softened, 4 minutes. Add 12 oz. **Yukon Gold potatoes** (peeled and cubed) and 3 minced **garlic cloves**; cook, stirring constantly, 1 minute. Add 4 cups **unsalted chicken stock**. Bring to a boil over medium-high. Cook until potatoes are semitender, 8 minutes. Add 1½ tsp. **kosher salt** and the asparagus pieces; cook 5 to 6 minutes. Remove from heat; stir in ½ cup chopped **fresh parsley**. Process using an immersion blender until smooth. Stir in ½ cup **heavy cream** and 2 Tbsp. **orange juice**. Drizzle servings with **heavy cream**; top with cooked asparagus tips, chopped **cooked bacon**, and additional **parsley**.

ASPARAGUS RIBBON CROSTINI

CLOSE SHAVE
Make asparagus ribbons by shaving the stalks upward a few times with a Y peeler. Rotate spears, and repeat on other sides.

Asparagus Ribbon Crostini

ACTIVE 20 MIN. - TOTAL 30 MIN.
MAKES 12

Place 12 (½-inch-thick) diagonal **baguette** slices on a baking sheet. Drizzle with 2 Tbsp. **olive oil**; sprinkle with ¼ tsp. **kosher salt**. Bake at 450°F until golden brown, 6 to 8 minutes. Cool completely. Stir together ¾ cup **whole-milk ricotta**, ¼ cup grated **Parmesan**, 1 Tbsp. chopped **fresh mint**, 1 tsp. **lemon zest**, and ½ tsp. each **kosher salt** and **black pepper** in a bowl. Whisk together 1 Tbsp. each **olive oil** and **lemon juice** and ½ tsp. **kosher salt** in a separate bowl; add 1 lb. trimmed **asparagus** (shaved into thin ribbons), and toss gently to coat. Spread ricotta mixture on baguette slices. Top with asparagus ribbons. Garnish with **lemon zest** and torn **mint**.

RHUBARB CUSTARD PIE
(PAGE 54)

Think Pink

Rhubarb is one of spring's most underappreciated ingredients.
This year, it stars in six beautiful desserts

I DIDN'T GROW UP EATING RHUBARB.
I can't remember ever seeing it at the Sunflower grocery store when I was a kid in Grenada, Mississippi, and I know my grandparents never had it in their garden a few miles away. Years later, as an adult in my adopted hometown of Birmingham, I'd occasionally notice rhubarb at Whole Foods Market. Sometimes I'd even buy it, inspired to try something new, but I'd chicken out and end up tossing it into the compost bucket. It was completely unfamiliar to me and outside my comfort zone.

It turns out there's good reason rhubarb wasn't a staple in my youth. The stalks grow best in cooler climates, and it's not like the local nurseries carried it for home gardeners who were interested in trying to plant it in the South anyway. But last spring, I started seeing it around area farmers' markets, so I figured folks had found a way to make it work down here. And if they could do that, I could at least teach myself how to cook with it.

To my surprise, rhubarb is simple to prepare. Why had I been so intimidated? The bright red stalks felt celery-firm as I sliced through them. I swear I detected a musty, grapey smell emerge, a fragrance like that of muscadines. I tasted some raw. It was crunchy and quite tart, akin to a hard green plum.

I didn't expect such a dense vegetable (yes, it is a vegetable) to soften so quickly as it cooked, giving way easily to something like a puree after just a few minutes of sautéing. When tossed raw onto or under batter, it became completely tender by the time a cake was done.

Best of all, I learned that rhubarb's tangy bite is a wonderful way to usher in spring, when you naturally move away from the heartier flavors of winter (like chocolate, spice, and nuts) toward something brighter and livelier, like the following desserts. —Ann Taylor Pittman

Four Rules for Rhubarb

What to know about selecting, storing, and prepping the stalks

1
Seek out firm, blemish-free stalks, and bypass any that feel limp. Field-grown rhubarb tends to have deep red stalks, while hothouse varieties are often bright pink or light red (and milder in flavor).

2
Cut off and throw away any leaves still attached (they're toxic). To keep the stalks fresh and juicy for up to two weeks, bundle them together, wrap in foil (nothing airtight like plastic wrap), and store in the refrigerator.

3
Slice or chop the rhubarb when you're ready to use it; don't cut it ahead of time.

4
Consider frozen rhubarb (if fresh is not available) for recipes that call for sliced or chopped stalks. Be sure to thaw it completely; then blot it dry with paper towels.

**RHUBARB-BUTTERMILK
UPSIDE-DOWN CAKE
(PAGE 53)**

RHUBARB-CREAM
CHEESE SPOKE CAKE
(PAGE 53)

NO-CHURN RHUBARB-
RASPBERRY ICE CREAM

No-Churn Rhubarb-Raspberry Ice Cream

You don't need to have an ice cream maker to pull off this recipe—but you do need to plan ahead, as it takes several hours to freeze solid.

ACTIVE 15 MIN. - TOTAL 1 HOUR, 15 MIN., PLUS 6 HOURS FREEZING

SERVES 8

¼ cup unsalted butter, cut into small pieces

2½ cups sliced (½-inch) fresh (or frozen, thawed, and patted dry) rhubarb (11¼ oz.)

2 cups fresh raspberries (from 2 [6-oz.] containers)

3 Tbsp. granulated sugar

1 (14-oz.) can sweetened condensed milk

2 tsp. vanilla extract

2 cups heavy whipping cream

1. Preheat oven to 400°F. Place a 9- x 5-inch loaf pan in freezer. Place butter in a 13- x 9-inch baking dish; bake until butter browns, about 10 minutes. Remove baking dish from oven, and add rhubarb, raspberries, and sugar; stir to combine. Return to oven; continue baking at 400°F until rhubarb is very tender, about 20 minutes, stirring halfway through cook time. Remove from oven; let stand until mixture cools to room temperature, about 20 minutes. Gently mash using a fork or the side of a silicone spatula. Set aside.
2. Whisk together condensed milk and vanilla in a large bowl. Beat whipping cream in a separate large bowl with an electric mixer on high speed until stiff peaks form, 2 to 3 minutes. Add about one-fourth of the whipped cream to condensed milk mixture, gently folding until just combined. Fold remaining whipped cream into condensed milk mixture until combined.
3. Dollop mashed rhubarb mixture over whipped cream mixture in bowl; fold gently until just combined, 2 to 3 folds (it can be streaky/slightly swirled). Remove loaf pan from freezer. Spoon mixture into chilled loaf pan, gently shaking pan to level top; cover with plastic wrap. Freeze until firm, 6 to 8 hours. Let stand 10 minutes at room temperature. Scoop and serve.

Rhubarb-Buttermilk Upside-Down Cake

(Photo, page 50)

Many upside-down cake recipes use brown sugar to create a caramelized topping when the cake is inverted, but this one is made with granulated sugar and strawberry jam to preserve the rhubarb's vibrant color.

ACTIVE 15 MIN. - TOTAL 1 HOUR, 30 MIN.

SERVES 12

2 Tbsp. unsalted butter, melted

2¼ cups granulated sugar, divided

¼ cup seedless strawberry jam

4 large rhubarb stalks, trimmed and cut into 2¾- x ⅓-inch pieces (about 60 pieces total, 8 oz.)

3 cups all-purpose flour

1½ tsp. baking soda

1 tsp. kosher salt

2 large eggs

½ cup canola oil

1 Tbsp. vanilla extract

1½ cups whole buttermilk
Crème fraîche, for serving

1. Preheat oven to 350°F. Line a 13- x 9-inch metal baking pan with parchment paper. Drizzle butter evenly over bottom of parchment paper in pan, and sprinkle evenly with ¼ cup of the sugar. Place jam in a small microwavable bowl. Microwave on HIGH until melted, 30 to 45 seconds. Brush jam over sugar in pan. Arrange 4 or 5 rhubarb pieces, skin side (pink side) facing down, horizontally in 1 corner of pan. Arrange 4 or 5 rhubarb pieces vertically next to first section. Repeat process, alternating between horizontal and vertical positioning, to create a grid pattern.
2. Whisk together flour, baking soda, and salt in a medium bowl. Beat eggs, oil, vanilla, and remaining 2 cups sugar with a stand mixer fitted with a paddle attachment on medium speed until creamy, about 2 minutes. Reduce mixer speed to low, and beat in flour mixture alternately with buttermilk, beginning and ending with flour mixture. Pour batter evenly over rhubarb in pan. Bake in preheated oven until a wooden pick inserted in center comes out clean, about 50 minutes.
3. Transfer pan to a wire rack; cool 10 minutes. Carefully invert cake onto wire rack; remove parchment paper. Let cake cool on wire rack at least 15 minutes or up to 1 hour. Slice and serve warm or at room temperature with crème fraîche.

Rhubarb-Cream Cheese Spoke Cake

(Photo, page 51)

Named for its wheel-like appearance, this dessert has the dense crumb of a pound cake and an irresistibly crunchy top.

ACTIVE 15 MIN. - TOTAL 2 HOURS, PLUS 1 HOUR, 50 MIN. COOLING

SERVES 10

2 cups all-purpose flour

1½ tsp. baking powder

1⅛ tsp. kosher salt, divided

1 (8-oz.) pkg. cream cheese, softened

¾ cup plus 1½ Tbsp. unsalted butter, softened, divided

2 cups plus 1½ Tbsp. granulated sugar, divided

3 large eggs

2 tsp. vanilla extract

12 (4½- x ½-inch) pieces rhubarb (4½ oz., from about 2 large stalks)

1. Preheat oven to 325°F. Line bottom of a 9-inch springform pan with parchment paper. Coat paper and sides of pan with cooking spray; set aside. Whisk together flour, baking powder, and 1 teaspoon of the salt in a medium bowl. Beat cream cheese and ¾ cup of the butter with a stand mixer fitted with a paddle attachment on medium speed until light and fluffy, 2 to 3 minutes. Gradually add 2 cups of the sugar, beating until combined, about 1 minute. Add eggs, 1 at a time, beating well after each addition. Beat in vanilla. Reduce mixer speed to low; gradually add flour mixture, beating just until combined (batter will be thick).
2. Spoon batter into prepared pan; spread into an even layer using a small offset spatula. Bake in preheated oven 30 minutes. Remove from oven. (Do not turn oven off.) Arrange rhubarb pieces in a spokelike pattern over top of batter, overlapping slightly in center of pan. Microwave remaining 1½ tablespoons butter in a small bowl on HIGH until melted, about 30 seconds; brush evenly over rhubarb. Stir together remaining ⅛ teaspoon salt and 1½ tablespoons sugar in a small bowl; sprinkle over top of rhubarb and batter. Return to oven; continue baking at 325°F until a wooden pick inserted in center comes out clean, 1 hour to 1 hour, 10 minutes. Remove from oven. Transfer pan to a wire rack; cool 20 minutes. Remove sides of pan, and let cake cool completely on rack, about 1 hour, 30 minutes.

Rhubarb-Amaretto Bars

The lemony dough is dry and crumbly but bakes to a crisp, light shortbread texture.

ACTIVE 35 MIN. - TOTAL 1 HOUR, 45 MIN., PLUS 2 HOURS CHILLING

MAKES 24 BARS

CRUST

- 1½ cups all-purpose flour
- ⅔ cup powdered sugar, plus more for dusting (optional)
- 2 tsp. grated lemon zest (from 1 lemon)
- ½ tsp. kosher salt
- ½ cup cold unsalted butter, cut into small pieces
- 3 Tbsp. canola oil

FILLING

- 3 cups sliced (½-inch) fresh (or frozen, thawed, and patted dry) rhubarb (13½ oz.)
- 1⅓ cups granulated sugar, divided
- ¼ cup fresh lemon juice (from 1 lemon)
- ¼ cup (2 oz.) amaretto (almond liqueur)
- ½ cup all-purpose flour
- ¼ tsp. kosher salt
- 4 large eggs, lightly beaten
- Red liquid food coloring (optional)

1. Prepare the Crust: Preheat oven to 350°F. Line a 13- x 9-inch metal baking pan with parchment paper, leaving a 1-inch overhang on all sides; set aside. Place flour, ⅔ cup powdered sugar, the lemon zest, and salt in a food processor; pulse until combined, 2 to 3 pulses. Add butter; pulse until mixture resembles coarse meal, about 10 pulses. Drizzle mixture with oil; pulse until barely moistened, 5 or 6 pulses (mixture will be crumbly). Pour mixture into prepared pan; pat firmly into an even layer. Rinse food processor, and pat dry. Bake Crust until light golden brown, about 20 minutes. Remove from oven.
2. While Crust bakes, prepare the Filling: Bring rhubarb and ⅓ cup of the granulated sugar to a boil in a small saucepan over medium, stirring often (rhubarb will release juices). Reduce heat to medium-low; cook, stirring occasionally, until rhubarb is very tender and broken down, about 10 minutes. Transfer to cleaned food processor; process until smooth, about 30 seconds. Add lemon juice and amaretto; process until well combined, about 30 seconds. Set aside.

3. Whisk together flour, kosher salt, and remaining 1 cup granulated sugar in a large bowl. Whisk in rhubarb mixture and eggs until well combined. Stir in food coloring, if desired. Pour mixture over hot Crust. Return to oven, and bake at 350°F until Filling is set, about 20 minutes. Remove from oven. Let cool to room temperature, about 30 minutes. Refrigerate, uncovered, until chilled, 2 to 3 hours. Remove mixture from pan using parchment paper overhang; cut evenly into 24 (2-inch) squares.
4. Right before serving, dust with powdered sugar, if desired.

Rhubarb Custard Pie

(Photo, page 48)

ACTIVE 15 MIN. - TOTAL 2 HOURS, 15 MIN., PLUS 2 HOURS COOLING

SERVES 8

- ½ (14.1-oz.) pkg. refrigerated piecrusts, at room temperature
- 2 large eggs
- 1 cup half-and-half
- 1 tsp. vanilla extract
- ½ tsp. grated orange zest (from 1 orange)
- ¼ tsp. kosher salt
- ¼ tsp. almond extract
- 1 cup plus 2 Tbsp. granulated sugar, divided
- 4 Tbsp. all-purpose flour, divided, plus more for work surface
- 3 cups sliced (½-inch-thick) fresh (or frozen, thawed, and patted dry) rhubarb (about 13½ oz.)

1. Preheat oven to 375°F. Roll piecrust out on a lightly floured work surface into a 12-inch circle. Fit crust inside a 9-inch pie plate, pressing into bottom and up sides of plate. Fold crust edges under; crimp as desired. Place a piece of parchment paper over crust in pie plate, leaving a 3-inch overhang. Fill with pie weights or dried beans. Bake 15 minutes. Carefully remove parchment paper and pie weights. Continue baking at 375°F until crust is light golden brown, about 5 minutes. Transfer to a wire rack; cool to room temperature, about 30 minutes. Meanwhile, reduce oven temperature to 350°F.
2. Whisk together eggs, half-and-half, vanilla, orange zest, salt, almond extract, 1 cup of the sugar, and 3 tablespoons of the flour in a large bowl. Place rhubarb and remaining 1 tablespoon flour in a separate large bowl; toss to coat. Place cooled pie

plate on a large rimmed baking sheet. Place coated rhubarb in cooled piecrust. Pour egg mixture over rhubarb. Sprinkle evenly with remaining 2 tablespoons sugar. Wrap edges of piecrust with aluminum foil. Bake at 350°F until filling is set and a thermometer inserted into center of pie registers 175°F, about 1 hour to 1 hour, 10 minutes. Transfer to a wire rack; cool completely, about 2 hours. Serve at room temperature or chilled.

Skillet Rhubarb-Strawberry Crisp with Salted-Almond Streusel

(Photo, page 2)

Marcona almonds make the streusel buttery and rich, but you can use regular almonds instead.

ACTIVE 15 MIN. - TOTAL 1 HOUR, 15 MIN.

SERVES 8

- 1 cup uncooked old-fashioned regular rolled oats
- ½ cup chopped salted roasted Marcona almonds
- ½ cup packed light brown sugar
- ¼ cup all-purpose flour
- ¾ tsp. ground cinnamon
- 8 Tbsp. unsalted butter, divided
- 4 cups sliced (½-inch) fresh (or frozen, thawed, and patted dry) rhubarb (1 lb., 2 oz.)
- 4 cups quartered fresh strawberries
- 1 cup granulated sugar
- 3 Tbsp. cornstarch
- Vanilla ice cream, for serving

1. Preheat oven to 350°F. Stir together oats, almonds, brown sugar, flour, and cinnamon in a medium bowl. Microwave 6 tablespoons of the butter in a small bowl on HIGH until melted, about 60 seconds. Drizzle melted butter over oat mixture; stir until fully moistened. Set aside.
2. Melt remaining 2 tablespoons butter in a 10-inch cast-iron skillet (or other ovenproof skillet) over medium-high. Add rhubarb; cook, stirring often, until softened, about 3 minutes. Remove from heat; stir in strawberries. Sprinkle with granulated sugar and cornstarch; stir gently to combine. Sprinkle evenly with oat mixture.
3. Transfer skillet to preheated oven; bake until filling is bubbly and streusel is browned, about 40 minutes. Let stand until slightly cooled, 20 to 30 minutes. Serve warm with vanilla ice cream.

RHUBARB-AMARETTO BARS

Freezes Beautifully

Tasty meals to serve tonight or in the future

Fire-Roasted Tomato-and-Beef Ragù

ACTIVE 40 MIN. · TOTAL 40 MIN.
SERVES 6

- 1 Tbsp. extra-virgin olive oil
- 1¼ lb. 85/15 lean ground beef
- 1 medium sweet onion, finely chopped (about ¾ cup)
- 3 large garlic cloves, finely chopped (about 3 Tbsp.)
- 1½ tsp. kosher salt, divided
- ½ tsp. black pepper
- 1 (14.5-oz.) can fire-roasted crushed tomatoes
- 1 (14.5-oz.) can fire-roasted diced tomatoes
- 1 (8-oz.) can tomato sauce
- 1 cup chicken or vegetable broth
- 1 Tbsp. granulated sugar
- 1 Tbsp. dried Italian seasoning
- ¼ tsp. crushed red pepper
- 1 lb. pasta of choice, cooked according to pkg. directions, for serving

  Grated Parmesan cheese, optional

  Fresh basil leaves, optional

1. Heat olive oil in a large nonstick skillet over medium-high. Add beef, sweet onion, garlic, 1 teaspoon of the salt, and the pepper; cook, stirring occasionally and breaking up beef, until browned, about 5 minutes. Drain beef mixture; return to skillet. Stir in crushed and diced tomatoes, tomato sauce, broth, sugar, Italian seasoning, red pepper, and remaining ½ teaspoon salt.

2. Bring sauce to a simmer over medium-high; reduce heat to medium. Cook, stirring occasionally, until thickened, 20 to 30 minutes. Serve with hot cooked pasta. Top with Parmesan and basil, if desired.

ENJOY IT LATER

FREEZE: Let cooked sauce cool to room temperature, 1 hour. Place in an airtight, freezer-safe container. Or fill a zip-top plastic freezer bag three-fourths full, and seal, pushing out any air. Freeze until solid, at least 4 hours or up to 6 months.
REHEAT: Thaw overnight in refrigerator or at room temperature (about 1 hour). Place sauce in a Dutch oven or saucepan; heat over medium, stirring often, until hot, about 15 minutes. Serve as directed.

Sesame Shrimp Stir-Fry
ACTIVE 20 MIN. - TOTAL 20 MIN.
SERVES 6

- ½ cup soy sauce
- 2 Tbsp. light brown sugar
- 1 Tbsp. sesame oil
- 1 Tbsp. ground fresh chile paste (such as sambal oelek)
- 1 Tbsp. cornstarch
- 3 garlic cloves, grated (about 1½ tsp.)
- 1 Tbsp. canola oil
- 2 large red bell peppers, cut into 1-inch pieces (about 4 cups)
- 3 medium carrots, sliced ⅛ inch thick (about 1½ cups)
- 1 medium-size white onion, cut into ¼-inch wedges (about 2 cups)
- 4 cups broccoli florets (from 1 small head)
- 1½ lb. large raw shrimp, peeled and deveined
- ¼ cup roughly chopped fresh cilantro
- Hot cooked rice, optional

Whisk together soy sauce, sugar, sesame oil, chile paste, cornstarch, and garlic in a small bowl. Heat canola oil in a large skillet over high. Add bell peppers, carrots, onion, and broccoli; cook, stirring often, until just beginning to become tender, about 4 minutes. Add shrimp and soy sauce mixture; cook, stirring often, until shrimp are fully cooked and sauce is slightly thickened, about 5 minutes. Sprinkle with cilantro. If desired, serve over rice.

ENJOY IT LATER
FREEZE: Let cooked shrimp mixture cool to room temperature, about 1 hour. Fill a zip-top plastic freezer bag three-fourths full, and seal, pushing out any air. Freeze until solid, at least 4 hours or up to 6 months. **REHEAT:** Allow bag to thaw overnight in refrigerator. Heat a large skillet over high; add thawed stir-fry mixture. Cook, stirring often, until heated through, 10 minutes. Sprinkle with cilantro, and serve with rice, if desired.

Creamy Artichoke, Kale, and Rice Gratin

ACTIVE 20 MIN. · TOTAL 35 MIN.

SERVES 6

- ¾ cup uncooked basmati rice
- ¾ tsp. kosher salt, divided
- 1 (10-oz.) container refrigerated Alfredo sauce (such as Giovanni Rana)
- 1 (8-oz.) pkg. cream cheese, softened
- 3 garlic cloves, finely chopped (1 Tbsp.)
- 2 Tbsp. sherry vinegar
- 1 tsp. grated lemon zest plus 1 Tbsp. fresh juice (from 1 lemon)
- ¼ tsp. black pepper
- 2 (14-oz.) cans quartered artichoke hearts, drained
- 4 cups packed chopped kale (from 1 bunch)
- ¾ cup Italian-seasoned panko breadcrumbs
- 2 oz. Parmesan cheese, grated (½ cup)
- 2 Tbsp. olive oil
   Crushed red pepper, optional
   Chopped fresh parsley, optional

1. Preheat oven to 400°F. Spray a 2-quart (11- x 7-inch) baking dish with cooking spray. Bring 2 cups water, basmati rice, and ¼ teaspoon of the salt to a boil in a small saucepan over medium-high. Reduce heat to medium-low; cover and cook, 7 minutes. Drain well; place in even layer in bottom of prepared dish.

2. Whisk together Alfredo sauce, cream cheese, garlic, sherry vinegar, lemon zest and juice, black pepper, and remaining ½ teaspoon salt in a large bowl until smooth. Stir in artichokes and kale until evenly combined. Spoon over rice in prepared baking dish. Stir together breadcrumbs, Parmesan cheese, and oil in a small bowl. Sprinkle mixture evenly in baking dish. Bake in preheated oven until golden brown, about 15 minutes. Sprinkle with crushed red pepper and parsley, if desired.

ENJOY IT LATER

FREEZE: Let baked dish cool to room temperature, 1 hour. Wrap tightly with plastic wrap and then aluminum foil. Freeze until solid, at least 4 hours or up to 6 months. **REHEAT:** Thaw overnight in refrigerator. Preheat oven to 350°F. Let stand at room temperature while oven preheats, 30 minutes. Unwrap; discard plastic wrap. Cover with aluminum foil; bake 30 minutes. Uncover; continue baking until a thermometer inserted registers 165°F, 15 to 20 minutes.

Green Chile-Chicken Soup

ACTIVE 20 MIN. · TOTAL 20 MIN.

SERVES 6

- 1 Tbsp. olive or canola oil
- 1 large poblano chile, seeded and chopped (about ½ cup)
- 1 cup chopped sweet onion (from 1 medium onion)
- 4 small garlic cloves, finely chopped (about 1 Tbsp.)
- 4 cups unsalted chicken broth
- 2 (15½-oz.) cans white Great Northern beans, drained and rinsed
- 1 (15-oz.) can green enchilada sauce
- 1 tsp. kosher salt
- 1 tsp. ground cumin
- ½ tsp. ground coriander
- 3 cups coarsely shredded cooked chicken (about 1 rotisserie chicken)
- ¼ cup chopped fresh cilantro, plus more for garnish
  Thinly sliced radishes
  Sour cream

Heat oil in a large Dutch oven over medium-high. Add poblano and sweet onion; cook, stirring occasionally, until tender, about 5 minutes. Add garlic; cook, stirring constantly, until fragrant, about 30 seconds. Stir in broth, beans, enchilada sauce, salt, cumin, and coriander. Bring to a simmer, and cook, stirring occasionally, about 5 minutes. Using back of spoon, gently mash beans. Stir in chicken; continue simmering until heated through, about 5 minutes. Stir in cilantro. Garnish with radishes, sour cream, and additional cilantro. Serve immediately.

ENJOY IT LATER
FREEZE: Let cooked soup cool to room temperature, 1 hour. Place in an airtight, freezer-safe container. Or fill a zip-top plastic freezer bag no more than three-fourths full, and seal, pushing out any air. Freeze until solid, at least 4 hours or up to 6 months. **REHEAT:** Thaw overnight in refrigerator or at room temperature (1 hour). Place soup in Dutch oven; heat over medium-high, stirring often, until hot, about 15 minutes. Garnish as desired.

Shepherd's Pie with Scalloped Potatoes and Pesto

ACTIVE 15 MIN. · TOTAL 45 MIN.
SERVES 6

- 1 tsp. olive oil
- 1 lb. ground lamb
- 1½ tsp. kosher salt, divided
- ¾ tsp. black pepper, divided
- 2 medium parsnips, halved lengthwise and sliced ¼ inch thick (about 1 cup)
- 1 cup sliced leeks (from 1 small leek)
- 2 Tbsp. all-purpose flour
- ½ cup chicken broth
- 1 cup frozen sweet peas
- ¼ cup crème fraîche
- ¼ cup jarred basil pesto (such as Giovanni Rana)
- ¼ cup chopped fresh flat-leaf parsley, plus more for garnish
- 1 (4.7-oz.) pkg. scalloped potatoes (such as Betty Crocker)
- ¾ cup boiling water
- ⅓ cup whole milk

1. Preheat oven to 450°F. Lightly spray a 2-quart (7- x 11-inch) baking dish with cooking spray. Heat oil in a large skillet over medium-high. Add ground lamb, ¾ teaspoon of the salt, and ¼ teaspoon of the pepper; cook, using a spoon to break up meat, until browned, about 5 minutes. Remove using a slotted spoon, and let drain on a plate lined with a paper towel, reserving drippings in pan. Add parsnips and leeks to drippings, and cook, stirring occasionally, until just beginning to become tender, about 2 minutes. Sprinkle flour over vegetable mixture; cook, stirring constantly, about 1 minute. Gradually stir in broth until smooth; cook, stirring often, until thickened, about 2 minutes. Remove from heat; stir in sweet peas, crème fraîche, pesto, ¼ cup parsley, cooked lamb, and remaining ¾ teaspoon salt and ½ teaspoon pepper. Spoon into prepared dish.

2. Arrange dried potatoes over filling in even layer. Whisk together sauce mix from potato box, boiling water, and milk in a small heatproof bowl until smooth; pour mixture evenly over potatoes. Bake, uncovered, in preheated oven until golden brown and edges are crispy, about 20 minutes. Let stand 10 minutes before serving. Sprinkle with additional parsley.

ENJOY IT LATER

FREEZE: Let baked dish cool to room temperature, 1 hour. Wrap tightly with plastic wrap and then aluminum foil. Freeze until solid, at least 4 hours or up to 6 months. **REHEAT:** Thaw overnight in refrigerator. Preheat oven to 350°F. Let stand at room temperature while oven preheats, 30 minutes. Unwrap; discard plastic wrap. Cover with aluminum foil; bake 20 minutes. Uncover; continue baking until a thermometer inserted registers 165°F, 10 to 15 minutes.

Ham It Up

Deceptively simple savory pastries perfect for weekend brunch

**Ham-and-Cheese Puff Pastries
with Creole Mustard**

ACTIVE 10 MIN. - TOTAL 40 MIN.
SERVES 10

- 3 Tbsp. Creole mustard
- 1 Tbsp. honey
- 1 (17.3-oz.) pkg. frozen puff pastry sheets, thawed
  All-purpose flour for work surface
- 8 deli ham slices (preferably Black Forest, 4 oz.)
- 4 (½-oz.) Gruyère cheese slices
- ¾ tsp. chopped fresh thyme leaves, plus more for garnish
- 1 large egg, lightly beaten

1. Preheat oven to 425°F with racks in upper third and lower third positions. Line 2 large baking sheets with parchment paper, and set aside. Stir together Creole mustard and honey in a small bowl; set aside.
2. Unfold each puff pastry sheet on a lightly floured work surface. Roll each sheet into a 15- x 12-inch rectangle. Transfer pastry rectangles to prepared baking sheets. Spread mustard mixture evenly over half of each rectangle lengthwise, leaving a ½-inch border around edges. Layer ham and Gruyère slices evenly over mustard mixture, leaving a ½-inch border. Sprinkle evenly with thyme.
3. Whisk together egg and 1 tablespoon water in a small bowl. Brush edges of both pastry rectangles with egg wash, and fold in half lengthwise over filling, creating 2 (15- x 6-inch) rectangles, and crimp edges with a fork to seal. Brush top of each puff pastry with egg wash. Cut 5 or 6 (3-inch) diagonal slits on top of each pastry, and gently separate slits to slightly reveal filling.
4. Bake in preheated oven until puff pastries are deep golden brown, 20 to 25 minutes, rotating baking sheets between top and bottom racks halfway through bake time. Remove from oven; cool slightly, about 5 minutes. Transfer to a cutting board; cut each puff pastry crosswise into 5 pieces. Transfer to a serving plate. Garnish with additional thyme, and serve.

PREP-AHEAD POINTER
Save time by filling and sealing the puff pastry dough a day or two before. Cover and chill (or freeze up to 2 weeks) until you're ready to bake.

Relishing Spring

Tailgating is a family tradition for Test Kitchen Pro and *Hey Y'all* host Ivy Odom, who turns seasonal vegetables into a party-worthy tray

I HAVE ALWAYS LOVED A GOOD PICKLE.
While most kids reached for the ketchup bottle, I went for the relish. I was eager to pile my plate full of pickles and thinly sliced Vidalia onions so I could add them to every bite.

Relish trays have graced Southern supper tables for generations. Ubiquitous but understated, these platters of fresh, pickled, and marinated veggies add a welcome dose of acidity and crunch to our region's creamy casseroles, cooked vegetables, and fried meats. Some plates are simply prepared with fresh onions and pickled cucumbers, while others are adorned with a wide array of salty, sweet, and tangy condiments.

Sweet Heat Spring Garden Pickles are so fresh and colorful that they would have made my childhood self giddy. And the adult in me sees their potential to shine as an accompaniment to a Bloody Mary bar—especially the Garlicky Variation (at bottom right).

Even better, they are ridiculously easy to make because they don't require fussy canning or any special equipment. Plus, they look beautiful packed in containers and stored in the fridge. Whether you enjoy them as a garnish or eat them straight out of the jar, I hope you'll relish every sweet-and-spicy bite.

Sweet Heat Spring Garden Pickles
ACTIVE 25 MIN. - TOTAL 25 MIN., PLUS 1 HOUR COOLING AND OVERNIGHT CHILLING
MAKES 4 (1-PT.) JARS

7½	oz. radishes, small radishes left whole and large radishes cut in half (from 1 medium bunch)
6	oz. asparagus, trimmed to 5-inch pieces
6	oz. whole small carrots, cut in half lengthwise (from 1 medium bunch)
6	oz. haricots verts (French green beans), trimmed to 5-inch pieces
2	large jalapeños, thinly sliced
2	tsp. black peppercorns
2	tsp. mustard seeds
2	tsp. crushed red pepper
2¾	cups white vinegar
1	cup granulated sugar
3½	Tbsp. kosher salt

1. Place radishes, asparagus, carrots, and haricots verts in 4 separate pint jars. Evenly divide jalapeño slices, peppercorns, mustard seeds, and crushed red pepper among jars.
2. Heat white vinegar, 1½ cups water, sugar, and kosher salt in a medium saucepan over medium-high. Cook, stirring often, until sugar is completely dissolved, about 5 minutes. Pour hot liquid evenly into jars.
3. Cover jars with lids and bands; cool completely to room temperature, about 1 hour. Transfer to refrigerator, and chill at least overnight or up to 2 weeks.

Garlicky Variation
To make Garlicky Spring Garden Pickles, omit jalapeños, reduce sugar to ½ cup, and add 3 smashed garlic cloves and 1 Tbsp. fresh dill (1 large sprig) to each jar. Pour liquid into jars as directed.

PICKLES IN A SNAP
This recipe doesn't even require canning. The jars will keep in the refrigerator for up to 2 weeks.

Soup of the Day

This simple two-step recipe can be made with many delicious flavors

WASTE NOT
This soup is a smart way to use up a small amount of any root vegetable. Mix and match to make your own version.

Super Spin-Offs

Sweet Potato-Carrot Soup

Season with 1½ tsp. **ground cumin.** Use 5 cups cubed peeled **sweet potatoes** (from 3 medium-size sweet potatoes) and 3 cups cubed **carrots** (from 7 large carrots). Garnish with **roasted pumpkin seed kernels (pepitas)** and diced **jalapeño.**

CALORIES: **207** – CARBS: **33 G** – FAT: **6 G**

Potato-Beet Soup

Season with 1½ Tbsp. finely chopped peeled **fresh ginger** (from 1 [1½-inch] piece). Use 5 cups cubed peeled **red beets** (from about 7 medium beets) and 3 cups cubed peeled **russet potatoes** (from about 4 medium potatoes). Garnish with plain **whole-milk Greek yogurt** and chopped **fresh chives.**

CALORIES: **210** – CARBS: **32 G** – FAT: **6 G**

Turnip-Parsnip Soup

Season with 2 tsp. chopped **fresh thyme.** Use 5 cups cubed peeled **turnips** (from about 5 medium turnips) and 3 cups cubed peeled **parsnips** (from 6 to 7 medium/large parsnips). Garnish with crumbled **vegetable chips** (such as Terra) and chopped **fresh flat-leaf parsley.**

CALORIES: **166** – CARBS: **25 G** – FAT: **6 G**

Any-Veggie Soup

ACTIVE 35 MIN. - TOTAL 1 HOUR
SERVES 6

- 2 Tbsp. olive oil
- 1 cup chopped yellow onion (from 1 medium onion)
- ½ cup finely chopped celery (from 1 large celery stalk)
- 2 tsp. finely chopped garlic (from 2 garlic cloves)
  Seasoning (see recipe variations at right)
- 8 cups chopped (½-inch cubes) peeled root vegetables (see recipe variations at right)
- 6 cups lower-sodium chicken broth or vegetable broth
- 1 tsp. kosher salt, divided
- ¼ cup half-and-half
  Garnishes (see recipe variations at right)

1. Heat olive oil in a large Dutch oven over medium-high. Add onion and celery. Cook, stirring often, until onion is translucent and softened, about 6 minutes. Stir in garlic and seasoning; cook, stirring constantly, 1 minute. Stir in root vegetables, broth, and ½ teaspoon of the salt; bring to a boil over high. Cover and reduce heat to low. Simmer, stirring occasionally, until vegetables are very soft, about 25 minutes.
2. Remove soup from heat. Using an immersion blender, process until very smooth, 2 to 3 minutes. Stir half-and-half and remaining ½ teaspoon salt into pureed soup. Garnish.

Gimme Some Sugar

This Louisiana specialty lets an iconic Southern ingredient—cane syrup—shine

IN SOUTH LOUISIANA, winter is harvest time for sugarcane. In some areas, the air is filled with the smell of burning bagasse (the fiber that remains after the juice has been extracted from the cane) and the noise from the mills is a 24-hour-a-day backdrop to life. During that season, cane's cultivation and harvest so influence the rhythms of life in some Louisiana parishes that it seems as if the plant were native to the area.

Cane was in fact brought to the region in 1751 by the Jesuits. Early colonists grew a cultivar known as Creole cane, but it was not well suited to the Louisiana terroir. In 1795, Etienne de Boré, a New Orleans plantation owner, was the first to unlock the secrets of creating wealth from the sugar-bearing reed after learning how to produce granulated sugar from two enslaved Cubans.

Planters from the French colony of Saint-Domingue fled the Haitian Revolution and brought other kinds of sugarcane and their knowledge of planting and harvesting with them to Louisiana. It did not become an important crop until 1817, when ribbon cane, a type that agreed with the Southern climate, was introduced. By the antebellum period, almost all of the cane consumed in the United States came from Louisiana and the state was the sugar capital of the nation.

I can't discuss sugarcane without thinking of my friend Father Ken Smith and his recipe for Gâteau de Sirop, or syrup cake. Today, he is a Roman Catholic priest who brings comfort to the sick, but when I first met him decades ago, he was Chef Ken and brought comfort through cooking delicious food at the legendary Upperline Restaurant in New Orleans. In those days, he regaled me with tales of the Cane River region of Louisiana, where sugar has a deep history and his people have roots. He also shared a recipe for Gâteau de Sirop, a satisfying dessert that celebrates the cane-growing traditions of the area. –Jessica B. Harris

Stock Up

Cane syrup, similar to molasses, has a sweet, delicate flavor. Here are a few Louisiana-based brands to try

Steen's 100% Pure Cane Syrup
Based in Abbeville, Steen's has been making syrup since 1910 and is still one of the most widely available brands. Their cane syrup is rich and buttery with a slight bitterness that balances out the sweetness. steenssyrup.com

Bien-Aimé Cane Knife Cane Syrup
Grown and processed on an organic farm in Church Point, this small-batch syrup adds lagniappe to waffles, pancakes, biscuits, and even coffee. bienaimefarm.square.site

Poirier's Real Cane Syrup
Many chefs and food lovers consider this the Holy Grail of cane syrups. In Youngsville, Charles Poirier uses an old family recipe to make caramel-sweet, earthy syrup in limited batches that sell out every year. realcanesyrup.com

Gâteau de Sirop (Syrup Cake)

ACTIVE 10 MIN. - TOTAL 55 MIN., PLUS 1 HOUR COOLING

SERVES 9

	Unsalted butter, for greasing
1	large egg
1½	cups 100% pure cane syrup, plus more for serving (optional)
½	cup vegetable oil
¾	cup hot water
1½	tsp. baking soda
2½	cups all-purpose flour, sifted, plus more for pan
1	tsp. ground cinnamon
1	tsp. ground ginger
¼	tsp. ground cloves
	Powdered sugar
	Sweetened whipped cream, for serving (optional)

1. Preheat oven to 350°F. Grease a 10-inch round (or 9-inch square) baking pan with butter, and dust with flour.
2. Whisk together egg, cane syrup, and oil in a medium bowl until well blended. Whisk together hot water and baking soda in a small bowl. Whisk together flour, cinnamon, ginger, and cloves in a second medium bowl. Stir flour mixture into syrup mixture, alternating with water mixture, stirring until just combined after each addition, beginning and ending with flour mixture.
3. Pour into prepared pan. Bake in preheated oven until a wooden pick inserted into center comes out clean, about 45 minutes. Let cool completely in pan, about 1 hour. Remove from pan; dust with powdered sugar. If desired, top with sweetened whipped cream and drizzle with additional cane syrup.

The Skinny on Butter
From basic to mind-blowingly good

UNSALTED BUTTER

Often called "sweet butter," it has no added sodium, which gives cooks and bakers more control over the amount of salt in recipes. However, if the label says "sweet cream butter," check the ingredients because it may contain additional salt.

Best for: Baked goods, pan sauces, and pastas

- -

SALTED BUTTER

No surprise here—these sticks contain extra sodium. Serve this butter with a bread basket or alongside (or on top of) a dish. The added salt also extends its shelf life a bit longer than the unsalted kind.

Best for: Spreading on pancakes, waffles, and baked potatoes

- -

PLANT BUTTER

Made with plant oils such as avocado, canola, coconut, or olive, this soft nondairy spread has the richness and flavor of butter but works for lactose-free and vegan diets. Most brands can be used in recipes just like the real deal.

Best for: Vegan and dairy-free cooking and baking

- -

CULTURED BUTTER

Live bacterial cultures (like in yogurt) are added to pasteurized cream and allowed to ferment before the mixture is churned into butter. The result is extra creamy with a pleasant tang.

Best for: Recipes in which butter is a prominent flavor, like biscuits or pound cake

- -

IRISH BUTTER

Genuine Irish butter is deep yellow (because the milk comes from grass-fed cows) with a spreadable texture and rich flavor. Like other European butters, it is higher in fat—around 82% compared to regular American butter, which has around 80%.

Best for: Bread baskets, especially when company's coming

> "My go-to method for quickly softening butter is to microwave a whole stick (in the wrapper) on HIGH in 10-second intervals, rotating it 90 degrees after each 10 seconds, for about a minute. Rotating is key; otherwise it will begin to melt before the entire stick has had a chance to soften."
>
> **—John Somerall**
> **Test Kitchen Professional**

The Gold Standard

LAND O'LAKES
Our Test Kitchen pros prefer this brand because it whips nicely, melts evenly, and has consistent amounts of water and salt. This comes in handy when you're testing a dozen different piecrust recipes.

HOW TO MAKE CLARIFIED BUTTER

Remove water and milk solids for pure butterfat that won't burn over high heat

In a saucepan, melt butter over low heat until the bubbling and foaming subside. Remove from heat; set aside 5 minutes. Skim and discard foam. Line a fine mesh sieve with cheesecloth; place over a heat-safe bowl or container. Leaving the white milk solids at the bottom of the pan, carefully pour butterfat through the sieve. Let cool; refrigerate up to 1 month.

April

SIMPLE CUCUMBER-AND-
VIDALIA ONION SALAD

Viva Vidalia!

Delicious cooked or raw, these sweet Georgia-grown onions are coming back into season now

Simple Cucumber-and-Vidalia Onion Salad

ACTIVE 10 MIN. - TOTAL 10 MIN.
SERVES 4

Vigorously whisk together ⅓ cup **white vinegar**, 2 Tbsp. **extra-virgin olive oil**, 2 tsp. **granulated sugar**, 1 tsp. **kosher salt,** and ½ tsp. cracked **black pepper** in a medium bowl until sugar dissolves. Add 4 cups thinly sliced **English cucumbers**, 1 cup thinly sliced **Vidalia onion,** and 2 Tbsp. torn fresh **dill sprigs;** stir to combine. Let stand, stirring occasionally, 5 minutes.

Caramelized Vidalia Onion Pasta with Herbed Breadcrumbs

ACTIVE 25 MIN. - TOTAL 25 MIN.
SERVES 4

Cook 1 lb. **bucatini or spaghetti** in boiling **salted** water according to package directions. Drain; reserve 1 cup cooking water. Heat 1 Tbsp. **extra-virgin olive oil** in a large nonstick skillet over medium. Add ½ cup **panko breadcrumbs** and ½ tsp. **kosher salt;** cook, stirring often, until light golden, 2 minutes. Remove from heat; stir in ¼ cup each chopped **fresh parsley** and grated **Parmesan cheese.** Transfer to a bowl; set aside. Wipe skillet clean, then return to heat over medium-high. Add 3 cups **Slow-Cooker Caramelized Onions** (recipe at right), 1 Tbsp. **tomato paste**, and 1 tsp. **crushed red pepper;** cook, stirring occasionally, until onions are heated through and tomato paste darkens, 3 minutes. Add pasta and ½ cup reserved cooking water to skillet; toss to combine. If needed, add remaining ½ cup cooking water until desired consistency. Stir in ½ cup **capers**, ¼ cup grated **Parmesan,** 1 tsp. **kosher salt,** and 1 tsp. **sherry vinegar or red wine vinegar.** Sprinkle with panko mixture.

CARAMELIZED VIDALIA ONION PASTA WITH HERBED BREADCRUMBS

Slow-Cooker Caramelized Onions

ACTIVE 1 HOUR, 10 MIN. - TOTAL 1 HOUR, 10 MIN., PLUS 10 HOURS SLOW-COOKING
MAKES 4 CUPS

Place ¼ cup **unsalted butter** (cubed) in a 5- to 6-qt. slow cooker. Stir in 3 lb. **Vidalia onions** (thinly sliced, about 14 cups) and 1 tsp. **kosher salt.** Cover and cook on LOW until evenly golden, about 10 hours. Uncover and stir. Cook, uncovered, stirring occasionally, until most of the liquid has evaporated, about 1 hour.

SAVE FOR LATER
Caramelized onions can be frozen in a zip-top plastic bag (press out the air) up to 3 months.

Shaking Things Up

Atlanta mixologist Tiffanie Barriere serves her seasonal cocktails with a side of history

LOVELY 'RITA

FRESH IDEA
Enliven a typical margarita with grapefruit juice and rosemary.

"**WHEN YOU KNOW MORE,** drinks taste better," says Tiffanie Barriere. While working at a high-end bar at Hartsfield-Jackson Atlanta International Airport, she became as renowned for her animated stories about ingredients and techniques as for her inventive recipes. When the pandemic hit, Barriere–who's now an independent mixologist known as The Drinking Coach (thedrinkingcoach.com)–homed in on something she felt would have a bigger impact: the African American influence on cocktails.

"I wanted to raise a glass to those who helped execute some of our favorite drinks and never had the pleasure of being recognized for their talents," she says. On Instagram, she writes about beverage geniuses like John Dabney (a 19th-century Richmond, Virginia, bartender who was beloved for his mint juleps) and Jupiter Evans (an enslaved man who helmed the cider making at Thomas Jefferson's Monticello). Here, Barriere celebrates spring with delicious drinks that toast some of the season's herbaceous bounty.

GARDEN PLEASURES

Garden Pleasures

ACTIVE 5 MIN. - TOTAL 5 MIN.

MAKES 1

- ¼ cup (2 oz.) clear spirit (gin, vodka, white rum, blanco tequila)
- ¼ cup unsweetened green tea, chilled
- 1½ Tbsp. fresh lemon juice (from 1 lemon)
- 1 Tbsp. Honey Water (recipe follows)
- 4 fresh basil leaves, plus more for garnish
  Ice
  Club soda
  Champagne

Combine spirit, green tea, lemon juice, Honey Water, and basil leaves in a cocktail shaker filled with ice. Shake hard until cold, about 20 seconds. Double strain into a red wine glass filled halfway with ice. Top with club soda and Champagne. Stir; garnish with additional basil leaves.

Honey Water

Combine 3 parts **honey** and 1 part **warm water** in a small bowl. Stir to loosen.

Lovely 'Rita

ACTIVE 5 MIN. - TOTAL 5 MIN.

MAKES 1

   Margarita salt
- ¼ cup (2 oz.) blanco tequila
- 2 Tbsp. fresh grapefruit juice (from 1 grapefruit)
- 1½ Tbsp. fresh lime juice (from 1 lime)
- 1 Tbsp. (½ oz.) elderflower liqueur (such as St-Germain)
   Pinch of kosher salt
   Ice
- 1 (4-inch) fresh rosemary sprig, for garnish

Salt the rim of a rocks glass with margarita salt. Combine tequila, grapefruit juice, lime juice, elderflower liqueur, and kosher salt in a cocktail shaker filled with ice. Shake hard until cold, about 10 seconds. Strain into a prepared glass with fresh ice; garnish with a rosemary sprig.

Right on Thyme

ACTIVE 5 MIN. - TOTAL 5 MIN.

MAKES 1

- 1½ Tbsp. simple syrup
- 4 fresh thyme sprigs, divided

RIGHT ON THYME

- 4 dashes Angostura bitters
- ¼ cup (2 oz.) dark spirit (whiskey, cognac, dark rum)
   Ice, plus large ice cube for serving

Combine syrup and 3 of the thyme sprigs in a cocktail mixing glass (or tall glass). Gently muddle thyme into the syrup, about 30 seconds. Add bitters; stir. Add spirit and ice; stir until cold, about 30 seconds. Double strain into a rocks glass with a large ice cube. Garnish with remaining thyme sprig.

GRILLED RADISH-AND-FENNEL SALAD WITH GOAT CHEESE TOASTS

Fresh Off the Grill

The market is overflowing with spring produce, and the weather is just right.
It's time to light a fire and celebrate the season with a little smoke

Grilled Radish-and-Fennel Salad with Goat Cheese Toasts

The fennel and radishes sweeten after being tossed in butter and grilled. If you can find them, use Easter egg radishes, which are a bit larger than the regular red kind and won't fall through the grill grates. Their mix of colors makes this salad look pretty, too.

ACTIVE 25 MIN. - TOTAL 35 MIN.

SERVES 4

- 1 large fennel bulb
- 10 medium-size Easter egg radishes, trimmed and halved
- 6 Tbsp. unsalted butter, melted, divided
- ¾ tsp. kosher salt, divided
- ¾ tsp. black pepper, divided
- 1 large garlic clove, grated (½ tsp.)
- 8 (½-inch-thick) baguette slices
- 4 oz. goat cheese, softened
- 1 Tbsp. chopped fresh dill
- 12 butter lettuce leaves (from 1 head)
- 3 Tbsp. extra-virgin olive oil
- 1 tsp. grated Meyer or regular lemon zest plus 2 Tbsp. fresh juice (from 1 lemon)
- 1 tsp. Dijon mustard

1. Preheat grill to medium-high (400°F to 450°F). Cut and discard stalks from fennel bulb; remove and discard any browned spots on outside of bulb using a vegetable peeler. Stand fennel bulb upright on cutting board; cut straight down into 8 even slices, and place in a medium bowl. Add radishes, 3 tablespoons of the melted butter, ½ teaspoon of the salt, and ¼ teaspoon of the pepper; toss gently to coat. Place fennel and radishes on unoiled grates; grill, covered, until well marked and tender-crisp, 4 to 5 minutes per side. Remove from grill, and set aside until ready to use.

2. Stir together garlic and remaining 3 tablespoons melted butter in a small bowl; brush evenly over both sides of bread slices. Arrange bread on unoiled grates; grill, uncovered, until well marked on bottoms, 1 to 2 minutes. Remove from grill, and turn to face grilled side up. Stir together goat cheese, dill, and remaining ½ teaspoon pepper in a small bowl; spread evenly over top (grilled) sides of toasts. Return toasts, goat cheese side up, to grates; grill, covered, until bottoms of bread slices are toasted and cheese softens, 1 to 2 minutes. Remove from grill.

3. Arrange lettuce leaves on a large platter, and top with fennel and radishes. Whisk together oil, lemon zest and juice, mustard, and remaining ¼ teaspoon salt in a bowl (or shake together in a sealed jar). Drizzle salad with dressing. Serve alongside toasts.

Spring Onion Grilled Pizza

(Photo, page 74)

This unconventional pizza has a sauce made from whipped cream that's taken in a savory direction with the addition of thyme and garlic. When that's sprinkled with Pecorino Romano, the two melt together on the dough to form a creamy topping that's a perfect match for prosciutto and charred spring onions.

ACTIVE 25 MIN. - TOTAL 30 MIN.

SERVES 4

- ⅓ cup heavy whipping cream
- 1½ tsp. chopped fresh thyme
- ½ tsp. black pepper
- 2 medium garlic cloves, grated (½ tsp.)
- ¼ tsp. kosher salt
- 1 lb. fresh prepared pizza dough, at room temperature
- 3 Tbsp. olive oil, divided
- 6 spring onions
- 1 oz. Pecorino Romano cheese, grated (about ¼ cup)
- 3 (about 2 oz. total) slices prosciutto

1. Preheat grill to medium-high (400°F to 450°F). Beat cream in a medium bowl with an electric mixer on high speed until stiff peaks form, about 2 minutes. Stir in thyme, pepper, garlic, and salt. Refrigerate until ready to use.

2. Stretch pizza dough into a 14- to 16-inch-long oval shape on a large sheet of parchment paper. Brush top of dough with 1 tablespoon of the oil. Holding parchment paper, flip dough, oiled side down, onto oiled grill grates. Peel parchment paper off dough. Grill, covered, until well marked on bottom, 2 to 3 minutes. Remove from grill, and transfer to a work surface; brush top (ungrilled side) with 1 tablespoon of the oil. Set aside until ready to use.

3. Trim spring onions to 6 inches long from root end; reserve removed tops for another use. Cut trimmed spring onions in half lengthwise; place in a bowl. Drizzle evenly with remaining 1 tablespoon oil, and toss gently to coat. Arrange onions on oiled grates; grill, covered, until well marked, 1 to 2 minutes per side. Remove from grill.

4. Flip pizza dough over to face grilled side up. Spread evenly with cream-thyme mixture, leaving a 1-inch border. Sprinkle evenly with cheese. Top with grilled onions. Place pizza on oiled grates, and grill, covered, until well marked on bottom, 2 to 3 minutes. Remove from grill. Tear prosciutto into pieces, and arrange on pizza. Cut into 8 wedges.

SPRING ONION
GRILLED PIZZA
(PAGE 73)

GRILLED BABY
ARTICHOKES WITH
BROWN BUTTER AÏOLI
(PAGE 77)

SMOKED VIDALIA DIP
WITH GRILLED CRUDITÉS

Smoked Vidalia Dip with Grilled Crudités

This creamy dip gets its depth from buttery smoked onions and pairs beautifully with spring vegetables that have been grilled just long enough to get a little charred but not so long that they lose their crunch.

ACTIVE 15 MIN. - TOTAL 40 MIN.

SERVES 8

- 1 cup wood chips
- 1 large Vidalia onion, chopped (about 2 cups)
- 2 Tbsp. unsalted butter, melted
- 2 tsp. chopped fresh thyme
- 1¼ tsp. kosher salt, divided
- 4 oz. cream cheese, softened
- ¾ cup sour cream
- 1½ Tbsp. Worcestershire sauce
- ½ tsp. black pepper
- ¼ cup chopped fresh chives
- 1 lb. fresh thick asparagus spears, trimmed
- 8 oz. fresh sugar snap peas, trimmed
- 1 bunch multicolor baby carrots (8 to 10 carrots), trimmed and halved lengthwise
- 1 bunch multicolor radishes (8 to 10 radishes), trimmed and halved lengthwise
- 3 Tbsp. olive oil

1. Preheat grill to medium (350°F to 400°F). Arrange wood chips on a large sheet of heavy-duty aluminum foil; crimp all sides of foil to make a tightly sealed packet. Pierce top of foil several times using a knife (this will allow smoke to escape the packet). Place packet on unoiled grates; grill, covered, until smoke starts to appear, about 5 minutes.

2. Arrange onion on a large double-layer piece of foil; fold up edges of foil to make a "bowl." Drizzle onion with butter; sprinkle with thyme and ½ teaspoon of the salt. Stir to coat. Place onion mixture in foil bowl on unoiled grates; grill, covered, stirring occasionally, until onion is almost tender, about 20 minutes. Remove onion bowl and wood chip packet from grill. Increase grill temperature to medium-high (400°F to 450°F).

3. Stir together warm onion mixture, cream cheese, sour cream, Worcestershire, pepper, and ¼ teaspoon of the salt in a bowl until well combined. Fold in chives.

4. Toss together asparagus, snap peas, carrots, radishes, and oil on a large baking sheet; sprinkle evenly with remaining ½ teaspoon salt. Arrange carrots and radishes (cut side down) and asparagus on unoiled grates; arrange snap peas on a mesh or silicone grill mat on unoiled grates. Cover grill. Grill carrots and radishes, covered, until tender-crisp and grill marks appear on cut sides, about 3 minutes. Grill asparagus and peas, covered, turning or stirring occasionally, until tender-crisp, about 3 minutes. Serve grilled vegetables alongside dip.

Grilled Baby Artichokes with Brown Butter Aïoli

(Photo, page 75)

Baby artichokes are so much easier to prep than their larger counterparts. There's no need to scoop out the choke, and there are far fewer tough leaves to remove. Homemade mayo, which gets a nutty boost from brown butter and a pungent kick from fresh garlic, makes a lovely accompaniment.

ACTIVE 35 MIN. - TOTAL 1 HOUR

SERVES 4

- ½ cup unsalted butter
- 1 lemon, halved crosswise, divided
- 12 fresh baby artichokes
- 1 large egg
- 1½ Tbsp. fresh lemon juice (from 1 lemon)
- ½ tsp. Dijon mustard
- ½ tsp. kosher salt
- 1 large garlic clove, grated (½ tsp.)
- 5 Tbsp. canola oil, divided
- ½ tsp. flaky sea salt

1. Melt butter in a small saucepan over medium. Continue cooking, stirring occasionally, until butter is well browned and deeply fragrant, 6 to 8 minutes. Pour butter into a spouted measuring cup, and let cool to room temperature, about 20 minutes.

2. Meanwhile, squeeze 1 of the lemon halves into a large bowl of cold water. Working with 1 artichoke at a time, cut off and discard top ½ inch of artichoke. Cut off and discard stem to within 1 inch of base; peel trimmed stem using a vegetable peeler. Remove bottom leaves and tough outer leaves, letting tender hearts and bottoms remain. Cut trimmed artichoke in half lengthwise; rub cut sides with remaining lemon half. Place in bowl with lemon water. Repeat process with other artichokes. Set aside until ready to use.

3. Preheat grill to medium-high (400°F to 450°F). Meanwhile, bring a large pot of salted water to a boil over high. Drain artichokes. Add to boiling water, and cook until almost tender, about 5 minutes. Drain and rinse under cold water. Drain well, and pat dry. Set aside.

4. Place egg, lemon juice, mustard, kosher salt, and garlic in a mini food processor; pulse until well combined, about 15 pulses. With processor running, slowly drizzle in cooled butter and 3 tablespoons of the oil, processing until creamy and emulsified, about 1 minute. Spoon aïoli into a bowl; set aside until ready to serve.

5. Gently toss together artichokes and remaining 2 tablespoons oil in a bowl to coat. Place artichokes on unoiled grates; grill, covered, until well marked, 4 to 5 minutes per side. Arrange artichokes on a platter; sprinkle evenly with flaky salt. Serve alongside aïoli.

GRILLED LAMB CHOPS
WITH GREEN GARLIC
CHIMICHURRI (PAGE 80)

GARLIC-OREGANO
CHICKEN WITH
GRILLED LEEKS AND
LEMON (PAGE 80)

Grilled Lamb Chops with Green Garlic Chimichurri

(Photo, page 78)

Earthy spices imbue the lamb with heady flavor, and a tangy-herby chimichurri sauce provides a bright contrast to the rich meat. Green garlic (also called spring garlic) is often found at farmers' markets this time of year and can vary a lot in size. For this recipe, you'll want to choose smaller stalks.

ACTIVE 20 MIN. - TOTAL 30 MIN.

SERVES 4

- 2 (2-lb.) racks of lamb (8 bones each), frenched
- 1 tsp. ground cumin
- ½ tsp. ground coriander
- ½ tsp. black pepper
- 1¼ tsp. kosher salt, divided
- 6 Tbsp. olive oil, divided
- 5 small green garlic stalks or large scallions
- ⅓ cup chopped fresh flat-leaf parsley
- 2 Tbsp. red wine vinegar
- ¼ tsp. crushed red pepper
- 1 medium garlic clove, grated (¼ tsp.)

1. Preheat grill to medium-high (400°F to 450°F). Cut lamb racks between bones to form 16 rib chops total. Stir together cumin, coriander, black pepper, and 1 teaspoon of the salt in a small bowl. Brush both sides of lamb chops evenly with 1½ tablespoons of the oil; sprinkle evenly with cumin mixture. Let stand at room temperature 15 minutes.
2. While lamb stands, drizzle garlic stalks evenly with 1½ teaspoons of the oil in a bowl; toss gently to coat. Arrange garlic stalks on oiled grates; grill, uncovered, turning often, until lightly charred, 4 to 5 minutes. Transfer to a cutting board; let cool slightly, about 3 minutes.
3. Stir together parsley, vinegar, crushed red pepper, grated garlic, and remaining ¼ teaspoon salt and ¼ cup oil in a medium bowl. Chop grilled garlic stalks, and stir into parsley mixture.
4. Place lamb chops on oiled grates; grill, covered, just until grill marks appear, about 2 minutes per side. Serve lamb alongside chimichurri.

Garlic-Oregano Chicken with Grilled Leeks and Lemon

(Photo, page 79)

Rich and meaty chicken thighs pick up tons of garlicky, citrusy flavor in this quick marinade. Blanching the leeks first before grilling them ensures they'll be tender. Avoid cutting away too much from the root end so the halves will hold together.

ACTIVE 20 MIN. - TOTAL 50 MIN.

SERVES 4

- 1 Tbsp. grated lemon zest plus 3 Tbsp. fresh juice (from 2 lemons), divided
- 2 Tbsp. extra-virgin olive oil
- 3 garlic cloves, grated (about 1½ tsp.)
- 1 tsp. dried oregano
- ½ tsp. crushed red pepper
- 1¼ tsp. kosher salt, divided
- 8 (about 2 lb. total) boneless, skinless chicken thighs
- 4 medium leeks
- 2 Tbsp. unsalted butter, melted
- 2 lemons, halved crosswise

1. Place lemon juice, oil, garlic, oregano, crushed red pepper, 2 teaspoons of the lemon zest, and ½ teaspoon of the salt in a large bowl. Add chicken; toss well to coat. Let marinate at room temperature, stirring occasionally, 30 minutes.
2. Meanwhile, preheat grill to medium-high (400°F to 450°F). Bring a large pot of water to a boil over high. Trim roots off leeks, leaving bases intact so leeks will hold together when halved. Trim and discard dark green tops from leeks; cut in half lengthwise. Rinse well under running water, separating leaves without removing them from the base. Add leeks to boiling water, and cook until just softened, 2 to 3 minutes. Plunge into a bowl filled with ice water; drain well, and pat dry.
3. Stir together melted butter and remaining 1 teaspoon lemon zest in a small bowl. Brush generously over both sides of leeks. Place leeks, chicken, and lemon halves, cut side down, on oiled grates. Cover grill. Grill leeks, covered, until well marked and tender, 3 to 4 minutes per side. Grill lemons, covered, until well marked on cut sides, about 5 minutes. Grill chicken, covered, until a thermometer inserted into thickest portion of thighs registers 165°F, about 5 minutes per side. Remove from grill. Sprinkle chicken and leeks evenly with remaining ¾ teaspoon salt.

Grilled Endive-and-Halloumi Salad with Strawberries

Grilling endive mellows its sharpness and adds a rich, savory note that's completely unlike the way it tastes in its raw state. Peppery arugula, juicy berries, grilled salty cheese, and a sweet white balsamic vinaigrette make this salad one to remember. Serve it as soon as it's done, before the cooked cheese hardens.

ACTIVE 15 MIN. - TOTAL 20 MIN.

SERVES 4

- 2 Tbsp. white balsamic vinegar
- 1 tsp. Dijon mustard
- 1 tsp. honey
- ½ tsp. kosher salt
- ¼ tsp. black pepper
- 5 Tbsp. extra-virgin olive oil, divided
- 5 oz. baby arugula
- 1½ cups sliced fresh strawberries
- ⅓ cup thinly sliced red onion (from 1 small onion)
- 4 Belgian endives, halved lengthwise
- 5 oz. Halloumi cheese, cut into (½-inch-thick) slices

1. Preheat grill to medium-high (400°F to 450°F). Whisk together vinegar, mustard, honey, salt, pepper, and 3 tablespoons of the oil in a small bowl (or shake together in a sealed jar). Place arugula, strawberries, and onion in a large bowl. Set aside.
2. Brush endives and cheese evenly with remaining 2 tablespoons oil. Place on unoiled grates; grill, covered, until well marked, about 2 minutes per side. Remove from grill.
3. Add endives to arugula mixture in bowl; drizzle with dressing, and toss gently to coat. Nestle cheese into salad, and serve immediately.

GRILLED ENDIVE-
AND-HALLOUMI
SALAD WITH
STRAWBERRIES

Dressed to Impress

Four flavorful ways to liven up your salad bowl

Creamy Herb Dressing

ACTIVE 10 MIN. - TOTAL 10 MIN.
MAKES 2 CUPS

Whisk together 1 small minced **shallot**, 1 Tbsp. **Champagne vinegar**, 1½ tsp. f**resh lemon juice** (from 1 lemon), 1 tsp. **Dijon mustard**, ½ tsp. **black pepper**, ¼ tsp. **kosher salt**, and 1 small grated **garlic clove** in a small bowl until combined. In a thin, steady stream, whisk in ¼ cup **extra**-**virgin olive oil** until combined. Slowly whisk in ⅔ cup whole **buttermilk**, ⅔ cup **plain whole**-**milk strained yogurt** (such as Greek), and ½ cup finely chopped **mixed fresh tender herbs** (such as chives, tarragon, basil, and flat-leaf parsley).

CALORIES: **101** – CARBS: **3 G** – FAT: **9 G**

Pair with: *butter lettuce, radishes, packaged crunchy chickpeas, snap peas, avocado, and additional fresh tender herbs*

Carrot-Ginger Dressing

ACTIVE 10 MIN. - TOTAL 10 MIN.
MAKES 2 CUPS

Place 1½ cups coarsely chopped **carrots** (from 4 medium carrots), ½ cup **grapeseed oil**, ¼ cup **water**, 3 Tbsp. chopped **fresh ginger** (from 1 piece), 3 Tbsp. **rice vinegar**, 1 Tbsp. **toasted sesame oil**, 2 tsp. **honey**, and ½ tsp. **kosher salt** in a blender. Process until smooth and creamy, 1 minute, 30 seconds.

CALORIES: **152** – CARBS: **4 G** – FAT: **15 G**

Pair with: *cabbage, cucumber, chow mein noodles, bean sprouts, fresh cilantro, and sesame seeds*

CARROT-GINGER
DRESSING

Tangy Raspberry Dressing

ACTIVE 10 MIN. - TOTAL 10 MIN.
MAKES ABOUT 1¾ CUPS

Process 2 cups fresh **raspberries** (from 1 pt.), ½ cup **olive oil**, 2 Tbsp. **seedless raspberry jam**, 1 Tbsp. **apple cider vinegar**, 1½ tsp. **Dijon mustard**, and ½ tsp. **kosher salt** in a food processor until smooth and creamy, about 1 minute, stopping to scrape down sides as needed. Pour dressing through a fine mesh strainer into a bowl; discard seeds

CALORIES: **145** – CARBS: **6 G** – FAT: **14 G**

Pair with: *arugula, blue cheese crumbles, raspberries, and chopped pecans*

TANGY RASPBERRY
DRESSING

Spicy Avocado Dressing

ACTIVE 10 MIN. - TOTAL 10 MIN.
MAKES 2 CUPS

Process 2 cups packed fresh **cilantro** leaves, 1 large chopped **avocado**; ½ cup plus 2 Tbsp. **water**; ⅓ cup **olive oil**; 2 small chopped, seeded **jalapeño chiles**; 3 Tbsp. **fresh lime juice** (from 2 limes); ½ tsp. **kosher salt**; and 1 grated **garlic clove** in a food processor until smooth, 1 minute.

CALORIES: **118** – CARBS: **3 G** – FAT: **12 G**

Pair with: *romaine, grilled chicken, Cotija cheese, packaged crispy tortilla strips, and radishes*

SPICY AVOCADO
DRESSING

The Pastas of Spring

Seasonal ingredients shine in these simple dishes

Pesto Primavera Ravioli with Ham

ACTIVE 15 MIN. - TOTAL 25 MIN.

SERVES 4

- 2 Tbsp. olive oil
- 1 cup packaged diced ham (about 5 oz.)
- 1 small shallot, thinly sliced
- 2½ cups chicken broth
- 1 cup dry white wine
- 2 (10-oz.) pkg. refrigerated spinach-and-ricotta ravioli (such as Giovanni Rana)
- 3 Tbsp. unsalted butter
- 1 lb. fresh asparagus, trimmed and cut into 1½-inch pieces
- 1 cup frozen sweet peas, thawed
- 4 cups baby arugula (4 oz.)
- 2 oz. Parmesan cheese, finely shredded (about ½ cup)
- ¼ cup refrigerated basil pesto
  Crusty bread

1. Heat oil in a large, deep lidded skillet over medium–high. Add ham and shallot; cook, stirring often, until ham is beginning to brown, about 3 minutes. Add broth and wine, and bring to a low boil over medium–high. Add ravioli and butter, spreading in a single layer in liquid. Cover skillet, and cook 2 minutes.
2. Uncover skillet, and add asparagus pieces and peas; cook, stirring gently to incorporate vegetables, until pasta is tender, asparagus is tender–crisp, and peas are still bright green, 1 to 2 minutes. Remove skillet from heat.
3. Divide arugula evenly among 4 shallow bowls. Top evenly with ravioli mixture, Parmesan, and pesto. Serve hot with crusty bread for dipping.

PICK YOUR FAVORITE
For this recipe, you can use any flavor of ravioli. Be sure to select the fresh refrigerated (not frozen) kind.

Sausage-Pimiento Cheese Pasta Rollups

ACTIVE 25 MIN. - TOTAL 40 MIN.

SERVES 6

- 1 lb. mild or sweet Italian chicken sausage, casings removed
- 12 oz. pimiento cheese
- 1 cup whole-milk ricotta cheese (from 1 [15-oz.] container)
- 8 oz. low-moisture part-skim mozzarella cheese, shredded (about 2 cups), divided
- 4 cups coarsely chopped arugula, divided
- 2 (5-oz.) jars diced pimientos, drained and divided
- 2 (15-oz.) jars Alfredo sauce (such as Rao's)
- 1 (8.8-oz.) pkg. refrigerated pasta sheets (such as Giovanni Rana)

1. Preheat oven to 425°F. Cook sausage in a 10-inch ovenproof skillet over medium-high, stirring often, until crumbled and browned, 6 to 7 minutes. Remove from heat; cool 10 minutes.

2. While sausage cooks, stir together pimiento cheese, ricotta, 1 cup of the shredded mozzarella, 1 cup of the chopped arugula, and 3 tablespoons of the diced pimientos in a medium bowl. Remove sausage from skillet using a slotted spoon; stir into cheese mixture.

3. Without wiping skillet, add Alfredo sauce, ¼ cup water, 2½ cups of the chopped arugula, and ⅓ cup of the diced pimientos; bring to a simmer over medium, stirring occasionally. Reduce heat to low.

4. Place 1 pasta sheet on a work surface; top with about 1 cup cheese mixture, and spread evenly to the short edges, leaving a ½-inch border along the long edges. Starting at 1 long edge, roll up pasta; place on work surface seam side down. Using a sharp knife, cut crosswise into fourths. Repeat with remaining pasta sheets and cheese mixture to make 24 rollups.

5. Carefully arrange rollups (cut side up) in warm sauce in skillet, starting in the center and working toward the edges. Nestle rollups closely together to prevent unrolling. Sprinkle with remaining 1 cup mozzarella and 2 to 3 tablespoons diced pimientos. Bake in preheated oven until sauce is bubbly, pasta is softened, and top is golden, 15 to 18 minutes. Top with remaining ½ cup chopped arugula, and serve hot.

STICK WITH CHICKEN
We recommend using chicken (not pork) sausage in this recipe because it has less fat and will keep the sauce from being greasy.

Smoky Sausage-and-Collard Stuffed Shells

ACTIVE 25 MIN. · TOTAL 45 MIN.

SERVES 4

- 20 uncooked jumbo pasta shells (from 1 [1-lb.] pkg.)
- 2 Tbsp. olive oil
- 1 lb. mild or hot Italian turkey sausage, casings removed
- 4 cups chopped stemmed collard greens (from 1 [12-oz.] pkg. collard greens)
- 1½ cups thinly sliced Vidalia onion (from 1 onion)
- 2 (15-oz.) jars Alfredo sauce (such as Rao's)
- 6 oz. smoked Gouda cheese, shredded (about 1½ cups), divided
- 1½ cups whole-milk ricotta cheese (from 1 [15-oz.] container)
- ¼ cup panko breadcrumbs

1. Preheat oven to 425°F with rack about 10 inches from heat source. Cook pasta in a large pot of boiling salted water according to package directions for al dente, about 9 minutes. Drain and rinse with cold water. Arrange in 1 layer on a clean, lint-free kitchen towel; set aside until ready to use.

2. While pasta cooks, heat oil in a 12-inch high-sided broiler-safe skillet over medium-high. Add sausage; cook, stirring often, until sausage crumbles and begins to brown, 6 minutes. Add collard greens and onion; cook, stirring often, until softened, about 6 minutes. Transfer mixture to a large bowl; wipe skillet clean.

3. Return skillet to medium heat; add Alfredo sauce and ¾ cup of the Gouda. Cook, stirring occasionally, until cheese melts, about 2 minutes. Remove from heat; keep covered.

4. Add ricotta and remaining ¾ cup Gouda to sausage mixture in bowl; stir to combine. Spoon about ¼ cup mixture into each pasta shell; place, filled side up, in sauce in skillet. Sprinkle panko evenly over top. Bake in preheated oven until sauce is bubbly around edges of skillet, about 15 minutes.

5. Keep skillet in oven, and increase oven temperature to broil. Broil until panko is golden brown, 4 to 7 minutes.

MAKE IT MEATLESS
Swap out the turkey sausage for a plant-based version (such as MorningStar Farms Veggie Italian Sausage Style Crumbles).

One-Pot Pasta Primavera with Bacon and Feta

ACTIVE 30 MIN. - TOTAL 30 MIN.
SERVES 6

- 12 oz. extra-thick-cut bacon (about 6 slices), cut crosswise into 1-inch piece
- 1 large red onion, cut into ¾-inch wedges, petals separated (about 2 cups)
- 1 pt. cherry tomatoes
- 4 cups chicken stock
- ¼ cup sun-dried tomato pesto (such as Rao's)
- 1 tsp. kosher salt
- ½ tsp. black pepper
- 1 lb. uncooked mini farfalle pasta
- 1 (5-oz.) pkg. fresh baby spinach
- 1 tsp. sherry vinegar
- 3 oz. feta cheese, crumbled (about ¾ cup)

1. Heat a large Dutch oven over medium-high. Add bacon, and cook, stirring often, until fat is rendered and bacon is crisp, 8 to 10 minutes. Using a slotted spoon, transfer to a paper towel-lined plate, reserving ¼ cup drippings in pot. Crumble bacon; set aside.

2. Add onion and tomatoes to drippings; increase heat to high. Cook, stirring often, until onion softens and begins to brown and tomatoes burst, about 6 minutes. Add stock, 1 cup water, the pesto, salt, and pepper; stir using a wooden spoon to scrape any browned bits from bottom of pot. Add pasta; partially cover pot. Cook, uncovering and stirring often, until al dente, about 8 minutes. Add spinach; cook, uncovered, stirring often, until spinach wilts and sauce thickens, about 3 minutes. Remove from heat; stir in vinegar.

3. Divide pasta evenly among 6 bowls; top with crumbled bacon and feta.

LOVE YOUR LEFTOVERS
Any extra pasta will taste great the next day. If it seems a little dry when reheating, stir in a bit of chicken stock to loosen things up.

Creamy Linguine with Corn, Leeks, and Mushrooms

ACTIVE 30 MIN. - TOTAL 30 MIN.
SERVES 6

- 1 lb. uncooked linguine
- 3 Tbsp. olive oil
- 1 cup chopped country ham slices (about 4½ oz.)
- 1 (8-oz.) pkg. sliced white mushrooms
- 2 cups fresh corn (from 4 ears) or frozen corn kernels
- 2 cups sliced leeks (from 1 large leek)
- 2 Tbsp. chopped fresh thyme leaves, divided
- 1 tsp. coarsely ground black pepper, divided

- ¾ cup dry white wine
- ½ cup chicken broth
- 1½ cups heavy whipping cream
- 3 oz. Parmesan cheese, grated (about ¾ cup), divided

1. Bring a large pot of salted water to a boil over high. Add pasta; cook according to package directions for al dente, 10 to 11 minutes. Drain, reserving 1 cup water. Return pasta to pot; cover to keep warm.
2. While pasta cooks, heat oil in a large skillet over medium-high. Add ham; cook, stirring often, until ham begins to brown, about 3 minutes. Add mushrooms; cook, stirring occasionally, until mushrooms begin to soften and release moisture, about 4 minutes. Add corn, leeks, 1 tablespoon of the thyme, and ½ teaspoon of the pepper.

Cook, stirring often, until vegetables are softened and ham is crisp, about 5 minutes. Transfer to pot with cooked pasta.
3. Return skillet to medium-high. (Do not wipe clean.) Add wine and broth to skillet; bring to a boil over medium-high. Cook, stirring to loosen up browned bits in skillet, 1 minute. Stir in cream; return to a boil over medium. Cook, stirring often, until liquid thickens slightly, 4 minutes; stir in 1½ teaspoons of the thyme, ½ cup of the Parmesan, and remaining ½ teaspoon pepper. Pour over pasta mixture in pot; toss to coat. (Add reserved cooking water as needed to reach desired consistency.) Divide among 6 bowls; top with remaining 1½ teaspoons thyme and ¼ cup Parmesan.

This Kugel's a Keeper

A cast-iron skillet gives this dish a crisp crust

GRATE IDEA

For this recipe, save yourself (literal) tears by grating the onion and potatoes in a food processor with the shredding attachment.

Cast-Iron Potato Kugel

Often served at Passover, kugel is a savory or sweet baked casserole that's made with potatoes (like this one) or with noodles. It's also great for brunch.

ACTIVE 30 MIN. - TOTAL 1 HOUR, 30 MIN.

SERVES 8

- 4 lb. russet potatoes, peeled and cut into medium-size chunks
- 1 large (12-oz.) yellow onion, peeled and cut into chunks
- 1 Tbsp. plus 1 tsp. kosher salt
- 1 tsp. black pepper
- ½ cup peanut oil, canola oil, or chicken schmaltz (rendered chicken fat), divided
- 6 large eggs
- Chopped fresh chives

1. Place a 10-inch cast-iron skillet in oven; preheat oven to 400°F. Grate potatoes and onion using shredding disk attachment on a food processor or large holes of a box grater. Working in 4 or 5 batches, place shredded potatoes and onion in a cheesecloth or clean, lint-free kitchen towel; squeeze out liquid into a large glass bowl. Place squeezed potato mixture in a large clean bowl; repeat procedure with remaining potato mixture. Let liquid stand for 5 minutes; starch will settle in bottom of bowl. **2.** Carefully pour off and discard liquid, leaving starch in bowl. Scrape starch into bowl with potato mixture. Add salt, pepper, and ¼ cup of the oil; stir to combine. Place eggs in a medium bowl; beat with an electric mixer on medium-high speed until foamy, 1 minute. Pour into potato mixture; toss to combine. **3.** Remove skillet from oven. Add 2 tablespoons of the oil to pan; tilt to completely coat bottom and slightly up sides. Gently spoon potato mixture into hot pan (don't pack it in). Drizzle with remaining 2 tablespoons oil. Bake in preheated oven until crispy on top and tender in center, 55 minutes to 1 hour. Let stand 5 minutes. Top with chives; slice and serve warm.

BEET PICKLED
DEVILED EGGS

GOOD EGGS
While the pink pickling liquid doesn't
make the eggs taste like beets, it will
permeate the whites completely in
24 hours. Don't let them sit any longer,
or the whites might be too tough.

The Devil's in the Details

Four new ways to enjoy the quintessential Southern appetizer

I GREW UP in North Carolina, and like many Southerners, I inherited a deviled-egg plate from my mother. The amber-colored glass dish was still in the box, with the bow attached, and had been stuffed in a closet.

Whoever gave it to her knew nothing about her. She hated deviled eggs and even claimed she was allergic to eggs, though she produced no evidence. My mother didn't cook anything that she didn't like to eat, so none appeared at my house when I was growing up.

I turned to my grandmother, who made them only one way: with mayonnaise, yellow mustard, white vinegar, and black pepper. Adding anything else was, for her, like wearing white after Labor Day—just not done. Besides, there was no need to mess with their tart, silky perfection. I was in love.

Later, I learned that making deviled eggs could be a competitive sport. You'll always see at least two plates of them at any church picnic or potluck family reunion, and those who bring them monitor the consumption of theirs versus their rivals' with side glances and outright stares. I've witnessed quiet battles among sweet little aunties or church ladies to be queen of the classic. No one is that invested in broccoli salad. The more eggs eaten from one's tray, the closer to glory. And it's no coincidence that the empty plate looks a lot like a tiara. –Debbie Moose

Beet Pickled Deviled Eggs

ACTIVE 30 MIN. - TOTAL 55 MIN., PLUS 12 HOURS CHILLING
MAKES 16

- 1 cup bottled beet juice
- 1 cup white wine vinegar
- 2½ Tbsp. granulated sugar
- 2 tsp. black peppercorns
- 2¼ tsp. kosher salt, divided
- 8 large hard-cooked eggs, peeled
- ⅓ cup mayonnaise
- 2 Tbsp. finely chopped cornichons (from 3 to 4 cornichons)

TURMERIC PICKLED DEVILED EGGS

- 1½ Tbsp. prepared horseradish
- 1 Tbsp. chopped fresh dill, plus more for garnish
- 2 tsp. Dijon mustard

1. Place beet juice, vinegar, ⅓ cup water, the sugar, peppercorns, and 2 teaspoons of the salt in a small saucepan. Bring to a boil over high, stirring occasionally to dissolve sugar. Remove from heat, and cool 25 minutes.

2. Place eggs in a 1-quart canning jar or medium-size container. Pour vinegar mixture over eggs. Loosely cover with lid; chill at least 12 hours or up to 24 hours. (If needed, press plastic wrap directly onto surface of eggs to keep submerged.)

3. Drain eggs; pat dry with paper towels. Cut eggs in half lengthwise. Carefully remove yolks; place in a medium bowl. Set aside egg white halves. Mash yolks using a fork; add mayonnaise, cornichons, horseradish, dill, mustard, and remaining ¼ teaspoon salt, and stir until smooth. Transfer yolk mixture to a zip-top plastic bag, and seal. Snip a hole in tip of plastic bag. Pipe about 1 tablespoon yolk mixture onto each egg white half. Garnish with dill.

Turmeric Pickled Deviled Eggs

Prepare recipe as directed in Step 1, substituting 1 cup **water** for 1 cup bottled beet juice and adding 2 tsp. ground **turmeric** to saucepan. Prepare Step 2 as directed. In Step 3, substitute 1 Tbsp. **plain whole-milk yogurt**, 2 tsp. **yellow mustard**, ½ tsp. **curry powder**, and ⅛ tsp. **cayenne pepper** for the cornichons, horseradish, dill, and Dijon mustard. Substitute snipped fresh chives for dill to garnish.

Spicy Fried Deviled Eggs

ACTIVE 55 MIN. - TOTAL 1 HOUR, 20 MIN.
MAKES 16

10	large eggs, divided
6	cups canola oil
⅓	cup mayonnaise
2½	Tbsp. dill pickle relish
1½	tsp. yellow mustard
½	tsp. hot sauce
¼	tsp. cayenne pepper
½	tsp. kosher salt, divided
⅓	cup all-purpose flour
1⅓	cups panko breadcrumbs
½	tsp. Creole seasoning (such as Tony Chachere's)
	Paprika

1. Bring a large pot of water to a boil over high. Carefully lower 8 of the eggs into water using a slotted spoon. Cook 10 minutes. Meanwhile, fill a large bowl with cold water and ice. Immediately transfer boiled eggs to ice water; chill 15 minutes. Peel eggs.

2. Heat oil in a medium-size Dutch oven over medium-high until oil reaches 350°F. Meanwhile, cut boiled eggs in half lengthwise. Carefully remove yolks; place in a medium bowl. Set aside egg white halves. Mash yolks using a fork; add mayonnaise, relish, mustard, hot sauce, cayenne, and ¼ teaspoon of the salt; stir until smooth. Transfer mixture to a zip-top plastic bag; seal and set aside.

3. Place flour in a shallow dish. Whisk remaining 2 eggs in a second shallow dish. Place panko in a third shallow dish. Working with 1 egg white half at a time, dredge in flour, gently shaking off excess. Dip in beaten eggs, letting excess drip off; dredge in panko.

4. Working in 3 batches, fry coated egg white halves in hot oil until golden brown, 60 to 90 seconds. Transfer to a rimmed baking sheet lined with paper towels to drain. Sprinkle evenly with Creole seasoning and remaining ¼ teaspoon salt.

5. Snip a hole in tip of plastic bag with egg yolk mixture. Pipe about 1 tablespoon egg yolk mixture onto each fried egg white half. Sprinkle with paprika, and transfer to a serving platter.

No-Stuff Deviled Eggs

ACTIVE 15 MIN. · TOTAL 15 MIN.

MAKES 24

Stir together 2½ Tbsp. **mayonnaise**, 1½ Tbsp. **Dijon mustard**, and a dash of **hot sauce** in a small bowl. Trim off and discard ends from 4 peeled hard-cooked **eggs**. Using an egg slicer or chef's knife, cut each egg crosswise into 6 slices. (For clean slices, dip knife into water and wipe clean often.) Dollop ½ teaspoon mayonnaise mixture onto 24 **round buttery crackers** (such as Ritz). Top each cracker with 1 egg slice. Garnish each slice with a sprinkle of **paprika**, **black pepper**, **kosher salt**, and **fresh dill**.

A Little Cake Tradition

For *Hey Y'all* host Ivy Odom, it wouldn't be Easter without
this beloved old-fashioned dessert

LITTLE LAYER CAKES are becoming a lost art in the South. Beloved throughout parts of Georgia, Alabama, Maryland, and Louisiana, these heirloom confections were a huge part of my childhood in southwest Georgia. No gathering was ever complete without one—or three.

The thin but sturdy layers are held together by chocolate, caramel, or lemon fillings. The diameter is just 8 inches, but there's nothing little about this dessert; the number of layers can range from 6 to 18. Although recipes are prized and passed down through generations, it seems as if these once ubiquitous cakes are slowly fading away. Since I joined *Southern Living* in 2016, I've made it my mission to see that these incredible vintage desserts never go out of style.

My Lemon-Cheese Layer Cake (properly pronounced with no pause between "lemon" and "cheese") is not like a cheesecake, as the name might suggest. The perfect balance of Lemon Curd Filling and cake is what gives it that creamy consistency. My updated version is frosted with buttercream (unlike traditional recipes iced with lemon curd), which balances the tang and makes it more beautiful. It takes some effort, but once you slice into it, you'll know why these desserts have stood the test of time.

Lemon-Cheese Layer Cake

ACTIVE 1 HOUR, 20 MIN. - TOTAL 1 HOUR,
40 MIN., PLUS 5 HOURS CHILLING

SERVES 12

CAKE LAYERS
- 1 cup unsalted butter, softened
- 2 cups granulated sugar
- 6 egg whites
- 1½ tsp. vanilla extract
- 1 tsp. grated lemon zest (from 1 lemon)
- 3⅓ cups bleached cake flour
- 1 Tbsp. baking powder
- ¼ tsp. kosher salt
- 1 cup whole milk

LEMON CURD FILLING
- 12 egg yolks
- 2¼ cups granulated sugar
- 2 Tbsp. cornstarch
- 1 Tbsp. grated lemon zest plus ¾ cup fresh juice (from 5 large lemons)
- ¼ tsp. kosher salt
- ¾ cup cold unsalted butter, cut into ½-inch pieces

LEMON BUTTERCREAM
- 1 cup unsalted butter, softened
- 3½ cups powdered sugar
- 1 tsp. grated lemon zest (from 1 lemon)
- 1 tsp. vanilla extract
- ⅓ cup heavy whipping cream

1. Prepare the Cake Layers: Preheat oven to 375°F with racks in middle and lower third positions. Coat 4 (8-inch) round cake pans with cooking spray, and line with parchment paper; set aside. Beat butter with a stand mixer fitted with a paddle attachment on medium speed until creamy, about 1 minute. Gradually add granulated sugar, beating until light and fluffy, 3 to 4 minutes. Stop mixer; scrape down sides. With mixer running on low speed, add egg whites, 1 at a time, stopping to scrape down sides as needed. Add vanilla and lemon zest; beat until just combined, about 30 seconds.

2. Whisk together cake flour, baking powder, and salt in a medium bowl. Add to butter mixture alternately with milk, beginning and ending with flour mixture, beating on low speed until just combined after each addition. Spread about ⅔ cup of batter into each of the prepared pans.

3. Bake cakes in preheated oven until a wooden pick inserted in center of cakes comes out clean, about 12 minutes. Cool in pans on wire racks 5 minutes. Remove cakes from pans; place directly on wire racks to cool completely, about 30 minutes. Meanwhile, coat pans again with cooking spray, and line again with parchment. Divide remaining batter evenly among pans (about ⅔ cup batter per pan). Bake cakes per previous instructions. (Cake Layers can be chilled overnight; separate the layers with plastic wrap.)

4. While cakes are cooling, prepare the Lemon Curd Filling: Whisk together egg yolks, granulated sugar, cornstarch, lemon zest and juice, and salt in a medium-size heavy saucepan until combined. Cook mixture over medium, stirring constantly with a wooden spoon, until mixture is thick and coats the back of spoon, 8 to 10 minutes. Remove from heat. Add cold butter; stir until melted and smooth.

5. Pour mixture through a fine mesh strainer into a medium bowl; discard any lumps. Place bowl with strained Lemon Curd Filling into a large bowl filled with ice water. Let stand, stirring often, until mixture is cool, about 20 minutes. Remove medium bowl from ice water bowl, and place a piece of plastic wrap directly on top of filling (to prevent a film from forming). Cover and chill until filling is firm, at least 4 hours or up to 3 days.

6. Prepare the Lemon Buttercream: Beat butter with an electric mixer on medium speed until creamy, about 1 minute. Gradually add powdered sugar, beating on low speed until combined, about 1 minute. Add lemon zest and vanilla, beating until just combined, about 10 seconds. With mixer running on medium speed, gradually add cream, beating until fluffy and spreadable, about 30 seconds.

7. Assemble the cake: Place 1 Cake Layer on a serving platter or a cake stand. Spoon ¼ cup Lemon Curd Filling onto cake; spread evenly to edges using an offset spatula. Repeat process with 6 more Cake Layers and Lemon Curd Filling. Top with remaining Cake Layer. (You should have about 1¼ cups filling remaining. Place in a piping bag or zip-top plastic bag; chill until ready to use.) Chill cake, uncovered, 1 hour.

8. Spread Lemon Buttercream over top and sides of cake. Snip a ½-inch tip off piping bag. Pipe dots of reserved Lemon Curd Filling, about the size of a quarter, around the top of cake to create a ring, leaving about a 1-inch border around edge. Using an offset spatula, drag dots of filling toward center of cake to create a flowerlike pattern.

OPEN SESAME
Toasted sesame oil has a richer, nuttier flavor than regular sesame oil, but either will work in this lively salad dressing.

Singing the Praises of Strawberries

They may not technically be berries, but they are a sure sign of spring

"THEY'RE SO FRESH AND SO FINE, and they're just off the vine ...strawberries, strawberries, strawberries." These lyrics from the opera *Porgy and Bess* celebrate Charleston, South Carolina's street vendors, whose cries provided the soundtrack for the city for generations. This song exalts a fruit that's a spring treat in many parts of the South.

But the lyrics got it wrong. Strawberries don't grow on vines but rather on runners that spread on the ground. The sweet fruit is one of the first to ripen in the spring and one of the few to have "seeds" on the outside, which are actually the true fruits, not the juicy flesh.

Members of the rose family that were originally found in the temperate regions of the northern hemisphere, strawberries come in many types, including various wild ones. Native Americans were some of the first people to use the fruit that is now cultivated virtually around the world. In fact, the strawberries we eat today are hybrids of the Virginia strawberry that is native to North America. It was taken to Europe by explorers in the 1600s and was readily adopted because it was larger and sweeter than the wild varieties that had previously been eaten there.

One of King Henry VIII's courtiers, Thomas Wolsey, is reputed to have been the first to come up with the combination of strawberries and cream, a pairing that has been enjoyed at the Wimbledon tennis matches since the first tournament was held back in 1877.

While biscuit-like shortcakes existed in Britain, strawberry shortcake seems to be a uniquely American creation. One of its earliest mentions in print is a recipe for Strawberry Cakes (layers of cake, icing, and mashed berries) in *Miss Leslie's Lady's New Receipt-Book* from 1850. As time went on, the recipes evolved to include whipped cream, pound cake, sponge cake, and other ingredients.

Strawberries can go in a savory direction, too. This salad, which features Boston lettuce, avocados, and a ginger-sesame–white balsamic dressing, is another way of enjoying the beloved fruit that isn't exactly a berry but is, for many, a delicious harbinger of spring. –Jessica B. Harris

Strawberry-Avocado Salad with Sesame-Ginger Dressing

ACTIVE 10 MIN. - TOTAL 10 MIN.
SERVES 6

- 1 head Boston lettuce, torn into pieces
- 3 cups fresh strawberries, stemmed and halved (quartered, if large)
- 2 medium avocados, cut into ½-inch cubes (about 2 cups)
- 2 Tbsp. white balsamic vinegar
- 1 Tbsp. toasted sesame oil
- 1 Tbsp. canola oil
- 2 tsp. honey
- 1 tsp. grated fresh ginger (from 1 [1-inch] piece)
- ½ tsp. kosher salt
- ¼ tsp. black pepper

1. Arrange lettuce on a serving platter. Top with strawberries and avocados.
2. Place vinegar, sesame oil, canola oil, 1 tablespoon water, the honey, ginger, salt, and pepper in a small jar. Seal jar; shake to combine well. Drizzle dressing over salad; serve immediately.

Strawberry Salads Forever

Use this simple recipe as the jumping-off point for all sorts of tasty variations

As spring moves into summer, you can ring in the changes by adapting this Strawberry-Avocado Salad. Arrange a mix of equal amounts of strawberries, tomatoes, and watermelon (or other fruits) on the lettuce for a warm-weather treat. Or try adding crisp crumbled bacon and/or cloves of roasted garlic atop the salad for a slightly different taste. The dressing can also be used on other salads that would benefit from the addition of a slightly sweet and spicy note.

Secrets to a Great Potato Gratin

Simple tweaks to make this cheesy classic even better

1

2

3

4

Scalloped or Au Gratin?

Both dishes are delicious, but they aren't the same. Scalloped potatoes are cooked in milk or cream, and au gratin ones have cheese.

PICK THE RIGHT POTATO

BAKING AND FRYING
Sweet potatoes and russets have a drier texture and are starchy and absorbent.

SALADS AND STEWS
Creamy and waxy red, new, and fingerling kinds have thin skins and hold their shape better when cooked.

ALL-PURPOSE
For roasting, mashing, or baking, try Yukon Golds, which are starchy but tender.

1

SLICE
Use a chef's knife (or a mandoline) to cut peeled potatoes crosswise into ⅛-inch-thick rounds. Thin, uniform slices will cook through quickly and at the same time.

2

SHINGLE
When arranging the potatoes in the baking dish, overlap the top layer at an angle to help them crisp up more in the oven.

3

SMOTHER
After the potatoes have baked and are tender, add a generous layer of shredded cheese with a bold flavor, like sharp Cheddar or Gruyère.

4

SERVE
When the gratin is done, set it aside for 10 minutes to let the sauce thicken a bit before digging in.

May

Mint Condition

This tenacious herb tends to overtake yards and gardens in the summer—but that's
a good thing, because there are so many refreshing ways to use it

MINT JULEP
SWEET TEA

Mint Julep Sweet Tea

ACTIVE 10 MIN. - TOTAL 10 MIN., PLUS 1 HOUR COOLING

SERVES 8

Combine 6 cups **water,** 1½ cups **fresh mint,** and 1 cup **granulated sugar** in a medium saucepan over high, stirring occasionally, until sugar is dissolved and mixture comes to a boil, about 3 minutes. Remove from heat. Add 6 **mint herbal tea bags.** Steep until cooled to room temperature, about 1 hour. Strain into a pitcher, and stir in 1½ cups (12 oz.) **bourbon** and 1 sliced **lemon.** Serve over **crushed ice,** and garnish with additional **fresh mint.**

SAUTÉED SNAP PEAS AND MINT

NO-CHURN FRESH MINT CHIP ICE CREAM

No-Churn Fresh Mint Chip Ice Cream

ACTIVE 15 MIN. - TOTAL 45 MIN., PLUS 4 HOURS CHILLING AND 4 HOURS FREEZING

SERVES 6

Combine 2½ cups **heavy whipping cream,** 2 cups **fresh mint,** and ⅛ tsp. **kosher salt** in a saucepan over medium, stirring occasionally, until it begins to steam (do not boil). Remove from heat. Cover; steep 30 minutes. Discard mint. Pour into a large metal bowl. Cover; chill 4 hours. Beat cream with an electric mixer on high speed until stiff peaks form, about 1 minute, 30 seconds. Fold in 1 (14-oz.) can **sweetened condensed milk** and 1 chopped (4-oz.) **60% bittersweet chocolate bar.** Transfer to a 9- x 5-inch loaf pan. Cover; freeze until firm, 4 hours.

Sautéed Snap Peas and Mint

ACTIVE 10 MIN. - TOTAL 10 MIN.

SERVES 4

Heat 1 Tbsp. **olive oil** in a large skillet over medium-high until it just begins to smoke. Add 1 lb. **fresh sugar snap peas** (with ends trimmed and strings removed); cook, undisturbed, until peas begin to brown and blister on bottoms, about 2 minutes. Stir once to redistribute in skillet. Cook, undisturbed, until peas are tender-crisp, about 3 minutes, adding 1 thinly sliced **small garlic clove** during final 1 minute cook time. Transfer to a serving bowl. Toss with 3 Tbsp. torn **fresh mint,** ½ tsp. grated **lemon zest** and 1 tsp. **fresh juice,** ½ tsp. **flaky sea salt,** and a pinch of **crushed red pepper.**

Lost Salads of the South

Our region might be known for salads of the congealed sort, but Southerners had an appetite for bowls of leafy greens and other fresh produce long before Marshmallow Fluff was invented

CAJUN-STYLE
POTATO SALAD

I LOVE SALAD—A LOT. I actually love it so much that I started a newsletter about it, "The Department of Salad: Official Bulletin." I'm so obsessed that I'm constitutionally incapable of truly disliking it in any form. So it always hurts my feelings if someone disparages one.

As a Southerner, however, I would like to request that the rest of the country stop blaming the South for congealed/gelatin salads. I may prefer a nice tomato-and-cucumber salad with a bit of red onion, but I'm not ashamed to say I have a nostalgic affection for those outlandish contrivances full of nuts and fruit and shredded vegetables. This explains why I get upset at Thanksgiving if I don't see at least one on the table. ("Hey, where's the Lime-Cabbage-Pecan-Marshmallow Surprise? No, I don't want to eat any. I'm just making sure it's here.")

Contrary to what so many of my dog-eared, spiral-bound Junior League and vintage Southern cookbooks imply with their abundant "Fluffs" and "Delights," we did not invent the trick of suspending food in jiggling gelatin. That practice can be traced to ancient savory aspics—some historians claim they date to medieval France, and others say as far back as 10th-century Arabic cooking. Instead, blame food manufacturers' marketing campaigns for the early- to midcentury explosion of congealed salads.

If you travel farther back into our culinary past, salads reflect the produce grown here much more than the rise of convenience foods. We grow almost every single vegetable found throughout the rest of the United States, as the great Southern journalist John Egerton pointed out in his 1987 classic *Southern Food: At Home, On the Road, In History.* He referred to our region as America's "primary and perennial orchard grove and truck garden."

So back in 1824, when Mary Randolph published *The Virginia Housewife* (considered to be the country's first real cookbook), she included many ways to prepare artichokes, asparagus, eggplant, sea kale, sorrel, spinach, sugar beans, turnips, and peas. She also gave

instructions for dressing a salad that are so bossy and up-to-the-minute that they could have been written yesterday–by me. ("To have this delicate dish in perfection, the lettuce, pepper grass, chervil, cress, &c. [sic] should be gathered early in the morning, nicely picked, washed, and laid in cold water, which will be improved by adding ice...") *The Williamsburg Art of Cookery*, a collection of recipes from Virginia households in the 18th and early 19th centuries, has a section called "Garden Stuff and Salads." And *The Carolina Housewife*, published in 1847, has a tomato salad, of course.

Southerners were salad people almost a hundred years before the "garden salad" became ubiquitous at home and in restaurants. But here's the thing: We've never crowed about our salads. Unlike the Caesar, the Cobb, the Waldorf, the Niçoise, and other famous ones named after chefs, restaurants, or cities, our recipes grew out of the everyday eating habits of gardeners and home cooks.

The five following recipes could be considered our lost salads, but the truth is that we have them memorized. They're as second nature to us as putting on a pot of beans or making a pan of cornbread. –Emily Nunn

Cajun-Style Potato Salad

Imagining a Louisiana picnic or cookout without a side of potato salad is almost impossible. And for some folks, this is a preferred stand-in for rice when eating a bowl of gumbo. The texture of the potato salad can range from smooth and creamy to chunky, depending on who's in the kitchen, but in its most basic form, it's a sumptuous mix of exactly what you'd expect: potatoes, mayo, a little Creole mustard, hard-cooked eggs, and Cajun seasoning. We took it beyond the limit, adding thick-cut bacon, bell peppers, celery, and freshly chopped dill pickles.

ACTIVE 20 MIN. - TOTAL 1 HOUR, 20 MIN.
SERVES 10

- 1 (24-oz.) bag gold new potatoes, cut into 1½-inch pieces
- 6 thick-cut bacon slices, cut into 1-inch pieces
- ¾ cup mayonnaise
- 2 Tbsp. pickle juice (from a jar of dill pickles)
- 2 Tbsp. Creole mustard
- 2 tsp. Cajun seasoning
- 1 cup (1-inch) chopped red bell pepper (from 1 medium bell pepper)
- 1 cup (1-inch) chopped yellow bell pepper (from 1 medium bell pepper)
- ½ cup (1-inch) chopped green bell pepper (from 1 medium bell pepper)
- ½ cup coarsely chopped dill pickles
- ½ cup (¼-inch) diagonally sliced celery (from 1 medium celery stalk)
- 5 hard-cooked eggs, peeled and cut into eighths (quartered lengthwise, then halved crosswise)
- ¼ cup sliced scallions (2 small scallions), plus more for garnish

1. Bring a large pot of water to a boil over high. Add new potatoes, and cook until tender when pierced with a knife, about 15 minutes. Drain and spread on a large rimmed baking sheet to cool to room temperature, about 45 minutes.
2. Meanwhile, cook bacon in a large skillet over medium, stirring often, until crisp, about 12 minutes. Remove from skillet, and place on a paper towel-lined plate. Set aside.
3. Stir together mayonnaise, pickle juice, Creole mustard, and Cajun seasoning in a large bowl. Add bell peppers, pickles, celery, hard-cooked eggs, scallions, cooled potatoes, and three-fourths of the bacon pieces; stir gently until evenly coated (trying not to break bacon pieces or eggs). Transfer to a serving bowl, and garnish with remaining bacon pieces and additional scallions. Store, covered, in refrigerator until ready to serve.

CITRUS-AVOCADO SALAD
WITH GRAPEFRUIT
VINAIGRETTE (PAGE 106)

SALMAGUNDI (PAGE 106)

Citrus-Avocado Salad with Grapefruit Vinaigrette

(Photo, page 104)

This ethereal combination seems to be the salad we make the most and include in our cookbooks least. But the great Georgia newspaper columnist and cookbook author Mrs. S.R. Dull knew that the ladies who lunch wanted a light, refreshing salad at their bridge-club gatherings, so she included an "avocado-and-grapefruit" version in her 1928 book, Southern Cooking. *This salad almost always includes a light vinaigrette; ours is made with grapefruit juice and a hint of mustard. You can mix up the citrus to make an extra-pretty plate or stick to just grapefruit.*

ACTIVE 20 MIN. - TOTAL 20 MIN.

SERVES 4

- ½ cup canola oil
- 1 tsp. Dijon mustard
- ½ tsp. ground coriander
- ¼ tsp. kosher salt
- ¼ tsp. black pepper
- ½ cup plus 1 Tbsp. fresh grapefruit juice (from 1 large grapefruit), divided
- 3 medium avocados, each cut into 8 wedges
- 2 medium grapefruits (white, pink, or Ruby Red), peeled, pith removed, and cut crosswise into ¼-inch-thick slices
- 1 medium-size orange (navel or Cara Cara), peeled, pith removed, and cut crosswise into ¼-inch-thick slices
- 2 medium blood oranges, peeled, pith removed, and cut crosswise into ¼-inch-thick slices
- ½ tsp. flaky sea salt
- ¼ cup chopped lightly salted pistachios

1. Whisk together oil, mustard, coriander, salt, pepper, and ½ cup of the grapefruit juice in a medium bowl until emulsified. Gently toss avocados and remaining 1 tablespoon grapefruit juice in a separate bowl until evenly coated.

2. Arrange grapefruit, orange, and blood orange slices on a platter, overlapping slightly. Place avocado wedges on top of the citrus slices.

3. Sprinkle with flaky sea salt, and drizzle with half of the dressing. Top with chopped pistachios. Serve with remaining dressing.

Salmagundi

(Photo, page 105)

Before the Cobb came along, there was the salmagundi. This early composed salad, which originated in 17th-century England, usually included anchovies, chicken, egg, nuts, grapes, and onion. It's one of the few true salad "receipts" that Mary Randolph recorded in her 1824 book, The Virginia Housewife: or, Methodical Cook. *She recommended putting "a little pyramid of butter on the top" along with an egg for dressing. Our interpretation has fresh produce (though, like Randolph, you can use what you have on hand) and a cooked dressing instead of butter.*

ACTIVE 1 HOUR - TOTAL 1 HOUR, 45 MIN.

SERVES 6

- 3 large egg yolks
- 1 Tbsp. all-purpose flour
- 1 tsp. kosher salt
- 1 tsp. dry mustard
- 1¼ cups half-and-half
- 3 Tbsp. unsalted butter, cut into small cubes
- 2 Tbsp. whole-grain mustard
- 1 Tbsp. chopped fresh chives
- 1 tsp. grated lemon zest plus ¼ cup fresh juice (from 2 lemons), divided
  - Ice
- 1 Tbsp. olive oil
- 1 tsp. garlic salt
- ½ tsp. black pepper
- 1 lb. medium peeled, deveined raw shrimp (about 48 shrimp)
- 1½ cups drained pickled okra pods (or 18 okra pods)
- 6 hard-cooked eggs, peeled and halved lengthwise
- 1 lb. red beefsteak tomatoes, cut into wedges (about 12 wedges)
- 3 oz. mixed baby salad greens
- 3 (2-oz.) pkg. thinly sliced prosciutto
- 2 cups English cucumber slices
- 6 lemon wedges, for serving

1. Combine egg yolks, flour, kosher salt, and dry mustard in a medium-size, heavy-bottom saucepan; whisk until smooth. Slowly add half-and-half, and whisk until blended. Cook over medium, stirring constantly with a flat-edge spatula or wooden spoon, until mixture is thick enough to coat the back of the spoon without running off, 5 to 7 minutes. Remove from heat, and pour through a fine mesh strainer into a medium metal bowl. While mixture is still hot, whisk in butter, whole-grain mustard, chives, and 2 tablespoons of the lemon juice. Place bowl over a larger bowl filled with ice; let mixture cool, stirring occasionally, about 20 minutes. Once cool, transfer dressing to a serving bowl, and cover surface directly with plastic wrap. Chill in refrigerator about 30 minutes. (Dressing will continue to thicken as it chills.)

2. Preheat grill to medium-high (400°F to 450°F). Combine olive oil, garlic salt, and pepper in a medium bowl; add shrimp, and toss to coat. Thread shrimp onto skewers. Place skewers on oiled grates, and grill until grill marks appear and shrimp are cooked through, 2 to 3 minutes per side. Remove from grill, and place shrimp in a medium bowl with lemon zest and remaining 2 tablespoons lemon juice; toss to coat shrimp evenly.

3. Arrange shrimp, okra, eggs, tomato wedges, mixed greens, prosciutto slices, and cucumber slices on a large serving platter. Serve with chilled dressing and lemon wedges.

Heirloom Tomato-Cracker Salad

(Photo, page 3)

This simple but heavenly concoction has been showing up on summertime tables for as long as we can remember—it's like a tomato sandwich in salad form. But you don't see it much in cookbooks or glossy magazines, because a mash-up of tomatoes, mayonnaise, and saltines isn't exactly gorgeous. This new version solves the image problem by turning it into a composed salad, with each element layered beautifully atop the creamy dressing. We also brightened up those traditional flavors with fresh herbs, sweet corn, and garlicky crisped crackers.

ACTIVE 20 MIN. - TOTAL 30 MIN.

SERVES 6

- 12 saltine crackers
- 1 Tbsp. unsalted butter, melted
- ¾ tsp. garlic salt, divided
- 1½ cups mayonnaise
- 2 Tbsp. chopped fresh chives
- 1 Tbsp. apple cider vinegar
- 2½ lb. heirloom tomatoes (assorted sizes and colors), sliced
  - Black pepper
- ¾ cup fresh corn kernels (1 ear)
- 2 Tbsp. small fresh basil leaves

1. Preheat oven to 375°F. Line a rimmed baking sheet with parchment paper; place crackers in a single layer on prepared baking sheet. Brush tops of crackers liberally with melted butter; sprinkle with ¼ teaspoon of the garlic salt. Bake until golden brown and fragrant, 8 to 10 minutes. Cool completely, about 20 minutes.

2. Meanwhile, stir together mayonnaise, chives, apple cider vinegar, and remaining ½ teaspoon garlic salt in a small bowl.

3. Spread mayonnaise mixture evenly on a large platter. Arrange tomato slices on top of mayonnaise mixture, overlapping slightly. Season tomatoes with pepper to taste; sprinkle with corn. Coarsely crush crackers over salad; sprinkle with basil.

Herbed Chicken-and-Rice Salad

Incorporating two mainstays of the Southern diet—chicken and rice—this salad is an example of the kind of delicious home cooking that grew out of the necessity of using every bit of food. From the 1920s on, rice salads also went in a sweet direction with ambrosia-like concoctions (with names like Million Dollar Rice Salad or Glorified Rice) made with canned fruit, gelatin, and marshmallows. Our recipe keeps things light and savory, pairing basmati rice with vegetables and rotisserie chicken. Herbs and a bright lemon dressing give it vivid colors and a fresh taste.

ACTIVE 35 MIN. - TOTAL 45 MIN.

SERVES 8

- 2 (8½-oz.) pkg. microwavable basmati rice
- ½ cup loosely packed fresh tender herbs (such as dill, parsley, and chives), plus more for garnish
- ¼ cup plus 2 Tbsp. olive oil
- ¼ cup fresh lemon juice (from 2 large lemons)
- 2 Tbsp. chopped shallot (from 1 small shallot)
- ½ Tbsp. Dijon mustard
- 2 tsp. honey
- ½ tsp. kosher salt
- ¼ tsp. black pepper
- 2½ cups shredded rotisserie chicken breast (from 1 chicken)
- 2 cups halved multicolor cherry tomatoes (from 1 [12-oz.] pkg.)
- 1¼ cups (¼-inch) diagonally sliced Persian or mini cucumbers (about 3 cucumbers)

HERBED CHICKEN-AND-RICE SALAD

- 1 cup sliced almonds, toasted
- 4 oz. feta cheese, crumbled (about 1 cup)
- ½ cup (¼-inch) sliced celery (from 1 large celery stalk)
- ¼ cup coarsely chopped celery leaves
- ¼ cup coarsely chopped fresh flat-leaf parsley

1. Microwave rice according to package directions; transfer to a large bowl, and cool completely, about 20 minutes.

2. Meanwhile, place herbs, olive oil, lemon juice, shallot, mustard, honey, salt, and pepper in a food processor or blender; process until smooth, about 30 seconds.

3. Add chicken, tomatoes, cucumbers, almonds, feta, celery, celery leaves, and parsley to bowl with cooled rice; drizzle with dressing, and toss to coat. Transfer to a large serving platter or bowl, and garnish with additional herbs.

CUCUMBER SALAD (PAGE 112)

LEMON-BARBECUE CHICKEN

JANIE MAY'S BAKED BEANS

The Art of the Party

Celebrating the 50th anniversary of our most popular entertaining book

LONG BEFORE you could text or email a party invite or scroll through endless recipes and table settings right in the palm of your hand, we published the *Southern Living Party Cookbook* in 1972. The way we entertain today is different from how we did back then—though fondue and flared pants seem to be coming back in style—but 50 years later, this beloved best-selling book still has recipes and menus to inspire as well as wisdom to share.

Author Celia Marks, a food writer from Chattanooga, Tennessee, who died in 2005, created it as a handbook for the Southern host who wants to entertain well and still enjoy the party. In her world, that meant being prepared. The *Party Cookbook* includes diagrams on how to set a table; instructions for assembling a bar and writing invitations; and advice on saying grace, seating arrangements, small budgets, plus more.

One of the most remarkable things about the book is its reassuring tone. Marks is an experienced friend right beside you in the kitchen who knows how to carve a standing rib roast and how much ice you'll need on hand for a large cocktail party (350 cubes for 50 people). And if something doesn't go as planned, that's perfectly alright. She makes it clear that the key to gracious hospitality is for everyone to feel comfortable, including the hosts.

That said, it's not a party without food. She provides menus for the expected occasions like holiday celebrations (with recipes for roasted turkey, lamb, and even goose), casual and fancy dinners, and brunches of all types. Plus, there are gatherings that seem charmingly dated now, like a Garden Tea for 40 to 50 guests (featuring Horns of Plenty filled with Chicken Salad) or a Summertime Bridge Luncheon (including Lime-Grape Gelatin Molds). The following menu for the Lemon-Barbecue Chicken Cookout has been adapted a bit, but like Marks' best advice, it works just as well today.
—Lisa Cericola

A Cookout Menu

With a few updates, these recipes are just as tasty today. Serve with plenty of iced tea and lemonade, as Marks suggests

Lemon-Barbecue Chicken

ACTIVE 45 MIN. - TOTAL 55 MIN.,
PLUS 3 HOURS CHILLING
SERVES 8

- 1 cup olive oil
- ½ cup fresh lemon juice (from 3 lemons)
- 2 tsp. dried basil
- 2 tsp. onion powder
- ½ tsp. dried thyme leaves
- 1 garlic clove, smashed
- 1 Tbsp. plus 1½ tsp. kosher salt, divided
- 2 (3½- to 4-lb.) whole chickens, cut lengthwise in half, backbones removed
- Lemon halves, for garnish (optional)
- Fresh basil, for garnish (optional)

1. Whisk together olive oil, lemon juice, dried basil, onion powder, thyme, garlic, and 1 tablespoon of the salt in a large bowl. Add chicken halves; toss to coat. Cover; chill for 3 to 5 hours, turning chicken halves occasionally.

2. Preheat grill to medium (350°F to 400°F). Remove chicken from marinade; discard marinade. Sprinkle evenly with remaining 1½ teaspoons salt. Place skin side up on oiled grates, and grill, covered, turning occasionally, until a meat thermometer inserted into thickest portion registers 165°F, 35 to 45 minutes.
3. Transfer chicken to a platter; let rest for 10 minutes before serving. Garnish with lemon halves and fresh basil, if desired.

Janie May's Baked Beans

ACTIVE 20 MIN. - TOTAL 1 HOUR, 20 MIN.
SERVES 8

- 2 tsp. canola oil
- 1 lb. smoked spicy pork sausage, thinly sliced crosswise
- 1 medium-size yellow onion, chopped (about 1¾ cups)
- 3 medium garlic cloves, chopped
- 2 (28-oz.) cans baked beans
- ¼ cup light brown sugar
- 2 Tbsp. yellow mustard
- 2 Tbsp. apple cider vinegar
- 2 Tbsp. unsulphured molasses
- ½ tsp. dry mustard
- ½ tsp. kosher salt
- ¼ tsp. black pepper

1. Preheat oven to 350°F. Heat oil in a skillet over medium. Add sausage; cook, stirring occasionally, until browned on both sides, 8 to 10 minutes. Using a slotted spoon, transfer sausage to a paper towel-lined plate. Add onion and garlic to drippings in skillet. Cook over medium, stirring and scraping occasionally to loosen browned bits from bottom of skillet, until softened, about 6 minutes. Transfer to a bowl.
2. Add beans, sugar, yellow mustard, vinegar, molasses, dry mustard, salt, and pepper to bowl with onion mixture. Stir in sausage. Transfer to a 2½-quart baking dish. Bake in preheated oven, uncovered, until bubbly and sauce has thickened, 50 minutes to 1 hour. Let stand 10 minutes before serving.

SIDNEY'S
POTATO SALAD

MRS. R'S
COLESLAW

Sidney's Potato Salad

ACTIVE 25 MIN. - TOTAL 50 MIN.,
PLUS 1 HOUR CHILLING
SERVES 6

2½ lb. baby yellow potatoes, halved

1 fresh or dried bay leaf

¼ cup chopped fresh flat-leaf parsley, plus 8 parsley sprigs, divided

6 whole black peppercorns

¼ cup kosher salt, plus more to taste

2 medium celery stalks, finely chopped (about ½ cup), tops reserved

¾ cup mayonnaise

½ cup sour cream

1 medium bunch scallions, thinly sliced (about ¾ cup), plus more for garnish

2 Tbsp. chopped fresh tarragon

1 Tbsp. apple cider vinegar

1½ tsp. seasoned salt (such as Lawry's)

½ tsp. garlic salt

¾ tsp. black pepper

1. Combine halved potatoes, bay leaf, parsley sprigs, peppercorns, kosher salt, and reserved celery tops in a large saucepan. Add 1 quart cold water, adding additional water as needed to cover potatoes by 2 inches. Bring to a boil over medium-high. Reduce heat to medium-low; simmer, stirring occasionally, until potatoes are fork-tender, 15 to 18 minutes. Drain. Let cool for 10 minutes. Discard bay leaf, parsley sprigs, peppercorns, and celery tops.
2. While potatoes are boiling, stir together mayonnaise, sour cream, scallions, tarragon, apple cider vinegar, seasoned salt, garlic salt, black pepper, chopped parsley, and chopped celery in a large bowl.
3. Add potatoes to mayonnaise mixture, and stir until well combined. Cover and chill at least 1 hour or up to 2 days. Just before serving, season to taste with additional kosher salt. Stir well. Garnish with additional sliced scallions.

Mrs. R's Coleslaw

ACTIVE 20 MIN. - TOTAL 20 MIN.,
PLUS 1 HOUR CHILLING
SERVES 8

1 medium-size green bell pepper, chopped (about 1 cup)

1 medium-size red bell pepper, chopped (about 1 cup)

A Note on Hospitality
An excerpt from the author's introduction

"PLEASANTEST of all ties is the tie of host and guest." –Aeschylus, 500 B.C.

It is the purpose of this book to help you in all seasons, on all occasions, to be at your best while entertaining.

A good party doesn't just happen, not even for the hostess who is regarded as having an inborn flair for entertaining. The successful party is the result of careful planning of the food to be offered as well as an awareness of just what makes an occasion memorable.

So often in organizing our entertaining, we tend to forget why we're doing it at all. We're so busy with the mechanics of the affair that we overlook the real purpose–the pleasure of dispensing hospitality. It should be our aim that afterward our guests will be warmed by the memory of a happy, exciting party and that they'll think back on an interesting discussion, a challenging turn of the conversation, an exciting newcomer with a different viewpoint–and wonder, too, what magic you worked with the food you served. These intangibles are so much more important than the guest seeing her reflection in the shine on your furniture.

The old French proverb puts it succinctly: "The company makes the feast." But you as hostess can create the climate surrounding the feast, one that promotes the enjoyment of people when they get together.

It's impossible to bring about this ambience if you're in the kitchen tasting and fussing instead of being with your guests, seeing that the shy are not ignored, that the glasses are refilled before you hear the ice rattle, that everyone gets a chance at the nibbles you've prepared ahead of time (for as a famous American columnist once complained, "There's someone at every party who eats all the celery").

If entertaining is to be done with confidence and pleasure–and often if it is to be done at all–much of the food should be prepared ahead of time, allowing for catastrophes and recovery therefrom. Because where entertaining is concerned, most of us feel we operate according to Murphy's Law, anyhow: "If anything can go wrong, it will go wrong."

Equal to the problem of timing is the greatest stumbling block in the path of even a veteran hostess–what goes with what. Many women may be great at producing one superb dish; but however wonderfully constructed, to exploit its virtues, the entrée must be surrounded by dishes that complement rather than compete with it. As an artist is concerned with relationships in a painting, so you, an artist in your own kitchen, are concerned with the relationship of one dish to another, with the creation of a harmonious unit rather than a heterogeneous assortment of parts, good as each may be.

We hope the menus we've selected will solve your entertaining problems so that when the last guest has departed and you lock up, take off your shoes, and turn to your mate and ask, "Well, how do you think it went?" you'll know the happy answer before you get it. –Celia Marks

1 small yellow onion, chopped (about 1 cup)

2 medium celery stalks, chopped (about ½ cup)

1 cup mayonnaise

¼ cup apple cider vinegar

2 Tbsp. yellow mustard

2 tsp. kosher salt

1 tsp. black pepper

1 small head green cabbage, cored and shredded (about 8 cups)

Stir together bell peppers, onion, celery, mayonnaise, apple cider vinegar, mustard, salt, and black pepper in a large bowl until well combined. Stir in cabbage. Cover and chill for at least 1 hour or up to overnight (12 hours). Stir well before serving.

Words of Wisdom

*Advice from the book that
stands the test of time*

ON CREATING A MENU: "Consider
the mood; elegantly dressed dinner
guests are apt to take only token
bites of corn on the cob."

- -

ON GETTING READY FOR COMPANY:
"Give the bathroom a last-minute
once-over just prior to party time.
See that hand towels are fresh
and individual guest soap is out in
a clean, dry dish, and give a quick
swipe to the sink and toilet bowl."

- -

ON KEEPING YOUR COOL: "A harried
hostess who spends all day in the
kitchen can only succeed in giving
her guests a guilty feeling, even
though the dinner is a masterpiece.
After all, guests have not come
primarily to eat but to enjoy
your company."

Cucumber Salad

(Photo, page 108)
ACTIVE 25 MIN. · TOTAL 25 MIN.,
PLUS 1 HOUR CHILLING
SERVES 8

- 2 small English cucumbers, thinly sliced into half-moons (about 4 cups)
- 4 medium scallions, thinly sliced (about ¾ cup)
- ¼ cup dry white wine
- 1½ tsp. kosher salt, divided, plus more to taste
- 3 Tbsp. olive oil
- 1½ Tbsp. fresh lemon juice (from 1 lemon)
- ½ tsp. black pepper
- 2 medium romaine lettuce hearts, chopped (about 6 cups)
- 1½ cups cherry tomatoes, halved
- ½ cup loosely packed fresh basil leaves, thinly sliced, plus more for garnish

1. Toss together cucumbers, scallions, wine, and ½ teaspoon of the salt in a medium-size nonreactive bowl. Cover and chill, tossing occasionally, until flavors meld, about 1 hour.
2. Whisk together olive oil, lemon juice, pepper, and remaining 1 teaspoon salt in a large bowl. Add lettuce, cherry tomatoes, and cucumber mixture (with liquid); toss to combine. Gently stir in basil. Season to taste with additional salt. Garnish with basil, and serve.

Chocolate Icebox Cake

ACTIVE 35 MIN. · TOTAL 45 MIN.,
PLUS 12 HOURS CHILLING
SERVES 12

- 1 (4-oz.) 100% cacao unsweetened chocolate baking bar, roughly chopped
- ¼ cup unsalted butter, plus more for greasing pan
- 6 large pasteurized eggs, separated, at room temperature
- ¼ tsp. kosher salt
- ½ cup plus 2 Tbsp. granulated sugar, divided
- 1 tsp. vanilla extract
- ½ tsp. almond extract
- 2½ cups heavy whipping cream, divided
- 1 (7-oz.) pkg. crisp ladyfingers
- 1 cup sliced almonds, toasted, plus more for garnish
- Unsweetened cocoa for dusting

1. Fill a small saucepan with water to a depth of 1 inch, and bring to a simmer over medium. Combine chocolate and butter in a medium heatproof bowl; set bowl over pan of water, ensuring bottom of bowl doesn't touch water. Heat, stirring often, until melted and smooth, about 5 minutes. Remove from heat; cool slightly, about 10 minutes.
2. Vigorously whisk together egg yolks, kosher salt, and ¼ cup of the granulated sugar in a large bowl until pale and thickened, about 3 minutes. Gradually stream in cooled chocolate mixture, whisking constantly until well combined. Whisk in vanilla and almond extracts. Set aside.
3. Beat egg whites with a stand mixer fitted with a whisk attachment on medium speed until frothy, about 45 seconds. With mixer running on medium speed, gradually add ¼ cup of the sugar, beating until stiff peaks form, about 2 minutes. Gently fold egg white mixture into chocolate mixture in 3 additions.
4. Beat 1 cup of the heavy whipping cream with stand mixer fitted with whisk attachment on medium speed until stiff peaks form, about 1 to 2 minutes. Fold whipped cream into chocolate mixture.
5. Lightly grease a 9-inch springform pan with butter. Arrange half of ladyfingers in a single layer on bottom of pan, breaking cookies as needed. Spread half of chocolate mixture (about 3½ cups) in an even layer on top of cookies. Sprinkle with ½ cup sliced almonds. Repeat layering with remaining ladyfingers, chocolate mixture, and ½ cup almonds. Cover and chill overnight, about 12 hours.
6. Just before serving, beat remaining 1½ cups whipping cream with stand mixer fitted with whisk attachment on medium-high speed until frothy, about 30 seconds. Gradually add remaining 2 tablespoons sugar, beating until soft peaks form, 1 to 2 minutes.
7. Run a small offset spatula around edges of pan to loosen. Remove sides of pan, and smooth sides of cake with spatula. Top cake with whipped cream; spread in an even layer. Dust lightly with cocoa, and garnish with additional toasted sliced almonds.

CHOCOLATE
ICEBOX CAKE

For Pudding Lovers Only

It's hard to improve upon a beloved banana dessert, but that didn't stop our
Test Kitchen from whipping up three new creamy, dreamy recipes

BANANA PUDDING PIE

Banana Pudding Pie

ACTIVE 30 MIN. - TOTAL 55 MIN.,
PLUS 2 HOURS CHILLING
SERVES 8

Brown Butter-Vanilla Wafer Crust
(recipe, below right)
1½ cups whole milk
½ cup heavy whipping cream
½ cup granulated sugar
⅛ tsp. kosher salt
4 large egg yolks
¼ cup cornstarch
2 Tbsp. unsalted butter, plus more
for greasing pie plate
1½ tsp. vanilla extract
4 medium bananas, divided
Vanilla Bean Whipped Cream
(recipe, bottom right)
Crushed vanilla wafers

1. Preheat oven to 325°F. Lightly grease a 9-inch deep-dish pie plate with butter, and press Brown Butter-Vanilla Wafer Crust into bottom and up sides of prepared pie plate. Bake until golden brown and firm, 10 to 12 minutes. Remove from oven; let cool on a wire rack while preparing filling.
2. Whisk together milk, cream, sugar, and salt in a medium saucepan. Cook over medium, whisking often, until steaming, about 5 minutes (do not let milk mixture boil). Remove from heat. Whisk together egg yolks and cornstarch in a medium heatproof bowl until smooth. Using a ladle, slowly drizzle ½ cup steaming milk mixture into egg mixture, whisking constantly until combined. Slowly drizzle egg mixture into remaining warmed milk mixture in saucepan, stirring constantly until combined. Cook milk mixture over medium, whisking constantly, until mixture thickens and begins to simmer (about 200°F), about 5 to 7 minutes. Remove saucepan from heat; whisk in butter and vanilla. Transfer pudding to a medium bowl, and cover with plastic wrap, pressing plastic wrap directly on pudding surface to prevent a skin from forming. Let pudding stand 15 minutes.
3. Cut 3 of the bananas into ½-inch-thick slices; arrange slices in bottom of cooled crust. Top with pudding; spread into an even layer using a small offset spatula. Cover with plastic wrap, pressing plastic wrap directly on pudding surface to prevent a skin from forming, and chill until set, at least 2 hours or up to 12 hours.
4. Just before serving, remove pie from refrigerator. Cut remaining banana into ½-inch-thick slices. Pipe Vanilla Bean Whipped Cream on pie. Arrange banana slices as desired, sprinkle pie with crushed vanilla wafers, and serve.

Banana Pudding Cheesecake Bars

(Photo, page 117)
ACTIVE 25 MIN. - TOTAL 1 HOUR, 30 MIN., PLUS
1 HOUR COOLING AND 6 HOURS CHILLING
SERVES 12

Brown Butter-Vanilla Wafer Crust
(recipe follows)
3 medium (about 6 oz. each)
bananas, divided
2 Tbsp. light brown sugar
1 Tbsp. fresh lemon juice (from
1 lemon)
1 Tbsp. (½ oz.) banana liqueur
(optional)
3 (8-oz.) pkg. cream cheese, softened
1 cup granulated sugar
3 large eggs
2 tsp. vanilla extract
Vanilla Bean Whipped Cream
(recipe, below right)
Vanilla wafers

1. Preheat oven to 325°F. Line bottom and sides of a 9-inch square baking pan with parchment paper, allowing 2 inches to extend over sides; set aside. Press Brown Butter-Vanilla Wafer Crust into bottom of prepared pan. Bake until golden brown and firm, 10 to 12 minutes. Remove from oven; let cool on a wire rack while preparing filling. Increase oven temperature to 350°F.
2. Chop 2 of the bananas; place in a small saucepan with brown sugar and lemon juice. Cook over medium-high, stirring constantly, until sugar is dissolved, about 1 minute. Remove from heat, and stir in banana liqueur, if using; cool 10 minutes.
3. Beat cream cheese and granulated sugar with a stand mixer fitted with a paddle attachment on medium speed until light and creamy, about 3 minutes. Reduce speed to medium-low; add eggs, 1 at a time, beating until just combined and scraping bowl as needed. Add vanilla; beat until smooth, about 30 seconds. Add banana mixture; beat until just combined, about 30 seconds.

Pour filling over cooled crust in pan; smooth top with a spatula.
4. Bake at 350°F until center is set and no longer jiggles when gently shaken, 45 to 55 minutes. Remove from oven; cool completely on a wire rack, about 1 hour. Cover with plastic wrap; chill at least 6 hours or up to 24 hours.
5. Carefully remove cheesecake from baking pan using parchment paper as handles. Cut into 12 (1½- x 4½-inch) rectangles, and arrange on a platter. Pipe Vanilla Bean Whipped Cream on each cheesecake bar as desired. Cut remaining banana into ½-inch-thick rounds. Top bars with banana rounds and vanilla wafers as desired; serve immediately.

Brown Butter-Vanilla Wafer Crust

ACTIVE 10 MIN. - TOTAL 10 MIN.
**MAKES ENOUGH CRUST FOR A 9-INCH
SQUARE BAKING PAN OR A 9-INCH
DEEP-DISH PIE PLATE**

Melt 6 Tbsp. **unsalted butter** in a small saucepan over medium. Cook, whisking constantly, until butter reaches a deep golden brown and smells nutty, about 3 to 5 minutes. Stir together brown butter, 1½ cups finely ground **vanilla wafer crumbs** (from about 50 vanilla wafers), ¼ cup **granulated sugar**, ½ tsp. **kosher salt**, and ¼ tsp. **ground nutmeg** in a bowl. Form crust in baking pan or pie plate as directed in recipe. Cover and store in refrigerator up to 2 days, or freeze up to 2 months.

Vanilla Bean Whipped Cream

ACTIVE 5 MIN. - TOTAL 5 MIN.
MAKES ABOUT 2 CUPS

Cut 1 **vanilla bean pod** in half lengthwise. Using back of a paring knife or edge of a small spoon, scrape vanilla seeds from 1 pod half into bowl of a stand mixer fitted with a whisk attachment. Reserve remaining pod half for another use. Add 1 cup **heavy whipping cream**, ⅛ tsp. **kosher salt**, and 3 Tbsp. **powdered sugar** to bowl. Beat on medium speed until frothy, about 1 minute. Increase speed to medium-high, and beat until stiff peaks form, 2 to 3 minutes. Use immediately, or store in refrigerator until ready to use (up to 4 hours).

New-Fashioned Banana Pudding

ACTIVE 35 MIN. - TOTAL 35 MIN.,
PLUS 4 HOURS CHILLING

SERVES 12

- 4 large egg yolks
- ¼ cup cornstarch
- 2 cups whole milk
- 1 cup heavy whipping cream
- ¾ cup granulated sugar
- ½ tsp. ground nutmeg
- ¼ tsp. kosher salt
- 2 Tbsp. unsalted butter
- ½ Tbsp. vanilla extract
- 2½ cups crushed vanilla wafers (from 1 [11-oz.] pkg.), plus whole wafers for garnish, if desired
- 4 medium bananas, peeled and cut into ½-inch-thick rounds

  Vanilla Bean Whipped Cream (recipe, page 115)

1. Whisk together egg yolks and cornstarch in a medium-size heatproof bowl until well combined. Whisk together milk, whipping cream, sugar, nutmeg, and salt in a medium saucepan. Cook over medium, whisking often, until steaming, 4 to 6 minutes (do not let milk mixture boil). Remove from heat. Using a ladle, slowly drizzle 1 cup steaming milk mixture into egg mixture, whisking constantly until combined. Slowly drizzle egg mixture into remaining warmed milk mixture in saucepan, stirring constantly until combined. Cook milk mixture over medium, whisking constantly until mixture thickens and begins to simmer (about 200°F), 8 to 10 minutes. Remove saucepan from heat, and whisk in butter and vanilla. Transfer pudding to a medium bowl; cover with plastic wrap, pressing wrap directly to surface to prevent a skin from forming. Refrigerate until completely chilled, about 3 hours.

2. Spoon 3 tablespoons crushed vanilla wafers into each of 12 stemless wineglasses or other 8-oz. glasses; top each with about one-third of a sliced banana and ⅓ cup pudding. Dollop each with about 2 tablespoons Vanilla Bean Whipped Cream, and sprinkle with 1 teaspoon crushed vanilla wafers. Cover loosely, and chill for at least 1 hour (or up to 4 hours) before serving. Garnish each glass with a whole vanilla wafer, if desired.

SCALE IT UP FOR A CROWD
Double the pudding, bananas, and Vanilla Bean Whipped Cream. Layer in a 13- x 9-inch baking dish with 60 vanilla wafers as desired. Chill at least 3 hours.

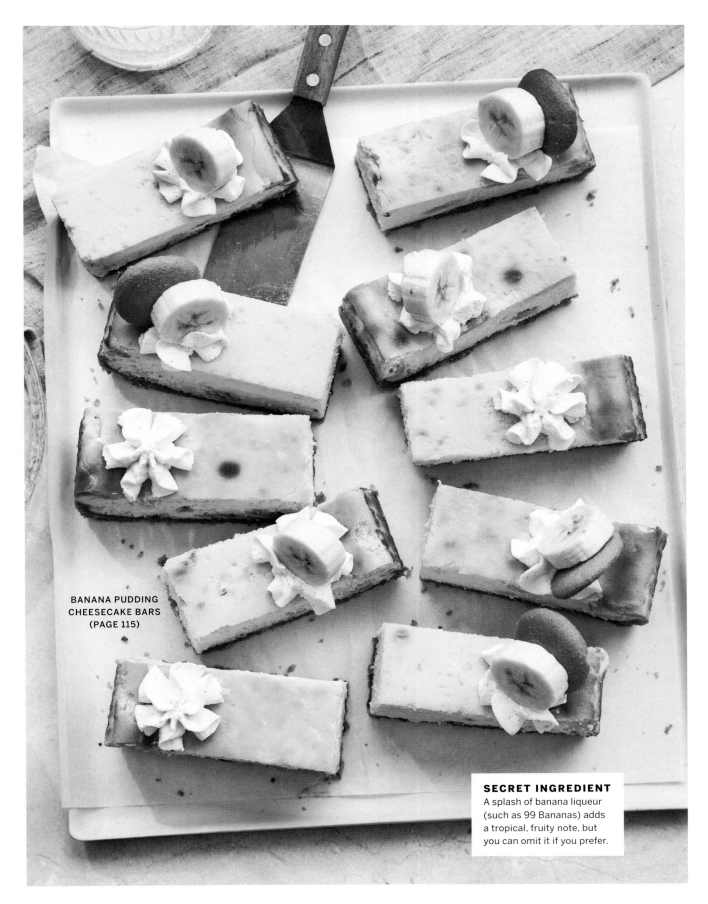

BANANA PUDDING CHEESECAKE BARS (PAGE 115)

SECRET INGREDIENT
A splash of banana liqueur (such as 99 Bananas) adds a tropical, fruity note, but you can omit it if you prefer.

Good Eggs

Just-fancy-enough recipes to wow your brunch crowd

Bacon-and-Egg Tarts with Goat Cheese

ACTIVE 30 MIN. · TOTAL 1 HOUR

SERVES 8

- 1 (17.3-oz.) pkg. frozen puff pastry sheets, thawed
- All-purpose flour, for dusting
- 2 (4-oz.) containers goat cheese crumbles
- 8 large eggs
- 8 bacon slices, cooked
- 8 (¼-inch-thick) plum tomato slices (from 2 plum tomatoes)
- ¼ cup chopped fresh parsley
- 1 tsp. kosher salt
- ½ tsp. ground black pepper

1. Preheat oven to 400°F. Line 2 rimmed baking sheets with parchment paper; set aside.

2. Roll each puff pastry sheet into a 12- x 10-inch rectangle on a lightly floured surface. Cut each sheet into 4 (6- x 5-inch) rectangles. With floured fingertips, fold about ½ inch of each edge over toward center of pastry, pinching corners with fingertips to form a border. Place rectangles on prepared baking sheets. Using a fork, lightly prick the bottom of each inside border. Bake in preheated oven until puffed and light golden brown, about 14 minutes.

3. Working quickly, lightly press the center of each tart with a clean kitchen towel to deflate and form a well for eggs. Sprinkle about 1 tablespoon goat cheese over each tart; then crack an egg into each well. Top each egg with 1 crumbled bacon slice, 1 tomato slice, a sprinkle of parsley, ⅛ teaspoon salt, a pinch of pepper, and about 1 tablespoon goat cheese.

4. Return tarts to oven; bake at 400°F until egg whites are cooked and yolks are slightly runny, 13 to 15 minutes. Serve hot or at room temperature.

REMEMBER THIS STEP
Lightly pressing the center of the baked tarts with a clean kitchen towel will help the pastry deflate a bit to form a well for the eggs.

Creamy Baked Eggs with Leeks and Spinach

ACTIVE 15 MIN. - TOTAL 30 MIN.
SERVES 4

- 3 Tbsp. unsalted butter, divided
- 1 large leek, trimmed, halved lengthwise, and thinly sliced (about 1½ cups)
- 1 (10-oz.) pkg. fresh spinach
- ¼ cup heavy cream
- ½ tsp. kosher salt
- 8 large eggs
- 2 oz. feta cheese, crumbled (about ½ cup)
- ¼ tsp. black pepper
- 1 Tbsp. thinly sliced chives
  Toasted English muffins, for serving

1. Preheat oven to 375°F with an oven rack in top third of oven. Grease an 11- x 7-inch baking dish with 1 tablespoon of the butter; set aside.
2. Melt remaining 2 tablespoons butter in a medium skillet over medium-high. Add leek, and cook, stirring occasionally, just until softened, 3 minutes. Add spinach in 3 batches, stirring to wilt spinach after each addition. Continue cooking, stirring occasionally, until spinach is wilted and liquid has almost completely evaporated, 2 to 3 minutes. Stir in cream and salt; remove from heat. Spoon spinach mixture into prepared baking dish; let cool 5 minutes.
3. Make 8 evenly spaced wells in spinach mixture, and crack an egg into each well. Sprinkle eggs with feta and pepper. Bake in preheated oven until egg whites are set but yolks are still soft, 14 to 16 minutes. Sprinkle with chives; serve with English muffins.

Southern Salmon Benedict

ACTIVE 30 MIN. - TOTAL 30 MIN.

SERVES 4

- 4 frozen biscuits
- ¼ cup cold water
- 8 large eggs plus 4 large egg yolks, divided
- ½ cup unsalted butter, melted
- ½ tsp. kosher salt
- 2 tsp. grated lemon zest plus 2 Tbsp. fresh juice, divided (from 1 lemon)
- 1½ Tbsp. white vinegar
- 2 (4-oz.) pkg. thinly sliced smoked salmon
- 2 Tbsp. chopped fresh chives
- ¼ tsp. ground black pepper

1. Bake biscuits according to package directions, and keep warm.

2. Meanwhile, whisk together the water and 4 egg yolks in a small saucepan. Cook over medium, whisking constantly, until mixture is foamy and begins to thicken slightly, about 2 minutes. Gradually add melted butter, 1 tablespoon at a time, whisking constantly until each addition of butter is incorporated and mixture is thick, about 6 minutes. Remove pan from heat. Stir in salt and lemon juice; set aside.

3. Add water to a depth of 3 inches in a wide, shallow stockpot or Dutch oven. Add vinegar; bring to a boil over medium-high. Reduce heat to low; adjust temperature as needed to maintain a simmer (there should be a few small bubbles at bottom of pot). Crack 8 eggs into individual small bowls or ramekins. Working with 1 egg at a time, add 4 of the eggs to simmering water as close to the surface as possible. Simmer until whites are done and look unified, 3 to 5 minutes. Using a slotted spoon, carefully remove cooked eggs and transfer to a paper towel-lined plate. Repeat process with remaining 4 eggs.

4. Split biscuits; place them open-face on a platter. Top each biscuit half with 1 ounce salmon and 1 poached egg; drizzle evenly with hollandaise sauce. Sprinkle with chives, lemon zest, and pepper; serve immediately.

EASIER EGGS

If you don't feel like poaching the eggs, cooking them sunny-side up or over easy will work just as well.

Oven-Baked Omelet

ACTIVE 25 MIN. - TOTAL 50 MIN.

SERVES 10

12	large eggs
1	cup heavy cream
2	medium scallions, finely chopped (½ cup)
1	tsp. kosher salt
1	tsp. garlic powder
½	tsp. ground black pepper, plus more for serving
8	oz. shredded Cheddar-Jack cheese (about 2 cups), divided
½	cup coarsely chopped soft fresh herbs (such as parsley, chives, dill, tarragon, or cilantro)

1. Preheat oven to 400°F. Grease a 13- x 9-inch baking dish with cooking spray. Whisk together eggs, cream, scallions, salt, garlic powder, pepper, and 1 cup of the cheese in a large bowl. Pour egg mixture into prepared baking dish; top with remaining 1 cup cheese.
2. Bake in preheated oven until eggs are puffed and lightly golden around edges, about 25 minutes. Top with herbs and additional pepper. Serve immediately with desired toppings (below). The omelet will deflate as it cools.

HAVE IT YOUR WAY

Southwestern Omelet
Top with chopped avocado, salsa, fresh cilantro, and hot sauce.

French Omelet
Top with sautéed mushrooms and shallots, fresh tarragon and parsley, and crumbled goat cheese.

Denver Omelet
Top with sautéed onions and peppers, diced ham, fresh chives, and shredded Cheddar.

CATCH THE MESS
Before placing this casserole in the oven, put the dish on a rimmed baking sheet to contain any drips as it cooks.

Cheesy Tomato-and-Sausage Strata

ACTIVE 20 MIN. - TOTAL 1 HOUR, 30 MIN., PLUS 4 HOURS CHILLING

SERVES 10

- 1 lb. hickory-smoked sausage (such as Conecuh), halved lengthwise and sliced ½ inch thick
- 2 cups grape or cherry tomatoes
- 1 small (8-oz.) yellow onion, chopped (1 cup)
- 1 (1-lb.) hearty bakery-style bread loaf, cut into 1-inch cubes (about 9 cups)
- ¼ cup chopped fresh parsley, divided
- 8 large eggs, lightly beaten
- 2½ cups whole milk
- 8 oz. shredded Italian blend cheese (about 2 cups), divided
- 1 (6.5-oz.) container garlic-and-herb spreadable cheese (such as Alouette), divided

1. Heat a large skillet over medium-high. Add sausage. Cook, stirring occasionally, until sausage begins to brown, about 5 minutes. Add tomatoes and onion; cook, stirring occasionally, until onion is softened and tomatoes have burst, about 5 minutes. Remove skillet from heat.

2. Toss together sausage mixture, bread, and 2 tablespoons of the parsley in a very large bowl. Whisk eggs, milk, 1 cup of the shredded cheese, and half of the garlic-and-herb cheese in a medium bowl. Pour egg mixture over bread mixture; toss gently to combine. Spoon mixture into a 13- x 9-inch (3-quart) baking dish lightly greased with cooking spray; pour any remaining liquid over bread in dish. Cover with aluminum foil; chill at least 4 hours or up to 12 hours.

3. Preheat oven to 375°F. Uncover baking dish; sprinkle with remaining 1 cup shredded cheese, and dollop with remaining garlic-and-herb cheese. Cover with foil; place on a rimmed baking sheet. Bake until almost set, about 40 minutes. Uncover; continue baking until golden brown and a knife inserted in center comes out clean (with no liquid egg), 15 to 20 minutes. Let stand at room temperature 15 minutes. Sprinkle with remaining 2 tablespoons parsley before serving.

Fuss-Free Biscuit

Delight everyone at breakfast—and keep your countertop clean—with this savory bread

Bacon-and-Cheddar Skillet Biscuit

ACTIVE 10 MIN. - TOTAL 45 MIN.

SERVES 8

- 2½ cups all-purpose flour
- 1 Tbsp. granulated sugar
- 2½ tsp. baking powder
- 1 tsp. kosher salt
- ¼ tsp. baking soda
- ½ cup cold unsalted butter, cubed, plus more for greasing pan
- 3 oz. sharp yellow Cheddar cheese, shredded (about ¾ cup)
- ¾ cup sour cream
- ½ cup crumbled cooked bacon
- ⅓ cup whole buttermilk
- 3 Tbsp. chopped fresh chives
- 1 large egg, lightly beaten

1. Preheat oven to 400°F. Grease a 10-inch cast-iron skillet with butter.
2. Stir together flour, sugar, baking powder, salt, and baking soda. Using a pastry blender or 2 forks, cut in cold butter until mixture is crumbly. Stir in cheese, sour cream, bacon, buttermilk, and chives until dough starts to come together. Knead a few times to incorporate any dry pieces.
3. Place dough in prepared skillet, pressing top lightly to spread evenly. Brush top with beaten egg. Bake in preheated oven until golden brown and cooked through, 26 to 28 minutes. Cool 10 minutes before serving.

PREP POINTER
For flaky layers and lift, make sure the butter is cold when it's cut into the flour mixture.

LEMONY BAKED COD,
POTATOES, AND ARTICHOKES
IN PARCHMENT

Dinner, Unwrapped

Three simple yet impressive ways to steam fish fillets in parchment

Lemony Baked Cod, Potatoes, and Artichokes in Parchment

ACTIVE 15 MIN. - TOTAL 30 MIN.
SERVES 4

- 1 lb. new potatoes, sliced ¼ inch thick
- 1 (12-oz.) jar marinated quartered artichokes, drained and patted dry
- ½ tsp. black pepper
- 4 tsp. olive oil, divided
- 1½ tsp. kosher salt, divided
- 4 (6-oz.) skinless cod fillets
- 4 tsp. chopped capers
- 2 Tbsp. unsalted butter, cut evenly into 8 pieces
- 4 (4-inch) fresh dill sprigs, plus chopped dill for garnish
- 1 lemon, sliced

1. Preheat oven to 425°F with racks in upper and lower third positions. Toss together potatoes, artichokes, pepper, 2 teaspoons of the oil, and ½ teaspoon of the salt in a large bowl.
2. Lay 4 (18- x 15-inch) sheets of parchment paper flat on a work surface. Fold each parchment sheet in half crosswise; make a crease down the center, and open back up. Divide prepared vegetable mixture, and place evenly on half of each sheet.
3. Rub cod evenly with remaining 2 teaspoons oil; sprinkle with remaining 1 teaspoon salt. Place 1 fillet diagonally on top of vegetable mixture on each parchment sheet. Top each fillet with 1 teaspoon capers and 2 butter pieces. Top fillets evenly with dill sprigs and lemon slices.
4. Fold parchment over fish, making small overlapping folds along edges until fully sealed. Place 2 packets on each of 2 rimmed baking sheets. Roast in preheated oven until parchment puffs, about 10 minutes. Remove from oven. Transfer each packet to a plate, and carefully cut packets open, avoiding any escaping steam. Discard herb sprigs and lemon slices. Garnish with chopped dill, and serve.

CALORIES: **331** – CARBS: **23 G** – FAT: **15 G**

Smoky-Sweet Baked Salmon in Parchment

Prepare Step 1 as directed, replacing potatoes and artichokes with 12 oz. trimmed **haricots verts** (French green beans) and 2 (2 oz. each) **shallots** (sliced). Prepare Step 2 as directed. Omit Step 3. Instead, place 4 (6-oz.) **skin-on or skinless salmon fillets** over vegetable mixture, and sprinkle with 1 tsp. **kosher salt**. Stir together ¼ cup **stone-ground mustard**, 1½ Tbsp. **dark brown sugar**, and 1 tsp. **smoked paprika**; spread evenly over fillets. Top fillets with 4 **fresh thyme sprigs** and **orange slices**. Proceed with Step 4 as directed, omitting dill garnish. Discard thyme sprigs and orange slices, if desired. Serve over hot cooked **rice**.

CALORIES: **348** – CARBS: **1 G** – FAT: **14 G**

Spicy Baked Snapper, Greens, and Carrots in Parchment

Prepare Step 1 as directed, omitting potato-and-artichoke mixture. Instead, toss together 1 lb. **carrots** (sliced diagonally ½ inch thick), 2 cups packed torn **mustard greens**, 1 (1-oz.) thinly sliced **red Fresno chile**, 2 tsp. chopped **garlic**, 2 tsp. **olive oil**, ½ tsp. **kosher salt**, and ½ tsp. **black pepper** in a large bowl. Prepare Step 2 as directed. Omit Step 3. Instead, place 4 (6-oz.) skin-on or skinless red snapper fillets over vegetable mixture. Rub fish evenly with 2 tsp. olive oil and 2 tsp. grated **fresh ginger**; sprinkle with 1 tsp. kosher salt. Top fillets with 4 **cilantro sprigs**. Proceed with Step 4 as directed, replacing dill garnish with chopped fresh cilantro. Serve over hot cooked **couscous**.

CALORIES: **267** – CARBS: **13 G** – FAT: **7 G**

Party in a Bite

A little taste of New Orleans that packs a whole lot of flavor

Mini Muffuletta Sandwiches

ACTIVE 20 MIN. - TOTAL 20 MIN.

MAKES 32

- 2 cups Italian olive salad (such as Boscoli Family Italian Olive Salad; from 1 [32-oz.] jar)
- 1 Tbsp. chopped fresh basil
- 1 Tbsp. white balsamic vinegar
- ¼ tsp. crushed red pepper (or more if desired)
- 8 sesame seed hamburger buns
- 8 oz. thinly sliced capocollo
- 8 oz. thinly sliced provolone cheese
- 8 oz. thinly sliced deli ham
- 8 oz. thinly sliced mozzarella
- 8 oz. thinly sliced dry salami
  Wooden picks
- 16 pimiento-stuffed olives, cut in half crosswise

1. Place olive salad, basil, vinegar, and crushed red pepper in the bowl of a food processor, and pulse just until chopped (you do not want it finely chopped), 4 to 5 times.

2. Top the bottom half of each hamburger bun with 2 tablespoons olive salad mixture. Top each bun with 1 ounce capocollo, 1 ounce provolone, 1 ounce ham, 1 ounce mozzarella, and 1 ounce salami. Top each with 2 tablespoons olive salad mixture and bun tops. Cut each sandwich into quarters. Secure each quarter with a wooden pick topped with an olive half.

Anything Goes with Pound Cake

Our best-ever brown sugar dessert is incredible however you choose to top it

MASCARPONE CHEESE + STRAWBERRY JAM + STRAWBERRIES + MINT

LEMON CURD + BLUEBERRIES + LEMON ZEST

PEANUT BUTTER + BANANAS + HONEY + PEANUTS

BOURBON WHIPPED CREAM + PECANS + ORANGE ZEST

VANILLA ICE CREAM + CHOCOLATE SAUCE + CINNAMON + CAYENNE + PEPITAS

VANILLA GREEK YOGURT + RASPBERRIES + PISTACHIOS

Brown Sugar Pound Cake

ACTIVE 15 MIN. - TOTAL 1 HOUR,
35 MIN., PLUS 2 HOURS COOLING

SERVES 16

Baking spray with flour
1½ cups butter, softened
1 (8-oz.) pkg. cream cheese, softened
1 (16-oz.) pkg. light brown sugar (about 2¼ cups firmly packed)
¾ cup granulated sugar
6 large eggs, at room temperature
3 cups all-purpose flour
¼ tsp. kosher salt
¼ cup whole milk
2 tsp. vanilla extract

1. Preheat oven to 325°F. Heavily spray a 15-cup Bundt pan with baking spray; set aside. Beat butter and cream cheese in the bowl of a stand mixer fitted with a paddle attachment at medium speed until creamy, 2 to 3 minutes. Gradually add brown sugar and granulated sugar, beating at medium speed until light and fluffy, 4 to 6 minutes. Add eggs, 1 at a time, beating just until incorporated after each addition (do not overbeat).
2. Whisk together flour and salt in a medium bowl. Gradually add flour mixture to butter mixture in 3 additions alternately with milk, beginning and ending with flour mixture and beating on low speed just until blended after each addition. Stir in vanilla with a spatula just until blended. Pour batter into prepared pan, and spread evenly.
3. Bake in preheated oven until a wooden pick inserted in center comes out clean, 1 hour, 10 minutes, to 1 hour, 20 minutes. Cool in pan on a wire rack 10 to 15 minutes. Gently loosen sides of cake from pan with an offset spatula, if needed, and turn cake out of pan onto a wire rack. Cool completely, about 2 hours.

Fancy Up a Tomato Sandwich
A warm–weather favorite gets dressed for company

THE UPPER CRUST
Spread two slices of thin white bread with mayonnaise. Add sliced tomato to one piece of bread; season with salt and black pepper. Cover with other piece of bread. Cut off crusts; slice diagonally twice. Spread mayonnaise on one cut edge of each triangle. Dip into a mixture of breadcrumbs and finely chopped cooked bacon until coated.

THE OPEN BOOK
Remove crusts from thin wheat bread; cut into quarters. Spread each quarter with mayonnaise. Add cherry tomato slices. Top with a basil leaf, salt, and black pepper.

THE BATON
Spread two slices of toasted thin white bread with mayonnaise. Add sliced tomato to one piece of bread, and season with salt and black pepper. Cover tomato with other bread slice. Remove crusts; cut sandwich into thirds. Attach a basil leaf to each with a toothpick.

TEA-SANDWICH SECRETS

Choose the Right Bread
Whether you go for pumpernickel, rye, or white, make sure it is thinly sliced and has a soft texture. Traditionally the crusts are removed to make a more tender sandwich. Do this step once the sandwiches are assembled for neat, crumb-free results.

Spread to the Edges
Keep the sandwiches from drying out by smearing a thin, even layer of cream cheese, mayo, or butter all the way to the sides on each piece of bread. A small offset spatula is a good tool for the job.

Use the Correct Knife
A serrated blade makes the cleanest cuts. To avoid squishing the sandwiches, use a gentle sawing motion and don't press down.

Serve Them Soon
Tea sandwiches are best enjoyed shortly after they are made. To prevent them from drying out, cover loosely with a slightly damp paper towel.

June–July

Seeing Red

Summer's most delicate berry packs a big punch of sweet–tart flavor

FRESH RASPBERRY-
CREAM CHEESE
FROSTING

Fresh Raspberry-Cream Cheese Frosting

ACTIVE 20 MIN. - TOTAL 20 MIN.
MAKES ABOUT 5 CUPS

Process 1 (6-oz.) pkg. **fresh raspberries** (1½ cups) in a mini food processor or blender until smooth, about 1 minute. Pour through a fine mesh strainer set over a bowl; discard seeds. Beat 8 oz. **cream cheese** and ½ cup **unsalted butter** (both at room temperature) with an electric mixer on medium speed until smooth, 1 to 2 minutes. Gradually add berry puree, beating on low speed until combined, about 30 seconds. Gradually add 2 lb. **powdered sugar**, beating until combined, about 2 minutes. Add ⅛ tsp. **kosher salt**, and beat on high speed until smooth and fluffy, 45 seconds.

BERRY PATCH COCKTAIL

KEEP 'EM FRESH
Store berries near the front of the refrigerator. The back gets too cold, and the crisper drawer stays too humid.

Tangy Raspberry Salad

ACTIVE 20 MIN. - TOTAL 20 MIN.
SERVES 6

Place ½ cup **raspberries**, ¼ cup **olive oil**, 2 Tbsp. **white balsamic vinegar**, 1 Tbsp. **fresh lemon juice**, 1 tsp. **honey**, and ½ tsp. **kosher salt** in a blender or mini food processor; process until smooth, about 30 seconds. Tear 1 (6-oz.) head **Bibb lettuce** into pieces, and place in a wide, shallow bowl. Add 1 medium **avocado** (cubed), 2½ cups **raspberries**, ½ cup crumbled **feta**, and ⅓ cup thinly sliced **red onion**. Toss to combine. Drizzle with desired amount of dressing.

Berry Patch Cocktail

ACTIVE 15 MIN. - TOTAL 15 MIN.
SERVES 1

Place ¼ cup **fresh raspberries**, 2 Tbsp. (1 oz.) **gin**, and 2 Tbsp. (1 oz.) **elderflower liqueur** (such as St-Germain) in a cocktail shaker; muddle mixture using a muddler or a wooden spoon handle until berries are crushed. Add ¾ cup **ice** and ¼ cup **limeade**; place lid on shaker, and shake vigorously for 30 seconds. Pour into a tall Collins glass. Thread 3 **fresh raspberries** onto a wooden pick. Garnish drink with berry pick and 1 **lime wheel**. Serve.

A Feast for the Eyes

This time of year, tomatoes come in just about every shape and hue.
Celebrate the season with these gorgeous color-inspired salads

Grilled Green Tomatoes with Jalapeño-Honey Vinaigrette

(Photo, page 135)

Rather than breading and frying unripe tomatoes, we grilled them in this recipe. Mix slices with cucumber ribbons, smoked almonds, and goat cheese; then toss in a tangy-sweet vinaigrette.

ACTIVE 20 MIN. · TOTAL 55 MIN.

SERVES 4

- 1½ lb. green (unripe) tomatoes (about 3 medium), cored and cut into ¼-inch-thick slices
- 1½ tsp. granulated sugar
- 1½ tsp. kosher salt, divided
- 1 small jalapeño chile
- 2 Tbsp. honey
- 2 Tbsp. apple cider vinegar
- 2 Tbsp. extra-virgin olive oil
- ¼ tsp. black pepper, plus more for garnish
- 1 small English cucumber, halved crosswise and shaved lengthwise into thin ribbons
- 2 oz. goat cheese, crumbled
- ¼ cup smoked almonds, chopped
- ½ tsp. flaky sea salt
- ½ cup loosely packed fresh herb leaves (such as basil, parsley, and cilantro)

1. Arrange tomato slices in a single layer on a paper towel–lined baking sheet. Sprinkle both sides evenly with sugar and 1 teaspoon of the kosher salt. Let stand while preheating grill to very high (about 550°F), about 15 minutes.
2. Grill tomatoes and jalapeño, uncovered, until lightly charred, turning occasionally, 4 to 6 minutes. Set tomatoes aside. Let jalapeño stand until cool enough to handle, 10 minutes. Thinly slice; discard stem.
3. Whisk together honey, vinegar, oil, black pepper, and remaining ½ teaspoon kosher salt in a small bowl. Stir in jalapeño slices. Let stand 10 minutes.
4. Arrange tomato slices and cucumber ribbons on a serving platter. Sprinkle with goat cheese, almonds, and flaky sea salt. Drizzle with dressing. Sprinkle with herbs; garnish with black pepper.

Yellow Tomatoes and Burrata with Watermelon-Beet Salsa

(Photo, page 137)

Any yellow-orange heirloom variety will work well in this summertime dish. Instead of sliced tomatoes, you can substitute halved cherry tomatoes, if you prefer. A relish of golden beets and watermelon adds tang, and burrata (an Italian cheese made from mozzarella and cream) brings just the right amount of richness.

ACTIVE 20 MIN. · TOTAL 50 MIN., PLUS 20 MIN. COOLING

SERVES 6

- 2 small golden beets, stemmed
- 2 cups small (¼-inch) yellow watermelon cubes (from 1 seedless watermelon)
- 1 small shallot, minced (about ¼ cup)
- 2 Tbsp. finely chopped fresh mint
- 2 Tbsp. extra-virgin olive oil, divided
- 4 tsp. Champagne vinegar, divided
- 1¾ tsp. flaky sea salt, divided
- 3 medium-size yellow-orange heirloom tomatoes, cut into ½-inch-thick slices
- 2 (4-oz.) balls burrata cheese, split open
  Black pepper

1. Place beets in a saucepan; add water to cover by 3 inches. Bring to a boil over medium–high. Reduce heat to medium–low; cook, uncovered, until fork–tender, 30 to 40 minutes. Transfer to a plate; cool 20 minutes. Peel; cut into ¼-inch cubes.
2. Stir together beets, watermelon, shallot, mint, 1 tablespoon of the oil, 2 teaspoons of the vinegar, and 1 teaspoon of the salt in a bowl. Arrange tomato slices and burrata on a serving platter. Top with melon mixture and any liquid in bowl. Drizzle with remaining 1 tablespoon oil and 2 teaspoons vinegar. Sprinkle with remaining ¾ teaspoon salt; garnish with pepper.

Escabèche-Style Marinated Tomatoes

(Photo, page 141)

Escabèche is typically a meat or vegetable that is marinated in a blend of vinegar, peppers, onions, and spices. Tomatoes get a similar treatment in this recipe, which softens them and makes them extra juicy. Serve with bread to soak up the marinade.

ACTIVE 20 MIN. · TOTAL 20 MIN., PLUS 1 HOUR MARINATING

SERVES 6

- 2 lb. firm, ripe red heirloom tomatoes (about 3 large), cored and cut into ½-inch-thick slices
- 2¼ tsp. kosher salt, divided
- 1 tsp. coriander seeds
- 1 tsp. cumin seeds
- ½ tsp. black peppercorns
- ¾ cup extra-virgin olive oil
- 1 small yellow onion, thinly sliced
- 1 small red bell pepper, thinly sliced
- 1 small red Fresno chile, thinly sliced
- 6 medium garlic cloves, smashed
- 2 fresh bay leaves
- ½ cup apple cider vinegar
- 2 Tbsp. finely chopped fresh oregano
- 1 Tbsp. granulated sugar

1. Arrange tomato slices, slightly overlapping, in a rimmed serving dish. Sprinkle with 1¼ teaspoons of the salt.
2. Toast coriander, cumin, and peppercorns in a small saucepan over medium, stirring often, until fragrant, 1 to 2 minutes. Add oil, onion, bell pepper, Fresno chile, garlic, and bay leaves. Cook, stirring, until vegetables are tender but not browned, 6 to 8 minutes. Stir in vinegar, oregano, sugar, and remaining 1 teaspoon salt. Bring to a simmer, stirring often to dissolve sugar. Pour hot mixture over tomatoes. Marinate at room temperature at least 1 hour or up to 4 hours. Marinated tomatoes can be covered and chilled up to overnight. Remove bay leaves before serving.

GREEN TOMATO
STACKS WITH HERB OIL
AND CRISPY CAPERS
(PAGE 142)

GRILLED GREEN
TOMATOES WITH
JALAPEÑO-HONEY
VINAIGRETTE (PAGE 133)

GOLDEN TOMATO-
AND-CORN SALAD
(PAGE 142)

YELLOW TOMATOES
AND BURRATA WITH
WATERMELON-BEET SALSA
(PAGE 133)

BLT PANZANELLA
WITH QUICK-PICKLED
SHALLOTS (PAGE 143)

BLISTERED CHERRY
TOMATOES WITH RED
PEPPER-FETA SPREAD
(PAGE 143)

GRILLED OKRA-
AND-TOMATO
SALAD (PAGE 142)

ESCABÈCHE-STYLE
MARINATED TOMATOES
(PAGE 133)

Golden Tomato-and-Corn Salad

(Photo, page 136)

Featuring yellow cherry tomatoes (like Sun Gold), this sunny salad is plated with a vibrant yogurt sauce made with the smoky-tart juice from grilled lemons and ground turmeric.

ACTIVE 25 MIN. - TOTAL 30 MIN.
SERVES 4

- 1 medium ear fresh yellow corn, husked
- 1 medium lemon, halved crosswise
- 5 Tbsp. extra-virgin olive oil, divided
- 1½ tsp. kosher salt, divided
- 1 tsp. honey
- 1 tsp. fennel seeds
- ¼ tsp. black pepper
- ¾ cup whole-milk Greek yogurt
- ¾ tsp. ground turmeric
- 10 oz. small yellow or orange tomatoes (such as Sun Gold) or teardrop cherry (pear-shape), halved
- 1 large yellow or orange tomato, cored, halved lengthwise, and thinly sliced

1. Preheat grill to high (450°F to 500°F). Drizzle corn and lemon halves with 1 tablespoon of the oil. Sprinkle corn with ¼ teaspoon of the salt. Grill lemon halves (cut side down) and corn, turning corn occasionally, until tender and charred in spots, 5 to 8 minutes. Set aside to cool. Cut kernels from cob; set aside. Discard cob.
2. Squeeze 1 grilled lemon half to make about 1½ tablespoons juice. Whisk together lemon juice, honey, fennel seeds, black pepper, 1 teaspoon of the salt, and remaining 4 tablespoons oil in a small bowl. Stir together yogurt, turmeric, and 1½ tablespoons of the lemon juice mixture in a small bowl; reserve remaining lemon juice mixture for drizzling.
3. Spread yogurt mixture on a serving platter. Top with tomatoes and corn. Sprinkle with remaining ¼ teaspoon salt; drizzle with reserved lemon juice mixture. Serve with remaining grilled lemon half.

Grilled Okra-and-Tomato Salad

(Photo, page 140)

Purple probably isn't the first color that comes to mind when you think about tomatoes, but there are many delicious varieties, like Cherokee Purple and Black Cherry, that range from shades of plum to almost black. When paired with purple okra, it's like a painting on a plate.

ACTIVE 35 MIN. - TOTAL 35 MIN.
SERVES 6

- ¼ cup unsalted butter
- ¼ cup olive oil
- 4 garlic cloves, grated
- 2 oil-packed anchovies, finely chopped
- 1¼ tsp. kosher salt, divided
- ¾ tsp. black pepper, divided
- 4 small Fairy Tale eggplants, halved lengthwise, or 1 small Globe eggplant, sliced into ½-inch-thick rounds
- 6 oz. purple okra, halved lengthwise
- 1 small red onion, cut into ½-inch wedges
- 2 tsp. sherry vinegar
- 2 lb. purple or black tomatoes (such as Cherokee Purple, Kumato, or Black Cherry), cut into wedges or halved
  Fresh purple basil leaves and shaved radishes (such as Watermelon or Purple Ninja)

1. Cook butter, oil, garlic, anchovies, ½ teaspoon of the salt, and ¼ teaspoon of the pepper in a saucepan over medium-low, stirring often, until butter is melted and anchovies have mostly dissolved, 4 to 6 minutes. Set butter mixture aside.
2. Preheat grill to medium-high (400°F to 450°F). Toss eggplant, okra, onion, 2 tablespoons butter mixture, ½ teaspoon of the salt, and ¼ teaspoon of the pepper in a large bowl. Place seasoned vegetables on oiled grates. Grill, turning occasionally, until lightly charred and tender, 3 to 5 minutes for okra, 8 to 12 minutes for eggplant, and 14 to 18 minutes for onion.

3. If remaining butter mixture has solidified, reheat in a small saucepan over low, stirring often, until melted. Remove from heat; whisk in sherry vinegar. Arrange tomatoes, eggplant, okra, and onion on a serving platter. Sprinkle with remaining ¼ teaspoon each salt and pepper. Drizzle with butter mixture. Garnish with purple basil and radishes.

Green Tomato Stacks with Herb Oil and Crispy Capers

(Photo, page 134)

Prepare to wow with this elegant first-course presentation. An ideal choice for a sit-down supper, these stacks showcase ripe green heirlooms, such as Green Zebra. Crisp and salty fried capers—the surprise ingredient everyone will talk about—balance the sweetness of the tomatoes and avocado.

ACTIVE 25 MIN. - TOTAL 40 MIN.
SERVES 4

- 1 cup packed fresh parsley leaves
- ¼ cup roughly chopped fresh chives
- 2 Tbsp. fresh tarragon leaves, plus more for garnish
- ¾ cup grapeseed oil, plus more for frying
- 2 Tbsp. drained capers, patted dry
- 4 medium green tomatoes (such as Green Zebra and green heirloom, about 6 oz. each)
- 1 Tbsp. fresh lemon juice (from 1 lemon)
- 1½ tsp. flaky sea salt, divided
- ¾ tsp. black pepper, divided
- 2 medium avocados, thinly sliced

1. Place parsley, chives, tarragon, and grapeseed oil in a blender. Secure lid on blender; process mixture until smooth, about 3 minutes. Pour through a fine mesh strainer into a bowl (do not press on solids); discard solids.
2. Meanwhile, pour oil to a depth of ¼ inch in a small skillet; heat over medium. Add capers; cook, stirring occasionally, until crispy, about 2 minutes. Using a slotted spoon, transfer to a paper towel-lined plate; set aside.

3. Trim off tops and bottoms of tomatoes; cut each tomato into 3 slices. Place 1 slice onto each serving plate. Brush top of tomato slices lightly with lemon juice; sprinkle evenly with ¼ teaspoon salt and ⅛ teaspoon pepper. Top each slice with 3 to 4 avocado slices, brush lightly with lemon juice, and sprinkle with ¼ teaspoon salt and ⅛ teaspoon pepper. Repeat alternating layers with remaining tomato and avocado slices, brushing with lemon juice and seasoning between layers, to build 4 stacks that are 6 layers tall.

4. Drizzle each stack with about 1 tablespoon herb oil. Reserve any remaining herb oil for another use, or serve on the side. Sprinkle with crispy capers, and garnish with additional tarragon leaves.

Blistered Cherry Tomatoes with Red Pepper–Feta Spread

(Photo, page 139)

You can pull together this recipe with any cherry tomatoes, but ones that are still on the vine make a striking presentation placed atop the crimson-hue red pepper spread.

ACTIVE 25 MIN. - TOTAL 35 MIN.,
PLUS 1 HOUR STANDING AND 1 HOUR CHILLING

SERVES 6

- 1 cup cooked red quinoa
  Canola oil
- 1¼ tsp. kosher salt, divided
- 1 cup drained jarred roasted red bell peppers
- 4 oz. feta cheese, crumbled
- 1 Tbsp. fresh lemon juice (from 1 lemon)
- 1 garlic clove, smashed
- ¼ tsp. crushed red pepper, plus more for garnish
- ¼ cup plus 2 Tbsp. extra-virgin olive oil, divided
- 1½ lb. red cherry tomatoes (on the vine, if possible)
- 4 (6-inch) fresh thyme sprigs, plus more for garnish
  Toasted pita wedges

1. Spread quinoa in an even layer on a paper towel-lined plate. Let stand at room temperature for at least 1 hour or up to overnight (12 hours) to dry out. Pour oil to a depth of ½ inch in a medium Dutch oven; heat over medium to 375°F. Fry quinoa in 2 batches, stirring occasionally, until crisp, 1 to 2 minutes. Using a fine mesh strainer, transfer to a paper towel-lined baking sheet. Sprinkle with ¼ teaspoon of the salt. Set aside.

2. Process red peppers, feta, lemon juice, garlic, crushed red pepper, ¼ cup of the olive oil, and ¼ teaspoon of the salt in a food processor until smooth and creamy, 2 minutes, stopping to scrape down sides as needed. Transfer mixture to a bowl. Cover; chill until ready to serve, at least 1 hour or up to overnight (12 hours).

3. Preheat oven to 475°F. Heat remaining 2 tablespoons olive oil in a large cast-iron skillet over medium-high. Remove from heat; add tomatoes (still on vine) in a single layer. Add thyme sprigs; sprinkle with ¼ teaspoon of the salt. Transfer skillet to oven; roast until tomatoes begin to burst open, 8 to 12 minutes. Sprinkle with remaining ½ teaspoon salt.

4. Spread red pepper–feta mixture on a serving platter. Top with roasted tomatoes and crispy quinoa. Garnish with additional crushed red pepper and thyme sprigs; serve with toasted pita wedges.

BLT Panzanella with Quick-Pickled Shallots

(Photo, page 138)

Consider yourself warned: This is not your usual panzanella. Our version, made with two kinds of red tomatoes (be sure they are at the peak of ripeness), is full of bold textures and robust flavors from crumbled bacon, sharp radicchio, and crisp croutons cooked in bacon drippings and seasoned with paprika.

ACTIVE 25 MIN. - TOTAL 55 MIN.

SERVES 6

- 2 shallots, thinly sliced (about ⅔ cup)
- ½ cup red wine vinegar
- ¼ cup granulated sugar
- 2 Tbsp. plus 1 tsp. kosher salt, divided
- 6 thick-cut bacon slices
- ½ tsp. smoked paprika
- 4 white bread slices, cut into 1-inch pieces (3 cups)
- 1 small head radicchio, quartered, cored, and cut into ½-inch strips (3 cups)
- 1½ lb. red heirloom tomatoes (about 2 medium), cored and cut into ¾-inch wedges
- ½ lb. red cherry, grape, or teardrop cherry (pear-shape) tomatoes, halved

1. Place shallots in a medium heatproof bowl; set aside. Bring vinegar, ½ cup water, the sugar, and 2 tablespoons of the salt to a boil in saucepan over medium, stirring to dissolve sugar. Pour vinegar mixture over shallots. Cool slightly, 30 minutes.

2. Meanwhile, cook bacon in a large nonstick skillet over medium until crisp, 10 to 12 minutes. Drain on a paper towel-lined plate, reserving 6 tablespoons drippings in a bowl. Return 3 tablespoons reserved drippings to skillet. Heat drippings, paprika, and ¼ teaspoon of the salt over medium. Add bread; toss to coat. Cook, stirring occasionally, until bread is crispy, 5 to 6 minutes. Transfer to plate with bacon. Crumble bacon; set aside.

3. Drain shallots, reserving 5 tablespoons liquid. Combine radicchio, tomatoes, shallots, and remaining ¾ teaspoon salt in a large bowl. Heat remaining 3 tablespoons drippings in skillet over medium until hot, 1 to 2 minutes. Remove from heat; stir in reserved 5 tablespoons liquid. Pour hot dressing over tomato mixture; toss gently. Let stand 10 minutes, tossing occasionally. Gently fold in bacon and bread just before serving.

Double Your Greens

Pile on the arugula and broccoli for a satisfying salad

Lemony White Bean Salad with Broccoli

This gluten-free salad is packed with ingredients (like onion and beans) that support your gut microbiome. The combination of arugula and broccoli gives a double dose of cruciferous vegetables, which can reduce inflammation and may help lower your risk of cancer.

ACTIVE 30 MIN. · TOTAL 30 MIN.

SERVES 6

- 1 (16-oz.) pkg. fresh broccoli florets (7 cups florets)
- ½ cup, plus 1½ Tbsp. olive oil, divided
- 1 tsp. kosher salt, divided
- ½ tsp. black pepper, divided
- ½ tsp. lemon zest plus ¼ cup fresh juice (from 2 lemons)
- 2 Tbsp. chopped fresh flat-leaf parsley
- 1 garlic clove, minced
- 1 Tbsp. whole-grain mustard
- 1 Tbsp. apple cider vinegar
- ½ tsp. honey
- 1 (15½-oz.) can no-salt-added cannellini beans, drained and rinsed
- 4 cups baby arugula
- 1 cup thinly sliced red onion (from 1 onion)
- 1 oz. Parmesan cheese, shaved (about ½ cup)

1. Preheat oven to 400°F with oven rack 6 inches from heat. Toss together broccoli, 1½ tablespoons of the oil, ½ teaspoon of the salt, and ¼ teaspoon of the pepper in a large bowl. Spread broccoli in a single layer on a rimmed baking sheet. Roast in oven until just tender, 20 to 25 minutes.

2. Meanwhile, whisk together lemon zest and juice; parsley; garlic; mustard; vinegar; honey; and remaining ½ cup oil, ½ teaspoon salt, and ¼ teaspoon pepper in a medium bowl. Set aside.

3. Increase oven temperature to broil; cook broccoli until slightly charred, 1 to 2 minutes. Cool about 5 minutes.

4. Combine broccoli, beans, baby arugula, and red onion in a large bowl. Toss with dressing; sprinkle with Parmesan.

CALORIES: **336** – CARBS: **21 G** – FAT: **25 G**

Peach Wars

South Carolina, Georgia, and Texas face off over which state has the best fruit

IF YOU WANT TO SEE the most powerful way that people from the same region can be locked in a perpetual argument with one another, you should bring up peaches. Yes, I know about intense college-football rivalries. I also happen to live in between Duke University and the University of North Carolina at Chapel Hill, so I'm very familiar with the basketball ones. But if you think you've seen pride of place, it's even more intense when a South Carolinian meets up with a Georgian while there's a peach pie in the oven. Petty rivalries aside, real battles over fruit science, soil mineral content, degrees of sweetness, and economic well-being come to the fore along with faded recipe cards, weather charts, and almanacs. This has been going on for at least 100 years, and in the end, the fruit is what's at stake. The ideal peach is juicy, sweet, free of bruises, and at peak ripeness. It should be fragrant (but not too fragrant, or it's going to rot) and neither rock-hard nor soft enough for your thumb to make an imprint. From there, though, it's up for debate. So we let three of the South's top peach states—South Carolina, Georgia, and Texas—duke it out. Apologies to other producers like Alabama, Tennessee, New Jersey, and California. We await your comments. –Kelly Alexander

WHAT'S A PEACH?
It's a drupe, the botanical term for fruits with stonelike pits, also including apricots and olives.

South Carolina

We've Got the Science

THE TRUTH about a peach tree is that it lives only about 10 years, 20 if you're lucky. Today's popular selection could soon give way to tomorrow's newer, juicier, hardier, and more flavorful variety—especially when scientists at major state-funded university agricultural programs (like at Clemson University) are involved in developing new kinds all the time. Thanks to this group, South Carolina had overtaken Georgia by the late 20th century as the biggest peach-producing state in the region.

The Peach Team in the College of Agriculture, Forestry and Life Sciences at Clemson says that while Georgia may be called the Peach State, South Carolina should be known as "The Tastier Peach State." This oft-repeated taunt—circulated all over Twitter and other social media—was first popularized in 2011 by Desmond R. Layne, a former peach specialist at Clemson. He should know; his father was a peach breeder for Agriculture Canada, and his first job was picking the fruit for his dad. Layne loves all South Carolina peaches, especially the 'Winblo' variety. "It has a perfect creamy, melting texture and a fabulous blend of sugar and acidity," he says.

The town of Gaffney, South Carolina, even has its own peach statue, a 135-foot water tower that anyone traveling on I-85 through the state can tell you looms large. The Peachoid, as it has come to be known, was built in 1981 and holds 1 million gallons of water. When it was repainted in 2015, Claire Huminski, Gaffney's then communications intern,

said that it became a cause of national concern. "We have actually had a lot of people complain to us via social media and call to say that we are taking down the Peachoid and that we do not need to do that because it is a landmark," Huminski said at the time. "They were really upset, tweeting angry tweets at me. I'm like, 'We're not taking it down! I promise!'"

McLeod Farms' Fresh Peach Pound Cake

Family-owned McLeod Farms in McBee, South Carolina, has grown peaches since 1916 and even has its own cookbook.
ACTIVE 25 MIN. - TOTAL 2 HOURS, 40 MIN.
SERVES 12

PEACH POUND CAKE
- 1 cup unsalted butter, softened, plus more for greasing pan
- 2 cups, plus 1 Tbsp. granulated sugar, divided
- 4 large eggs
- 1 tsp. vanilla extract
- 1 tsp. baking powder
- 1 tsp. kosher salt
- 3 cups all-purpose flour, divided
- 2 cups fresh peeled peaches, cut into ¾-inch cubes (from 5 small peaches, about 1 lb., 4 oz.)

PEACH GLAZE
- 1 Tbsp. cornstarch
- 4 peaches (1 lb.), peeled and halved
- ¼ cup granulated sugar

1. Prepare the Peach Pound Cake: Preheat oven to 325°F. Grease a 10-inch tube pan with butter, and sprinkle with 1 tablespoon of the sugar.
2. Beat butter and remaining 2 cups sugar with a stand mixer fitted with a paddle attachment on medium-high speed until light and fluffy, about 3 minutes. Add eggs, one at a time, on medium-low speed, beating just until blended after each addition, about 1 minute. Beat in vanilla.
3. Stir together baking powder, salt, and 2¾ cups of the flour. With mixer running on low speed, gradually add flour mixture to butter mixture, beating just until combined, about 1 minute.
4. Combine peaches and remaining ¼ cup flour in a medium bowl, and toss until peaches are fully coated. Fold floured peaches into batter. Spread batter evenly in prepared pan.
5. Bake in preheated oven until toothpick inserted in center comes out clean, 60 to 70 minutes. Let cool in pan on a wire rack 10 minutes; run an offset spatula or knife around edges of cake, and remove from pan to rack. Cool completely, about 1 hour.
6. Prepare the Peach Glaze: Stir together ¼ cup water and cornstarch in a small bowl until cornstarch is completely incorporated; set aside.
7. Add peeled peach halves to a blender, and process until smooth, about 45 seconds. Pour peach mixture into a small saucepan, and add sugar. Bring to a simmer over low. Stir in cornstarch mixture; cook, stirring often, until mixture has thickened, about 5 minutes. Drizzle Peach Glaze over cooled pound cake before serving.

Georgia
We've Got the History

PEACH FARMERS in Georgia claim that time is on their side, and they're not wrong: This state has been growing peaches commercially for longer than any other. A farmer named Raphael Moses was among the first to ship the fruit in 1851. Because fresh peaches have delicate skin, he nestled them in Champagne boxes to help preserve their flavor and texture (a technique that's still used for shipping fine fruit).

It was not until the late 19th century, though, that the Georgia peach gained its fame. Samuel H. Rumph, another farmer, helped things along: In 1870 in Macon County, he grafted a Chinese peach variety onto another tree and named the large, juicy, yellow-fleshed result after his wife, Elberta. This kind was not only tender and sweet but also hardy and produced abundantly.

By the late 1800s, the Elberta was being shipped to markets up and down the East Coast. In the process, it became so valuable that it helped fund the expansion of the Georgia Southern Railway line. The fruit became synonymous with Georgia and, over the years, landed on the state quarter and license plates. Any native Atlantan can reel off the city's dozens of streets with "Peachtree" in their names.

Sadly for Georgians, in the 1960s the Elberta lost ground to more disease-resistant peaches. Today you'll be hard-pressed to find this one in a supermarket, though local farmers have carried on admirably with popular varieties including 'Belle of Georgia' and 'Rich Lady.'

And they admit no defeat. "Our peaches are the best because they are grown with love and a lot of TLC, and they're also sweeter," says Tisa Horton, director of the Georgia Peach Festival. This 36-year-old event is held in early June, peak harvest season in towns like Fort Valley and Byron in the aptly named Peach County. "We want to honor area farmers, local agriculture, and Georgia's nationwide contribution to the food industry," she says.

One of Horton's favorite dishes ever served at the festival was the peach-rum dumplings from chef Scottie Johnson of Blessed & Highly Flavored Cuisine in the nearby town of Kathleen, around 100 miles southeast of Atlanta. Even with flaky dough and a buttery sauce, the flavor of the peaches still shines through in his recipe. Johnson says, "My dumplings are awesome because our Georgia peaches are just so fresh. I get them from Lane Southern Orchards right here in Fort Valley. They're firm and just the tastiest ones in the whole world."

Spiced Rum-Peach Dumplings

Georgia chef Scottie Johnson uses a fizzy secret ingredient in this decadent dessert.
ACTIVE 15 MIN. · TOTAL 1 HOUR
SERVES 8

- ¾ cup salted butter, plus more for baking dish
- 2 fresh peaches (12 oz.), peeled
- 1 (8-oz.) can refrigerated crescent rolls (such as Pillsbury Crescent Rolls)
- ¾ cup packed dark brown sugar
- 3 Tbsp. spiced rum
- ½ tsp. vanilla extract
- ¾ cup citrus-flavored soft drink (such as Mountain Dew)
- ¼ tsp. ground cinnamon
- Whipped cream, for serving

1. Preheat oven to 350°F. Butter an 11- x 7-inch (2-quart) baking dish, and set aside.
2. Cut each peach into 4 wedges (about 1 to 1¼ inches thick). Unroll crescent rolls, and place triangles side by side on a clean work surface. Place 1 peach wedge along wide end of each triangle, and roll up each triangle, starting with wide end. Place wrapped peaches, point sides up, in prepared baking dish.
3. Melt butter and dark brown sugar in a small saucepan over medium-low, and cook, whisking often, until sugar is dissolved and mixture is well combined, about 3 minutes. Stir in rum and vanilla.
4. Pour sugar mixture evenly over crescent rolls. Top with citrus-flavored soft drink, and sprinkle evenly with ground cinnamon.
5. Bake in preheated oven until crescent rolls are evenly browned and liquid is bubbling rapidly, 35 to 40 minutes. Remove dish from oven, and let stand 5 minutes. Top warm dumplings with whipped cream, and serve immediately.

Texas

We've Got Presidential Approval

PEACHES MADE THEIR WAY to Texas in the late 1840s courtesy of German settlers. Those early farmers found the Hill Country's climate, altitude, and calcium-rich soil well suited for the fruit trees. Texas peaches were little more than a local treasure, though, until they were popularized on the national stage by a man named Gilbert Onderdonk, a New Yorker who had moved to Texas on doctor's orders to improve his fragile health. He set up a nursery near Victoria and the Gulf of Mexico and became a respected horticulturist. Onderdonk developed numerous varieties of peaches adapted to the Texas climate. He even showed them off at the state's horticultural exhibit at the world's fair of 1904 in St. Louis and won the grand prize.

Commercial peach production in the Hill Country began in earnest in the early 1900s and has thrived ever since. Peaches are the leading fruit crop in Texas, and roughly 40% of those grown in the state come from Gillespie County, home to the towns of Fredericksburg and Stonewall.

Having two U.S. Presidents who cherished this region helped boost the reputation of its peaches. After Texans Lyndon B. and Lady Bird Johnson took up residence in the White House, they brought in their longtime cook, Zephyr Wright, whose repertoire of Southern staples had already made them popular hosts. In an official oral history of her White House years, the First Lady recalled entertaining at the "Texas White House" (now part of Lyndon B. Johnson National Historical Park) in the Hill Country: "In summertime, homemade peach ice cream was one of our favorites. Every year I would manage to get down to the farmers market and buy several bushels of peaches. We'd have just loads of ice cream, fresh fruit, and corn on the cob."

Although George W. Bush was born in New Haven, Connecticut, he was raised in Texas from the age of 2 on. In 2001, he also brought peaches into the White House—most notably in his favorite dessert, a cream pie that First Lady Laura Bush shared in the cookbook *Recipes from the President's Ranch: Food People Like to Eat*. It's no wonder, since the family's beloved Prairie Chapel Ranch is in Crawford—where the Hill Country meets the Blackland Prairie.

So what makes these peaches so darn presidential, anyway? They're known for being as juicy and sweet as this fruit can get but are also about as stubborn and strong-willed as any Texan. Some years see a boom in plantings and varieties, but you never know what you're going to get each season because of the weather. Locals say you can tell it's going to be a good year by how many peach stands, some no more than pickup trucks with signs hanging off the back, pop up along the highways in and around the Hill Country in mid-May.

The best of these have been run for decades by farmers and their families, like Gold Orchards (established in 1940) or Vogel Orchard, which started in the 1950s and is known for the Flameprince, a yellow-fleshed selection prized for its slight acidic tang.

Peach Cream Kuchen

This simple cake from the Hill Country Fruit Council celebrates the German influence on the region's cuisine.

ACTIVE 15 MIN. - TOTAL 45 MIN.

SERVES 8

- 2 cups all-purpose flour
- 1 tsp. kosher salt
- ¼ tsp. baking powder
- ¾ cup granulated sugar, divided
- ½ cup unsalted butter
- 3 large ripe peaches, peeled and sliced (about 3 cups)
- 1 tsp. ground cinnamon
- 1 cup sour cream
- 2 large egg yolks

1. Preheat oven to 400°F. Whisk together flour, salt, baking powder, and ¼ cup of the sugar in a large bowl. Cut in butter with a pastry blender or 2 knives until mixture resembles fine crumbs. Transfer to a lightly greased (9-inch square) baking pan, and press crumbs firmly against bottom and 1 inch up sides of pan.

2. Arrange peach slices evenly over crust. Stir together cinnamon and remaining ½ cup sugar, and sprinkle over peach slices. Bake in preheated oven until most of the sugar is melted, about 15 minutes.

3. Meanwhile, beat sour cream and egg yolks in a medium bowl until smooth. Spoon over peaches, and continue baking until crust is golden brown and sour cream mixture is just set, 15 to 20 minutes. Serve warm or chilled.

Take Five

Pantry staples and fresh ingredients team up in these no-fuss recipes

Goat Cheese-and-Summer Squash Pizza

ACTIVE 25 MIN. - TOTAL 25 MIN.

SERVES 4

- 12 oz. summer squash (2 small zucchini and/or yellow squash)
- 3 Tbsp. olive oil, divided
- ½ tsp. kosher salt, divided
- 1 lb. fresh prepared pizza dough, at room temperature
- ¼ tsp. black pepper, divided
- 8 oz. low-moisture part-skim mozzarella cheese, shredded (about 2 cups)
- 4 oz. goat cheese, crumbled (about 1 cup)
- 2 Tbsp. thinly sliced and seeded red Fresno chile (from 1 small chile)
- Balsamic glaze (optional)

1. Preheat a gas grill to high (450°F to 500°F) on 1 side; keep other side unlit. Trim ends of squash; discard. Slice lengthwise into ¼-inch-thick planks (10 to 12 planks total).
2. Toss together squash, 1 tablespoon of the olive oil, and ¼ teaspoon of the salt on a rimmed baking sheet. Arrange squash slices on oiled grates over lit side of grill. Grill, uncovered, until marks appear, 1 to 2 minutes; flip and grill until marks appear on other side, 1 to 2 minutes. Transfer to baking sheet.
3. Stretch dough into a 14-inch round; brush with 1 tablespoon of the oil. Sprinkle with ⅛ teaspoon each of the salt and black pepper. Place dough, oiled side down, on grates over lit side of grill. Grill, uncovered, until it starts to puff and marks appear on bottom, about 2 minutes, rotating on grates if burning in spots. Brush remaining 1 tablespoon oil over top of dough. Sprinkle with remaining ⅛ teaspoon each salt and pepper. Flip dough to unlit side of grill using tongs or a large spatula. Top with mozzarella, goat cheese, squash, and chile. Grill, covered, 2 to 3 minutes. Slide dough onto grates over lit side of grill using tongs or a large spatula. Grill, uncovered, until dough starts to puff and marks appear on bottom, about 2 minutes, rotating on grates if burning in spots.
4. Remove pizza from grill. Drizzle with balsamic glaze, if desired. Slice and serve.

A GREAT WAY TO GRILL DOUGH
Stretch the pizza dough out on the back of a lightly floured baking sheet, and then slide it off onto the grill.

Scallops with Pesto, Corn, and Tomatoes

ACTIVE 35 MIN. · TOTAL 35 MIN.
SERVES 4

- 2 thick-cut applewood-smoked bacon slices, chopped (about ½ cup)
- 3 cups fresh corn kernels (from 4 large ears)
- 2 cups multicolor cherry tomatoes (about 12 oz.), halved
- ¼ cup jarred refrigerated basil pesto
- ¼ tsp. black pepper
- 1½ tsp. kosher salt, divided
- 16 large sea scallops, patted dry and side muscles removed and discarded
- 2 Tbsp. olive oil, divided
  Fresh basil leaves (optional)

1. Cook bacon in a large cast-iron skillet over medium-high, stirring occasionally, until fat is rendered and bacon is crispy, 6 to 8 minutes. Transfer to a plate, reserving 1 tablespoon drippings in skillet. Add corn kernels; cook, stirring often, until tender-crisp, about 4 minutes. Remove skillet from heat; stir in cherry tomatoes, basil pesto, pepper, and ½ teaspoon of the salt. Transfer to a medium bowl; cover to keep warm. Wipe skillet clean.

2. Sprinkle scallops evenly with remaining 1 teaspoon salt. Heat 1 tablespoon of the oil in skillet over medium-high. Add half of the scallops, and press gently using a spatula. Cook, undisturbed, until edges are browned, about 3 minutes. Flip; cook until firm to touch and center is slightly translucent, about 30 seconds, or to desired level of doneness. Transfer to a plate. Wipe skillet clean; repeat with remaining 1 tablespoon oil and scallops.

3. Divide corn mixture among 4 bowls; top with scallops and bacon. Add basil (if desired).

THE SECRET TO A PERFECT SEAR
Cook the scallops undisturbed until the edges are browned. Then flip them once, and cook until the centers feel firm.

Lemon-Dill Chicken Skillet

ACTIVE 25 MIN. - TOTAL 40 MIN.

SERVES 4

1½ lb. small Yukon Gold potatoes (about 6 potatoes), quartered (about 5½ cups)

  1 Tbsp. olive oil

  4 (7-oz.) bone-in, skin-on chicken thighs, trimmed

½ tsp. black pepper

  2 tsp. kosher salt, divided

¼ cup fresh lemon juice (from 2 lemons), plus lemon wedges for serving

  2 oz. feta cheese, crumbled (about ½ cup)

Fresh dill fronds

1. Preheat oven to 375°F. Pour 4 cups water into a large microwavable bowl; add potatoes. Cover with plastic wrap; microwave on HIGH until potatoes are easily pierced with a knife, 10 to 12 minutes. (Potatoes will not be cooked through.) Drain.

2. While potatoes microwave, heat olive oil in an ovenproof 12-inch skillet over medium-high. Sprinkle chicken evenly with pepper and 1½ teaspoons of the salt. Place chicken, skin side down, in skillet. Cook, undisturbed, until fat has rendered and skin is golden brown, 10 to 12 minutes. Transfer to a plate, reserving drippings in skillet.

3. Add potatoes, cut side down, to drippings in skillet. Cook over medium-high, undisturbed, until browned on bottoms, 4 to 6 minutes. Add remaining ½ teaspoon salt, stirring to combine. Remove from heat. Arrange chicken, skin side up, on top of potatoes. Drizzle with lemon juice. Bake in preheated oven until potatoes are tender and a thermometer inserted into thickest portion of chicken registers 165°F, 15 to 20 minutes.

4. Sprinkle feta evenly over chicken mixture. Garnish with dill; serve with lemon wedges.

FAT = FLAVOR
It may look like there's a lot of drippings in the skillet when it goes into the oven, but don't worry. The potatoes absorb the fat, making them extra tasty.

THICK OVER THIN
Pick a jarred salsa with a chunky consistency. "Restaurant-style" and "cantina" salsas are too watery for this recipe.

Chipotle Chicken Tacos

ACTIVE 20 MIN. - TOTAL 50 MIN.
SERVES 4

- 1½ lb. boneless, skinless chicken thighs
- 1 (16-oz.) jar mild salsa
- 3 Tbsp. honey
- 1½ Tbsp. finely chopped canned chipotle chiles in adobo sauce (from 1 [7-oz.] can)
- 1½ tsp. kosher salt, plus more to taste
- 1 tsp. garlic powder
- 12 (6-inch) corn or flour tortillas, warmed

Optional toppings: crema, lime wedges, chopped fresh cilantro, sliced avocado

1. Toss together chicken, salsa, honey, chipotle chiles, salt, and garlic powder using tongs in a programmable pressure multicooker, such as Instant Pot. (Times, instructions, and settings may vary according to cooker brand or model.) Cover with lid; lock in place. Turn steam release handle to SEALING position. Select MANUAL/PRESSURE COOK setting. Select HIGH pressure for 8 minutes. (It will take 12 to 14 minutes for cooker to come up to pressure before cooking begins.)

2. Carefully turn steam release handle to VENTING position; let steam fully escape (float valve will drop). This will take 1 to 2 minutes. Remove lid. Transfer chicken to a bowl, leaving chile mixture in cooker.

3. Select SAUTÉ setting on cooker. Select HIGH temperature setting; bring chile mixture to a boil. Boil, stirring occasionally, until sauce thickens, about 15 minutes. Press CANCEL.

4. While chile mixture thickens, shred chicken using 2 forks. Return shredded chicken to cooker; stir to coat in sauce. Add additional salt to taste, stirring to combine. Serve with warmed tortillas and desired toppings.

Pasta with Pancetta, Artichokes, and Roasted Red Peppers

ACTIVE 25 MIN. - TOTAL 25 MIN.
SERVES 4

¼ tsp. kosher salt, plus more for salting water

12 oz. uncooked bow tie pasta

1 (4-oz.) pkg. diced pancetta

1 (24-oz.) jar marinated quartered artichoke hearts, drained, 2 Tbsp. liquid reserved

1 (12-oz.) jar roasted red bell peppers, drained and coarsely chopped (about 1⅓ cups)

2 Tbsp. olive oil

¼ tsp. black pepper

3 cups baby arugula (3 oz.)

   Grated Parmesan cheese (optional)

1. Bring a large pot of salted water to a boil over high. Add pasta, and cook according to package directions for al dente, about 10 minutes. Drain, reserving 1 cup cooking water.
2. While pasta cooks, cook pancetta in a large nonstick skillet over medium-high, stirring often, until fat is rendered and pancetta is crisp, 8 to 10 minutes. Transfer pancetta to a plate, reserving drippings in skillet.
3. Add artichokes, cut side down, to drippings in skillet; spread in an even layer. Cook, undisturbed, until evenly golden on bottom, about 7 minutes. Add bell peppers, oil, salt, black pepper, pasta, reserved artichoke liquid, and ½ cup of the reserved cooking water, stirring to combine. Cook, stirring constantly, until a creamy, emulsified sauce forms and coats pasta, 2 to 3 minutes, adding more cooking water if needed until desired sauce consistency. Remove skillet from heat, and cool 2 minutes. Stir in arugula and pancetta. Divide pasta mixture evenly among 4 bowls. Garnish with Parmesan, if desired.

CHOOSE THE RIGHT 'CHOKES
Marinated artichokes (not the plain brined kind) work best in this recipe because the marinade helps flavor the pasta.

Flapjacks They'll Flip For

When zucchini is overflowing in the garden, whip up a stack of these light and fluffy pancakes

Zucchini Bread Pancakes

If you can't find mascarpone (Italian-style cream cheese), replace it with the same amount of full-fat Greek yogurt or cream cheese.

ACTIVE 40 MIN. - TOTAL 45 MIN.
SERVES 6

- 2 cups grated zucchini (from 2 small zucchini)
- 1¾ cups unbleached all-purpose flour
- 2 tsp. baking powder
- 1 tsp. baking soda
- 1 tsp. kosher salt
- 1 tsp. ground cinnamon
- ¼ tsp. ground nutmeg
- 2 cups whole buttermilk
- ½ cup packed light brown sugar
- 2 tsp. vanilla extract
- 2 large eggs
- ¼ cup butter, melted, plus more for greasing skillet
- ½ cup chopped toasted pecans, plus more for garnish
- 1 (8-oz.) container mascarpone cheese
- 3 Tbsp. pure maple syrup, plus more for serving

1. Place zucchini in an even layer on 3 layers of paper towels. Place 3 more layers on top; roll up. Gently squeeze to remove excess moisture from zucchini. (No need to repeat; a little moisture left is okay.) Set aside.

2. Whisk together flour, baking powder, baking soda, salt, cinnamon, and nutmeg in a large bowl. Whisk together buttermilk, brown sugar, vanilla, and eggs in a medium bowl. Add buttermilk mixture to flour mixture, stirring just until flour mixture is moistened. Drizzle melted butter over batter; gently stir to combine. Fold in zucchini and pecans (there should be lumps). Let stand 5 minutes.

3. Grease a large nonstick skillet with butter. Heat over medium. Working in 6 batches, pour ¼ cupfuls of batter into hot pan (3 pancakes per batch). Cook until tops are covered with bubbles and edges look dry and cooked, 2 to 3 minutes. Flip; cook 2 to 3 minutes more. (Between batches, wipe pan and grease again as needed.) Set aside until ready to serve. (Or place in 1 layer on a baking sheet; keep warm in a 200°F oven up to 30 minutes.)

4. Stir mascarpone cheese in a bowl until loosened. Add maple syrup, gently stirring until combined. Dollop over pancakes; top with additional pecans and maple syrup.

The Power of the Pod

Okra is in season, and it's time to show it some love

OKRA IS the Rodney Dangerfield of the vegetable world: It gets no respect. Many people screw up their faces into tight knots when it is mentioned and spend much of their time trying to figure out how to keep it from doing what it does naturally. Cookbooks abound with recipes for okra that begin by demonizing it for its slipperiness. I, on the other hand, am an avowed lover of the mucilaginous pod. I even have it on my stationery.

I delight in okra's history and in knowing that it's botanically related to sorrel (the red pod used in a favorite Caribbean beverage that's served at Christmastime) as well as to the tropical hibiscus plant and—most surprisingly—to cotton. I take particular pleasure in the irony that those who were forced to work in the cotton fields gave the South the gift of okra, without which New Orleans gumbos and many a summer succotash certainly would not be the same.

The trick to cooking this vegetable is to avoid fighting its natural tendencies. The more it's sliced, the more it exudes its slipperiness. So if you don't like the slime, the solution is easy: Cut it as little as possible, or leave it intact. The young pods can also be eaten raw or simply blanched like string beans. You can even cook them whole in the oven or grill them, like in my recipe for Grilled Okra-and-Pepper Skewers.

Growing up, I was never forced to eat this veggie because my mother could not abide it. One of my personal culinary points of pride is that I was able to convince her, a formidable okra naysayer, to not only taste it but also to enjoy it, even if only annually in a stew that I made. She admitted it wasn't too bad, and I have no doubt that she would have been able to accommodate herself to these skewers as well.
—Jessica B. Harris

Grilled Okra-and-Pepper Skewers with Dijon Dipping Sauce

ACTIVE 15 MIN. - TOTAL 25 MIN.

SERVES 4

- 16 medium-size (8 oz. total) fresh okra pods
- 12 (12 oz. total) sweet mini peppers
  Olive oil, for brushing pan
- ¼ cup mayonnaise
- 1 Tbsp. Dijon mustard
- 2 tsp. anchovy paste
- 1 tsp. fresh lemon juice (from 1 lemon)
- ½ tsp. hot sauce

1. Thread okra and peppers alternately onto 4 (10-inch) wooden skewers (4 okra pods and 3 peppers per skewer).
2. Heat a grill pan over high, and brush lightly with oil. Add skewers to grill pan, and cook until vegetables are charred and tender, 6 to 8 minutes, turning once halfway through cook time.
3. Meanwhile, stir together mayonnaise, mustard, anchovy paste, fresh lemon juice, and hot sauce in a small bowl.
4. Serve skewers immediately alongside dipping sauce.

Even More to Know About Okra

The South's most underappreciated vegetable might also be its most interesting

THE ENGLISH word "okra" probably comes from one of the Akan languages of Ghana, in which the plant is known as nkruma, or the Igbo word okuru from Nigeria. In the Bantu languages of Central Africa, it is known in Tshiluba as kingombo and in Umbundu as ochingombo, hence our word "gumbo." In fact, anyone who wants to prepare this recipe in France will require some gombo, the word in contemporary French for the veggie.

In the garden, okra plants grow tall with beautiful hibiscus-like flowers in shades of yellow, pink, and red. Some types have burgundy-color pods, which look striking but taste like their green counterparts. (The red hue fades when cooked.)

You can also eat raw okra leaves or add them to thicken a stew. The seeds are useful as well. Oliver Farm Artisan Oils in Georgia cold-presses them into a golden oil that they describe as having "a hint of spice without being spicy." Perhaps even more unusual is okra coffee, which is made from dried, toasted, and ground seeds that are then brewed like regular coffee beans.

Some Like It Hotter

Spice up grilled chicken with three lively sauces

Spicy Grilled Chicken Breasts

ACTIVE 15 MIN. - TOTAL 20 MIN.,
PLUS 30 MIN. CHILLING
SERVES 4

- ¼ cup kosher salt
- 4 (6- to 8-oz.) boneless, skinless chicken breasts
  Nashville-Style Hot Sauce, Ginger-Garlic-Chile Sauce, or Sweet Heat Brown Sugar Sauce (recipes below)
- 1 Tbsp. olive oil
- ½ tsp. black pepper

1. Stir together 4 cups water and the salt in a large bowl until salt dissolves. Add chicken; chill, uncovered, 30 minutes.
2. Meanwhile, preheat grill to high (450°F to 500°F) on 1 side and medium-low (300°F to 350°F) on other side.
3. Prepare desired sauce; set aside 4 tablespoons.
4. Remove chicken, discarding brine; pat dry. Coat with oil; sprinkle with pepper. Place on oiled grates over hotter side of grill. Cover and grill, undisturbed, 2 to 3 minutes. Flip chicken; place on oiled grates over cooler side of grill. Cover and grill until a thermometer inserted in center registers 160°F, 10 to 15 minutes, brushing each breast with about 1 tablespoon of reserved sauce after 5 minutes. Transfer to a plate; cover with aluminum foil. Let rest 5 to 10 minutes. Serve with remaining sauce, if desired.

SPICY GRILLED
CHICKEN BREASTS
WITH NASHVILLE-
STYLE HOT SAUCE

Nashville-Style Hot Sauce

ACTIVE 5 MIN. - TOTAL 5 MIN.
MAKES ⅔ CUP

Stir together ½ cup **canola oil**; 2 Tbsp. each **cayenne pepper** and **light brown sugar**; 1 tsp. each **paprika**, **garlic powder**, and **kosher salt**; and ½ tsp. **black pepper** in a microwavable bowl. Microwave, covered, on HIGH until sizzling and fragrant, about 1 minute.

CALORIES: **324** – CARBS: **4 G** – FAT: **19 G**
(PER SERVING WITH CHICKEN)

Ginger-Garlic-Chile Sauce

ACTIVE 10 MIN. - TOTAL 10 MIN.
MAKES ⅔ CUP

Cook ¼ cup each **canola oil** and finely chopped **scallions** (3 medium scallions), 3 Tbsp. grated **fresh ginger**, and 1 tsp. grated **garlic** in a small skillet over medium-low until sizzling and fragrant, 1 minute. Remove from heat, and stir in 1 Tbsp. **sambal oelek** (ground fresh chile paste), 2 tsp. **soy sauce**, and 1 tsp. each **sesame oil** and **rice vinegar**. Stir until slightly cooled, 1 minute. Stir in 3 Tbsp. finely chopped **fresh cilantro**.

CALORIES: **266** – CARBS: **1 G** – FAT: **13 G**
(PER SERVING WITH CHICKEN)

Sweet Heat Brown Sugar Sauce

ACTIVE 5 MIN. - TOTAL 5 MIN.
MAKES ABOUT 1 CUP

Whisk together ½ cup **bottled chili sauce**, 3 Tbsp. each **light brown sugar** and minced **canned chipotle chiles in adobo sauce**, 1 Tbsp. **apple cider vinegar**, and 2 tsp. each **Worcestershire sauce** and **paprika** in a bowl until smooth.

CALORIES: **232** – CARBS: **6 G** – FAT: **7 G**
(PER SERVING WITH CHICKEN)

The Sweetest Heat

Homemade pepper jelly is one of summer's tastiest treats

Red Chipotle Pepper Jelly

ACTIVE 20 MIN. - TOTAL 50 MIN.,
PLUS 6 HOURS CHILLING

MAKES 6 (½-PT.) JARS

- **4** large red bell peppers, roughly chopped (about 4 cups)
- **3** large canned chipotle chiles in adobo sauce (from 1 [7-oz.] can), seeded and chopped (about 1½ Tbsp.)
- **4½** cups granulated sugar
- **1⅓** cups apple cider vinegar
- **½** cup plus 1 Tbsp. liquid pectin (from 2 [3-oz.] pkg.)
- **¼** tsp. kosher salt
- **¼** tsp. garlic powder

1. Pulse bell peppers and chipotle chiles in a food processor until finely chopped, about 6 pulses. Transfer to a large saucepan, and cook over medium-high, stirring occasionally, until liquid evaporates, 8 minutes.
2. Add sugar and vinegar to saucepan, stirring to combine; bring to a boil over medium-high. Reduce heat to medium, and cook, stirring occasionally, 5 minutes. Add pectin, salt, and garlic powder, stirring to combine; cook, undisturbed, 1 minute. Remove from heat.
3. Spoon jelly evenly into 6 (½-pint) sterilized canning jars, filling to the top (leave ½ inch headspace if freezing); wipe jar rims. Cool 30 minutes. Screw on lids, and refrigerate until set, about 6 hours. Store in refrigerator for up to 3 weeks or in freezer for up to 1 year.
Serving Idea: Serve with buttermilk biscuits and sliced ham.

RED CHIPOTLE PEPPER JELLY

YELLOW PEPPER JELLY WITH GINGER

GREEN PEPPER JELLY WITH BASIL

Green Pepper Jelly with Basil

Prepare recipe as directed at left, substituting 4 large poblano chiles for red bell peppers and 2 large jalapeño chiles, seeded and chopped, for chipotle chiles in Step 1. Omit garlic powder; stir in 2 tablespoons chopped fresh basil after removing mixture from heat in Step 2.
Serving Idea: Spread over baguette slices topped with ricotta cheese and basil.

Yellow Pepper Jelly with Ginger

Prepare recipe as directed at left, substituting 4 large yellow bell peppers for red bell peppers and omitting chipotle chiles in Step 1. Substitute 2 teaspoons grated fresh ginger for garlic powder in Step 2.
Serving Idea: Use as a glaze and dipping sauce for chicken wings.

Daddy's Biscuits

When Test Kitchen professional and *Hey Y'all* host Ivy Odom makes her family's recipe, a very special bowl is the secret ingredient

IN THE SOUTH, biscuit recipes aren't always committed to paper. Instead, they are often passed down through memories shared with loved ones in the kitchen. Our favorite version is probably the one we grew up eating, and the regional takes can vary greatly.

For my daddy, there is only one way to make a biscuit. Soft, fluffy, and almost cakelike in crumb, it's very different from the buttery, flaky, crunchy-top kind that's popular at modern brunch joints.

He remembers his grandfather gently incorporating shortening and buttermilk into a giant wooden bowl of flour. Like magic, the buttermilk and shortening would cling to the perfect amount of flour needed to make the dough, leaving the rest of it completely dry. Any flour that remained in the bowl was covered with a towel and set atop a cabinet for the next biscuit-making day.

I'm now the keeper of my great-great-grandfather's wooden biscuit bowl that was hand-carved and passed down to his son, then from my great-grandfather to his grandson, and now from my daddy to me. It's weathered, cracked, and stained. Over the years, it's been used as a catchall and a serving piece. But on those days when I need something to sop up a taste of home, I pull out the bowl that knows just what to do. –Ivy Odom

Biscuit-Bowl Biscuits

"Practice makes perfect" definitely applies to biscuit making. Use as little flour as possible to prepare this dough; it should be soft but not too wet. Don't worry if some sticks to your hands.
ACTIVE 20 MIN. · TOTAL 35 MIN.
MAKES 12

- ¼ cup vegetable shortening, at room temperature, plus more for greasing pan
- 1 (2-lb.) pkg. enriched bleached self-rising flour (such as White Lily)
- 1 cup whole buttermilk

1. Preheat oven to 500°F. Grease a small or medium (no smaller than 8-inch) round cast-iron griddle pan with shortening. Place flour in a large bowl. Spoon 2½ cups of the flour into a sifter; sift flour back into bowl. Using the back of your hand, create a nestlike shape in flour in center of bowl, pressing and packing flour down firmly.
2. Pour buttermilk directly into nest. Add shortening to buttermilk (Fig. 1). Squeeze together using 1 hand to incorporate until no large pieces remain (Fig. 2). Using a circular motion with your hands, gradually begin incorporating flour from sides of bowl into buttermilk mixture, working as quickly and gently as you can and incorporating only as much flour as needed until a soft dough forms. (You will not need to use all the flour in the bowl.) The dough should be soft but not wet, and it can be a bit sticky. Reserve remaining flour in bowl for flouring and, if desired, for another batch of biscuits.
3. Flour your hands, and transfer dough to a lightly floured work surface. Pat dough to about 1-inch thickness. Using a 2-inch biscuit cutter, cut out 8 biscuits, flouring cutter after each cutting (Fig. 3). Reroll dough scraps, and pat to 1-inch thickness. Cut remaining 4 biscuits using floured cutter. Discard any remaining scraps.
4. Arrange biscuits as close together as possible (they should be touching) on prepared griddle pan (Fig. 4). Bake in preheated oven until tops are golden, 10 to 12 minutes. Cool 5 minutes before serving.

FIG. 1

FIG. 2

FIG. 3

FIG. 4

COOKING SCHOOL

An Easy Way to Drain Zucchini

Three steps to remove moisture when shredding a lot of squash

STEP 1

Place a few paper towels under a box grater. Grate zucchini using the large holes so it collects on the paper towels.

STEP 2

Using the paper towels, transfer the shredded zucchini to a fine mesh strainer placed over a bowl. Discard paper towels. Toss the zucchini with a pinch of salt. Set aside for 10 minutes.

STEP 3

Press the zucchini against the sides of the strainer with a spoon to get out excess moisture. Remove zucchini from strainer, and use as desired.

The Hard Truth About Parmesan

Know what you're really getting when shopping for this classic cheese

PARMIGIANO-REGGIANO

Made from cow's milk, salt, and rennet, this version is produced in certain parts of Italy and is labeled as such. It must be aged for at least a year and is prized for its nutty, slightly sweet flavor.

PARMESAN

Unless labeled otherwise, it is not produced in Italy; the word "Parmesan" is typically used generically to refer to a hard cow's milk cheese. While it's still tasty, it has less complexity.

Southern Staple

Zatarain's Cheddar Jalapeño Cornbread Mix and Martha White's Buttermilk Cornbread & Muffin Mix

BEST SWEET

This moist, cakelike cornbread has enough sweetness to balance the savory Cheddar and spicy chiles. (Add more cheese to make it extra tasty.)

BEST SAVORY

In a mix that's as basic as they come, the flavors of toasty cornmeal and tangy buttermilk really shine. It's ideal for folks who don't like sugar in their cornbread.

August

Tomatoes for Breakfast?

Absolutely! Enjoy this savory quiche any time of day

Roasted Tomato Quiche

Removing and discarding the tomato seeds keeps them from releasing moisture as they cook, which can make the filling watery.
ACTIVE 20 MIN. · TOTAL 2 HOURS, 5 MIN.
SERVES 8

- 1½ lb. assorted heirloom tomatoes (about 3 medium tomatoes), seeded and sliced ¼ inch thick
- ½ (14.1-oz.) pkg. refrigerated piecrusts (1 crust), at room temperature
- All-purpose flour, for dusting
- 4 large eggs
- 1 cup whole milk
- ½ cup chopped red onion (from 1 small onion)
- 1 tsp. kosher salt
- ¼ tsp. garlic powder
- ¼ tsp. black pepper
- 5 oz. Colby Jack cheese, shredded (about 1¼ cups), divided
- ¾ cup cooked and crumbled bacon (8 slices), divided
- Chopped scallions

1. Preheat oven to 350°F with rack in lower third position. Line a large rimmed baking sheet with aluminum foil. Arrange tomatoes in a single layer on baking sheet. Bake in preheated oven until lightly browned around edges, about 30 minutes. Set aside. Do not turn oven off.

2. While tomatoes are baking, roll out piecrust on a lightly floured work surface into a 12-inch round. Place in an ungreased 9-inch deep-dish pie plate, pressing into bottom and up sides of pie plate; fold excess dough under edges, and crimp as desired. Freeze until crust is cold and filling is ready to use, 5 to 15 minutes.

3. Whisk together eggs, milk, onion, salt, garlic powder, pepper, 1 cup of the cheese, and ½ cup of the bacon in a large bowl until combined. Pour into prepared crust.

4. Bake at 350°F until filling is partially set, about 25 minutes. Carefully remove from oven; top evenly with tomato slices and remaining ¼ cup cheese and ¼ cup bacon. Bake until filling is set and crust is golden brown, about 20 minutes. Let cool slightly on a wire rack, about 30 minutes. Garnish with chopped scallions, and serve warm.

Berry Picking with Bill

Despite a lifetime of pricks and scratches, North Carolina chef
Bill Smith still loves this late-summer fruit

WILD BLACKBERRIES and I have a long history. When I was a kid growing up in New Bern, North Carolina, my great-grandmother would make a pie if I picked 4 cups of them for her. They grew along the railroad tracks that ran through the woods behind our house. As I recall, this was the only assistance that I was ever allowed to provide in her kitchen. She was a fabulous cook but didn't want anyone underfoot, no matter how helpful. I credit her with much of my later success as a chef, even though I learned by watching from a distance.

Blackberries like to grow along the edges of clearings. Right across the street from Crook's Corner, the restaurant where I was chef for over 25 years, there was just such a spot. When I would go out in late spring to pick honeysuckle flowers to make sorbet, I could also scope out the season's blackberry crop, because they prefer to grow in the same places and bloom at the same time. I picked them every summer for our dessert menu. Early on, I would try to show some restraint with the number of blackberry items on the menu, but as I grew more confident in my role as a chef, I began to take liberties. I was the boss, after all. There might have been

nights when we served three different blackberry desserts.

When you go picking, face the fact that you are probably going to get scratched up by thorns. There are also ticks and "red bugs" (as we used to call chiggers) to consider. Wearing the proper clothing helps, but when we were young, we discovered that applying the lotion that's used to get rid of lice around the ankles and groin assured that we wouldn't get any bites. Of course, there is also the question of who in your crew won't be too embarrassed to be seen buying this product, but at least you don't have to ask for it at the counter anymore like you used to. (It's on the shelves now.)

Wild blackberries tend to grow in clusters of six to eight. About a week before a whole bunch ripens, one berry at the end of each group will suddenly plump up and be ready. It's as if they're sending out a scout. More generally, they ripen by location. Those that can get sun from both sides are first, followed by those in mostly shade. They are slower, but because their spot stays more damp, the fruit is larger.

Blackberries take on a certain luster when they're just right. Then the sheen dulls, but they'll still be good for another day or two. Ripe ones will come away in your hand without much tugging. If a whole group looks ready, put down your basket or bowl and hold an open palm beneath the branch before starting to pick. (The berries on the bottom of the cluster ripen first, and the motion of picking may cause those to fall from their stems and be lost.) When you think you've collected everything in one spot,

move a few steps to the left or right while keeping your eyes on the same place. Invariably, more ripe fruit will reveal itself. June bugs love blackberries and are dark and shiny like the fruit. If you grab one of them by mistake, you might get an "electric handshake" from the beetle vibrating as it tries to buzz away.

Even though I've retired, I continue to gather berries every summer, so I sometimes find myself with a kitchen full of desserts. During the pandemic, I arranged for friends to do driveway pickups of cobblers and cakes. But I kept the sabayon—a runny, boozy custard—for myself. I'm not complaining, but just imagine what that much sugar and alcohol at once can do to a person. But after all, blackberry season is short and comes only once a year. –Bill Smith

Blackberries in Sabayon

(Photo, page 172)

I love most desserts, but sabayon is the one that I have the least success resisting. There are a million variations: It can be either hot or cold. And in some Italian restaurants, where it's called zabaglione, it's served warm over strawberries. I generally prefer it cold, which means chilling the custard and then folding in whipped cream. While I like to use blackberries, many other fruits can work.

ACTIVE 25 MIN. - TOTAL 45 MIN.,
PLUS 4 HOURS CHILLING

SERVES 8

- 3 large eggs
- 5 large egg yolks
- Pinch of kosher salt
- 1½ cups granulated sugar, divided
- ¾ cup (6 oz.) Madeira
- ¾ cup (6 oz.) dry vermouth
- 1 cup heavy whipping cream
- 8 cups fresh blackberries (from 6 [6-oz.] pkg.)

> "About a week before a whole bunch ripens, one berry at the end of each group will suddenly plump up and be ready. It's as if they're sending out a scout."

Continued on page 170

Continued from page 169

1. Pour water to a depth of 1½ inches in a large saucepan; bring to a boil over high. Reduce heat to low, maintaining a gentle simmer. Whisk together eggs, egg yolks, salt, and 1¼ cups of the sugar in a large heatproof bowl until thoroughly combined; whisk in Madeira and vermouth. Place bowl over simmering water. Cook, whisking constantly and vigorously, until mixture is foamy, triples in size, begins to give off steam, and reaches a temperature between 145°F and 150°F, 8 to 10 minutes. (Do not bring mixture to a boil.)

2. Chill custard, uncovered, stirring occasionally, until cold, about 4 hours. Beat cream with an electric mixer on medium speed until foamy, about 30 seconds. Increase mixer speed to medium-high; gradually add remaining ¼ cup sugar, beating until soft peaks form, 1 to 2 minutes. Gently fold whipped cream into custard using a rubber spatula; cover and chill 20 minutes. Place about ½ cup blackberries in 8 dishes; top with custard. Garnish each with about ½ cup berries.

Rum Babas with Fresh Blackberries

(Photo, page 173)

When I was at Crook's Corner, I generally would make rum babas only during the holidays. They seem extra festive but are also a bit more trouble than the simpler recipes that I prefer. I don't recall how they suddenly popped back up on the menu in midsummer, but I'm glad it happened because they are exquisite with fresh wild blackberries.

ACTIVE 1 HOUR · TOTAL 1 HOUR, 30 MIN., PLUS 1 HOUR, 30 MIN. RISING

SERVES 12

BABAS
- 1 (¼-oz.) pkg. active dry yeast
- 3 Tbsp. warm water
- 2 large eggs
- ¼ cup butter, melted and cooled slightly
- 2 Tbsp. granulated sugar
- 1½ cups all-purpose flour, plus more for dusting

RUM SYRUP
- 1 cup granulated sugar
- ½ cup (4 oz.) dark rum

ADDITIONAL INGREDIENTS
- 4 cups fresh blackberries (from 3 [6-oz.] pkg.)
  Sweetened whipped cream

1. Prepare the Babas: Dissolve yeast in warm water in a large bowl; let stand until foamy, about 5 minutes. Whisk in eggs, butter, and sugar until smooth and completely incorporated. Fold in flour using a rubber spatula until mixture is smooth. Knead dough in bowl until it sticks to itself more than it does to your hands, about 5 minutes, dusting it with a little flour to help prevent sticking. (Don't use too much flour.) Shape into a ball. Place in a large bowl lightly greased with cooking spray; dust the top with a little flour. Cover with a damp cloth; let rise in a warm (75°F to 80°F) place until doubled in size, 1 hour to 1 hour, 30 minutes.

2. Punch dough down, and knead 2 or 3 times (still in bowl). Generously coat wells of a 12-cup mini Bundt pan with cooking spray. Divide dough evenly among wells (about 1¼ ounces each), pressing gently into bottom of each well. (You don't need to smooth the tops. That will take care of itself when rising.) Let rise, uncovered, in a warm place until doubled in size, 30 to 45 minutes.

3. Preheat oven to 375°F. Bake until Babas are golden brown and spring back when lightly pressed, 12 to 15 minutes. Remove from oven; cool on a wire rack 10 minutes.

4. While Babas bake, prepare the Rum Syrup: Bring 1¼ cups water and the sugar to a boil in a small saucepan over medium-high. Boil mixture, stirring occasionally, until sugar is completely dissolved, about 2 minutes. Remove from heat; stir in rum.

5. Remove Babas from mini Bundt pan. Pierce tops several times using a wooden pick; drizzle with enough warm syrup so they are moist but not soggy (about 1¼ cups syrup total).

6. Place Babas on 12 dessert plates, and garnish each with blackberries. Drizzle each with a little more syrup. Garnish with whipped cream. This dessert should be served warm, but the cakes and the syrup hold well, so you can reheat both to serve later.

Blackberry-Buttermilk Sherbet

In May 2008, Southern Living *published a recipe for Strawberry-Buttermilk Sherbet. It must have been around blackberry season, because I switched the fruit when I tried a batch. It was fabulous. Plus, it doesn't have to be cooked and sets up quickly. Ordinarily as a chef, I would wait awhile before stealing a recipe from a magazine, but in this instance, it was so good that I put it on the menu while that issue was still on newsstands.*

ACTIVE 15 MIN. · TOTAL 1 HOUR, PLUS 4 HOURS CHILLING AND 2 HOURS FREEZING

MAKES ABOUT 6 CUPS

- 2 cups fresh blackberries, plus more for garnish
- 1 cup granulated sugar
  Pinch of kosher salt
- 2 cups whole buttermilk
- 1 tsp. vanilla extract
  Small fresh basil or mint leaves, for topping (optional)

1. Toss together blackberries, sugar, and salt in a large bowl; let stand, stirring occasionally, 30 minutes to 1 hour. Transfer mixture to a blender or a food processor; process until completely smooth, about 2 minutes. Press puree through a fine mesh strainer into a large bowl; discard solids.

2. Stir buttermilk and vanilla into strained puree. Cover and chill until thoroughly cold, about 4 hours. Pour mixture into the freezer container of a 4-quart ice-cream maker; freeze according to manufacturer's instructions. Transfer to a freezer-safe container; cover and freeze 2 hours. Serve sherbet in bowls; top each with additional berries and a few herb leaves, if desired.

BLACKBERRY-
BUTTERMILK
SHERBET

BLACKBERRIES
IN SABAYON
(PAGE 169)

RUM BABAS
WITH FRESH
BLACKBERRIES
(PAGE 170)

SECRET INGREDIENT: BAKING SODA
It might sound strange, but a pinch of this kitchen staple combats any bitterness and keeps the tea from turning cloudy when chilled.

How Do You Take Your Tea?

Southern-style sweet tea is freshly brewed black tea that's sweetened with sugar while hot, chilled until cold, and served over ice. Change any of those variables, and you have a beverage–perhaps a nice one–but not classic sweet tea

IT'S A STAPLE IN OUR FRIDGES and cup holders, and we appreciate the free refills when we go out, a bottomless fount of refreshment. Some people drink sweet tea daily. Some sip all day long. Others indulge once in a blue moon as a treat or a trip down memory lane. No matter the frequency, if you ever crave this drink's incomparable quenching relief and comfort, you understand why it is a Southern culinary masterpiece.

Tea was first grown in the South nearly 300 years ago, but it didn't do well. The most successful early effort happened in 1795 when botanist André Michaux planted *Camellia sinensis* in Charleston, South Carolina. (Yes, aromatic tea is a cousin to fragrant camellias.) The first known recipe for iced tea (made with green tea) can be traced back to *Housekeeping in Old Virginia*, an 1878 cookbook by Marion Cabell Tyree. Sweet tea as we know it today didn't become a mainstay until refrigeration and inexpensive imported black tea, sugar, and ice became commonplace after WWII.

Before long, households often had special pitchers and tall glasses just for this drink, and silverware drawers included long-handled iced tea spoons. Many of us still make it regularly, even if we've traded an heirloom pitcher for a Mason jar and footed glasses for go-cups.

Loyalty to this beverage remains strong in many Southern restaurants as well. Kahlil Arnold of Arnold's Country Kitchen, a legendary meat 'n' three in Nashville, says they sell upwards of 35 gallons of sweet tea a day, with sweet outpacing unsweet three to one. Their customers drink more tea than carbonated soft drinks, with no dropping off in the winter. "Some of our folks won't take their first bite until after they've finished their first glass of tea," Arnold says. He thinks it's because many grew up drinking it, at least with Sunday dinner and on holidays, and developed a lifelong taste for it.

Some of us have cut back on the amount of sugar in our tea. Most restaurant servers understand exactly what we mean when we order ours "half-and-half" or "unsweet with a splash of the good stuff." It's also true that not all Southerners like it. No recipe, no matter how iconic, is universally beloved.

Sweet tea requires nothing more than tea, sugar, water, ice, and a little know-how, and that's why it's well worth learning to make this Southern classic right at home.

Perfect Southern Sweet Tea

ACTIVE 5 MIN. - TOTAL 50 MIN.
SERVES 6

- 2 family-size (7 oz. each) black tea bags
- ¼ tsp. baking soda
- 6 cups filtered or spring water, at room temperature, divided
- ½ cup granulated sugar
- Ice

1. Place tea bags and baking soda in a large glass jar or pitcher.
2. Bring 4 cups of the water to a rolling boil in a saucepan over high; immediately pour over tea bags, making sure they are submerged. Steep for 15 minutes. Remove bags, and gently squeeze. Discard bags.
3. Stir in granulated sugar until dissolved. Stir in remaining 2 cups water.
4. Refrigerate, uncovered, until chilled, about 30 minutes. Serve over ice. Store covered in refrigerator up to 2 days.

Key Components

Each element of sweet tea matters, so choose wisely

TEA Use black tea that is grown or blended for iced drinks, usually a type known as orange pekoe. The bags must be fresh and fragrant enough to release their aroma each time the container, preferably an airtight one, is opened.

WATER Filtered or spring water eliminates any odd flavors or odors in treated tap water. Distilled, however, is bland and can make it taste flat. (Not all bottled water is spring; some brands are treated city water from another town.)

SUGAR Southern-style sweet tea relies on granulated cane sugar, though it's fine to adjust the amount to taste. Granulated sugar, white or unbleached, works better than water-based simple syrup, which dilutes the brew.

"Sweet tea tastes best when freshly brewed and no more than a day old, two tops. You can recognize stale tea on the first sip, which is why store-bought bottles and jugs never measure up."
–Kahlil Arnold

Superfast Shrimp Suppers

Stir up these easy, breezy meals in 25 minutes or less

Shrimp Salad Rolls
ACTIVE 10 MIN. - TOTAL 10 MIN.
SERVES 6

- 1½ lb. large shrimp, peeled and deveined
- 2½ tsp. kosher salt, divided
- 2 celery stalks, finely chopped (1 cup)
- ⅓ cup mayonnaise
- 2 Tbsp. chopped fresh chives, plus more for garnish
- 2 Tbsp. chopped fresh dill
- 1 Tbsp. Dijon mustard
- 1 Tbsp. fresh lemon juice (from 1 lemon)
- 1 tsp. Old Bay seasoning
- 2 Tbsp. butter, softened
- 6 potato hot dog buns, split and toasted
   Bibb or Boston lettuce leaves, for serving

1. Cook shrimp in a large pot of boiling water seasoned with 2 teaspoons of the salt until cooked through, about 2 minutes. Drain and rinse with cold water until cool to the touch. Pat dry, and chop into bite-size pieces.
2. Stir together celery, mayonnaise, chives, dill, Dijon mustard, lemon juice, Old Bay seasoning, and remaining ½ teaspoon salt until combined. Fold in chopped shrimp.
3. Spread butter on toasted buns, and top with lettuce. Fill each bun with shrimp mixture, and garnish with additional chives, if desired.

DON'T SKIMP ON THE SALT
Cooking the shrimp in salted water makes them more flavorful right out of the pot.

Shrimp and Burst Cherry Tomato Pasta

ACTIVE 25 MIN. · TOTAL 25 MIN.
SERVES 4

- 6 Tbsp. extra-virgin olive oil, divided
- 1 lb. large shrimp, peeled and deveined
- 2 tsp. kosher salt, divided, plus more for salting water
- 6 garlic cloves, thinly sliced
- 2 lb. red and yellow cherry tomatoes
- ¼ tsp. crushed red pepper
- 1 lb. uncooked spaghetti
- 2 oz. Parmesan cheese, grated (about ½ cup), plus more for serving
- Fresh basil, for garnish

1. Heat 2 tablespoons of the oil in a large deep skillet over medium-high. Pat shrimp dry with paper towels. Season shrimp with ½ teaspoon of the salt, and add to skillet. Cook, stirring often, until shrimp are cooked through, about 3 minutes. Transfer to a plate; set aside.
2. Heat remaining 4 tablespoons oil in same skillet over medium-high. Add garlic, and cook, stirring often, until aromatic, about 1 minute. Add tomatoes, crushed red pepper, and remaining 1½ teaspoons salt. Cover and cook, stirring occasionally, until tomatoes are tender and release their juices, about 14 minutes.
3. Meanwhile, bring a large pot of salted water to a boil over high. Cook spaghetti until al dente. Drain spaghetti, reserving ½ cup pasta water.
4. Add cooked shrimp and any accumulated juices to tomatoes, and cook over medium. Add cooked spaghetti, Parmesan, and reserved pasta water, tossing to coat. Cook, stirring occasionally, until sauce clings to pasta. Remove from heat. Garnish with fresh basil, if desired. Serve with additional Parmesan.

Grilled Shrimp and Herbed Couscous Salad

ACTIVE 20 MIN. - TOTAL 20 MIN.

SERVES 4

- 2 cups uncooked Israeli couscous
- 1 tsp. grated lemon zest plus 3 Tbsp. fresh juice (from 1 large lemon)
- 1 small garlic clove, grated
- ¼ tsp. black pepper
- ¼ cup plus 1 Tbsp. extra-virgin olive oil, divided
- 1¾ tsp. kosher salt, divided, plus more for salting water
- 1 lb. large shrimp, peeled and deveined
- 1 tsp. smoked paprika
- 1 cup loosely packed fresh flat-leaf parsley leaves, chopped, plus more for garnish
- ¼ cup chopped fresh dill, plus more for garnish
- 4 oz. feta cheese, crumbled (about 1 cup)

1. Bring a medium saucepan of salted water to a boil over high. Add couscous; cook, stirring occasionally, until tender, 5 to 7 minutes. Drain couscous, and rinse with cool water.

2. Stir together lemon zest and juice, grated garlic, black pepper, ¼ cup of the oil, and 1¼ teaspoons of the salt in a large bowl. Stir into cooked couscous; set aside.

3. Pat shrimp dry with paper towels. Sprinkle shrimp with paprika and remaining ½ teaspoon salt. Thread shrimp onto skewers. Preheat grill to high (450°F to 500°F). Drizzle shrimp with remaining 1 tablespoon oil, and place shrimp skewers on oiled grates. Grill, covered, until charred and cooked through, 1 to 2 minutes per side.

4. Stir parsley and dill into couscous mixture. Remove skewers from shrimp, and arrange shrimp over couscous. Top with crumbled feta. Garnish with additional parsley and dill.

MAKE IT AHEAD
This pasta salad tastes great served cold or at room temperature, and the flavors only intensify if prepared a day in advance.

REMEMBER THIS STEP
Use paper towels to thoroughly pat the thawed shrimp dry so they cook and sear (not steam) in the pan.

Chipotle Shrimp Tacos

ACTIVE 15 MIN. - TOTAL 15 MIN.

SERVES 4

- 1 lb. frozen cooked salad-size shrimp, thawed
- 1 tsp. chipotle chile powder
- ¼ tsp. garlic powder
- 1 tsp. kosher salt, divided
- 1 Tbsp. olive oil
- 3 cups shredded coleslaw mix
- ½ small red onion, thinly sliced (about ½ cup)
- ⅓ cup chopped fresh cilantro, plus more for garnish
- 3 Tbsp. fresh lime juice (from 2 limes)
- 3 Tbsp. mayonnaise
- ½ tsp. granulated sugar
- 8 (6½-inch) flour tortillas, toasted
  Lime wedges, for serving
  Hot sauce, for serving

1. Pat shrimp dry with paper towels. Mix together shrimp, chipotle chile powder, garlic powder, and ½ teaspoon of the salt until combined.

2. Heat oil in a large nonstick skillet over medium-high. Add shrimp, and cook, stirring occasionally, until heated through, about 1 minute.

3. Stir together coleslaw mix, red onion, cilantro, lime juice, mayonnaise, sugar, and remaining ½ teaspoon salt in a medium bowl.

4. Top each toasted tortilla with about ½ cup coleslaw mixture and ⅓ cup cooked shrimp. Serve tacos with lime wedges and hot sauce. Garnish with cilantro.

BUILD YOUR OWN BOWL
Make this recipe with other grains like quinoa or farro. Or turn it into a salad by swapping out the rice for chopped romaine lettuce.

Blackened Shrimp Rice Bowl

ACTIVE 20 MIN. - TOTAL 20 MIN.
SERVES 4

- 2 ears yellow corn
- 1 large poblano chile
- 2/3 cup plain whole-milk strained yogurt (such as Greek yogurt)
- 1/3 cup fresh flat-leaf parsley leaves
- 1/4 cup chopped fresh chives
- 1 1/2 tsp. kosher salt, divided
- 1 lb. extra-large shrimp, peeled and deveined
- 2 tsp. chili powder
- 1 tsp. ground cumin
- 1/2 tsp. garlic powder
- 1/4 tsp. black pepper
- 2 Tbsp. extra-virgin olive oil
- 3 cups cooked white rice
- 1 (14-oz.) can black beans, drained and rinsed
- 2 avocados, halved, peeled, and chopped

1. Preheat grill to high (500°F and up). Place corn and poblano on oiled grates; grill, uncovered, until char marks form, turning occasionally, about 10 minutes.
2. Remove and discard skin, seeds, and stem of poblano. Place in a blender with yogurt, parsley, chives, and 1 teaspoon of the salt. Blend 1 minute. Cut corn from cob; reserve kernels.
3. Toss together shrimp, chili powder, cumin, garlic powder, pepper, and remaining 1/2 teaspoon salt in a bowl. Thread shrimp onto skewers; drizzle with oil. Place on oiled grates; grill, covered, until charred and cooked, 2 minutes per side.
4. Divide rice among 4 serving bowls. Top with shrimp, beans, avocados, and reserved corn kernels. Drizzle with dressing.

Lean and Green

An easy and refreshing blender soup for the most sweltering days

Green Tomato Gazpacho

ACTIVE 15 MIN. · TOTAL 45 MIN.

SERVES 6

- 6 unripe green tomatoes, chopped (about 8 cups)
- 1 English cucumber, seeded and chopped (about 2 cups)
- 1 green bell pepper, chopped (about 1¼ cups)
- ½ cup chopped white onion (from 1 medium onion)
- ½ cup chopped mixed tender fresh herbs (such as parsley, cilantro, basil, tarragon, mint, and dill)
- 3 garlic cloves, smashed
- 1¾ tsp. kosher salt, divided
- ½ cup vegetable broth
- ½ cup extra-virgin olive oil
- ¼ cup white balsamic vinegar
- ¼ cup fresh lime juice (from 2 limes)

  Toppings: Greek yogurt, diced Fresno chile, fresh cilantro (see variations at right)

1. Stir together first 6 ingredients and 1½ teaspoons of the salt in a large bowl until thoroughly combined. Let stand at room temperature for 30 minutes.
2. Stir broth, oil, vinegar, and lime juice into tomato mixture. Working in batches, process in a blender until smooth, 45 seconds to 1 minute. Transfer to a bowl. Stir in remaining ¼ teaspoon salt. Serve immediately, or cover and store in refrigerator up to 24 hours. Top gazpacho as desired.

CALORIES: **246** – CARBS: **18 G** – FAT: **19 G**

3 More Creative Toppings

1. Chopped cooked bacon, fresh corn kernels, and fresh chives

- - - - - - - - - -

2. Olive oil, fresh basil leaves, and chopped pistachios

- - - - - - - - - -

3. Thinly sliced radishes, chopped fresh dill, and toasted sliced almonds

- - - - - - - - - -

One Chill Pie

Cold, sweet, and a little bit salty, this make-ahead recipe is everything you want in a summer dessert

SMOOTH FINISH
To make neat, round dollops of whipped cream, use an ice cream or cookie scoop.

Chocolate-Peanut Butter Icebox Pie

ACTIVE 20 MIN. · TOTAL 50 MIN., PLUS 8 HOURS CHILLING
SERVES 8

22	peanut butter sandwich cookies (such as Nutter Butter, from 1 [16-oz.] pkg.)
5	Tbsp. butter, melted
2	Tbsp. cornstarch
3	large egg yolks
1	(14-oz.) can sweetened condensed milk
1	cup whole milk
2	tsp. vanilla extract
¾	cup 60% cacao bittersweet chocolate chips (4½ oz.)
2	cups Best-Ever Whipped Cream (recipe, page 188)
	Chopped chocolate-covered peanuts

1. Preheat oven to 375°F. Lightly coat a 9-inch pie pan with cooking spray. Place cookies in a food processor; process until finely ground, 45 seconds to 1 minute. Measure 2¾ cups cookie crumbs into a medium bowl; discard any remaining crumbs. Stir melted butter into crumbs in bowl until combined. Press mixture into bottom and up sides of prepared pan. Bake in preheated oven until lightly browned, 8 to 10 minutes. Let cool completely on a wire rack, about 20 minutes.

2. During final 10 minutes of cooling time, whisk together cornstarch and egg yolks in a medium saucepan until smooth. Gradually whisk in sweetened condensed milk, whole milk, and vanilla extract until combined. Bring to a simmer over medium, whisking constantly. Continue simmering, whisking constantly, until thickened to a puddinglike consistency, about 2 minutes. Remove from heat; whisk in chocolate chips until melted and smooth, about 1 minute. Pour through a fine mesh strainer into cooled crust, and discard solids. Smooth pie top. Refrigerate, uncovered, until set, at least 8 hours or up to 2 days.

3. Top pie with whipped cream dollops around edge, and garnish with chopped chocolate-covered peanuts.

Irresistible Fried Pickles

Company's coming? Meet your new signature appetizer

Crispy Fried Pickle Spears with Ranch Dipping Sauce

ACTIVE 25 MIN. - TOTAL 25 MIN.
SERVES 6

- ¼ cup mayonnaise
- ¼ cup sour cream
- 1 Tbsp. chopped fresh chives
- 1 tsp. white wine vinegar
- ½ tsp. dried dill
- 1 cup plus 2 Tbsp. whole buttermilk, divided
- 3½ tsp. hot sauce, divided
- 1¼ tsp. kosher salt, divided
- 1 tsp. garlic powder, divided
- ¾ tsp. black pepper, divided
  Vegetable oil
- 1½ cups coarse stone-ground yellow cornmeal
- ½ cup all-purpose flour
- 1 (16-oz.) jar dill pickle spears
  Flaky sea salt
  Paprika

1. Whisk together mayonnaise, sour cream, chives, vinegar, dried dill, 2 tablespoons of the buttermilk, ½ teaspoon of the hot sauce, ¼ teaspoon of the kosher salt, ½ teaspoon of the garlic powder, and ¼ teaspoon of the pepper in a small bowl until combined. Cover and refrigerate until ready to use (up to 7 days).
2. Pour oil in a large Dutch oven to a depth of 1 inch. Heat oil to 375°F over medium-high.
3. Meanwhile, whisk together remaining 1 cup buttermilk and 3 teaspoons hot sauce in a shallow dish. Whisk together cornmeal, flour, and remaining 1 teaspoon kosher salt, ½ teaspoon garlic powder, and ½ teaspoon pepper in a separate shallow dish. Drain pickles; pat dry using paper towels. Cut each pickle spear in half lengthwise. Working in small batches, dip pickles in buttermilk mixture, and then dredge in cornmeal mixture, pressing gently to fully coat. Place on a large rimmed baking sheet.
4. Working in batches of about 4, add breaded pickle spears to hot oil; fry, turning as needed, until golden brown, about 2 minutes. Transfer to a paper towel-lined plate using a slotted spoon; drain. Garnish with flaky sea salt and paprika. Serve immediately with reserved sauce.

Chowing Down

Spicy, sweet, and tangy, this Southern relish enlivens so many dishes

CREATED FROM summer's garden bounty, chowchow is a classic condiment that's used to jazz up everything from veggies to fish cakes. There are several origin stories for the relish: Some believe that it traveled to the South from Canada with the Acadians, while others suggest that it may have come from China. I speculate on none of that because, for me, chowchow harks back to one person: my friend Charlotte Lyons, who worked in the neon orange *Ebony* magazine test kitchen for more than 25 years.

When I tasted her version, it was love at first nibble. As a historian who is curious about African American culinary matters, I immediately wanted to know about the recipe and her connection to it. Lyons grew up in Atlanta's Old Fourth Ward, and her grandparents lived right across the street. "My grandfather worked for one of the people who owned a bus company that became part of MARTA [the Metropolitan Atlanta Rapid Transit Authority], and he was allowed to plant a garden in the area where the buses were kept," she says. "He had an extensive plot, and I'd help him tend it. We had all the traditional things—green beans, tomatoes, watermelons, and greens."

At harvesttime, Lyons and her mother, grandmother, and great-grandmother put up the veggies for the winter. "As the oldest grandchild and the one who loved to cook, I would always help," she recalls. "One of the last things we made each season was chowchow. It became a family specialty. The recipe originated with my great-grandmother (Grandma Jessie) and was passed down through my grandmother (Eva) to my mother (Greenie-Mae) and finally to me. Each of us put our own spin on it."

Lyons' version is the perfect blend of sweet and hot, and it goes well with just about everything. She once marketed it as Greenie's Country Kitchen Chow Chow and managed to get Walmart interested. I never thought she'd share her cherished recipe, but she did—enjoy!
–Jessica B. Harris

Charlotte's Chowchow

ACTIVE 1 HOUR, 15 MIN. - TOTAL 1 HOUR, 20 MIN., PLUS 18 HOURS STANDING
MAKES 5 (1-PT.) JARS

- 1 small (2-lb.) head cabbage, coarsely chopped (about 10 cups)
- 5 small green heirloom tomatoes, chopped (about 5 cups)
- 2 white onions, chopped (about 4 cups)
- 1 small green bell pepper, chopped (about 1 cup)
- 1 small red bell pepper, chopped (about 1 cup)
- ¼ cup pickling salt
- 5 cups white vinegar
- 3 cups granulated sugar
- 1 Tbsp. ground allspice
- ½ Tbsp. dry mustard
- 2 to 3 tsp. dried pico de pájaro chiles, crushed, to taste (or 2 to 3 tsp. crushed red pepper, to taste)

1. Place chopped cabbage, green tomatoes, onions, and green and red bell peppers in a nonreactive container. Sprinkle with pickling salt, and toss to combine. Cover and let stand at room temperature at least 6 hours, or chill in refrigerator up to 12 hours.
2. Drain mixture well; rinse and drain again. Set aside.
3. Prepare a boiling-water canner. Heat 5 (1-pint) glass jars in simmering water until ready to use. Do not boil. Wash lids in warm, soapy water, and dry well. Set bands aside.
4. Stir together vinegar, sugar, allspice, dry mustard, and chiles in a large stockpot. Cover and bring to a boil over high. Uncover; reduce heat to medium-low, and simmer, undisturbed, 10 minutes. Add vegetable mixture, and stir to combine. Cover and bring to a boil over medium-high. Uncover; reduce heat to medium-low, and simmer, undisturbed, 10 minutes.
5. Remove mixture from heat, and ladle evenly into hot sterilized jars, filling to ¼ inch from top. Remove air bubbles, and wipe jar rims. Center lids on jars, and screw on bands; adjust to fingertip tight. Lower jars into boiling-water canner, and process, covered, for 10 minutes. Turn off heat, uncover, and let jars stand 5 minutes. Remove jars from canner, and let stand 12 to 24 hours. Check lids for seal (they should not flex when center is pressed). Store in a cool, dark, dry place for up to 18 months.

And Here's How to Use It

From seafood to salad, chowchow lends itself to experimenting

APPETIZERS Add a dollop to deviled eggs, blend it with sour cream and cream cheese to make a smooth and tangy dip, or serve it with crackers and goat cheese.

MAIN DISHES This relish is a good match for rich or fried proteins, from burgers and hot dogs to fried chicken and fish. It adds a special zing to a chopped barbecue sandwich.

SIDE DISHES Greens with chowchow and cornbread is a familiar combination in many parts of the South. This relish also brightens up bean dishes, from field pea salads to soupy bowls of pintos. Stir a spoonful or two into coleslaw or potato salad.

Field Day

Whether you go for black-eyed, lady, crowder, or zipper, this recipe will put any kind of summer peas to good use

SUMMER SALAD

FRESH FIELD PEA DIP

Marinated Field Pea Relish

ACTIVE 5 MIN. · TOTAL 5 MIN.

SERVES 6

Bring 2 Tbsp. **extra-virgin olive oil;** 1 Tbsp. **white wine vinegar;** 1 tsp. **granulated sugar;** and ¼ tsp. each **kosher salt, black pepper,** and **crushed red pepper** to a simmer in a small saucepan over medium. Stir in 2 cups cooked, cooled **field peas;** 1 cup chopped **cherry tomatoes;** 2 Tbsp. thinly sliced **shallot;** 2 Tbsp. finely chopped **dill;** and 1 Tbsp. chopped drained **capers.** Cook, stirring occasionally, until warm, about 3 minutes. Remove from heat. Serve warm, or cool completely (about 30 minutes) and serve at room temperature.

Summer Salad

Toss relish with arugula and feta for a light lunch.

Fresh Field Pea Dip

Serve it with chips for a happy hour snack.

Chicken with Field Pea Relish

Pair the marinated field peas with your favorite grilled meat or seafood.

Field Pea Pasta

(Photo, page 6)
Fold the relish into hot cooked linguine, and top each dish with shaved Parmesan and fresh basil.

CHICKEN WITH FIELD
PEA RELISH

COOKING SCHOOL

STIR UP SOME NEW FLAVORS

Four easy additions

COFFEE
Add 2 Tbsp. **instant espresso granules** *to whipping cream mixture before beating.*

PEANUT BUTTER
Add ¼ cup **creamy peanut butter** *to whipping cream mixture before beating.*

ORANGE
Add 2 Tbsp. grated **orange zest** *to whipping cream mixture before beating.*

BERRY
Add ¼ cup **seedless jam** *of choice to whipping cream mixture before beating.*

The Scoop on Whipped Cream
Follow these tips for results so dreamy you'll want to eat it straight from the bowl

1 KNOW YOUR DAIRY
Fat is the difference between heavy whipping cream (also called heavy cream) and whipping cream (aka light whipping cream). The first has at least 36% milk fat; the latter has 30% to 36%. More fat means stiffer peaks.

2 KEEP IT COLD
Whipped cream is best when made with cold dairy and a chilled metal bowl and whisk. Or skip prechilling, and use a food processor. It makes dense whipped cream quickly—but keep an eye on it, or you'll have butter.

3 MAKE IT LAST
Whip up everything a few hours in advance, and thank yourself later. Powdered sugar contains cornstarch, which helps stabilize the cream. Beat in a tablespoon for each cup of cream; chill until ready to serve.

Best-Ever Whipped Cream
ACTIVE 5 MIN. - TOTAL 5 MIN.
MAKES ABOUT 4 CUPS

Beat 2 cups **heavy whipping cream**, 1 tsp. **vanilla bean paste**, and ¼ cup plus 2 Tbsp. **powdered sugar** with a stand mixer fitted with a whisk attachment on medium speed until frothy, 1 minute. Increase speed to medium-high; continue beating until stiff peaks form, about 1 to 2 more minutes. Use immediately, or chill in an airtight container up to 4 hours.

September

A Roux Awakening

It takes practice and patience to replicate a beloved family recipe, and when that dish is gumbo, it requires all of that plus laser focus–and the will to get it right

I'M NOT GOING TO PRETEND for one moment that I'm qualified to tell you how to make roux or gumbo. I am neither Creole nor Cajun, but 38% of my DNA comes from Western Europe, which includes France–from whence came culinary techniques that greatly influenced both aforementioned groups. For you folks who are unfamiliar with roux, it is simply a mixture of equal parts fat and flour cooked to varying hues and used as a basis for sauces, gumbo in particular. The recipe is simple, but the process can be nerve-racking.

My precious mother-in-law, Ouida (pronounced WEE-duh) Rasberry, cooked gumbo for special occasions or anytime she could get her hands on some fresh Mississippi Gulf Coast shrimp. Served over hot rice, it was always the most requested meal for family birthdays.

Ouida's gumbo was top-notch, and as far as I knew, her recipe (which was included in a handwritten cookbook that she gave me for Christmas several years ago) was all I ever needed to know. Her mother showed her how to make it, and she passed it down to me. I've experimented and fine-tuned it over the years, but the base of her recipe remains. Both of our methods of cooking gumbo are part Creole (tomato-based) and part Cajun (roux-based).

Sooner than I would have liked, I became the matriarch of the Rasberry clan. Ouida died at the age of 97, but I had been practicing her recipe for years because her health was failing. It was a daunting task that terrified me when I stood over an iron skillet and started making the one thing that would turn my gumbo into something disastrous or legendary: the roux. The goal is to cook the flour and oil together–slowly, patiently, lovingly, confidently, and attentively–until it resembles the color of an old copper penny or darker. There's a fine line between dark enough and disaster. Only instinct, sight, and smell (which come with experience) can distinguish between the two.

The first time I attempted to make a roux, I scrounged around in my wallet and pulled out the oldest-looking penny in there. It was from 1972 and had obviously been around the U.S.A. a few times. You should have seen me eyeballing that coin in my left hand over the skillet and stirring with a wooden spoon in my right hand. The phone rang. I dropped the penny and the spoon to answer it. I swear it was for only a few seconds. The roux scorched and set off the smoke alarm. I pitched a hissy fit, stomped my feet, grabbed the pan, ran into the yard, and poured out the catastrophe. I wiped my eyes, fanned the smoke, and then pulled on my "Weeder" pants to start over.

That was a long time ago. I now have gallons of gumbo and dozens of skillets of (nearly) perfect roux under my cooking belt. I've learned that it can be unforgiving, selfish, and demanding. It has to be the center of attention, or it will give you a very roux awakening.
–Karen Clark Rasberry

Shrimp-and-Sausage Gumbo

ACTIVE 1 HOUR, 55 MIN. - TOTAL 1 HOUR, 55 MIN.
SERVES 6

- ½ cup plus 1 tsp. vegetable oil, divided
- 1 lb. hickory-smoked sausage (such as Conecuh Original), sliced ¼ inch thick
- 4 cups sliced fresh okra (from 1½ lb. okra pods) or frozen cut okra (from 1 [16-oz.] pkg.), thawed
- 1 large onion, chopped (2 cups)
- 1 (14½-oz.) can diced tomatoes
- 2 Tbsp. Worcestershire sauce
- 1 tsp. Old Bay seasoning
- ½ tsp. black pepper
- ½ tsp. garlic powder
- 3 fresh bay leaves
- 8 cups chicken broth, divided
- 3 Tbsp. tomato paste
- ½ cup all-purpose flour
- 2 lb. medium shrimp, peeled and deveined
- Hot cooked rice and crackers or garlic toast, for serving

1. Heat 1 teaspoon of the oil in a large stockpot over medium; add sausage, and cook, stirring occasionally, until fat renders and sausage is lightly browned, about 5 minutes. Add okra and onion; cook, stirring often, until vegetables are softened, about 3 minutes. Pour off any excess drippings in stockpot.

2. Add tomatoes, Worcestershire, Old Bay seasoning, pepper, garlic powder, bay leaves, and 7 cups of the chicken broth to sausage and vegetables in stockpot. Bring to a boil over medium-high; reduce heat to medium-low, and simmer, undisturbed, 20 to 30 minutes.

3. While tomato mixture simmers, whisk tomato paste and remaining 1 cup chicken broth in a small bowl or liquid measuring cup; set aside.

4. Combine flour and remaining ½ cup oil in a medium skillet; stir using a wooden spoon to remove any lumps. Cook over medium, stirring constantly, until roux is the color of an old penny, 20 to 30 minutes, adjusting heat as needed to maintain a gentle simmer.

5. Add tomato paste-broth mixture to roux in skillet, stirring until smooth. Add mixture to stockpot, stirring until combined. Bring to a boil over medium; reduce heat to low, and simmer, stirring often, until slightly thickened, about 45 minutes.

6. Add shrimp to stockpot, and cook over low, undisturbed, until shrimp are opaque, about 5 minutes. Remove and discard bay leaves. Serve over rice with crackers or garlic toast alongside a green salad.

STUFFED HAM-AND-
CHEESE CROISSANT
CASSEROLE

Breakfast Is Served

What's the secret to getting everyone around the table in the morning? A casserole!

Stuffed Ham-and-Cheese Croissant Casserole

ACTIVE 20 MIN. - TOTAL 1 HOUR, 10 MIN., PLUS 8 HOURS CHILLING

SERVES 10

- 10 (1¼-oz.) deli smoked ham slices (¼ inch thick)
- 10 mini croissants
- 10 (½-oz.) Swiss cheese slices
- 6 large eggs
- 2 cups heavy whipping cream
- 2 tsp. Dijon mustard
  Fresh thyme sprigs

1. Microwave ham slices between paper towels on a microwavable plate on HIGH 45 seconds. Blot with paper towels to remove excess moisture.
2. Split croissants open with a serrated knife. Top bottom half of each croissant with 1 ham slice and 1 Swiss cheese slice (folding ham and cheese to fit, if needed). Cover each with top half of croissant. Place stuffed croissants in a lightly greased (with cooking spray) 13- x 9-inch baking dish.
3. Whisk together eggs, cream, and mustard in a large bowl. Pour mixture slowly over stuffed croissants. Cover with plastic wrap, and refrigerate 8 hours or overnight.
4. Remove dish from refrigerator. Preheat oven to 350°F. Remove plastic wrap; bake until golden brown and a knife inserted in center comes out clean, 40 to 45 minutes, covering with aluminum foil during the last 15 minutes to prevent overbrowning. Garnish with thyme sprigs.

Breakfast Chilaquiles Casserole

(Photo, page 194)

ACTIVE 20 MIN. - TOTAL 45 MIN.

SERVES 6

- ¾ lb. fresh Mexican chorizo, casings removed
- 1 yellow onion, chopped (about 1 cup)
- 2 (8-oz.) pkg. red chile enchilada sauce (such as Frontera)
- 14 corn tostadas (from 1 [12.4-oz.] pkg., such as Olé)
- 1 (8-oz.) pkg. preshredded Mexican 4-cheese blend
- 2 Tbsp. butter
- 6 large eggs
  Toppings: chopped fresh cilantro, diced avocado, thinly sliced radishes, crumbled queso fresco, sour cream, salsa

1. Preheat oven to 375°F. Cook chorizo and onion in a large skillet over medium-high, stirring often to break up sausage, until cooked through and onion is tender, 6 to 8 minutes. Stir enchilada sauce into sausage mixture.
2. Arrange 7 of the corn tostadas in bottom of a 13- x 9-inch baking dish, breaking to fit. Top with half of the sausage mixture; sprinkle evenly with half of the shredded cheese. Repeat layers. Bake in preheated oven until cheese is melted and sauce is bubbling, about 20 minutes.
3. Meanwhile, heat butter in a large skillet over medium-high until bubbling. Carefully crack eggs, in batches, into frying pan 1 at a time. Cook until whites are set but yolks are still runny, 3 to 4 minutes. (For firmer yolks, flip eggs and cook 1 minute longer.)
4. Top hot casserole with fried eggs, and serve immediately with desired toppings.

A Better Breakfast Casserole

Simple ways to improve your favorite recipe

Set Aside the Streusel

If your dish has a streusel topping, mix the ingredients with melted butter until combined and let it stand for 30 minutes. This will give the dry ingredients more time to absorb the wet ingredients so you can break up the mixture into small and large chunks for the topping.

Use Full-Fat Dairy

Breakfast casseroles should be indulgent. Do not substitute low-fat milk for heavy cream (the custard will be watery) or cut back on the cheese. If you want to make a casserole healthier, look for recipes that are loaded with fruits or vegetables—or make it meatless.

Chill Thoroughly

For a recipe that includes bread, make sure that it spends enough time in the refrigerator so it can fully absorb the dairy-egg mixture. Don't rush this step, or you'll prevent it from baking evenly, which might make the casserole dry in spots. However, you also shouldn't let it sit too long before baking, because you don't want it to be soggy.

BREAKFAST CHILAQUILES
CASSEROLE (PAGE 193)

DEEP-DISH LOADED
HASH BROWN
CASSEROLE
(PAGE 197)

BAKED ALMOND FRENCH
TOAST WITH MAPLE-
BLACKBERRY SYRUP

Baked Almond French Toast with Maple-Blackberry Syrup

ACTIVE 25 MIN. - TOTAL 1 HOUR, 20 MIN.,
PLUS 8 HOURS CHILLING
SERVES 10

- 1 (8-oz.) pkg. cream cheese, softened
- ½ cup packed light brown sugar
- 2 tsp. vanilla extract
- ¾ tsp. almond extract
- ¼ tsp. kosher salt
- 8 large eggs
- 2 cups whole milk
- 1 cup heavy whipping cream
- 14 cups (1-inch) brioche bread cubes (16 oz.)
- ¾ cup sliced almonds
- 2 Tbsp. granulated sugar
- 1 cup pure maple syrup
- ¼ cup seedless blackberry jam
  Fresh blackberries and strawberries, for serving

1. Beat together cream cheese and brown sugar with a heavy-duty stand mixer on medium speed using the paddle attachment until smooth and creamy. Beat in vanilla extract, almond extract, and salt until well incorporated. Add eggs, 1 at a time, beating until well blended. Gradually add milk and cream, beating at low speed until well incorporated.
2. Place bread cubes in a lightly greased (with cooking spray) 13- x 9-inch baking dish. Slowly pour egg mixture evenly over bread cubes. Cover with plastic wrap, and refrigerate at least 8 hours or overnight.
3. Remove dish from refrigerator. Preheat oven to 350°F. Remove plastic wrap, and sprinkle casserole evenly with almonds and granulated sugar. Bake until golden brown and set in the middle, 50 to 55 minutes, covering with aluminum foil during the last 15 minutes.
4. Stir together maple syrup and jam in a small saucepan, and cook over medium-low until heated through and jam has melted and combined. Serve casserole warm with warm blackberry syrup. Top with fresh blackberries and strawberries.

Deep-Dish Loaded Hash Brown Casserole

(Photo, page 195)
ACTIVE 20 MIN. - TOTAL 1 HOUR, 30 MIN.
SERVES 12

- 8 thick-cut bacon slices
- ½ cup chopped sweet onion (from 1 small onion)
- 1 (32-oz.) pkg. frozen hash browns, thawed
- 10 oz. sharp Cheddar cheese, shredded (about 2½ cups), divided
- 1½ tsp. kosher salt, divided
- ½ tsp. black pepper, divided
- 6 large eggs
- 1 (8-oz.) container sour cream
- 1 cup whole milk
  Halved cherry tomatoes and chopped scallions, for garnish

1. Preheat oven to 350°F. Cook bacon in a large skillet over medium until crispy; transfer to a plate lined with paper towels to drain. Reserve 1 tablespoon bacon drippings in skillet. Add onion to skillet. Cook, stirring often, until tender, about 5 minutes. Remove from heat. Crumble 5 slices of the cooked bacon; reserve 3 slices.
2. Stir crumbled bacon, hash browns, 2 cups of the shredded cheese, ½ teaspoon of the salt, and ¼ teaspoon of the pepper into cooked onion in skillet until combined. Spoon mixture into a lightly greased (with cooking spray) 13- x 9-inch baking dish.
3. Whisk together eggs, sour cream, milk, and remaining 1 teaspoon salt and ¼ teaspoon pepper in a large bowl. Carefully pour egg mixture over hash brown mixture. Cover with aluminum foil, and bake in preheated oven 40 minutes. Remove aluminum foil, and sprinkle evenly with remaining ½ cup shredded cheese. Return to oven, and continue to bake until cheese is melted and casserole is bubbly, 10 to 15 minutes. Remove from oven, and let stand 10 minutes.
4. Crumble remaining 3 slices of bacon, and sprinkle over top of casserole. Garnish with halved cherry tomatoes and chopped scallions before serving.

Chocolate Chip Pancake Bake with Cinnamon-Pecan Streusel

(Photo, page 198)
ACTIVE 30 MIN. - TOTAL 1 HOUR, 30 MIN.,
PLUS 8 HOURS CHILLING
SERVES 12

PANCAKES
- 2⅔ cups all-purpose flour
- 2 Tbsp. packed light brown sugar
- 2 tsp. baking powder
- 1½ tsp. baking soda
- 1½ tsp. kosher salt
- 3 cups whole buttermilk
- 3 large eggs
- 6 Tbsp. butter, melted, plus more for griddle and skillet
- 1 cup semisweet chocolate chips, plus 2 Tbsp. for garnish

CASSEROLE
- 6 large eggs
- 1½ cups heavy whipping cream
- 1 cup whole milk
- ¼ cup packed light brown sugar
- 2 tsp. vanilla extract

STREUSEL
- 1 cup coarsely chopped pecans
- ½ cup all-purpose flour
- ¼ cup packed light brown sugar
- ½ tsp. ground cinnamon
- ¼ tsp. kosher salt
- ¼ cup butter, melted

ADDITIONAL INGREDIENT
  Warm maple syrup

1. Prepare the Pancakes: Stir together flour, brown sugar, baking powder, baking soda, and salt in a large bowl. Whisk together buttermilk and eggs in a medium bowl; gradually stir buttermilk mixture into flour mixture. Gently stir in melted butter (batter will be lumpy). Very gently stir in 1 cup of the chocolate chips. Let stand 5 minutes.
2. Pour about ¼ cup batter for each Pancake onto a hot (350°F) buttered griddle. Cook until tops are covered with bubbles and edges look dry, 3 to 4 minutes. Turn and cook until golden brown, about 3 minutes more. (You should have about 25 Pancakes.)
3. Generously butter a 12-inch cast-iron ovenproof skillet or a 13- x 9-inch baking dish. Reserve 2 Pancakes. Shingle remaining Pancakes in a circle

Continued on page 199

CHOCOLATE CHIP
PANCAKE BAKE WITH
CINNAMON-PECAN
STREUSEL (PAGE 197)

Continued from page 197

in skillet. Cut each reserved Pancake in half; place in center.

4. Prepare the Casserole: Whisk together eggs, cream, milk, brown sugar, and vanilla in a large bowl. Slowly pour egg mixture over Pancakes. Cover with plastic wrap, and refrigerate at least 8 hours or up to overnight.

5. Prepare the Streusel: Stir together pecans, flour, brown sugar, cinnamon, and salt in a medium bowl. Stir in melted butter until mixture is combined. Let stand 30 minutes. Remove skillet from refrigerator. Preheat oven to 350°F.

6. Uncover Casserole; sprinkle Streusel mixture over the top. Bake, uncovered, in preheated oven until center is set, 50 to 55 minutes. Garnish with the remaining chocolate chips; let stand 5 minutes before serving. Drizzle each serving with warm maple syrup.

Sausage-and-Spinach Breakfast Casserole with Cornmeal Biscuits

ACTIVE 25 MIN. - TOTAL 1 HOUR, 5 MIN.
SERVES 10

CASSEROLE
- 1 lb. smoked sausage, chopped (such as Conecuh)
- ¼ cup butter
- ¼ cup all-purpose flour
- 1 cup whole milk
- 1 cup heavy whipping cream
- 1 tsp. chopped fresh thyme
- ¼ tsp. kosher salt
- ¼ tsp. black pepper
- 8 oz. Gruyère cheese, shredded (about 2 cups)
- 4 oz. sharp Cheddar cheese, shredded (about 1 cup)
- 10 oz. fresh baby spinach

BISCUITS
- 1¼ cups all-purpose flour
- ⅔ cup finely ground yellow cornmeal
- 1½ tsp. baking powder
- ¼ tsp. baking soda
- ¼ tsp. kosher salt
- ¼ cup chilled butter, cut into small pieces
- 4 oz. sharp Cheddar cheese, shredded (about 1 cup)
- 1 cup whole buttermilk

SAUSAGE-AND-SPINACH BREAKFAST CASSEROLE WITH CORNMEAL BISCUITS

1. Prepare the Casserole: Preheat oven to 400°F. Cook sausage in a large skillet over medium-high until browned, 8 to 10 minutes. Transfer to a plate lined with paper towels, and set aside.

2. Melt butter in a Dutch oven over low, and whisk in flour until smooth. Cook, whisking constantly, 1 minute. Gradually whisk in milk, cream, thyme, salt, and pepper. Cook over medium, whisking often, until thickened and bubbly, 4 to 5 minutes. Stir in Gruyère and Cheddar cheeses until melted and smooth. Stir in spinach and cooked sausage until completely incorporated. Remove from heat, and spoon sausage-spinach mixture into a lightly greased (with cooking spray) 13- x 9-inch baking dish.

3. Prepare the Biscuits: Combine flour, cornmeal, baking powder, baking soda, and salt in a large bowl. Cut in butter pieces with a pastry blender or 2 knives until mixture resembles coarse meal. Stir cheese. Stir in buttermilk until just combined. Drop batter by heaping 2 tablespoons evenly over Casserole.

4. Bake in preheated oven until Biscuits are golden and Casserole is bubbly, 25 to 30 minutes. Let stand 10 minutes before serving.

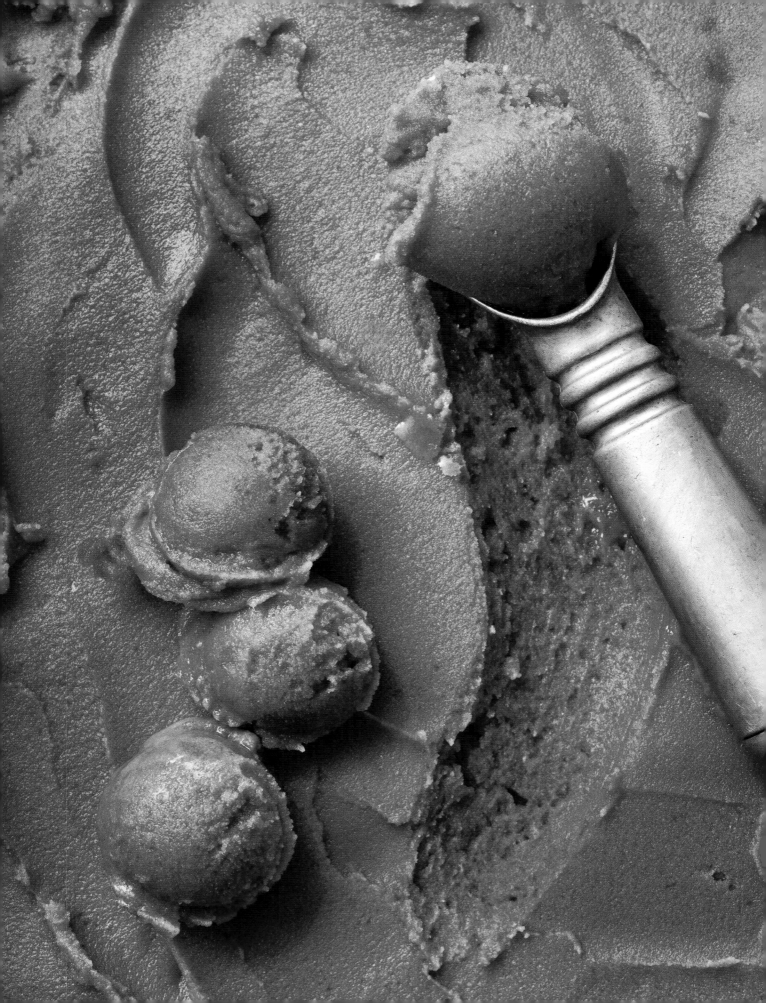

Muscadine Magic

The Southeast's native grape is in its prime right now.
Enjoy it scoop by frosty scoop this season

Know Your Grapes

The difference between two common types

Muscadine

Large, round, thick-skinned, and very sweet, these grapes come in shades ranging from black to green-gold. Vines grow wild throughout the Southeast and also on farms, bearing fruit from late summer to early autumn.

Scuppernong

Pronounced "SCUP-per-nong," this bronze-skinned muscadine is North Carolina's official state fruit. Slightly acidic in flavor, the grapes are tasty eaten out of hand and often used to make jelly.

Muscadine Sorbet

ACTIVE 15 MIN. - TOTAL 2 HOURS, 30 MIN., PLUS 4 HOURS FREEZING

SERVES 6

Cook 1 cup **water** and ½ cup **granulated sugar** in a medium saucepan over medium, whisking often, until dissolved, 2 to 3 minutes. Remove from heat. Process 8 cups (32 oz.) **muscadines** in a blender until almost smooth, 15 to 30 seconds. Pour through a fine mesh strainer into a large bowl, pressing on solids, to yield 2 cups juice. Discard solids. Whisk sugar mixture and 1 tablespoon **fresh lemon juice** into muscadine juice; chill, uncovered, until cold, 2 hours. Pour mixture into freezer bowl of a 1½-quart electric ice-cream maker; proceed according to manufacturer's instructions. Transfer mixture to an airtight freezer-safe container; freeze at least 4 hours or up to 1 month.

Apples to Apples

From Gala to Golden Delicious, autumn delivers a bounty of sweet varieties.
The seasonal star shines in these nine recipes

Apple-Spice Muffins with Oat Streusel

(Photo, page 204)

ACTIVE 15 MIN. - TOTAL 40 MIN.,
PLUS 30 MIN. COOLING

MAKES 12

MUFFINS
- ½ cup unsalted butter, softened
- ¾ cup granulated sugar
- ½ cup sour cream
- 1 tsp. vanilla extract
- 2 large eggs
- 1¾ cups all-purpose flour
- 1½ tsp. apple pie spice or pumpkin pie spice
- 1 tsp. baking powder
- 1 tsp. baking soda
- ½ tsp. kosher salt
- ¼ cup whole buttermilk
- 1 large (8-oz.) peeled Fuji apple, half chopped (¾ cup) and half grated (¾ cup)

STREUSEL
- ⅓ cup all-purpose flour
- ⅓ cup uncooked old-fashioned rolled oats
- ⅓ cup packed light brown sugar
- ⅓ cup chopped pecans
- ½ tsp. apple pie spice or pumpkin pie spice
- ¼ tsp. kosher salt
- 3 Tbsp. unsalted butter, softened

GLAZE
- 1 cup powdered sugar
- 2 Tbsp. apple cider

1. Prepare the Muffins: Preheat oven to 350°F. Line a 12-cup muffin tray with paper liners.
2. Beat butter and sugar with a stand mixer fitted with a paddle attachment on medium-high speed until light and fluffy, 3 to 4 minutes. Add sour cream, vanilla, and eggs, and beat on medium speed until just combined, about 30 seconds.
3. Whisk together flour, apple pie spice, baking powder, baking soda, and salt in a medium bowl. With mixer on low speed, gradually add flour mixture alternately with buttermilk, beginning and ending with flour mixture. Fold in chopped and grated apple until evenly combined. Spoon batter into prepared muffin cups (about 5 tablespoons batter per cup); set aside.
4. Prepare the Streusel: Whisk together flour, oats, brown sugar, pecans, apple pie spice, and salt in a medium bowl. Stir in butter until combined and crumbly. Top each filled muffin cup with about 1½ tablespoons of Streusel.
5. Bake in preheated oven until a wooden pick inserted in center comes out clean, 25 to 28 minutes. Cool in tray 10 minutes; transfer to a wire rack to cool completely, about 20 minutes.
6. Prepare the Glaze: Whisk together powdered sugar and apple cider in a small bowl until smooth. Drizzle over muffins.

Apple-Blackberry Cobbler

ACTIVE 15 MIN. - TOTAL 1 HOUR, 15 MIN.

SERVES 8

- 6 large Gala apples (3 lb. total), peeled and sliced (9 cups)
- 2 (6-oz.) containers fresh blackberries (about 3 cups)
- ½ cup packed light brown sugar
- ¼ cup cornstarch
- 1 tsp. ground cinnamon
- 1 tsp. grated lemon zest plus 2 Tbsp. fresh juice (from 1 lemon)
- 1½ cups all-purpose flour
- ½ cup granulated sugar
- 1½ tsp. baking powder
- ½ tsp. kosher salt
- ½ cup cold unsalted butter
- ⅔ cup whole buttermilk
- 2 Tbsp. sliced almonds
  Sweetened whipped cream, for serving

1. Preheat oven to 375°F. Combine apples, blackberries, brown sugar, cornstarch, cinnamon, and lemon zest and juice; toss together gently. Spoon into a 13- x 9-inch baking dish coated with cooking spray.
2. Whisk together flour, granulated sugar, baking powder, and salt in a medium bowl. Grate butter with large holes of a box grater into flour mixture; toss to combine. Stir in buttermilk just until dry ingredients are moistened. Drop 8 (¼-cup) scoops of dough over filling; sprinkle with almonds.
3. Bake in preheated oven until bubbly and browned on top, 45 to 55 minutes, covering with aluminum foil halfway through to prevent overbrowning. Cool 15 minutes before serving. Top with whipped cream.

Glazed Apple Tart

(Photo, page 205)

ACTIVE 10 MIN. - TOTAL 45 MIN.

SERVES 6 TO 8

- ½ (17.3-oz.) pkg. frozen puff pastry (1 sheet), thawed
- 1 large (8-oz.) Honeycrisp apple, cored and thinly sliced (⅛-inch-thick slices)
- ⅓ cup granulated sugar
- 3 Tbsp. unsalted butter, cubed
- 3 Tbsp. apricot preserves or apple jelly
  Fresh thyme, for garnish (optional)

1. Preheat oven to 350°F. Line a large rimmed baking sheet with parchment paper.
2. Place puff pastry sheet on prepared pan. Shingle apple slices evenly over pastry in diagonal lines, adjusting to cover dough completely. Sprinkle with sugar, and top evenly with butter cubes.
3. Bake in preheated oven until browned and puffed, 35 to 40 minutes. Stir together apricot preserves and 1 tablespoon water in a small bowl. Brush apricot mixture over warm tart. Garnish with fresh thyme, if desired.

APPLE-BLACKBERRY
COBBLER

APPLE-SPICE MUFFINS
WITH OAT STREUSEL
(PAGE 202)

GLAZED APPLE TART
(PAGE 202)

APPLESAUCE SNACK
CAKE WITH BROWN
SUGAR FROSTING

Applesauce Snack Cake with Brown Sugar Frosting

ACTIVE 15 MIN. - TOTAL 1 HOUR,
PLUS 1 HOUR COOLING

SERVES 12

CAKE

Baking spray with flour
- 3 large McIntosh apples (about 1½ lb. total), peeled and chopped (5 cups)
- 1¼ cups packed light brown sugar
- ¾ cup canola oil
- 2 tsp. ground ginger
- 1 tsp. ground cinnamon
- 1 tsp. grated lime zest (from 1 lime)
- 1 tsp. vanilla extract
- 2 large eggs
- 2½ cups all-purpose flour
- 1 tsp. baking powder
- 1 tsp. baking soda
- ½ tsp. kosher salt

FROSTING

- ½ cup unsalted butter
- 1 cup packed light brown sugar
- 2 Tbsp. whole milk
- 3 cups powdered sugar
- ¼ tsp. kosher salt
- 2 Tbsp. hot water (optional)
  Chopped toasted pecans, for garnish

1. Prepare the Cake: Preheat oven to 350°F. Coat a 13- x 9-inch pan with baking spray with flour. Place apples in a medium-size microwavable bowl. Cover loosely with plastic wrap; microwave on HIGH until softened, about 4 minutes. Transfer apples and any liquid to a food processor or blender, and puree until smooth, 20 to 30 seconds. Cool 10 minutes. (You should have 2 cups pureed apples.)
2. Whisk together brown sugar, oil, ginger, cinnamon, lime zest, vanilla, eggs, and pureed apples in a large bowl until combined. Whisk in flour, baking powder, baking soda, and salt just until combined. Spoon batter into prepared pan. Bake in preheated oven until a wooden pick inserted in the center comes out clean, 28 to 32 minutes. Transfer to a wire rack, and cool completely in pan, about 1 hour.

3. Prepare the Frosting: Melt butter in a medium saucepan over medium. Stir in brown sugar, and bring to boil. Cook, stirring constantly, 2 minutes. Stir in milk, and return to a boil. Remove from heat; whisk in powdered sugar and salt until smooth and thickened. If mixture is too thick, add hot water until desired consistency is reached. Spread Frosting over cooled Cake, and garnish with chopped toasted pecans.

Chewy Apple-Cran-Oatmeal Cookies

(Photo, page 209)

ACTIVE 25 MIN. - TOTAL 35 MIN.,
PLUS 30 MIN. COOLING

SERVES 12

- 2 cups uncooked old-fashioned rolled oats
- 1 cup all-purpose flour
- 1 tsp. ground cinnamon
- ½ tsp. baking soda
- ½ tsp. kosher salt
- ¼ tsp. ground nutmeg
- 1 cup packed light brown sugar
- ¼ cup unsalted butter, melted and cooled
- ¼ cup unsweetened applesauce
- 1 large egg
- ½ cup finely chopped, peeled Granny Smith apple (from 1 small [6-oz.] apple)
- ½ cup sweetened dried cranberries
- ½ cup chopped walnuts
- 1 cup powdered sugar
- 2 Tbsp. fresh orange juice (from 1 orange)

1. Preheat oven to 350°F with oven racks in upper and lower thirds of oven. Line 2 large rimmed baking sheets with parchment paper.
2. Whisk together oats, flour, cinnamon, baking soda, salt, and nutmeg in a large bowl until combined. Whisk together brown sugar, butter, applesauce, and egg in a medium bowl until combined. Add butter mixture to flour mixture, stirring just until combined. Stir in apple, cranberries, and walnuts until evenly combined. Place 1½-tablespoon scoops on prepared pans, spacing 2 inches apart. Gently press dough scoops with greased palms to flatten tops.

3. Bake both baking sheets in preheated oven until cookies are browned and lightly set on the edges, 10 to 12 minutes, rotating pans from top to bottom halfway through bake time. Cool on pans, about 30 minutes.
4. Whisk together powdered sugar and orange juice in a small bowl until smooth. Drizzle over cooled cookies.

Buttery Apple-Almond Cake

(Photo, page 208)

ACTIVE 15 MIN. - TOTAL 1 HOUR, 15 MIN.

SERVES 8

Baking spray with flour
- ¾ cup all-purpose flour
- ¼ cup almond flour
- ¾ tsp. baking powder
- ½ tsp. kosher salt
- ¼ tsp. ground ginger
- 2 large eggs
- ¾ cup granulated sugar
- ½ cup unsalted butter, melted and cooled
- 2 tsp. vanilla extract
- 3 medium Honeycrisp apples (about 1¼ lb. total), cored and cut into ¼-inch-thick slices (4 cups sliced)
  Powdered sugar, for garnish

1. Preheat oven to 350°F. Coat an 8-inch round cake pan with baking spray with flour; line bottom with parchment paper.
2. Whisk together all-purpose flour, almond flour, baking powder, salt, and ginger in a medium bowl until combined. Whisk eggs in a large bowl until frothy, about 30 seconds. Whisk in sugar, butter, and vanilla. Gradually whisk in flour mixture, stirring just until combined. Fold in half of the apple slices. Transfer batter to prepared pan. Arrange remaining slices on top of batter.
3. Bake in preheated oven until a wooden pick inserted in center comes out clean, 50 to 55 minutes, covering with aluminum foil halfway through baking, if necessary, to prevent overbrowning. Cool in pan 10 minutes; transfer to a serving plate. Sprinkle with powdered sugar. Serve warm, or let cool.

BUTTERY APPLE-
ALMOND CAKE
(PAGE 207)

CHEWY APPLE-CRAN-
OATMEAL COOKIES
(PAGE 207)

Granny Smith Slab Pie

ACTIVE 20 MIN. - TOTAL 2 HOURS, PLUS
1 HOUR COOLING

SERVES 12

CRUST

- 4 cups all-purpose flour, plus more for surface
- ½ cup granulated sugar
- 2 tsp. kosher salt
- ¾ cup cold unsalted butter, cubed
- ¾ cup cold water

FILLING

- 3½ lb. Granny Smith apples (7 large apples), peeled and chopped (about 10½ cups)
- 1 cup granulated sugar
- 3 Tbsp. cornstarch
- 2 Tbsp. fresh lemon juice (from 1 lemon)
- 1½ tsp. apple pie spice
- ¼ tsp. kosher salt
- 2 Tbsp. cold unsalted butter, cubed

ADDITIONAL INGREDIENTS

- 1 large egg yolk
- 3 Tbsp. turbinado sugar
- Vanilla ice cream, for serving

1. Prepare the Crust: Preheat oven to 375°F. Pulse together flour, sugar, and salt in a food processor until combined, 5 to 8 pulses. Add butter; pulse until mixture is crumbly, about 10 pulses. With food processor running, add cold water in a slow, steady stream until mixture just forms a dough, about 45 seconds. Divide dough in half. Shape each half into a square; wrap tightly in plastic wrap. Chill until firm, about 30 minutes.
2. On a lightly floured surface, roll 1 dough square into a 15- x 12-inch rectangle, about ⅛ inch thick. Transfer to a 13- x 9- x 1-inch baking pan, pressing into corners and letting dough hang over sides of pan. Chill, uncovered, while preparing Filling.
3. Prepare the Filling: Stir apples, sugar, cornstarch, lemon juice, apple pie spice, and salt in a large bowl until combined. Spread mixture over chilled piecrust. Sprinkle evenly with cubed butter.
4. On a lightly floured surface, roll out remaining dough square to a 15- x 12-inch rectangle, about ⅛ inch thick; drape over Filling. Fold edges under; crimp. Freeze for 10 minutes. Cut about 24 (2-inch) diagonal slits across top of pie. Whisk together egg yolk and

1 tablespoon water. Brush with egg wash; sprinkle with turbinado sugar.
5. Bake in preheated oven until bubbly and golden, 55 to 65 minutes. If Crust begins to brown too quickly, loosely tent with aluminum foil. Transfer to a wire rack; cool 1 hour.
6. Serve with vanilla ice cream.

Golden Delicious Sticky Buns

(Photo, page 213)

ACTIVE 25 MIN. - TOTAL 1 HOUR, 25 MIN.,
PLUS 2 HOURS, 15 MIN. RISING

MAKES 9

- 3 cups all-purpose flour, plus more for surface
- 1 (¼-oz.) envelope instant or quick-rising yeast
- 1½ cups packed light brown sugar, divided
- 1¾ tsp. kosher salt, divided
- ⅓ cup whole milk, warmed
- ⅓ cup sour cream
- 1 large egg, at room temperature
- 1¼ cups unsalted butter, softened and divided
- ½ cup apple cider
- ¼ cup maple syrup
- 1 large (8-oz.) Golden Delicious apple, peeled and chopped (about 1½ cups chopped)
- 2 tsp. ground cinnamon

1. Combine flour, yeast, ¼ cup of the brown sugar, and 1½ teaspoons of the salt in the bowl of a stand mixer fitted with a paddle attachment. With mixer on low speed, add warm milk, sour cream, egg, and ¼ cup of the butter. Beat just until combined, about 1 minute. Switch to a dough hook, and beat on medium-high speed until smooth and elastic, about 6 minutes (dough should clear sides of bowl but stick slightly to the bottom). Transfer to a large bowl coated with cooking spray. Cover with plastic wrap, and let rise in a warm, draft-free place until doubled in size, about 1 hour, 30 minutes.
2. Meanwhile, combine apple cider, maple syrup, ¾ cup of the brown sugar, ½ cup of the butter, and remaining ¼ teaspoon salt in a medium skillet. Bring to a boil over medium. Cook, stirring often, until mixture has thickened, 5 to 7 minutes. Remove from heat, and pour into a 9-inch square baking pan lightly coated with cooking spray; set aside.

3. Lightly punch down dough. On a lightly floured surface, roll dough into a 14- x 10-inch rectangle. Spread remaining ½ cup butter over dough. Sprinkle with apple, cinnamon, and remaining ½ cup brown sugar. Starting with 1 long side, roll dough into a tight log; pinch seam to seal. Using a serrated knife, slice log into 9 rolls, about 1½ inches wide. Place rolls on cooled caramel in pan. Cover with plastic wrap, and let rise in a warm, draft-free place until doubled in size, about 45 minutes. Preheat oven to 350°F.
4. Place pan on a foil-lined baking sheet, and bake, uncovered, in preheated oven until golden brown, 30 to 35 minutes. Cool in pan on a wire rack 10 minutes. Invert rolls onto a serving platter, and serve.

Big-Batch Apple-Cinnamon Pancakes

(Photo, page 212)

ACTIVE 10 MIN. - TOTAL 50 MIN.

SERVES 12

- 2½ cups all-purpose flour
- 2 Tbsp. baking powder
- ¾ tsp. kosher salt
- ½ tsp. ground cinnamon
- ¼ cup plus 1 Tbsp. granulated sugar, divided
- 2 cups whole milk
- ½ cup sour cream
- 6 Tbsp. unsalted butter, melted
- 1 tsp. vanilla extract
- 2 large eggs
- 1 small (6-oz.) Honeycrisp apple, cored and thinly sliced (about 2 cups)
- Maple syrup and butter, for serving

1. Preheat oven to 425°F. Coat a 13- x 9-inch baking pan with cooking spray.
2. Whisk together flour, baking powder, salt, cinnamon, and ¼ cup of the sugar in a large bowl. Create a well in center of dry ingredients; whisk in milk, sour cream, melted butter, vanilla, and eggs just until combined. Pour into prepared pan.
3. Bake in preheated oven until puffed, about 6 minutes. Stir together apple slices and remaining 1 tablespoon sugar in a medium bowl. Top pancake evenly with apple mixture, and continue baking until golden brown and a wooden pick inserted in center comes out clean, about 20 minutes. Let cool 10 minutes before serving. Slice and serve with maple syrup and butter.

GRANNY SMITH
SLAB PIE

BIG-BATCH APPLE-
CINNAMON PANCAKES
(PAGE 210)

GOLDEN DELICIOUS
STICKY BUNS
(PAGE 210)

MELTED QUESO
WITH CHORIZO
(PAGE 217)

CHUNKY GUACAMOLE WITH
JALAPEÑO AND CHILE DE
ÁRBOL (PAGE 217)

Secrets of the Tex-Mex Trail

Cookbook author and PBS host Pati Jinich explores the history and future
of this often misunderstood regional cuisine

THE FIRST TIME I tasted Tex-Mex cooking, I was perplexed. It was 1997, and I was at a San Antonio restaurant, having recently moved from my hometown of Mexico City to the United States. I knew how popular the food was, but I had also heard some of its negative connotations of being a washed-out, fake hybrid. I didn't quite understand the combo platter that was placed in front of me with enchiladas (tortillas blanketed with a cheesy sauce), red rice (with an intense taste of cumin), and refried beans (runny and mild in taste), but I licked the plate clean. I continued eating Tex-Mex wherever I found it, trying to grasp these familiar yet unfamiliar dishes. I now realize that part of my confusion was that many places advertised as being "authentic" Mexican, yet the food was so different from what I'd grown up with.

Once I settled in the U.S., I switched careers from political analysis to cooking so I could explore and share Mexican cuisine with the world. After 15 years of crisscrossing my home country, I have learned so much about its foodways and their expressions inside and outside Mexico. But it was my journey through the Texas-Mexico borderlands for my PBS docuseries *La Frontera* that gave me a deeper understanding of the Tex-Mex universe.

Tex-Mex, I humbly learned, is not trying to be Mexican food as it is found south of the border, nor should it. Neither is it an Americanized version of Mexican food. It is its own evolving regional cuisine that encompasses a geographical and cultural space that has historically belonged to both the U.S. and Mexico.

The roots of Tex-Mex precede the existence of Texas as a state, of both Mexico and the U.S. as independent countries, and of the Texas-Mexico border. The Tex-Mex territory that is now South Texas and northern Mexico was part of Spain's colony of New Spain for almost three centuries. During that time, the Old World brought by the Spanish became woven with the New World of people native to America in every aspect of life, including food. When Mexico gained independence from Spain in 1821, Texas remained part of Mexico until it became the Republic of Texas before finally being added as a U.S. state in 1845.

From then on, one of America's first regional cuisines took shape. In the kitchen, Tejanos (Mexicans native to Texas before it became a state or Texans of Mexican descent) began using American-style cheeses and wheat instead of corn. Foods such as tamales and tacos were introduced at fairs and in restaurants, often adapted and tweaked to please the American palate.

Most famously, around the 1860s, enterprising women called Chili Queens, practically all of Mexican origin, would set up open-air stands at plazas in San Antonio and sell chili as well as tamales, beans, enchiladas, and hot coffee. This tradition lasted until about the 1940s. Although the city council would shut down the stands, locals would complain so loudly that they would be set back up.

Whether I was in El Paso-Juárez, the Laredo and Nuevo Laredo area, the Rio Grande Valley, McAllen, or Brownsville, I found that the breakfast tacos, burritos, chili gravies, tamales, fajita platters, chiles rellenos, carnes asadas, botanas, guacamoles, and salsas all had different and defined culinary personalities.

You can find some common denominators, though. Queso is under, in between, and all over so many dishes. Flour tortillas are still adored in Texas, but people are getting pickier about their quality as more fresh flour tortillas appear in supermarkets. The "build," the over-the-top layering of ingredients, is also key. One example is Panchos, a version of nachos created by Juan Francisco Ochoa (also known as Don Pancho), owner of the Taco Palenque chain in the Laredo region. His chips covered in cheese sauce, fajitas, beans, and guacamole marry the Mex and the Tex.

Based on my travels, I believe that Tex-Mex is more complex and adventurous than ever. When I ate tacos at El Ultimo Taco Taqueria in Brownsville and crashed carne asada cookouts on Boca Chica Beach, I noticed new condiments, like candied (rather than pickled) jalapeños. The standard one-size-fits-all chili powder (see The Scoop on Chili Powder, page 217) is being replaced by dried chiles like chile de árbol, guajillo, and Cascabel. At Convenience West in Marfa, I tasted so many dried chiles in chefs Mark Scott and Kaki Aufdengarten-Scott's outrageously delicious smoked brisket.

Just like the Texas-Mexico borderlands, Tex-Mex food defies categorization. It is a cuisine caught in an evolving in-between space, a Mexican soul that's tucked inside Texas and is constantly changing—with incredible results. –Pati Jinich

Inside Pati's Pantry

Five of her Tex-Mex staples

Pickled Jalapeños
I've got enough cans of La Costeña pickled jalapeños to last me for weeks. The chiles are pickled in a seasoned brine that can shine in sauces and more.

Pinto Beans
Whether dried, canned whole, or already refried, these creamy and soft beans rule the Tex-Mex kitchen.

Rice
Mahatma Extra Long Enriched Rice is my go-to for red rice. The fluffy, separate grains have a soft texture that can absorb the flavors of the cooking broth.

Cumin
Judiciously used in most Mexican cooking, this spice has a big presence in Tex-Mex dishes, adding a layer of seasoning that is heavy, slightly bitter, and toasty.

Dried Oregano
You can now find Mexican oregano (it has a more intense scent, which I prefer) in addition to the more commonly available Mediterranean kind.

Tejano Red Rice

(Photo, page 219)
ACTIVE 35 MIN. - TOTAL 35 MIN.
SERVES 8

- 1 lb. ripe tomatoes, quartered, or 1 (14½-oz.) can tomato puree
- ⅓ cup coarsely chopped white onion
- 2 garlic cloves
- 1 tsp. kosher or coarse sea salt, or to taste
- 1 tsp. ground cumin
- 2⅔ to 3 cups chicken or vegetable broth, homemade or store-bought
- 3 Tbsp. vegetable oil
- 2 cups uncooked long-grain white rice
- ¾ cup diced carrot (optional)
- ½ cup fresh or frozen green peas (optional)
- ½ cup fresh or frozen corn kernels (optional)
- Chopped fresh cilantro, for topping (optional)

1. Puree tomatoes with onion, garlic, salt, and cumin in a blender or food processor until completely smooth. Pour tomato mixture into a large liquid measuring cup; note the amount, and reserve. Pour enough broth into another liquid measuring cup to make 4 cups total liquid (tomato puree and broth). Keep the tomato puree and broth separate, because you will add the puree first.
2. Heat oil in a medium saucepan over medium-high until hot but not smoking. Add rice; cook, stirring often, until rice becomes milky white, 3 to 4 minutes. Pour in tomato puree, and cook, stirring gently, until puree darkens, thickens, and has mostly been absorbed by the rice, about 3 minutes.
3. Stir in broth. If desired, add carrot, peas, and corn. Bring to a rolling boil; cover, and reduce heat to low. Cook until most of the liquid has been absorbed but there is still some moisture in the pan, about 15 minutes. Rice should be cooked and tender. (If rice is not tender but all liquid has been absorbed, add 1 to 2 tablespoons water, cover, and cook 2 minutes more.)
4. Remove from heat; let stand, covered, at least 5 minutes. Fluff rice with a fork. Top with cilantro, if desired; serve.

Beef Fajitas

(Photo, page 219)
ACTIVE 35 MIN. - TOTAL 1 HOUR, 35 MIN.
SERVES 6

- ½ cup olive oil
- ½ cup pickled jalapeño brine (from 1 [12-oz.] jar pickled jalapeños)
- ¼ cup fresh lime juice (from 1 lime)
- 3 Tbsp. soy sauce
- 2 Tbsp. Worcestershire sauce
- 1 tsp. brown sugar
- ½ tsp. ground cumin
- 3 garlic cloves, pressed or finely minced
- 1 tsp. kosher salt, divided
- 1 tsp. ground black pepper, divided
- 2 lb. bavette, flap steak, or skirt steak
- 1 red bell pepper, thinly sliced into rings
- 1 yellow bell pepper, thinly sliced into rings
- 1 green bell pepper, thinly sliced into rings
- 1 orange bell pepper, thinly sliced into rings
- 1 white onion, thinly sliced into rings
- 3 to 4 fresh jalapeño chiles
- Corn or flour tortillas
- Guacamole, for serving
- Salsa, for serving

1. Combine olive oil, jalapeño brine, lime juice, soy sauce, Worcestershire sauce, brown sugar, cumin, garlic, and ½ teaspoon each of the kosher salt and black pepper in a bowl; mix well with a whisk or fork. Place beef in a baking dish or container. Pour three-fourths of the marinade over beef, making sure beef is covered on all sides. Cover with plastic wrap, and chill at least 1 hour or up to 24 hours. Reserve remaining one-fourth of the marinade in a small container with a lid, and chill until ready to cook vegetables.
2. Preheat grill to medium-high. Remove beef from marinade; discard marinade. Grill beef until desired doneness, 3 to 4 minutes per side for medium. Remove beef to a cutting board; cover with foil, and let stand 10 minutes.
3. Brush bell pepper rings, onion rings, and jalapeño chiles with reserved one-fourth of marinade, and sprinkle with remaining ½ teaspoon each salt and

black pepper. Grill until soft and lightly charred, 2 to 3 minutes per side. Place bell peppers, onion, and jalapeños on a large platter. Slice beef across the grain, and serve on top of vegetables. Serve with tortillas, guacamole, and salsa.

Melted Queso with Chorizo

(Photo, page 214)
ACTIVE 35 MIN. - TOTAL 35 MIN.
SERVES 12

- 3 medium poblano chiles
- 1 lb. Mexican chorizo, casings removed
- 1 small white onion, chopped (1 cup)
- 2 ripe plum tomatoes, cored, seeded, and chopped
- ½ cup whole milk
- ½ cup heavy whipping cream
- 4 oz. cream cheese
- 2 lb. American cheese, shredded
  Tortilla chips, for serving

1. Preheat oven to broil with oven rack 6 inches from heat. Place poblanos on a baking sheet, and broil until skin is charred and blistered, about 5 minutes per side. Transfer to a medium bowl, and cover tightly with plastic wrap; let stand 10 minutes.
2. Uncover bowl, and peel poblanos. Discard peels. Cut poblanos in half lengthwise, and remove and discard stems and seeds. Chop poblanos.
3. Cook chorizo in a large cast-iron skillet over medium-high, stirring occasionally to break into smaller pieces, until browned and crisp, 6 to 8 minutes. Remove cooked chorizo with a slotted spoon, and set aside.
4. Reduce heat to medium. Add onion to drippings in skillet; cook until onion softens, 3 to 4 minutes. Add chopped poblanos and tomatoes, and cook until softened, about 2 minutes. Stir in milk, cream, cream cheese, and American cheese, stirring and scraping skillet to loosen browned bits. Simmer, stirring constantly, until thoroughly melted and combined, about 1 minute. Remove from heat. Scrape queso into a serving bowl, and garnish with cooked chorizo. Serve with tortilla chips.

Chunky Guacamole with Jalapeño and Chile de Árbol

(Photo, page 214)
ACTIVE 10 MIN. - TOTAL 10 MIN.
SERVES 6

- 1 jalapeño chile, stemmed, finely chopped, and (if desired) seeded
- 1 dried chile de árbol, stemmed, finely chopped, and (if desired) seeded
- ¼ cup fresh lime juice (from 2 limes)
- 1½ tsp. kosher salt
- 2 spring onions or 4 scallions, white and light green parts thinly sliced (¼ cup), divided
- ¼ cup coarsely chopped fresh cilantro leaves and upper parts of stems, divided
- 4 large ripe Mexican avocados, halved, pitted, and diced

Place jalapeño, chile de árbol, lime juice, kosher salt, and 3 tablespoons each of the spring onions and cilantro in a molcajete, mortar, or bowl. Mash or stir until pasty. Place diced avocados in a bowl, and stir in mashed chile mixture. Taste guacamole, and adjust seasoning if necessary. Garnish with remaining 1 tablespoon each spring onions and cilantro.

Charro Beans

(Photo, page 218)
ACTIVE 20 MIN. - TOTAL 20 MIN.
SERVES 6

- 6 oz. bacon slices, cut into 1-inch pieces
- ½ cup chopped white onion
- 2 jalapeño chiles, stemmed, chopped, and (if desired) seeded
- 1 lb. dried pinto beans, cooked (about 5 cups), or 5 cups drained and rinsed canned pinto beans
- 1 cup bean cooking liquid or tap water
- ¼ tsp. dried oregano
- ¼ tsp. smoked paprika
- ½ tsp. kosher salt

Cook bacon pieces in a 12-inch skillet over medium-high until beginning to crisp, 3 to 4 minutes. Add onion and jalapeños, and cook, stirring often, until vegetables are soft, 1 to 2 minutes. Stir in cooked beans, cooking liquid (or water), oregano, and paprika, and reduce heat to medium. Cook until beans are moist but not soupy, 8 to 10 minutes. Stir in salt, and serve hot.

The Scoop on Chili Powder

A German immigrant is credited with popularizing this now ubiquitous spice blend. In New Braunfels, an early German settlement in Texas, Willie Gebhardt opened a cafe in 1892 and started selling his own chili powder. Later sold as Gebhardt's Eagle Brand Chili Powder, this product spread like wildfire across the U.S. According to his 1923 cookbook, *Mexican Cookery for American Homes*, adding some of it to any meal (from meatballs to fried chicken) could quickly bring "that real Mexican tang."

CHARRO BEANS
(PAGE 217)

TEJANO RED RICE
(PAGE 216)

BEEF FAJITAS
(PAGE 216)

Pick-Up Sticks

Turn breakfast or brunch into a party with this fun take on French toast

French Toast Dippers

ACTIVE 15 MIN. - TOTAL 35 MIN.
SERVES 6

5	large eggs
1½	cups half-and-half
3	Tbsp. light brown sugar
1	tsp. vanilla extract
½	tsp. ground cinnamon
¼	tsp. kosher salt
8	oz. day-old Pullman (pain de mie) white bread or challah bread (from 1 unsliced loaf), cut into 3- x 1-inch sticks
2	Tbsp. unsalted butter, melted, divided
1	Tbsp. powdered sugar
	Dipping sauces (below)

1. Preheat oven to 375°F. Whisk together eggs, half-and-half, brown sugar, vanilla, cinnamon, and salt in a large bowl. Add bread sticks; turn to coat completely, and let excess drip off. Arrange sticks on a baking sheet lined with parchment paper. Brush sticks evenly with half of the melted butter.
2. Bake in preheated oven until sticks are slightly puffed and browned on bottoms, about 8 minutes. Remove from oven; flip sticks, and brush evenly with remaining butter. Return to oven; continue baking until sticks are puffed and browned on both sides, 7 to 8 minutes.
3. Arrange French toast sticks on a serving platter; dust evenly with powdered sugar. Serve immediately alongside dipping sauces.

Three Slam-Dunk Flavors
You can triple dip when you make all three

Vanilla Bean-Cream Cheese Dipping Sauce
Whisk together 3 oz. softened cream cheese and 2 Tbsp. powdered sugar in a small bowl until completely smooth. Whisk in 3 Tbsp. heavy whipping cream, 1 tsp. vanilla bean paste, and ⅛ tsp. kosher salt.

Strawberry-Ginger Dipping Sauce
Microwave ½ cup strawberry jam in a small microwavable bowl on HIGH until loosened and warmed through, about 20 seconds. Stir in 2 tsp. fresh lemon juice and ¼ tsp. grated fresh ginger.

Maple-Pecan Dipping Sauce
Stir together ¼ cup room-temperature pure maple syrup, 2 Tbsp. finely chopped pecans, 1 Tbsp. melted unsalted butter, and ⅛ tsp. kosher salt in a small microwavable bowl. (If butter starts to resolidify before serving, microwave on LOW for 1 minute.)

A Whole New Bowl Game

Colorful vegetables and grilled chicken team up in this simple yet satisfying meal

Cauliflower Rice Bowl with Tahini-Herb Chicken

Please everyone around the table with a meal that's as healthful as it is flexible. Riced cauliflower makes a low-carb, gluten-free base for grilled chicken, chickpeas, and a vivid mix of fresh veggies—use them all, or choose your own combination. The tahini marinade is also a dressing; marinate the chicken overnight for the most flavor.

ACTIVE 40 MIN. - TOTAL 40 MIN., PLUS
3 HOURS MARINATING

SERVES 4

- 1 cup plain 2% reduced-fat strained yogurt (such as Greek)
- ¾ cup packed fresh flat-leaf parsley leaves and tender stems, plus more for garnish
- ¼ cup tahini (sesame paste)
- 2 Tbsp. fresh dill, plus more for garnish
- 2 garlic cloves
- ½ tsp. grated lemon zest plus ¼ cup fresh juice (from 2 lemons)
- ¼ tsp. cayenne pepper
- ¾ tsp. Greek seasoning, divided
- 2 lb. boneless, skinless chicken thighs (about 6 thighs)
- ½ medium-size red onion, cut into 1-inch wedges with root intact (about 1 cup)
- 1 tsp. olive oil
- 1 (10-oz.) pkg. fresh or frozen riced cauliflower (about 1½ cups)
- 1 (15½-oz.) can no-salt-added chickpeas (garbanzo beans), drained and rinsed
- 1 small cucumber, diced (about 1 cup)
- 1 pt. cherry tomatoes, halved (about 2 cups)
- ¼ cup pitted Kalamata olives

1. Process yogurt, parsley, tahini, dill, garlic, lemon zest and juice, cayenne pepper, and ½ teaspoon of the Greek seasoning in a high-power blender or food processor until smooth, about 45 seconds.

2. Place half of yogurt dressing in a large ziptop plastic bag. Add chicken thighs and seal bag. Massage dressing into chicken; marinate in refrigerator at least 3 hours or up to 12 hours. Refrigerate remaining dressing in an airtight container until ready to serve.

3. Preheat grill to medium-high (400°F to 450°F). Combine onion, olive oil, and remaining ¼ teaspoon Greek seasoning in a small bowl; toss to coat. Place onion wedges on oiled grates. Remove chicken thighs from bag, discarding yogurt marinade. Place chicken on oiled grates. Grill onion wedges, uncovered, turning often, until charred and tender, 10 to 15 minutes. Grill chicken thighs, uncovered, until cooked through and an instant-read thermometer inserted in thickest part of thigh registers 165°F, 5 to 7 minutes per side. Remove onion wedges and chicken from grill; let rest 5 minutes. Cut 2 of the chicken thighs in half.

4. Prepare riced cauliflower according to the package instructions.

5. Divide riced cauliflower evenly among 4 bowls. Top evenly with chickpeas, cucumber, tomatoes, grilled onion wedges, olives, and chicken. Top each bowl with about 3 tablespoons of reserved yogurt dressing. Garnish with additional fresh parsley and/or dill.

CALORIES: **602** – CARBS: **35 G** – FAT: **26 G**

Reasons to Love Broccoli

The hearty veggie shines in five meals, from creamy soup to homemade pizza

Beef-and-Broccoli Stir-Fry

ACTIVE 15 MIN. - TOTAL 15 MIN.

SERVES 4

- ½ cup beef broth
- 6 Tbsp. soy sauce
- 3 Tbsp. light brown sugar
- 2 Tbsp. sesame oil
- 1½ Tbsp. cornstarch
- 2 garlic cloves, grated (1 tsp.)
- 1 (1-inch) piece fresh ginger, peeled and finely grated (1 tsp.)
- 2 Tbsp. canola oil, divided
- 6 cups small fresh broccoli florets (16 oz.)
- 1 lb. boneless sirloin steak (1 inch thick), thinly sliced (about ¼ inch thick)
- 2 cups hot cooked white rice

  Garnishes: Sesame seeds, crushed red pepper, and sliced scallions

1. Whisk together beef broth, soy sauce, brown sugar, sesame oil, cornstarch, garlic, and ginger in a small bowl until sugar dissolves. Set aside.

2. Heat 1 tablespoon of the canola oil in a large skillet over medium; add broccoli florets. Partially cover; cook, stirring occasionally, until broccoli is tender-crisp, about 5 minutes. Remove from skillet; set aside.

3. Increase heat to high; add remaining 1 tablespoon canola oil to skillet. Place steak slices in an even layer in skillet, and cook, stirring occasionally, until mostly browned, about 3 minutes. Stir in broth mixture, and reduce heat to medium-high. Cook, stirring constantly, until thickened, about 1 minute. Remove skillet from heat; add reserved broccoli, stirring until coated. Serve over rice; garnish with sesame seeds, crushed red pepper, and scallions.

THE SECRET TO SLICING STEAK
For the thinnest, most even results, freeze the raw meat for 15 minutes before cutting it.

Broccoli-Parmesan Soup with Grilled Cheese Croutons

ACTIVE 25 MIN. - TOTAL 25 MIN.
SERVES 4

- 3 Tbsp. extra-virgin olive oil
- 2 tsp. chopped garlic (from 2 garlic cloves)
- ¼ cup all-purpose flour
- 2 cups vegetable or chicken broth
- 2 cups whole milk
- 1 tsp. kosher salt
- ¾ tsp. black pepper, plus more for garnish
- 4 cups chopped fresh broccoli florets (12 oz.)
- 2 Tbsp. butter
- 2 (1½-oz.) hearty white bread slices
- 2 oz. sharp white Cheddar cheese, shredded (about ½ cup)
- 1 oz. Parmesan cheese, finely grated (about ⅔ cup), plus more for garnish
  Sliced chives

1. Heat oil in a large saucepan over medium. Add garlic, and cook, stirring frequently, until fragrant, about 1 minute. Stir in flour; cook, stirring constantly, until bubbly, about 3 minutes. Gradually whisk in broth and milk until smooth. Stir in salt and pepper, and bring to a simmer over medium, stirring occasionally. Reduce heat to medium-low. Add broccoli, and cook, stirring occasionally, until tender, about 10 minutes.

2. Meanwhile, melt 1 tablespoon of the butter in a medium skillet over medium. Place 1 white bread slice in skillet, and top evenly with Cheddar; cover with remaining bread slice. Cook, undisturbed, until golden brown, 1 to 2 minutes. Flip, and add remaining 1 tablespoon butter to skillet. Cook, undisturbed, until golden brown, 1 to 2 minutes. Cut into 12 equal pieces.

3. Carefully pour broccoli mixture and Parmesan into a blender. Secure lid on blender; remove center piece to allow steam to escape. Place a clean towel over opening. Process until smooth, about 1 minute. Divide soup among 4 bowls, and top evenly with Grilled Cheese Croutons; garnish with chives and additional pepper.

CHOOSE A BLOCK OF CHEESE
Freshly grated Parmesan melts smoothly, unlike the pregrated kind, which has additives to keep it from sticking together.

DON'T SKIP THIS STEP
Transfer the cooked broccoli from the boiling water to an ice bath to stop the cooking process and preserve the vegetable's bright green color.

Broccoli Pesto Pasta

ACTIVE 20 MIN. · TOTAL 35 MIN.

SERVES 4

Ice

- 1 Tbsp. plus 1¼ tsp. kosher salt, divided
- 6 cups small fresh broccoli florets (16 oz.)
- 1 (16-oz.) pkg. orecchiette pasta
- 2 cups lightly packed fresh basil leaves, plus more for garnish
- 2½ oz. Parmesan cheese, shredded (about 1 cup), plus shaved Parmesan for garnish
- ½ cup extra-virgin olive oil
- 1 Tbsp. fresh lemon juice
- 2 garlic cloves, coarsely chopped (1 Tbsp.)
- ½ cup chopped toasted walnuts, divided

Black pepper

1. Fill a large bowl with water and ice; set aside. Bring 12 cups water to a boil in a large saucepan over medium-high; stir in 1 tablespoon of the salt. Add broccoli, and cook, stirring occasionally, until tender, about 3 minutes. Using a slotted spoon, transfer broccoli to ice water; cool for 30 seconds. Drain well. Set aside.

2. Return water in saucepan to a boil over medium-high. Add pasta; cook, stirring occasionally, until al dente, about 10 minutes. Drain pasta, reserving ½ cup cooking water. Return pasta to saucepan; set aside.

3. Coarsely chop 3 cups broccoli. Place chopped broccoli, basil, shredded Parmesan, oil, lemon juice, garlic, ¼ cup of the walnuts, and remaining 1¼ teaspoons salt in the bowl of a food processor, and pulse until a coarse pesto is made, about 30 pulses, stopping to scrape down sides of bowl as needed.

4. Add pesto, remaining 3 cups broccoli, and reserved ½ cup cooking water to pasta in saucepan, and cook over medium-low, stirring often, until heated through, about 2 minutes. Top evenly with remaining ¼ cup walnuts, and garnish with additional basil, shaved Parmesan, and pepper.

Broccoli-Sausage Pizza

ACTIVE 25 MIN. · TOTAL 30 MIN.

SERVES 4

- 4 oz. mild Italian turkey sausage, casing removed
- 1 lb. fresh prepared pizza dough, at room temperature
- All-purpose flour, for dusting
- ½ cup pizza sauce (from 1 [13-oz.] jar, such as Rao's Margherita Pizza)
- 4 oz. fresh mozzarella cheese, torn (about 1 cup)
- 1½ cups small fresh broccoli florets (4 oz.)
- ½ cup halved grape tomatoes (from 1 pt.)
- 1 oz. Parmesan cheese, finely shredded (about ⅓ cup)
- ¼ tsp. black pepper
- Torn fresh basil

1. Preheat oven to 500°F with racks in top third and lower third positions. Lightly coat a large baking sheet with cooking spray. Cook turkey sausage in a small skillet over medium-high, stirring occasionally to break into smaller pieces, until no longer pink, about 5 minutes. Transfer from skillet to a paper towel-lined plate, and drain.

2. Roll and stretch dough on a lightly floured surface into a 12-inch round. Transfer to prepared baking sheet. Spread pizza sauce evenly over dough, leaving a 1-inch border around edges of dough. Place sausage, fresh mozzarella, broccoli, and tomatoes evenly over dough. Sprinkle evenly with Parmesan and pepper.

3. Bake in preheated oven on lower rack for 5 minutes. Carefully transfer baking sheet to top rack, and bake until crust is golden brown and cheese is melted, about 5 minutes. Let cool 5 minutes. Garnish with basil, and serve.

Sheet Pan Broccoli-and-Chicken Casserole

ACTIVE 20 MIN. - TOTAL 55 MIN.

SERVES 6

1½ cups panko breadcrumbs, divided

¼ cup plus 2 Tbsp. unsalted butter, divided

1 small red onion, chopped (about ⅔ cup)

4 large garlic cloves, minced (about 2 Tbsp.)

4 cups bite-size broccoli florets (12 oz.)

3 cups shredded rotisserie chicken

3 cups cooked white rice

1½ cups sour cream

1 cup mayonnaise

¼ cup fresh lemon juice (from 1 large lemon)

1½ tsp. kosher salt

½ tsp. black pepper

8 oz. sharp white Cheddar cheese, shredded (about 2 cups), divided

2 Tbsp. chopped fresh parsley, divided

1. Preheat oven to 400°F. Lightly spray a large rimmed baking sheet with cooking spray; sprinkle evenly with ¼ cup of the breadcrumbs.

2. Melt ¼ cup of the butter in a small skillet over medium-high. Add onion, and cook, stirring occasionally, until tender, about 3 minutes. Add garlic; cook, stirring often, until fragrant, about 1 minute. Remove skillet from heat.

3. Stir together onion mixture, broccoli, chicken, rice, sour cream, mayonnaise, lemon juice, salt, pepper, ¾ cup of the breadcrumbs, 1½ cups of the cheese, and 1 tablespoon of the parsley in a large bowl until combined. Spread broccoli mixture in an even layer over breadcrumbs on prepared baking sheet.

4. Microwave remaining 2 tablespoons butter in a medium-size microwavable bowl on HIGH for 30 seconds. Add remaining ½ cup breadcrumbs, ½ cup cheese, and 1 tablespoon parsley to butter, stirring to combine. Sprinkle breadcrumb mixture evenly over top of casserole. Bake in preheated oven until golden brown, about 30 minutes. Let stand 5 minutes; serve.

HEARTY AND HEALTHY
Add whole grains by using whole-wheat panko. Or replace the white rice with an equal amount of cooked brown rice, quinoa, or farro.

Too Good to Be Crackers

Turn pie dough into a buttery, savory treat that bakes up in minutes

Easy Piecrust Crackers

ACTIVE 10 MIN. - TOTAL 40 MIN.
MAKES ABOUT 8 DOZEN

- ½ (14.1-oz.) pkg. refrigerated piecrusts (1 crust)
  All-purpose flour, for dusting
- ½ Tbsp. olive oil
  Toppings (below)

1. Preheat oven to 450°F. Let piecrust dough stand at room temperature until softened, about 15 minutes. Line a baking sheet with parchment paper.
2. Roll out softened dough on a lightly floured work surface into a 12-inch circle. Brush with olive oil, and sprinkle with desired toppings, pressing gently with fingertips to adhere. Cut dough into 1-inch squares, cutting about 10 (1-inch-wide) strips lengthwise and about 10 (1-inch-wide) strips crosswise. (You will have a little waste but not much.) Transfer squares to prepared baking sheet.
3. Bake in preheated oven until crackers are lightly browned, 6 to 7 minutes. Let cool on pan 10 minutes. Serve immediately, or store in an airtight container at room temperature up to 5 days.

Choose Your Flavor

They're so simple, you can mix it up and make more than one

Rosemary and Sea Salt
2 tsp. chopped fresh rosemary leaves and 1 tsp. flaky sea salt

Parmesan and Herb
2 Tbsp. grated Parmesan cheese and 1 tsp. dried Italian seasoning

Poppy Seed and Onion
1 Tbsp. poppy seeds, 1 tsp. onion powder, and 1 tsp. flaky sea salt

THE SECRET TO THE CRISP
When working with the cracker dough, handle it as little as possible for a light and flaky texture.

Speedy Skillet Chili

All it takes is 30 minutes and one pan

Vegetarian Skillet Chili

ACTIVE 30 MIN. · TOTAL 30 MIN.

SERVES 4

- 1 bunch fresh cilantro sprigs
- 2 Tbsp. olive oil
- 1 lb. portobello mushroom caps, gills removed, chopped (about 5 cups)
- 1 medium-size red bell pepper, chopped (about 1 cup)
- 1 cup chopped white onion (from 1 medium onion)
- 1 medium jalapeño chile, seeded and chopped (1 Tbsp.)
- 2 Tbsp. minced garlic (from 2 garlic cloves)
- 3 Tbsp. tomato paste
- 2 (15-oz.) cans no-salt-added Great Northern beans, drained and rinsed
- 1 (14½-oz.) can fire-roasted diced tomatoes, undrained
- ¾ cup lower-sodium vegetable broth
- 2 tsp. ground cumin
- 2 tsp. ground coriander
- 1 tsp. kosher salt

    Shredded Cheddar cheese, chopped avocado, and lime wedges

1. Separate leaves and stems of cilantro sprigs; chop leaves and tender stems separately to equal about ⅓ cup each. Set aside.

2. Heat oil in a large cast-iron skillet over medium-high. Add mushrooms; cook, stirring occasionally, until browned, about 5 minutes. Stir in cilantro stems, bell pepper, onion, jalapeño, and garlic. Cook, stirring often, until tender, about 6 minutes. Stir in tomato paste; cook, stirring constantly, until caramelized, 1 minute. Stir in beans, tomatoes, broth, cumin, coriander, and salt. Bring to a boil over medium-high; reduce heat to medium-low. Simmer, stirring occasionally, until flavors meld and mixture thickens slightly, about 10 minutes.

3. Divide chili among 4 bowls. Top with cilantro leaves, cheese, avocado, and lime wedges.

CALORIES: **344** – CARBS: **53 G** – FAT: **9 G**

Batter Up!

One pumpkin bread recipe, three delicious ways to enjoy it this fall

Seeded Pumpkin Bread

ACTIVE 30 MIN. · TOTAL 1 HOUR, 20 MIN.,
PLUS 1 HOUR, 10 MIN. COOLING

MAKES 2 LOAVES

BATTER

- 1⅓ cups granulated sugar
- 1⅓ cups packed light brown sugar
- 1 cup unsalted butter, melted
- 4 large eggs
- 1 (15-oz.) can pumpkin
- ⅔ cup whole buttermilk
- 1 tsp. vanilla extract
- 3⅓ cups all-purpose flour
- 2 tsp. baking soda
- 1½ tsp. kosher salt
- 1½ tsp. ground cinnamon
- ½ tsp. baking powder
- ½ tsp. ground nutmeg
  Baking spray with flour

TOPPINGS

- ¼ cup raw pumpkin seed kernels (pepitas)
- 2 tsp. flaxseeds
- 2 tsp. sesame seeds

1. Prepare the Batter: Preheat oven to 350°F. Beat granulated sugar, brown sugar, and butter in a large bowl with an electric mixer at medium speed until creamy and lightened in color, about 2 minutes. Add eggs, 1 at a time, beating just until blended and stopping to scrape down sides of bowl after each addition. Add pumpkin, buttermilk, and vanilla; beat until blended, about 1 minute.
2. Whisk together flour, baking soda, salt, cinnamon, baking powder, and nutmeg in a large bowl until combined. Add flour mixture to butter mixture, and beat on low speed until just combined, about 30 seconds.
3. Coat 2 (9- x 5-inch) loaf pans with baking spray. Divide Batter evenly between loaf pans. Sprinkle 2 tablespoons of the pumpkin seeds and 1 teaspoon each of the flaxseeds and sesame seeds over Batter in each loaf pan.
4. Bake in preheated oven until a wooden pick inserted in center comes out clean, 50 minutes to 1 hour, covering

SEEDED
PUMPKIN
BREAD

with aluminum foil during last 10 to 15 minutes of baking time to prevent overbrowning, if needed. Cool in loaf pans on a wire rack 10 minutes. Run a knife around edges of bread to loosen; transfer to wire rack. Let cool completely, 1 hour.

Pumpkin-Pecan Coffee Cake

(Photo, page 230)

ACTIVE 30 MIN. · TOTAL 1 HOUR, 25 MIN.,
PLUS 20 MIN. STANDING

SERVES 16

Preheat oven to 350°F. Prepare Batter as directed, omitting Toppings. Coat a 13- x 9-inch baking pan with baking spray. Spread Batter into pan. Stir together ¾ cup all-purpose flour, ½ cup packed light brown sugar, ½ cup softened unsalted butter, ½ teaspoon ground cinnamon, and ⅛ teaspoon each ground nutmeg and kosher salt in a medium bowl until combined. Using hands, squeeze mixture into clumps. Stir in 1 cup chopped pecans; sprinkle over Batter. Bake in preheated oven until a wooden pick inserted in center comes out clean, 55 minutes to 1 hour and

5 minutes, covering with aluminum foil during last 10 to 15 minutes of baking time to prevent overbrowning, if needed. Let stand 20 minutes before serving, or cool completely in pan on a wire rack, 1 hour.

Chocolate Chip-Pumpkin Muffins

(Photo, page 231)

ACTIVE 30 MIN. · TOTAL 1 HOUR, 35 MIN.

MAKES 30 MUFFINS

Preheat oven to 350°F. Prepare Batter as directed, omitting Toppings. Gently stir 1½ cups semisweet chocolate chips into Batter. Line 3 (12-cup) muffin trays with 30 paper liners; spoon Batter into wells, filling each about three-fourths full (about ¼ cup Batter in each well). Sprinkle Batter in wells evenly with ½ cup semisweet chocolate chips. Bake in preheated oven, in 3 batches, until a wooden pick inserted in center comes out clean, 20 to 24 minutes. Let muffins cool in trays on wire racks for 5 minutes. Serve warm, or remove from trays and let cool completely on wire racks, about 30 minutes.

PUMPKIN-PECAN
COFFEE CAKE
(PAGE 229)

CHOCOLATE CHIP-
PUMPKIN MUFFINS
(PAGE 229)

Give Me a Ring!

Hey Y'all host and Georgia Bulldog superfan Ivy Odom
has a new favorite way to kick off football season

GAME DAYS IN THE SOUTH are about a lot more than football. They're about hospitality, camaraderie, and seriously good food. When I was in college at the University of Georgia, my parents tailgated for every home game. These were always done to the nines, with linen tablecloths, themed flower arrangements, and beautiful things to eat displayed on platters and tiered serving trays. If this sounds like a wedding to you, you haven't met my mama.

She spent the weeks leading up to football season planning different menus for each game, and her elaborate spreads went way beyond a to-go platter of chicken fingers. We rarely had the same entrée twice in one season. The tents (yes, there were two) were always filled with people because when you were there, you felt like you were home. Part of it had to do with the sense of togetherness that inevitably came with game day, but most of it had to do with the fact that "Mama O" (as my friends called her) wouldn't settle for anyone leaving her tents without at least two helpings of whatever she was serving.

These days, we don't make it back to Athens often, but it hasn't stopped our extensive game-day menu planning. In fact, we've become a lot more creative because our home kitchens can handle more than our tailgating burners did. In our newest go-to recipe for Crispy Onion Rings with Kickin' Ranch, freshly fried onions come together in a flash and disappear even faster. Best washed down with a glass of Big-Batch Lime Lager Shandy (recipe, below right), they'll have you reminiscing about your glory days with the first bite.

Crispy Onion Rings with Kickin' Ranch

ACTIVE 30 MIN. · TOTAL 45 MIN.

SERVES 6

- 1 medium-size sweet onion, cut crosswise into ½-inch-thick slices (about 2½ cups)
- 1 cup all-purpose flour
- 1 cup whole buttermilk
- 1 large egg
- 1½ tsp. kosher salt, divided
- 2 cups panko breadcrumbs, divided
- 3 cups vegetable oil, for frying
  Kickin' Ranch (recipe follows)

1. Separate onion slices into individual rings. Place in a large bowl with flour; toss to coat evenly. Transfer onions to a baking sheet. Add buttermilk, egg, and 1 teaspoon of the salt to flour; whisk until smooth. Place 1 cup panko in a medium shallow dish.

2. Working in batches, dredge coated rings in batter, allowing excess to drip off. Dredge in panko; place on wire racks. Once panko becomes too wet to coat rings, discard. Place remaining 1 cup panko in shallow dish; continue dredging. Let stand on wire racks 15 minutes before frying.

3. Meanwhile, heat oil in a medium Dutch oven over medium-high to 350°F. Fry in batches until golden and crisp, about 3 minutes, turning once halfway through. Drain on wire racks; sprinkle with remaining ½ teaspoon salt. Serve with Kickin' Ranch.

Kickin' Ranch

ACTIVE 5 MIN. · TOTAL 5 MIN.

MAKES 1⅓ CUPS

Whisk together 1 cup **sour cream,** 3 Tbsp. **whole buttermilk,** 2 Tbsp. very finely chopped **jalapeño chile** (from 1 medium), 1½ Tbsp. **sriracha chile sauce,** 1 (1-oz.) envelope **ranch dressing mix,** and ⅛ tsp. **kosher salt** in a medium bowl until smooth.

Big-Batch Lime Lager Shandy

ACTIVE 5 MIN. · TOTAL 5 MIN.

SERVES 6

Stir together 4 (12-oz.) cans chilled **Mexican-style lager** (such as Corona or Stone Buenaveza) and 4 cups cold **limeade** (such as Simply Limeade) in a gallon-size pitcher. Serve with **lime slices.**

COOKING SCHOOL

Bake a Better Quick Bread
Apply these smart tips to any loaf, from apple to zucchini

- 1 -
GREASE THE PAN
Even if you're using a nonstick one (wise move), always coat it thoroughly with butter, shortening, cooking spray, or oil.

- 2 -
TOAST THE NUTS
While entirely optional, this simple step gives quick breads an extra depth of flavor. Make sure nuts are completely cool before adding to the batter.

- 3 -
PREP MIX-INS
A light coating of flour helps prevent chocolate chips, nuts, fruits, and any other add-in ingredients from sinking to the bottom of the pan as the loaf bakes.

- 4 -
DON'T OVERMIX
Unlike bread dough, which is kneaded to develop gluten, quick bread batter should be stirred just until it comes together. Too much mixing can make the batter dense.

- 5 -
USE THE RIGHT KNIFE
When it's time to serve, be sure the loaf is completely cool before cutting with a serrated knife. A gentle sawing motion will make neat slices without squishing down the bread.

FIVE FANCY FINISHES
Dress up your go-to recipe with these topping ideas

Coconut chips

Crystallized ginger

Honey-roasted peanuts

Cacao nibs

Granola

October

SWEET AND TANGY
ROASTED PUMPKIN SALAD

Hello, Sugar!

Sure, the canned stuff is handy, but a fresh sugar pumpkin is a real fall treat, whether you go sweet or savory

Sweet and Tangy Roasted Pumpkin Salad

ACTIVE 15 MIN. - TOTAL 35 MIN.
SERVES 4

Toss 4 cups chopped unpeeled **sugar pumpkin**, 15 **fresh sage leaves**, ½ cup **pumpkin seeds** (from sugar pumpkin), 3 Tbsp. **extra-virgin olive oil**, 1½ Tbsp. **honey**, 1 tsp. **kosher salt,** and ¼ tsp. **black pepper** on a large rimmed baking sheet. Bake at 425°F until pumpkin is tender and golden, 20 to 25 minutes, flipping halfway through. Cool 10 minutes. Meanwhile, whisk together 3 Tbsp. each **extra-virgin olive oil** and **white wine vinegar,** 2 tsp. **Dijon mustard,** 1 Tbsp. **honey,** ½ tsp. **kosher salt,** and ¼ tsp. **black pepper** in a small bowl until emulsified. Combine 5 oz. **mixed baby greens,** 2 oz. **crumbled goat cheese,** ¼ cup **sweetened dried cranberries,** and roasted pumpkin and seeds on a large serving platter. Drizzle with vinaigrette and serve.

SUGAR-AND-PUMPKIN SPICE MUFFINS

Sugar-and-Pumpkin Spice Muffins

ACTIVE 25 MIN. - TOTAL 1 HOUR, 40 MIN.
MAKES 22

Bake 1 whole (3-lb.) **sugar pumpkin** on a large rimmed baking sheet at 400°F until fork-tender, 45 to 60 minutes. Cool 15 minutes. Cut pumpkin open; scoop flesh from skin. Discard skin and seeds. Mash with a fork; transfer 1½ cups to a large bowl (reserve remaining pumpkin for another use). Whisk in 2 **eggs,** 2 cups **granulated sugar,** ½ cup melted **butter,** ¼ cup **milk,** and 1 tsp. **vanilla extract.** Stir in 2½ cups **self-rising flour** and 1 Tbsp. **pumpkin pie spice** until just combined. Divide among 2 (12-cup) muffin trays lined with 22 paper liners. Stir together ⅔ cup **sugar** and 1 tsp. **pumpkin pie spice;** sprinkle over top. Bake at 350°F until a wooden pick inserted in the center comes out clean, about 22 minutes. Cool in tray 5 minutes.

Creamy Pumpkin Soup

ACTIVE 25 MIN. - TOTAL 1 HOUR, 30 MIN.
SERVES 4

Place 1 whole (3-lb.) **sugar pumpkin** and 1 medium **onion,** halved, on a large rimmed baking sheet. Cut the top third off 1 whole head of **garlic.** Place on a piece of foil; drizzle with ½ Tbsp. **extra-virgin olive oil.** Wrap tightly in foil; place on pan with pumpkin. Drizzle onion halves with ½ Tbsp. **olive oil;** place cut sides down. Bake at 400°F until pumpkin is fork-tender, 45 to 60 minutes. Cool 15 minutes. Cut pumpkin open; scoop flesh from skin. Discard skin and seeds. Transfer half of pumpkin and 2 cups **low-sodium vegetable broth** to a blender. Squeeze roasted garlic cloves from head; discard skins. Add cloves to blender. Discard onion peel; add onion to blender. Blend 1 minute; transfer to a medium saucepan. Repeat with remaining pumpkin and another 2 cups **broth.**

Bring to a simmer; stir in 2 tsp. **kosher salt** and ¼ tsp. **black pepper.** Remove from heat; ladle into bowls. Drizzle each with 1 Tbsp. **heavy whipping cream;** top with **fresh thyme leaves, pepitas,** and additional **pepper.**

SMOTHERED PORK
CHOPS WITH RICE
(PAGE 240)

Field of Dreams

It started with a father's wish for his daughters to take over the farm. Today, the women run one of the largest family-owned rice-producing companies in the region

ELTON KENNEDY CAME from a family of ministers in rural northeast Louisiana, but he always wanted to be a farmer. When given the chance to lease land with an option to buy in the town of Mer Rouge, he turned to the plow. He farmed his first rice crop in 1969, and over the years, his bulk-rice companies, Kennedy Rice Dryers and Kennedy Rice Mill, grew to include an average of 60 growers per year working over 15,000 acres. But to him, it was a family business all along. "I always thought that I would have a son to take over one day," Elton says. "As it turned out, having four daughters worked out just the same."

While building his business, he raised those daughters: Patchez, Felicity, Chantel, and Meryl. They spent their childhoods making regular "check on the farm" visits—or, as Felicity remembers, "times when Dad would share all kinds of knowledge, either farming related or just general life lessons." Chantel explains, "When we were growing up, our father always referred to his work as the family business and said it was up to us to carry on." The sisters had other plans, and their dreams didn't necessarily include working the land. In fact, they all went off to school and started their adult lives elsewhere.

The pull home, however, was stronger than they'd thought. After graduating from college, youngest sister Meryl planned to study abroad and struck a deal with her dad. If she agreed to work on the farm for a summer, he would pay for graduate school. As it turned out, studying overseas didn't happen—and neither did graduate school. "I think he knew that if he got me back to the farm, I would fall in love with the business," Meryl says. "It was the best deal of my life."

Chantel returned after college, married, and resumed working in the company. And so did Patchez. "Coming home with my children to family and childhood friends brought a sense of

comfort that cannot be replaced," she says. Felicity joined in, too, working from her home in Tennessee.

Knowing that the business was in good hands, Elton retired in 2010. Then in 2016, the women launched KenChaux, their first in-house packaging and retail brand. It was renamed 4Sisters in 2019 as a nod to their partnership. Meryl assumed the role of chief executive officer, Patchez became chief marketing officer, Felicity started traveling and promoting the company as a brand ambassador, and Chantel's interest in organic farming practices led her to take on the position of sustainability manager. "It was natural for us to tailor our roles to suit each of our skill sets," Felicity explains.

"Dad didn't have to pour his knowledge of this male-dominated

industry into four young girls, but he did it anyway," Meryl says. All those "check on the farm" visits ended up paying off. The company now works more than 25,000 acres of land, has a new state-of-the-art mill, enjoys relationships with national retailers such as Walmart and Whole Foods Market, and has launched an online store (4sistersrice.com). To answer the growing demand for natural products, they offer organic and sustainably grown rice along with the conventionally farmed kind.

Elton began his company with a vision to take a small grain and make a difference in the world. "Working with my girls has been extremely rewarding," he says. "I am beyond proud of the effort they put into growing what I started, something that will be here long after I'm gone."

THE FAMILY (FROM LEFT): PATCHEZ, MERYL, ELTON, CHANTEL, AND FELICITY

VEGETARIAN DIRTY RICE

Smothered Pork Chops with Rice

(Photo, page 238)

ACTIVE 1 HOUR · TOTAL 1 HOUR

SERVES 4

5	Tbsp. unsalted butter, divided
1½	cups uncooked long-grain white rice
1	Tbsp. plus 1 tsp. kosher salt, divided
1	tsp. smoked paprika
1	tsp. garlic powder
1	tsp. onion powder
1½	tsp. black pepper, divided
4	(1-inch-thick) bone-in pork chops (about 12 oz. each)
3	Tbsp. olive oil, divided
1	medium-size sweet onion, thinly sliced (about 2¼ cups)
4	garlic cloves, thinly sliced (about 2 tsp.)
¼	cup all-purpose flour
1½	cups beef stock
1	Tbsp. Worcestershire sauce
2	tsp. Creole mustard
½	cup heavy whipping cream
1	Tbsp. fresh thyme leaves

1. Melt 1 tablespoon of the butter in a medium saucepan over medium. Add rice; cook, stirring often, until shiny and starting to toast and sizzle, 2 to 3 minutes. Add 2½ cups water; bring to a boil over medium-high. Add 1 teaspoon of the salt; reduce to a simmer over medium-low. Cover and simmer, undisturbed, 20 minutes. Remove from heat. Let stand, covered, 5 minutes. Uncover; fluff rice with a fork. Stir in 1 tablespoon of the butter until melted. Cover to keep warm until ready to serve.
2. While rice cooks, stir together smoked paprika, garlic powder, onion powder, 2 teaspoons of the salt, and 1 teaspoon of the pepper in a small bowl; set aside. Pat pork chops dry with paper towels; sprinkle both sides evenly with smoked paprika mixture. Heat 2 tablespoons of the oil in a large cast-iron skillet over medium-high. Carefully add pork chops to skillet; cook, undisturbed, until browned on bottom, 4 to 5 minutes. Flip pork chops; cook until browned on other side, 4 to 5 minutes. Using tongs, lift each pork chop from skillet, and sear around the sides of chops until golden brown, about 1 minute per chop. Return chops to lie

ONE-POT SHRIMP-AND-SAUSAGE JAMBALAYA

flat in skillet, and cook, flipping every 2 minutes, until a thermometer inserted into center of each chop registers 140°F, about 6 minutes. Transfer to a large plate, and cover with aluminum foil. Let rest about 5 minutes.

3. Meanwhile, wipe skillet clean (some bits can remain). Add remaining 3 tablespoons butter and 1 tablespoon oil to skillet; heat over medium until butter is melted. Add onion; cook, stirring occasionally, until softened, 8 to 10 minutes. Add garlic; cook, stirring often, until onion is golden brown and softened, 8 to 10 minutes. (If some of the onion starts to burn before all is caramelized, add a splash of water to skillet.) Sprinkle evenly with flour; cook, stirring constantly, until flour starts to turn golden and smell nutty, about 1 minute. Stir in stock; cook, stirring constantly, until mixture thickens, 1 to 2 minutes. Stir in Worcestershire, mustard, and remaining 1 teaspoon salt and ½ teaspoon pepper. Reduce heat to low; stir in cream.

4. Nestle pork chops in gravy mixture in skillet, and spoon some gravy over chops. Remove from heat. Pile rice evenly on 4 plates, and place 1 pork chop over rice on each plate. Spoon ½ cup gravy on and around each chop. Sprinkle evenly with thyme. Serve immediately.

Vegetarian Dirty Rice

ACTIVE 30 MIN. - TOTAL 1 HOUR
SERVES 4

- 4 Tbsp. olive oil, divided
- 1 (8-oz.) pkg. fresh cremini mushrooms, stemmed and finely chopped (reserve stems for another use)
- 1 (6-oz.) pkg. smoky tempeh bacon (such as Lightlife), chopped
- 1 large poblano chile, finely chopped (about 1 cup)
- 1 small yellow onion, finely chopped (about 1 cup)
- 2 medium celery stalks, finely chopped (about ½ cup)
- 1 tsp. kosher salt
- ¼ cup dry white wine
- 1½ cups uncooked long-grain white rice
- 2 Tbsp. unsalted butter, divided
- 1 tsp. Creole seasoning (such as Tony Chachere's)

- 3½ cups vegetable stock, divided
- 2 Tbsp. thinly sliced fresh chives

1. Heat 2 tablespoons of the oil in a large skillet over medium-high. Add mushrooms; cook, stirring occasionally, until liquid has evaporated and mushrooms have cooked down to about 1 cup, about 5 minutes. Transfer mushrooms to a small bowl, and set aside. (Do not wipe skillet clean.)

2. Add remaining 2 tablespoons oil to skillet, and heat over medium-high. Add tempeh bacon, poblano, onion, celery, and salt; cook, stirring occasionally, until vegetables start to soften and tempeh bacon is golden brown, 4 to 5 minutes. Add wine to skillet; cook, stirring constantly to scrape up browned bits, until liquid is almost completely evaporated, about 1 minute. Add rice and 1 tablespoon of the butter to skillet; cook, stirring constantly, until rice has started to toast and turn golden brown, 1 to 2 minutes. Stir in Creole seasoning, reserved cooked mushrooms, and 3 cups of the stock.

3. Bring mixture to a simmer over medium-high. Cover and reduce heat to medium-low; simmer, undisturbed, 20 minutes. Uncover; stir in ¼ cup of the stock. Cover and continue to simmer, undisturbed, 5 minutes. Remove from heat. Uncover; stir in remaining 1 tablespoon butter and ¼ cup stock. Cover; let steam 5 minutes. Uncover; fluff mixture with a fork. Sprinkle with chives. Serve immediately.

One-Pot Shrimp-and-Sausage Jambalaya

ACTIVE 40 MIN. - TOTAL 1 HOUR
SERVES 6

- 1 medium bunch scallions
- 1 Tbsp. olive oil
- 12 oz. andouille sausage, cut in half lengthwise and crosswise into ½-inch half-moons (about 2½ cups)
- 3 Tbsp. unsalted butter, divided
- 1 medium-size yellow onion, chopped (about 1½ cups)
- 4 medium celery stalks, chopped (about 1¼ cups)
- 1 medium-size green bell pepper, seeded and chopped (about 1 cup)
- 5 medium garlic cloves, finely chopped (about 3 tsp.)

- 2 tsp. Creole seasoning
- 1 tsp. kosher salt
- 1½ cups uncooked long-grain white rice
- 1 (15-oz.) can diced tomatoes with roasted garlic
- 2½ cups chicken stock
- 2 tsp. Louisiana-style hot sauce
- 1 tsp. Worcestershire sauce
- 1 lb. medium shrimp, peeled and deveined
- 2 Tbsp. fresh lemon juice (from 1 lemon)
- ¼ cup finely chopped fresh flat-leaf parsley

1. Thinly slice white and light green parts of scallions; set aside. Thinly slice dark green parts of scallions; set aside separately. Heat oil in a Dutch oven over medium-high. Add sausage; cook, stirring occasionally, until deep golden brown on both sides, 4 to 5 minutes total. Transfer to a small bowl; set aside. Do not wipe Dutch oven clean.

2. Melt 1 tablespoon of the butter in Dutch oven over medium-high. Add onion, celery, and bell pepper; cook, stirring occasionally, until softened, 4 to 5 minutes. Add garlic, Creole seasoning, and salt; cook, stirring constantly, until garlic is fragrant, about 1 minute. Add 1 tablespoon of the butter; cook, stirring constantly, until butter is melted. Add rice; cook, stirring constantly, 1 minute. Add tomatoes, stock, hot sauce, Worcestershire sauce, and reserved cooked sausage. Bring mixture to a boil over medium-high. Cover and reduce heat to medium-low; cook, undisturbed, 8 minutes. Uncover; stir mixture, scraping bottom of Dutch oven to make sure rice doesn't stick. Cover and cook, undisturbed, until almost completely tender, 11 to 12 minutes. Uncover; stir in shrimp and white and light green parts of scallions. Stir to combine. Remove from heat. Let stand, covered, until rice is tender and shrimp are just cooked through, about 5 minutes.

3. Uncover Dutch oven; stir in lemon juice, 2 tablespoons of the parsley, and remaining 1 tablespoon butter. Divide evenly among 6 bowls; sprinkle evenly with dark green scallion parts and remaining 2 tablespoons parsley. Serve immediately.

The Superfood Salad

Whip up a delicious dinner that satisfies the mind and body

LIGHT AND BRIGHT
The weather might be turning cooler and the days shorter, but this recipe will liven up mealtime thanks to fresh baby kale, crunchy cucumber, and a tangy dill-infused vinaigrette. Leafy greens and omega-3-rich salmon deliver a double dose of goodness for your mental health, while the fish and pistachios support your heart.

Cast-Iron Salmon with Baby Kale Salad

ACTIVE 25 MIN. · TOTAL 25 MIN.
SERVES 4

4	(5- to 6-oz.) skin-on salmon fillets
½	tsp. kosher salt, divided
1	large cucumber
2	Tbsp. chopped fresh dill
1½	Tbsp. red wine vinegar
⅛	tsp. granulated sugar
5	Tbsp. olive oil, divided
1	lemon, cut in half crosswise
1	(5-oz.) pkg. baby kale (about 5 cups)
¼	cup shelled pistachios, chopped
¼	tsp. black pepper

1. Place a large cast-iron skillet on oven rack in top third position, and preheat to 425°F. Meanwhile, pat salmon dry with paper towels, and sprinkle evenly with ¼ teaspoon of the salt. Set aside.
2. Peel cucumber, and halve lengthwise; scoop out seeds using a spoon, and slice cucumber into half-moons. Whisk together dill, vinegar, sugar, and 3½ tablespoons of the oil in a medium bowl. Add cucumber, and toss to coat. Set aside.
3. Carefully remove hot skillet from oven (leave oven on), and place on stovetop over high heat. Add remaining 1½ tablespoons oil to hot skillet. Place salmon, skin side down, in skillet; cook until browned and crispy, 3 to 5 minutes. Flip salmon; add lemon halves, cut side down, to skillet. Immediately transfer skillet to oven. Bake in preheated oven until desired degree of doneness, about 5 minutes for medium.
4. Add kale and pistachios to cucumber mixture in bowl, and toss to combine. Sprinkle evenly with pepper and remaining ¼ teaspoon salt. Arrange salmon over salad; squeeze charred lemon halves over assembled salad.

CALORIES: **415** – CARBS: **6 G** – FAT: **30 G**

Party on the Porch!

Nashville entertaining pro Mary Hollis Huddleston has all the tips and tricks for a fuss-free fall bash

THE MONIKER "hostess with the mostest" has been bestowed upon Southerners with a knack for creating memorable events, and Mary Hollis Huddleston is an ideal example. As the founder of the lifestyle site Mrs. Southern Social (mrssouthernsocial.com) and the elevated event-rental company Please Be Seated, the Nashville native knows a thing or two about throwing a festive and stress-free party, thanks to her tasteful eye and tactful playbook. Her secret for breezy entertaining is making it simple, accessible, affordable, and—most importantly—enjoyable. "Don't obsess over perfection; just have fun," Huddleston says. "The hosts set the tone, so if they aren't having a good time, no one will." Here, she serves up her foolproof recipe for a fall porch party with all the autumnal flair and none of the jitters. Showstopping heirlooms, golden-hued centerpieces, a self-serve bar with a signature cocktail, and order-ahead favorites make it an elegant and effortless celebration.

Bourbon-Apple Cider-Thyme Punch

ACTIVE 10 MIN. - TOTAL 10 MIN.
SERVES 8

Stir together 4 cups **apple cider**, 2½ cups **bourbon**, 1 (10-oz.) bottle **club soda**, ½ cup **Thyme Simple Syrup**, and 12 dashes **Angostura bitters** in a punch bowl or pitcher. Serve over ice; garnish with thin **Fuji apple** slices and **fresh thyme sprigs**.

Thyme Simple Syrup

Combine 1 cup **granulated sugar**, 1 cup **water**, and ½ cup loosely packed **fresh thyme sprigs** in a small saucepan. Bring to a boil over medium-high, stirring until sugar dissolves. Remove from heat; cool to room temperature, about 30 minutes. Remove and discard thyme. Keep in an airtight container in the refrigerator up to 2 weeks.

RAISE THE BAR

"Encourage your guests to grab their own drinks so you won't be playing bartender," Huddleston advises. "This is especially important for larger parties so you don't spend the entire evening refilling people's cups. For my self-serve setups, I like to offer a big batch of a signature seasonal cocktail, like the Bourbon-Apple Cider-Thyme Punch from *Southern Living*."

Let's Start with Pie

Comforting, savory weeknight meals that will lure everyone to the table

DEEP-DISH HAM POT PIE

BAKE A BETTER PIE
Brush the egg wash over the top layer of the pastry before cutting the slits to help them stay open so steam can escape.

Deep-Dish Ham Pot Pie

ACTIVE 25 MIN. - TOTAL 1 HOUR
SERVES 6

- 1 (14.1-oz.) pkg. refrigerated piecrusts, at room temperature
- ¼ cup all-purpose flour, plus more for work surface
- 1 lb. fresh-cut cauliflower, broccoli, and carrot blend (about 2 cups, from 2 [12-oz.] pkg.)
- 3 Tbsp. unsalted butter
- 1 medium-size yellow onion, sliced (1½ cups)
- 1 lb. deli ham, cut into ½-inch cubes
- 1¼ cups whole milk
- 3 Tbsp. whole-grain Dijon mustard
- 2 tsp. dried tarragon
- ¾ tsp. black pepper, divided
- 6 oz. Swiss cheese, shredded (about 1½ cups), divided
- 1 large egg, lightly beaten

1. Preheat oven to 450°F. Coat a 9-inch deep-dish pie plate with cooking spray; place on a baking sheet. Roll 1 piecrust into a 12-inch round on a lightly floured work surface. Place in prepared pie plate; place parchment paper over piecrust, and fill with pie weights or dried beans.
2. Bake in preheated oven until crust is set and beginning to turn golden, about 12 minutes. Let cool on a wire rack with pie weights in place 5 minutes; remove parchment and pie weights, and let cool 10 minutes.
3. While piecrust bakes and cools, separate carrots from broccoli and cauliflower; cut all vegetables into bite-size pieces. Melt butter in a large skillet over medium-high. Add onion; cook, stirring often, until onion is softened and slightly brown, about 3 minutes. Add carrots, and cook, stirring occasionally, until softened, about 3 minutes. Add broccoli and cauliflower, and cook, stirring occasionally, until just tender, about 3 minutes. Stir in ham. Sprinkle flour evenly over mixture, and cook, stirring constantly, 1 minute. Stir in milk, mustard, tarragon, and ½ teaspoon of the pepper; cook, stirring constantly, over medium-high until mixture begins to boil and thicken, about 2 minutes. Set aside ⅓ cup of the cheese, and add remaining cheese to mixture in skillet, stirring until combined. Remove from heat.
4. Sprinkle reserved cheese evenly over bottom of prebaked crust; pour vegetable mixture over cheese. Roll second piecrust into a 12-inch round on a lightly floured work surface. Place over vegetable mixture in pie plate; carefully fold edges under, and crimp to seal. Brush lightly with beaten egg. Cut 5 slits in center of crust to allow steam to escape; sprinkle with remaining ¼ teaspoon pepper.
5. Bake at 450°F until crust is golden brown and filling is bubbly, 20 to 25 minutes. Let stand 10 minutes; serve.

CHICKEN-AND-BISCUIT POT PIE

Chicken-and-Biscuit Pot Pie

ACTIVE 25 MIN. - TOTAL 1 HOUR, 5 MIN.
SERVES 6

- 7 Tbsp. unsalted butter, divided, plus more for greasing
- 1 medium-size yellow onion, chopped (2 cups)
- 3 medium carrots, peeled and cut into ¼-inch-thick slices (2 cups)
- 3 celery stalks, sliced (1¼ cups)
- 1 (8-oz.) pkg. fresh green beans, trimmed and cut into 1-inch pieces (2 cups)
- ¼ cup plus 3 Tbsp. all-purpose flour
- 4 cups chicken broth
- 3 (about 1 lb., 12 oz. total) boneless, skinless chicken breasts, cut into 1-inch pieces
- 3 Tbsp. chopped fresh parsley, plus 12 fresh parsley leaves for biscuits
- 1½ Tbsp. chopped fresh thyme
- 2 tsp. kosher salt
- ½ tsp. black pepper, plus more for biscuits
- 12 frozen buttermilk biscuits (from 1 [25-oz.] pkg.)

1. Preheat oven to 375°F. Grease a 13- x 9-inch baking dish with butter.
2. Melt 6 tablespoons of the butter in a Dutch oven or large pot over medium-high. Add onion, carrots, and celery; cook, stirring often, until vegetables are starting to soften, about 5 minutes. Add green beans, and cook, stirring occasionally, 2 minutes. Sprinkle flour evenly over vegetables, and cook, stirring constantly, 1 minute. Stir in chicken broth; cook, stirring constantly, over medium-high until mixture begins to boil and thicken, about 3 minutes. Reduce heat to medium; stir in chicken, parsley, thyme, salt, and pepper. Cook, stirring occasionally, about 2 minutes (chicken will not be cooked through), and remove from heat.
3. Spoon mixture into prepared baking dish, and nestle biscuits slightly into filling. Microwave remaining 1 tablespoon butter in a small microwavable bowl on HIGH 20 seconds. Brush tops of biscuits with butter, and top each biscuit with a parsley leaf and additional pepper.
4. Bake in preheated oven until biscuits are golden brown, chicken is cooked through, and filling is bubbly, 28 to 30 minutes. Let stand 10 minutes; serve.

Mini Mushroom-and-Parsnip Pot Pies

ACTIVE 25 MIN. - TOTAL 50 MIN.

SERVES 4

- ¼ cup unsalted butter
- 2 shallots, chopped (½ cup)
- 2 (8-oz.) pkg. fresh cremini mushrooms, halved
- 1 tsp. kosher salt
- ½ tsp. black pepper, plus more for sprinkling
- 2 medium parsnips, peeled and cut into ¾-inch pieces (2 cups)
- ⅓ cup all-purpose flour, plus more for work surface
- 3 cups vegetable broth
- 1 cup frozen pearl onions (from 1 [14.4-oz.] pkg.), thawed and patted dry
- 2 Tbsp. Worcestershire sauce
- 5 oz. baby kale, coarsely chopped (5 cups packed)
- 2 tsp. chopped fresh thyme or rosemary, divided
- 1 frozen puff pastry sheet (from 1 [17.3-oz.] pkg.), thawed
- 1 large egg, lightly beaten

1. Preheat oven to 425°F. Place 4 mini cast-iron skillets (about 6 inches in diameter and 1¼ inches deep) on a rimmed baking sheet, and set aside.
2. Melt butter in a 10-inch cast-iron skillet over medium-high. Add shallots, and cook, stirring constantly, until transparent, about 2 minutes. Add mushrooms, salt, and pepper; cook, stirring often, until all liquid evaporates and mushrooms are beginning to brown, about 5 minutes. Add parsnips; cook, stirring often, until parsnips are beginning to brown and mushrooms are deeply browned, about 6 minutes. Sprinkle flour evenly over vegetables, stirring to coat; cook, stirring constantly, 1 minute. Add broth, onions, and Worcestershire sauce, stirring to release any browned bits from bottom of skillet. Bring to a boil over medium-high. Boil, stirring constantly, until liquid thickens, about 5 minutes. Remove from heat; add kale and 1 teaspoon of the thyme or rosemary, stirring until kale wilts.
3. Divide vegetable mixture among 4 prepared skillets. Cut puff pastry evenly into 4 squares on a lightly floured work surface; place 1 pastry square on top of filling in each skillet. Brush pastry lightly with beaten egg; sprinkle evenly with remaining 1 teaspoon thyme or rosemary, and sprinkle with additional pepper.
4. Bake in preheated oven until pastry is golden brown and filling is bubbly around edges, about 20 minutes. Let stand 5 minutes; serve.

FLAVOR BOOSTER
Browning the mushrooms and parsnips makes the filling extra savory and ensures that they will be cooked when the pastry is done baking.

Fall Squash Galette

ACTIVE 30 MIN. - TOTAL 1 HOUR, 15 MIN.
SERVES 6

- 4 thick-cut bacon slices, chopped
- 1½ lb. yellow onions, thinly sliced (6 cups)
- 1½ tsp. kosher salt, divided
- ½ tsp. black pepper, divided
- 1 (15-oz.) pkg. frozen butternut squash cubes (3 cups), thawed, well drained, and patted dry
- 1 Tbsp. olive oil
- 1½ tsp. chopped fresh rosemary
- ½ (14.1-oz.) pkg. refrigerated piecrusts
   All-purpose flour, for dusting
- 6 oz. goat cheese, softened, divided
- 1 large egg, lightly beaten

1. Preheat oven to 375°F. Cook bacon, stirring often, in a large skillet over medium until crisp, about 10 minutes. Transfer to a plate and crumble, reserving drippings in skillet; set aside. Transfer 2 tablespoons bacon to a bowl.

2. Add onions, 1 teaspoon of the salt, and ¼ teaspoon of the pepper to drippings in skillet; cook, stirring often, until onions are very soft and deep golden brown, about 20 minutes. (Add water, 1 tablespoon at a time, if onions brown too quickly.) Stir reserved bacon from plate into onion mixture. Remove skillet from heat.

3. Gently toss together squash, oil, rosemary, and remaining ½ teaspoon salt and ¼ teaspoon pepper in a medium bowl.

4. Roll out piecrust dough on a lightly floured work surface into a 13-inch round, and place on a parchment-lined baking sheet. Gently crumble ¾ cup of the goat cheese in center of dough, leaving a 3-inch border around edges. Arrange onion mixture over cheese; arrange squash mixture over onions. Brush dough edges with beaten egg; fold edges up and over filling (dough will only partially cover filling), pleating as you go. Brush edges with beaten egg. Top with reserved 2 tablespoons bacon and remaining ¼ cup of the cheese.

5. Bake in preheated oven until crust is golden and squash is tender, 35 to 40 minutes. Let stand 10 minutes; serve.

DON'T SKIP THIS STEP
The defrosted squash needs to be dry so it won't add extra moisture to the galette. Put it on three layers of paper towels, then gently pat dry with more paper towels.

Sweet Potato-Topped Southwestern Cottage Pie

ACTIVE 25 MIN. · TOTAL 1 HOUR, 5 MIN.

SERVES 6

- 3 lb. sweet potatoes (4 medium)
- 1½ Tbsp. canola oil
- 1½ lb. ground sirloin
- 2 medium-size red or yellow bell peppers, chopped (2 cups)
- 2 medium poblano chiles, chopped (1½ cups)
- 1 medium-size yellow onion, chopped (1¼ cups)
- 1 (16-oz.) jar green chile salsa (such as Chi-Chi's Salsa Verde Mild)
- 1 (15-oz.) can black beans, drained and rinsed
- 1 cup fresh corn kernels (from 2 ears) or frozen corn kernels, thawed
- 1 (1-oz.) envelope taco seasoning mix
- 2 Tbsp. adobo sauce from can
- 1 Tbsp. melted unsalted butter
- 1 tsp. garlic salt
- 1 tsp. chili powder
  Fresh cilantro leaves and diced fresh or pickled jalapeño chiles

1. Pierce sweet potatoes all over using a fork, and place on a microwavable plate. Microwave on HIGH until very soft when pierced with a knife, about 10 minutes. Remove from microwave, and let stand, covered with a clean dish towel, 10 minutes.

2. Meanwhile, preheat oven to 375°F. Coat a 13- x 9-inch baking dish with cooking spray. Heat oil in a large skillet over medium-high. Add ground sirloin; cook, stirring occasionally using a wooden spoon to break up meat, until partially cooked through, about 5 minutes. Add bell peppers, poblanos, and onion; cook, stirring occasionally, until vegetables are tender and beef is cooked through, about 5 minutes. Stir in salsa, black beans, corn, and taco seasoning; remove from heat.

3. Peel sweet potatoes, discarding skins. Place flesh in a large bowl, and mash using a fork. Stir in adobo sauce, butter, garlic salt, and chili powder until well combined.

4. Spoon beef-vegetable mixture into prepared baking dish. Top with dollops of sweet potato mixture; gently spread sweet potato mixture in an even layer using a fork to create a decorative pattern. Bake in preheated oven until sweet potatoes are golden in spots and filling is hot and bubbling, 25 to 28 minutes. Let stand 5 minutes. Garnish with cilantro and jalapeños; serve.

CUT DOWN CLEANUP TIME
Instead of using a baking dish, you can make this recipe in a single skillet if you prefer. Top the beef mixture with the potatoes, and bake as directed.

New-Fashioned Oats

This fruity baked oatmeal is a wholesome way to start your day

Skillet Baked Almond-and-Banana Oatmeal

ACTIVE 15 MIN. - TOTAL 55 MIN.

SERVES 6

- 3 Tbsp. unsalted butter, melted, plus more for greasing
- 2 very ripe large bananas
- 1 large egg
- 2½ cups whole milk
- ⅓ cup almond butter
- 1½ tsp. ground cinnamon, plus more for sprinkling
- 1 tsp. baking powder
- ¾ tsp. honey, plus more for drizzling
- ½ tsp. kosher salt
- 2½ cups uncooked old-fashioned regular rolled oats
- ½ cup sliced almonds
  Sliced bananas

1. Preheat oven to 350°F. Grease a 10-inch cast-iron skillet with butter.
2. Mash bananas in a large bowl until almost smooth. Whisk in egg, milk, almond butter, cinnamon, baking powder, honey, salt, and melted butter until well combined, and stir in oats. Quickly pour mixture into prepared skillet, and sprinkle sliced almonds evenly over top.
3. Bake in preheated oven until oatmeal is set and top is lightly golden, about 35 minutes. Remove from oven, and let cool 5 minutes. Garnish with sliced bananas. Then sprinkle with additional cinnamon and drizzle with additional honey.

The Globe-Trotting Meat Pie

No one knows the origin of the Natchitoches meat pie, but it has several international relatives. There are meat-stuffed empanadas in Spain and the Spanish-speaking Caribbean as well as early French references to a savory turnover known as a pâté, which is made with venison or other meats. It may be connected to England's beef, rutabaga, and potato Cornish pasty or Jamaica's meat patty with its curry-flavored filling—a traditional island snack.

A Legendary Little Pie

Natchitoches, Louisiana, has a history that's even richer than its famous delicacy

I AM NOT GOING TO LIE. It took me several years of living in New Orleans before I could wrap my tongue around the correct pronunciation of Natchitoches, the oldest permanent European settlement in the Louisiana Purchase. Eventually, my fascination with the Creoles of color as portrayed in novels (like Lalita Tademy's *Cane River*) and texts (like Sybil Kein's *Creole: The History and Legacy of Louisiana's Free People of Color*) gave me a reason to learn how to pronounce this place's name. Say it with me: "NACK–a–tish."

Established in 1714 and named for the Native American tribe from that area, the city has a history that includes the early European explorations of Louisiana. The colonization of this region is fraught with enough twists and turns as well as alliances and betrayals to give ample fodder for multiple television miniseries. The mix of Native American, Spanish, French, African, Anglo, and Creole cultures can still be seen today in Natchitoches' Cane River National Heritage Area. This region includes many historic sites and architectural gems such as the hipped–roofed African House at Melrose Plantation, a unique structure that blends African and French architecture and is home to the works of celebrated folk artist Clementine Hunter.

As important as the city is historically and culturally, it might be best known for the humble handheld Natchitoches meat pie. One year at the New Orleans Jazz & Heritage Festival, I joined the line at a meat pie stand and soon became an instant fan. A street snack that has been eaten in Natchitoches since the late 1700s, it's a fried flour turnover filled with a blend of beef and pork that's seasoned with what is simply called the culinary "trinity" in Louisiana: onion, bell pepper, and celery. It may also be flavored with one of the various Cajun spice mixtures and fired up with red chile flakes or a dash or two of hot sauce.

The annual Natchitoches Meat Pie Festival boasts both a pie–making contest and a pie–eating one in celebration of the savory treat that has become one of the symbols of the place with the difficult–to–pronounce name. –Jessica B. Harris

Natchitoches Meat Pies

ACTIVE 1 HOUR, 25 MIN. - TOTAL 1 HOUR, 55 MIN.
MAKES 16

DOUGH
- 5¾ cups all-purpose flour, plus more for work surface and baking sheet
- 1½ tsp. kosher salt
- 1¼ tsp. baking powder
- ¾ cup vegetable shortening
- 2 large eggs
- 1½ cups whole milk

FILLING
- 2 Tbsp. vegetable oil, divided, plus more for frying
- ½ lb. 80/20 ground beef
- ½ lb. ground pork
- 1½ Tbsp. Cajun seasoning
- ½ tsp. kosher salt
- 2 Tbsp. all-purpose flour
- 1 small yellow onion, finely chopped (½ cup)
- ¼ cup finely chopped green bell pepper (from 1 small bell pepper)
- 1 small celery stalk, finely chopped (about 3 Tbsp.)
- 3 garlic cloves, minced (about 1 Tbsp.)

ADDITIONAL INGREDIENT
- 1 large egg

1. Prepare the Dough: Whisk together all-purpose flour, salt, and baking powder in a large bowl. Using a pastry blender or 2 forks, cut in vegetable shortening until mixture is crumbly. Whisk together eggs and milk in a small bowl, and stir egg mixture into flour mixture until a shaggy Dough forms. Transfer to a lightly floured work surface; knead until soft and smooth, about 1 minute. Shape into a disk; cover tightly with plastic wrap. Refrigerate until chilled, at least 30 minutes or up to 1 day.

2. Meanwhile, prepare the Filling: Heat 1 tablespoon of the vegetable oil in a large skillet over medium–high. Add ground beef, ground pork, Cajun seasoning, and salt; cook, stirring often, until meat is browned and crumbled, about 5 minutes. Transfer to a medium bowl, and add flour, tossing to coat. Do not wipe skillet clean.

3. Heat remaining 1 tablespoon vegetable oil in skillet over medium–high. Add yellow onion, bell pepper, celery, and minced garlic. Cook, stirring occasionally, until tender, about 3 minutes. Add onion mixture to beef mixture in bowl, stirring to combine; set aside at room temperature to cool slightly, about 15 minutes.

4. Whisk together egg and 2 tablespoons water in a small bowl, and set aside. On lightly floured work surface, divide chilled Dough into 16 equal pieces, and shape each into a ball. Working with 1 ball at a time, roll out into a 6-inch round, about ⅛ inch thick. Spoon 2 tablespoons Filling in center of circle. Lightly brush edges of round with egg mixture, and fold round in half over Filling. Crimp edges using a fork to seal. Place on a lightly floured parchment paper-lined baking sheet. Repeat process with remaining Dough balls and Filling. Freeze pies, uncovered, for about 20 minutes.

5. Meanwhile, pour vegetable oil into a large Dutch oven to a depth of 2 inches, and heat oil to 370°F over medium–high. Working in batches, fry chilled pies, turning once, until golden brown, 1 to 2 minutes per side, adjusting heat as needed to maintain temperature. Drain on a paper towel-lined baking sheet. Serve immediately.

One-Pan Dinner Plan

Here's a complete chicken supper the whole family will love (surprise bonus: It's sneakily nutritious)

Crispy Chicken with Sweet Potato Fries and Green Beans

ACTIVE 15 MIN. · TOTAL 45 MIN.

SERVES 4

- **4** (6-oz.) bone-in, skin-on chicken thighs, skin removed
- **1** Tbsp. plus 1 tsp. Dijon mustard, divided
- **2** tsp. granulated garlic
- **2** tsp. granulated onion
- **2** tsp. Cajun seasoning
- **1½** tsp. kosher salt, divided
- **½** cup whole-wheat panko breadcrumbs
- **2** Tbsp. plus 1 tsp. olive oil, divided
- **1** sweet potato, cut into ½-inch-thick wedges (about 2 cups)
- **¼** cup finely chopped shallot (from 1 large shallot)
- **1½** Tbsp. orange marmalade
- **3** tsp. white wine vinegar
- **1** (12-oz.) pkg. fresh green beans, trimmed

1. Preheat oven to 400°F with racks in top third and middle positions. Rub chicken all over with 1 tablespoon of the mustard. Stir together garlic, onion, Cajun seasoning, and 1 teaspoon of the salt in a small bowl. Place 1 tablespoon of garlic mixture in a large bowl; set aside. Place panko, 1 tablespoon of the olive oil, and remaining garlic mixture in a small bowl; stir until well combined. Firmly press panko mixture onto tops of thighs. Place on 1 half of a baking sheet.

2. Add sweet potato wedges and 1 teaspoon of the oil to reserved garlic mixture in large bowl; toss to combine. Arrange wedges evenly on other half of baking sheet. Roast in preheated oven on middle rack for 15 minutes.

3. Meanwhile, add shallot, marmalade, vinegar, and remaining 1 teaspoon mustard, ½ teaspoon salt, and 1 tablespoon oil in a large bowl; whisk to combine. Add green beans; toss to coat.

4. Remove baking sheet from oven; flip sweet potato wedges. Place green beans on top of wedges, reserving any marmalade mixture in bowl. Return to oven; roast until vegetables are tender, chicken is golden brown, and a thermometer inserted into thickest portion of chicken registers 165°F, about 15 minutes. Remove baking sheet from oven; increase oven temperature to broil. Broil in preheated oven on top rack until green beans are blistered and chicken is golden brown, 1 to 3 minutes. Serve chicken with vegetables. Drizzle green beans with reserved marmalade mixture.

CALORIES: **324** – CARBS: **28 G** – FAT: **13 G**

Caramel Apples for Grown-Ups

Forget the fruit on a stick, and dig into this warm, tasty dessert

Apple Dumplings with Bourbon-Caramel Sauce

ACTIVE 40 MIN. - TOTAL 2 HOURS
SERVES 6

- 6 Tbsp. granulated sugar
- 1½ tsp. cornstarch
- 1 tsp. grated lemon zest (from 1 lemon)
- ¾ tsp. apple pie spice
- 2 (14.1-oz.) pkg. refrigerated piecrusts (4 crusts)
- All-purpose flour, for surface
- 6 small (6 to 7 oz. each) Gala apples, peeled and cored
- 6 Tbsp. finely chopped walnuts
- 1½ Tbsp. unsalted butter, cut into 6 (½-inch) cubes
- 1 large egg, lightly beaten
- 2 Tbsp. turbinado sugar
- Bourbon-Caramel Sauce (recipe, below right)

1. Stir together first 4 ingredients in a medium bowl; set aside.
2. Unroll 1 piecrust on a lightly floured surface; smooth into a 12-inch circle. Fold in 2 sides of circle until they meet in center of piecrust (about 3 inches on each side). Roll folded piecrust into a 14- x 7-inch rectangle. Cut rectangle in half, forming 2 (7-inch) squares. Repeat with 2 more piecrusts. (Reserve remaining piecrust.)
3. Place 1 apple in center of each dough square. Fill each apple with 1 tablespoon walnuts and 1 butter cube, and top with 1 tablespoon sugar mixture. Brush edges of dough with a small amount of the egg. Bring dough corners up to meet over center of apple; pinch side seams of dough to seal. Fold back dough ends over top of apple to leave a ¼-inch opening.
4. Cut leaf shapes out of remaining piecrust. Brush with a small amount of egg; press lightly onto top of dough-wrapped apples, being careful not to cover opening. Place on a parchment paper-lined rimmed baking sheet; freeze, uncovered, 30 minutes.

5. Preheat oven to 375°F. Remove apple dumplings from freezer. Brush evenly with remaining egg; sprinkle with turbinado sugar. Bake until dough is golden brown and apples are tender, 40 to 45 minutes. Cool 5 minutes; serve with Bourbon-Caramel Sauce.

Bourbon-Caramel Sauce

ACTIVE 10 MIN. - TOTAL 15 MIN.
MAKES 1½ CUPS

Cook ½ cup **granulated sugar** and ½ cup packed **dark brown sugar** in a medium-size heavy saucepan over medium, stirring occasionally, until mixture begins to bubble and smells nutty, about 6 minutes. Remove from heat, and whisk in 6 Tbsp. **butter**. Return to medium heat. Cook, whisking constantly, until mixture begins to boil, about 1 minute. Carefully add ½ cup **heavy whipping cream**. Cook, whisking constantly, until mixture is well combined and boiling, about 1 minute. Remove saucepan from heat; whisk in 1 tsp. **fine sea salt** and 2 Tbsp. **bourbon**. Cool 5 minutes before serving.

COOKING SCHOOL

Yep, a Skillet Can Do That

Cast-iron pans aren't just for frying chicken and cooking bacon

MAKE AN ICEBOX PIE

Ideal for baked sweets like cinnamon rolls and cobblers, skillets can also step in with chilled desserts like pies. Whether the recipe calls for a press-in cookie crust or pastry, use the pan as a pie plate. Avoid sudden temperature changes (oven to freezer), which can cause cracking.

SEPARATE GARLIC CLOVES

Break up a whole head of garlic without scattering cloves all over the kitchen. Set it in a skillet with the pointed end facing up. Place another pan on top, and then apply pressure until the head comes apart and the cloves separate.

DEFROST FROZEN MEAT

Quickly thaw thin cuts (1 inch thick or less) of meat. Remove from packaging, and place in a zip-top plastic bag. Set on an inverted skillet at room temperature. The pan's ambient heat will transfer to the meat and speed up defrosting.

BAKE PIZZA

Deep-dish pizza fans know the magic of cast iron, but if you prefer a thinner crust, flip the skillet over to use the underside as a pizza stone. Place the pan in the oven as it preheats to get the surface piping hot for when you add the dough.

THE RIGHT WAY TO RESEASON CAST IRON

1

Preheat oven to 450°F. Scrub the pan in hot, soapy water. Rinse and dry well.

2

Spread a thin layer of melted shortening or vegetable oil over the inside and outside of the pan.

3

Place the pan upside down on the middle rack. (Line lower rack with foil to catch drips.) Bake 1 hour; let cool in the oven.

November

BROWN SUGAR-GLAZED
BRUSSELS SPROUTS
WITH BACON

Sprouts to Savor

These cold-weather vegetables have become welcome guests at the holiday table.
Here are three new ways to serve them this year

Brown Sugar-Glazed Brussels Sprouts with Bacon

ACTIVE 20 MIN. - TOTAL 20 MIN.
SERVES 4

Cook 2 slices of **thick-cut applewood-smoked bacon,** chopped, in a large cast-iron skillet over medium-high, stirring often, until fat has rendered and bacon is crisp, 8 to 10 minutes. Transfer bacon to a paper towel-lined plate, reserving drippings in skillet. Reduce heat to medium, and add 1 lb. **fresh Brussels sprouts,** trimmed and halved, to skillet. Cook, stirring occasionally, until just tender and charred in spots, 8 to 10 minutes. Remove from heat; stir in cooked bacon, 2 Tbsp. **light brown sugar,** 1 Tbsp. **unsalted butter,** ¾ tsp. **kosher salt,** ¼ tsp. **black pepper,** and ¼ cup chopped **pecans** until butter melts.

Crispy Smashed Brussels Sprouts

ACTIVE 10 MIN. - TOTAL 35 MIN.
SERVES 8

Preheat oven to 425°F. Place 2 lb. trimmed **fresh Brussels sprouts** in a large microwavable bowl with ¼ cup water. Cover tightly with plastic wrap, and microwave on HIGH until just tender, 6 to 8 minutes. Carefully remove and discard plastic wrap; drain. Place cooked Brussels sprouts on a large rimmed baking sheet. Using flat bottom of a measuring cup or mug, smash each Brussels sprout, and pat dry with paper towels. Drizzle evenly with 2 Tbsp. **extra-virgin olive oil,** and sprinkle evenly with 2½ tsp. minced **fresh garlic,** 1 tsp. **kosher salt,** and ¼ tsp. **black pepper;** toss to coat. Bake 10 minutes. Remove from oven, and sprinkle with ⅓ cup grated **Parmesan cheese.** Bake until cheese is melted and set, about 5 minutes. Using a spatula, transfer Brussels sprouts mixture to a serving platter. Garnish with **fresh thyme leaves.**

CRISPY SMASHED
BRUSSELS SPROUTS

Brussels Sprout Spoon Bread

ACTIVE 20 MIN. - TOTAL 1 HOUR, 5 MIN.
SERVES 8

Preheat oven to 350°F. Melt ½ cup **unsalted butter** in a large skillet over medium-high. Add 1¼ cups chopped **sweet onion;** cook, stirring often, until tender, about 5 minutes. Transfer onion mixture to a large bowl. Melt 2 Tbsp. **unsalted butter** in skillet over medium-high. Add 12 oz. **fresh Brussels sprouts,** trimmed and halved, to skillet, cut side down. Cook without stirring until browned, about 2 minutes. Flip sprouts over, and remove from heat; set aside. Whisk 1 (8½-oz.) pkg. **corn muffin mix,** 1 (14¼-oz.) can **cream-style corn,** 1 cup **sour cream,** and 3 **large eggs** into cooked onion mixture in bowl until combined. Coat a 13- x 9-inch baking dish with **cooking spray.** Pour batter into prepared baking dish. Top with cooked Brussels sprouts, cut side up. Bake until puffed and golden brown, 40 to 45 minutes. Serve immediately.

Planting Good Seeds

New Orleans chef Emeril Lagasse is raising a new crop of young cooks
through his school gardens and teaching kitchens

WHEN YOU'RE A TV CELEBRITY chef and win $125,000 on *Who Wants to Be a Millionaire?*, what do you do with the money? For New Orleans' Emeril Lagasse, the answer was easy. He phoned his friend Sister Lillian McCormack, founder of St. Michael Special School in New Orleans (which is privately funded for students who have intellectual and developmental disabilities), and offered a lifeline in the form of his winnings.

For high-profile chefs, the options for giving back are endless, but that donation 22 years ago was Lagasse's first taste of what it meant to make a real difference. Grateful for his enormous success, not only on television but also with his award-winning cookbooks and restaurants throughout the nation, Lagasse (who grew up in Massachusetts and later made a home in New Orleans) found himself in a position to empower and inspire young people. Just two years after his game show win, he launched the Emeril Lagasse Foundation with the aim of mentoring youth through food. His organization has since granted

more than $18 million to children's charities, supporting nutrition, arts, and culinary programs.

But early on, the chef realized that a major obstacle for young children in the U.S. was a disconnect with food—not knowing where it comes from and not having access to enough good, fresh ingredients. Even kids who do have adequate meals sometimes still believe that juice comes from a carton or carrots from a can. In 2016, Lagasse turned his focus to establishing teaching kitchens and edible schoolyards nationwide, and his organization hired Katie Mularz to launch what's since become its signature outreach: Emeril's Culinary Garden & Teaching Kitchen. This initiative helps kids in kindergarten through eighth grade learn to seed, harvest, cook, and share the gifts of the garden.

The team began inviting families to come on Saturdays and harvest what they wanted out of the garden—as long as they did something with the food at home that included the child.

At Dr. John Ochsner Discovery Health Sciences Academy, one of the partner sites, seventh grader Nakira is gaining useful know-how as well as confidence in the kitchen. "She loves learning cooking techniques, which she then teaches her father and me," says her mother, Raina Edwards. They often make one of Nakira's favorite dishes, yakamein (a beloved local noodle soup that's spiced with Creole seasoning); each family often has its own secret ingredient. "The program has changed the way we cook," Edwards says. "We have decreased the amount of processed meals we eat and make a lot more fresh food together at home."

Emeril's Culinary Garden & Teaching Kitchen program currently has six official partner schools across the country, from Washington, D.C., to California. Even with nothing left to prove, the chef remains committed to mentoring the next generation of cooks, gardeners, and teachers. Everyone can give back in

small ways, he says, particularly when it comes to investing in people. "Volunteer your time; be present," Lagasse says. "You don't have to have means in order to have meaning."

Emeril's Maple-Butter Corn Muffins

ACTIVE 20 MIN. · TOTAL 45 MIN.

MAKES 1 DOZEN

- 1¼ cups all-purpose flour
- ½ cup fine yellow cornmeal
- 2 tsp. baking powder
- ½ tsp. baking soda
- ½ tsp. kosher salt
- 2 large eggs
- ½ cup whole milk
- ½ cup sour cream
- ¼ cup light brown sugar
- 3 Tbsp. melted unsalted butter, plus 7 Tbsp. softened unsalted butter, divided
- ½ cup plus 2 Tbsp. pure maple syrup, divided

1. Preheat oven to 350°F. Line a 12-cup muffin tray with paper liners; set aside.
2. Whisk together flour, cornmeal, baking powder, baking soda, and salt in a medium bowl until combined. Whisk together eggs, milk, sour cream, brown sugar, 3 tablespoons melted butter, and ½ cup of the maple syrup in a large bowl until smooth. Add flour mixture to egg mixture; whisk just until incorporated, being careful not to overmix. Divide batter evenly among prepared muffin liners.
3. Bake in preheated oven until golden brown, 18 to 20 minutes. Remove from oven. Let cool in muffin tray 5 minutes.
4. While muffins bake, whisk together the softened butter and remaining 2 tablespoons maple syrup in a small bowl until smooth. Set aside until ready to use. (Bowl of maple butter may be wrapped tightly with plastic wrap and stored in refrigerator up to 2 weeks.) Serve muffins warm with maple butter.

EMERIL'S MAPLE-BUTTER CORN MUFFINS

A Big Easy Thanksgiving

Inspired by his mother's epic holiday feasts, New Orleans chef Kevin Belton
cooks a small-scale meal with the same generous spirit

When Kevin Belton was growing up in New Orleans, his family had a strict hierarchy in the kitchen. "My grandmother was like the executive chef, my mom was the executive sous chef, and I was the hired helper," he recalls. Long before his celebrated career as a culinary instructor and his own PBS cooking series about Louisiana cuisine, Belton developed a love for food from those matriarchs.

In their household, Thanksgiving kicked off the Monday before, when his mom started prepping and meticulously organizing the refrigerator to accommodate the myriad groceries they would need. In her role as executive chef, his grandmother Magnolia Battle (known as Nan) was there to consult on ingredients. Meanwhile, Belton dutifully peeled the shrimp and snapped the ends of the green beans.

She always made enough food so that every household had their own turkey and pan of dressing to take home—nobody had to cook for an entire week. Over the years, Belton has tried to re-create his mother's menu, but the recipes never turn out quite the same without her; she passed away when he was just a teenager.

His holiday celebrations look a little different these days, and he cooks less at home because his two oldest sons live out of town. So along with his wife, Monica, and his youngest son, Noah, Belton picks a meal they can prepare together. They might experiment with something less traditional like a piña colada bread pudding or even a boudin-stuffed turkey breast instead of a whole bird. But that same spirit from his childhood gatherings remains.

His family's Thanksgiving is always an open house with an invitation for anyone to join and bring a dish to share. Although the food is always delicious, the time together is the real draw. "It's not so much what goes on the table as who's around it," Belton says.

Boudin-Stuffed Turkey Breast with Lemon-Garlic Butter

ACTIVE 55 MIN. - TOTAL 2 HOURS, 45 MIN.
SERVES 6

LEMON-GARLIC BUTTER
- ¼ cup unsalted butter, melted
- 2 Tbsp. fresh lemon juice (from 1 lemon)
- 5 garlic cloves, minced (about 1 Tbsp. plus 2 tsp.)
- ½ Tbsp. chopped fresh oregano
- ½ Tbsp. chopped fresh thyme

SPICE BLEND
- 1 Tbsp. Creole seasoning
- 1 tsp. sweet or smoked paprika
- 1 tsp. garlic powder
- 1 tsp. onion powder
- 1 tsp. dried thyme
- 1 tsp. dried oregano
- 1 tsp. kosher salt
- ½ tsp. chili powder
- 2 Tbsp. olive oil

TURKEY
- 1 cup Kevin's Boudin (recipe opposite) or store-bought boudin (such as Zummo Meat Co.), casings removed
- 1 cup chicken stock, plus about ¼ cup more if using store-bought boudin
- 1 (3-lb.) boneless, skin-on turkey breast roast, thawed
- 1 medium-size sweet onion, quartered
- 2 medium celery stalks
- 3 garlic cloves, cut in half lengthwise
- 4 (4-inch) fresh thyme sprigs

1. Prepare the Lemon-Garlic Butter: Whisk together butter, lemon juice, garlic, oregano, and thyme in a medium bowl. Set aside.

2. Prepare the Spice Blend: Stir together Creole seasoning, paprika, garlic powder, onion powder, thyme, oregano, salt, and chili powder in a small bowl; add olive oil, stirring until well combined. Set aside.

3. Prepare the Turkey: Preheat oven to 425°F. Place Kevin's Boudin in a small bowl, and set aside. (If using store-bought boudin, add about ¼ cup chicken stock, 2 tablespoons at a time, to moisten. Stir until mixture is moist and holds together when squeezed.) Pat turkey dry using paper towels. (If turkey is encased in netting, remove and discard.) Place turkey, skin-side down, on a clean cutting board; unroll to flatten. Holding the blade of a chef's knife parallel to cutting board, slice into thickest portion of breast, cutting along the length but not all the way through. Unfold so breast opens like a book. Place a piece of plastic wrap on top, and pound using a meat mallet or heavy skillet until turkey is about ¾ inch thick and is even in thickness. Remove plastic wrap. Spoon boudin into center of breast to create a log shape; roll 1 end of the breast over to encase boudin and meet the other end of breast. Using kitchen twine, tie rolled stuffed breast at 1- to 1½-inch intervals to secure. Place onion, celery, garlic, and thyme sprigs in a small roasting pan. Place rolled breast, skin-side up, on top of vegetables. Slowly spoon or pour Lemon-Garlic Butter over turkey, using your hands to massage it all around and under twine. Slather Spice Blend over outside of turkey. (If desired, cover with aluminum foil and refrigerate for up to 24 hours. Remove from refrigerator 1 hour before cooking.)

4. Pour 1 cup stock into pan. Place in preheated oven; reduce oven temperature to 325°F. Bake, uncovered, until a thermometer inserted into thickest part of the breast registers 155°F, 1 hour, 30 minutes to 1 hour, 45 minutes. (For crispier skin, baste every 30 minutes.) If it starts to brown too quickly, loosely tent a piece of aluminum foil over turkey, and continue to bake. Let rest 20 to 30 minutes. The temperature will continue to rise to 165°F. Carve and serve.

Kevin's Boudin

ACTIVE 1 HOUR · TOTAL 2 HOURS, 50 MIN.
MAKES ABOUT 13 CUPS

- 3 cups white short-grain rice, cooked and cooled
- 2 lb. boneless pork shoulder (Boston butt), cut into 1-inch cubes
- 1 lb. pork, beef, or calf liver, cut into large chunks
- 8 cups chicken stock
- 1½ cups chopped yellow onion (from 1 medium onion)
- ½ cup chopped green bell pepper (from 1 medium bell pepper)
- ½ cup chopped celery (from 2 medium celery stalks)
- 2 garlic cloves
- 2 Tbsp. Creole seasoning, divided
- 2 tsp. kosher salt, divided
- 2 tsp. cayenne pepper, divided
- 1¼ tsp. black pepper, divided
- 1 cup chopped fresh flat-leaf parsley, divided
- 1 cup chopped scallions, divided (from about 5 scallions)

1. Place rice in a large bowl; fluff using a fork. Set aside.

2. Stir together pork shoulder, liver, stock, onion, bell pepper, celery, garlic cloves, 1 tablespoon of the Creole seasoning, 1 teaspoon of the salt,

¼ teaspoon of the cayenne pepper, and ½ teaspoon of the black pepper in a large Dutch oven. Bring to a boil over high, and reduce heat to medium-low. Simmer, uncovered and undisturbed, until pork shoulder and liver are tender, about 1 hour, 30 minutes. Remove from heat, and drain, reserving 1½ cups cooking liquid, pork shoulder, and liver.

3. In a meat grinder fitted with a ¼-inch-hole grinder plate, grind pork shoulder, liver, ¼ cup of the parsley, and ¼ cup of the scallions. (Pork shoulder, liver, parsley, and scallions can also be coarsely chopped, in batches, in a food processor.)

4. Stir together pork mixture, reserved rice, and remaining 1 tablespoon of the Creole seasoning, 1 teaspoon salt, 1¾ teaspoons cayenne pepper, ¾ teaspoon black pepper, ¾ cup parsley, and ¾ cup scallions until well combined. Add reserved cooking liquid, about ½ cup at a time, stirring until mixture is moist but holds together when squeezed. Form mixture into 38 (3-ounce) balls or patties (about ⅓ cup each), or freeze in gallon-size zip-top plastic freezer bags for up to 3 months.

Savoring Sweet Potatoes

More than just a pie filling, this humble vegetable has been a source
of dessert inspiration across the South for centuries

SWEET POTATO PIE
SQUARES

EVERY FALL, sweet potatoes take a starring role at special occasions. For many Southern cooks, that means pie. The homey dessert has had remarkable staying power over many generations while other sweet potato–based treats, such as cobblers and puddings, have fallen out of favor. It seems like it's time for a dessert revival. Those old cookbooks gathering dust somewhere in your home are full of classic recipes that are eager to be reacquainted with today's palates and plates.

Perhaps the earliest dessert in the antebellum South was sweet potatoes roasted in the ashes of a slow fire. They were typically made by those with meager resources, namely enslaved Africans and the lower class, who often cooked in rudimentary hearths or over open fires. They required minimal effort to make, and people could work on other tasks while they were roasting. Some called them "candied yams" because of the glassy appearance from the natural sugars oozing to the surface or from being coated in lard during the cooking process. This, of course, differs from today's butter-spice-and-sugar-braised candied yams.

Southerners of means prepared complex desserts in a more elaborate hearth or even on a stove, and they had access to better cooking equipment and a variety of ingredients. One of their prized creations was the sweet potato pone. The indigenous Algonquian people used the words "poan" and "appoan" to describe foods that were roasted or baked in the ashes of a fire, particularly an eggless bread that was usually made of just cornmeal and salt with water or oil to bind it. Eventually, it became "pone" in English, but when describing sweet potatoes, it references a spiced pudding instead of a simple quick bread. Although some cooks claim there are differences, the words "pone" and "pudding" were used interchangeably for this dessert. One of the earliest documented recipes specifically calling this a "pone" appeared in the legendary 1847 cookbook *The Carolina Housewife* by Sarah Rutledge. It combined sweet potatoes, butter, ginger, milk, orange peel, and sugar in a shallow dish and was cooked in a slow oven. Many pone recipes printed in late 19th-century newspapers called for either grating or mashing the sweet potatoes.

In the middle of the 19th century, cobblers were increasingly popular. The earliest recipes typically used a deep cooking vessel (like a Dutch oven), which was filled with fruit and a sugary liquid, topped with raw biscuit dough, and baked over a fire. To cook the dough, hot coals were placed on a lid over the vessel. Cobbler recipes varied as to whether the sweet potatoes should be cut or mashed, but a number of them instructed bakers to alternate layers of the spiced veggies and dough until the vessel was completely filled. Otherwise, they were prepared and spiced similarly to fruit cobblers. As the cooking methods continued to evolve, chefs added a bottom crust to desserts, too.

This addition brought the cobbler more in line with the sweet potato pie. The biggest difference is that the pie usually did not have a top crust. It was likely inspired by carrot pudding, a popular British dessert during the colonial period. The recipes are so similar that one can see a cook swapping one sweet, orange-colored vegetable for another. It's believed that the iconic sweet potato pie recipe first appeared in 1824 in *The Virginia Housewife* by Mrs. Mary Randolph. She called it a "pudding," but it resembled an open-face pie and included brandy, butter, citron, eggs, lemon peel, nutmeg, and sweet potatoes. Today's versions tend to be less elaborate than Randolph's, but the template was set. Another tasty and popular riff on this dessert is the hand pie, which completely encases the sweet potato mixture in a crust.

Although not as well-known as the cobblers, pies, and pones, sweet potato cake recipes appeared in newspapers as early as the 1870s and 1880s. Southerners used a wide variety of ingredients including grated or mashed sweet potatoes, butter, cinnamon, powdered mace, eggs, flour, milk, nuts, nutmeg, shortening (Crisco, in particular, beginning during the early 1900s), and vanilla. Many of the recipes were for layer and tea cakes, but pound cake has since gained in popularity. During the first half of the 20th century, famed agricultural scientist George Washington Carver was one of the biggest sweet potato cheerleaders ever to walk the earth. Carver, who was known for his sliced sweet potato pie, heavily promoted the vegetable's

cultivation and consumption, especially in desserts.

Your holiday table may already be crowded, but these recipes are worthy additions. Everyone loves a comeback story—especially one with a sweet ending. –Adrian Miller

Sweet Potato Pie Squares

This amped-up version of a holiday classic is baked in a 9- x 13-inch dish, so there's plenty to feed the masses. And just like any crowd-pleaser, it has a few surprises: a pecan-studded pastry crust and a swooping meringue top.

ACTIVE 30 MIN. - TOTAL 1 HOUR, 45 MIN.

SERVES 15

CRUST
- 1¼ cups all-purpose flour
- ½ cup granulated sugar
- ½ cup unsalted butter, softened and cut into pieces
- ¼ tsp. kosher salt
- ⅔ cup toasted pecans, finely chopped

FILLING
- 2 lb. sweet potatoes (about 3 medium), peeled and cut into 1-inch cubes
- 5 Tbsp. unsalted butter, softened
- ⅔ cup granulated sugar
- 1¼ tsp. vanilla extract
- ½ tsp. ground cinnamon
- ¼ tsp. kosher salt
- ¼ tsp. ground nutmeg
- 1 (5-oz.) can evaporated milk
- 3 large eggs

MERINGUE
- 4 large egg whites
- ¼ tsp. cream of tartar
- ½ cup granulated sugar

1. Prepare the Crust: Preheat oven to 350°F. Line a 9- x 13-inch baking dish with parchment paper. Add flour, granulated sugar, softened butter, and salt to a food processor, and pulse until combined, 10 to 12 times. Add toasted pecans, and pulse until mixture forms a dough, 8 to 10 times. Break dough into pieces, and spread over bottom of prepared dish. Place a sheet of parchment paper over dough; press gently with the bottom of a measuring cup to smooth. Bake until edges are lightly browned, about 20 minutes.

Continued on page 264

SWEET POTATO PONE WITH CARDAMOM WHIPPED CREAM

BOURBON-SWEET POTATO BREAD PUDDING

Continued from page 263

2. Prepare the Filling: Bring a pot of water to a boil over medium-high. Add potatoes; reduce heat to medium-low, and simmer until tender, about 15 minutes. Drain potatoes, and transfer to a large bowl. Add butter, and mash until smooth. Add sugar, vanilla, cinnamon, salt, nutmeg, evaporated milk, and eggs; blend well. Spread evenly over Crust. Bake in preheated oven until center is set and Crust is deep golden, about 45 minutes. Let cool completely.

3. Prepare the Meringue: Beat egg whites in a stand mixer fitted with a whisk attachment on medium-high speed until soft peaks form, about 2 minutes. Add cream of tartar and 1 tablespoon of the sugar; beat well. Continue to slowly add sugar, 1 tablespoon at a time, letting mixture blend 1 to 2 minutes between additions. Once all sugar has been added and stiff peaks form, use a spoon to dollop Meringue over pie, making swoops and swirls. Use a torch to toast Meringue, or broil until browned, 2 to 3 minutes. (Glass dishes should not be set under the broiler.)

Sweet Potato Pone with Cardamom Whipped Cream

Even if you've never tried this concoction, you're likely familiar with its flavors. Similar to a sweet potato pie, it features warm spices along with the addition of molasses, which gives depth. The potatoes are shredded (rather than cooked and mashed); we recommend using the smallest hole on your grater to get this job done—it will require a little bit of elbow grease but will yield a more pleasant texture.

ACTIVE 20 MIN. - TOTAL 1 HOUR, 30 MIN.

SERVES 8

PONE

- 3 Tbsp. unsalted butter, melted, plus more for greasing the pie plate
- ½ cup granulated sugar
- 3 large eggs
- ½ cup heavy whipping cream
- 2 Tbsp. molasses
- 1 tsp. ground cinnamon
- 1 tsp. vanilla extract
- ½ tsp. kosher salt
- ½ tsp. ground ginger

- ¼ tsp. ground nutmeg
- 1¾ lb. (about 3 small) sweet potatoes, peeled and finely shredded (about 6 cups)

CARDAMOM WHIPPED CREAM
- ¾ cup heavy whipping cream
- ¼ tsp. ground cardamom
- ¼ tsp. vanilla extract
- 3 Tbsp. powdered sugar

1. Prepare the Pone: Preheat oven to 350°F. Grease a 9-inch deep-dish pie plate with butter. Whisk together sugar and eggs in a large bowl. Add heavy cream, melted butter, molasses, cinnamon, vanilla, salt, ginger, and nutmeg; whisk once more to combine. Fold in shredded sweet potato until completely incorporated.

2. Pour sweet potato mixture into prepared pie plate; cover with aluminum foil, and seal edges. Bake, covered, in preheated oven 45 minutes. Uncover and bake until edges are browned, 10 to 15 minutes. Remove to a wire rack, and let rest 10 minutes before serving.

3. Prepare the Cardamom Whipped Cream: Place heavy cream in a bowl, and beat with a hand mixer on medium-high speed until soft peaks form, 1 to 2 minutes. Add cardamom and vanilla; gradually add powdered sugar, beating until stiff peaks form, 2 to 3 minutes. Serve Pone warm or at room temperature topped with whipped cream. Cover and refrigerate any leftovers.

Bourbon-Sweet Potato Bread Pudding

A good bread pudding has just the right ratio of custard to bread, so it ends up rich and decadent rather than too eggy or soggy. To help avoid the latter, the bread here is lightly toasted to ensure it's dry enough to soak up all the bourbon-flavored goodness.

ACTIVE 20 MIN. - TOTAL 1 HOUR, 40 MIN., PLUS 1 HOUR STANDING

SERVES 8

- 1 large (12- to 14-oz.) sweet potato (makes about 1¼ cups mashed)
- 3 Tbsp. unsalted butter, plus more for greasing dish
- ¾ tsp. kosher salt, divided
- 10 cups (1-inch) cubed challah bread (from 1 [16-oz.] loaf)
- 5 large egg yolks
- 2¼ cups heavy whipping cream
- ½ cup packed light brown sugar
- ⅓ cup honey
- ⅓ cup bourbon
- 1½ tsp. vanilla extract
- 1 tsp. ground cinnamon
- 6 Tbsp. toasted chopped pecans

1. Preheat oven to 325°F. Pierce sweet potato several times using a fork, and place on a microwave-safe plate. Microwave potato on HIGH 4 minutes. Flip potato with a pair of tongs (it will be hot), and microwave 5 minutes more. Check for tenderness with a fork, and continue to microwave in 1-minute increments until cooked through, if needed. Let potato cool enough to be handled, about 10 minutes. Peel potato, and place flesh in a medium bowl. Add butter and ¼ teaspoon of the salt, and mash until well combined. Set aside.

2. Spread bread cubes on a baking sheet; bake in preheated oven until dried out but not browned, turning halfway through, 13 to 15 minutes. Let cool completely on pan, about 20 minutes.

3. Grease an 8-inch baking dish with butter. Whisk egg yolks in a large bowl, and set aside. Combine heavy cream, sugar, honey, bourbon, and vanilla in a medium saucepan. Gently warm over low until sugar and honey are dissolved, 2 to 3 minutes. Whisk in cinnamon and remaining ½ teaspoon salt. Remove from heat, and gradually whisk cream mixture into egg yolks in bowl until well combined. Add sweet potato mixture to cream mixture, and whisk until mostly smooth. Add bread cubes, and toss gently until moistened.

4. Spread half of the soaked bread cubes in prepared dish, and sprinkle with half of the pecans. Repeat with remaining soaked bread cubes and pecans. Pour any remaining custard from bowl over mixture, and let stand 15 minutes.

5. Bake in preheated oven until center is set, 50 to 60 minutes, rotating pan halfway through and covering with aluminum foil during last 10 to 15 minutes to prevent overbrowning, if needed. Let rest at least 15 minutes before serving.

Sweet Potato Cake with Cream Cheese Frosting

(Photo, page 266)

Mashed sweet potatoes give this cake an earthy flavor and a moist texture. You don't even need to spend time baking the potatoes in the oven; microwaving is a far quicker method with equally tasty results. While the cake is plenty irresistible with just the Cream Cheese Frosting, a sprinkling of chopped pecans or walnuts certainly doesn't hurt.

ACTIVE 40 MIN. - TOTAL 1 HOUR, 15 MIN., PLUS 1 HOUR COOLING

SERVES 12

CAKE LAYERS
- 1 large (12- to 14-oz.) sweet potato (makes about 1½ cups mashed)
  Baking spray with flour
- 2½ cups bleached cake flour
- 2 tsp. baking powder
- ¾ tsp. kosher salt
- ¾ tsp. ground ginger
- ½ tsp. baking soda
  Pinch of ground nutmeg
- ¾ cup whole milk
- ¼ cup molasses
- 1 tsp. vanilla extract
- 1¼ cups granulated sugar
- ¾ cup unsalted butter, softened
- 3 large eggs, at room temperature

CREAM CHEESE FROSTING
- 1½ (8-oz.) pkg. cream cheese, softened
- ¾ cup unsalted butter, softened
- 3 tsp. vanilla extract
- ¼ tsp. kosher salt
- 4½ cups powdered sugar, sifted
  Chopped pecans, for garnish (optional)

1. Prepare the Cake Layers: Preheat oven to 350°F with oven rack in center of oven. Pierce potato several times using a fork, and place on a microwave-safe plate. Microwave potato on HIGH 4 minutes. Flip potato with a pair of tongs (it will be hot), and microwave 5 minutes more. Check for tenderness with a fork, and continue to microwave in 1-minute increments until cooked through, if needed. Let cool enough to be handled, about 10 minutes; peel and mash in a small bowl.

2. Coat 2 (9-inch) cake pans with baking spray. Whisk together flour, baking powder, salt, ginger, baking soda, and a

Continued on page 266

SWEET POTATO CAKE WITH CREAM CHEESE FROSTING

Continued from page 265

generous pinch of nutmeg in a medium bowl. Whisk together milk, molasses, vanilla extract, and mashed sweet potato in a large glass measuring cup.

3. Beat sugar and butter in a stand mixer fitted with a paddle attachment on medium-high speed until pale yellow and fluffy, about 3 minutes. Add eggs, one at a time, and mix just until combined. Reduce speed to low; blend in one-third of the flour mixture. Add half of the milk mixture; blend until smooth. Repeat procedure, alternating dry and wet ingredients, blending fully between additions.

4. Divide batter between prepared pans. Bake in preheated oven until a wooden pick inserted in center of each cake comes out clean, about 25 minutes. Let cool in pans 15 minutes. Very carefully turn out Cake Layers onto a wire rack to cool completely, about 1 hour.

5. Prepare the Cream Cheese Frosting: Beat cream cheese and butter in a stand mixer fitted with a paddle attachment on medium speed until light and fluffy, about 3 minutes. Add vanilla and salt, and beat well. Reduce speed to low, and gradually add ½ cup of the powdered sugar. Beat until well blended. Gradually add remaining powdered sugar, 1 cup at a time, beating until smooth between additions. Continue to beat until frosting is light and fluffy.

6. Place 1 cooled Cake Layer on a serving plate. Cover generously with frosting; top with remaining layer, and frost top and sides of cake. Garnish with pecans, if desired. Refrigerate until ready to serve.

Sweet Potato Cobbler

Taking inspiration from a single-crust fruit cobbler, the sweet and syrupy filling is the star of this dessert. Fresh ginger and lemon juice add brightness without overpowering the taste of the potatoes. Sprinkling the buttery pastry crust with coarse sugar before it goes into the oven adds a satisfying crunch.

ACTIVE 30 MIN. - TOTAL 1 HOUR, 20 MIN.

SERVES 6

PASTRY
- 1¼ cups all-purpose flour, plus more for dusting
- 1 Tbsp. granulated sugar
- ½ tsp. kosher salt
- ½ cup cold unsalted butter, diced
- 3 Tbsp. ice water

FILLING
- 1½ lb. (about 3 small) sweet potatoes, sliced into ¼-inch-thick half-moons
- 6 Tbsp. unsalted butter
- ¾ cup granulated sugar
- 1 Tbsp. fresh lemon juice (from 1 lemon)
- 2 tsp. cornstarch
- 1½ tsp. grated fresh ginger
- ¾ tsp. kosher salt

ADDITIONAL INGREDIENTS
- 1 large egg
- 1 to 2 Tbsp. coarse sugar
  Vanilla ice cream, for topping (optional)

1. Prepare the Pastry: Combine flour, granulated sugar, and salt in a food processor; pulse to combine, 3 to 4 times. Add diced butter, and pulse until butter is combined with flour mixture forming pea-size pieces. Add ice water, and pulse until mixture forms a dough, 8 to 10 times. Turn dough out onto a lightly floured surface, and knead a few times. Roll into a ball, and flatten to form a disk. Wrap dough in plastic wrap, and refrigerate at least 1 hour or up to 24 hours.

2. Prepare the Filling: Preheat oven to 400°F. Bring 4 cups water to a boil in a large saucepan over medium-high. Add potatoes, and cook 10 minutes. Transfer potatoes to a bowl, reserving ½ cup of the cooking water.

3. Place butter in a 10-inch cast-iron skillet, and place skillet in hot oven until butter is melted, about 2 minutes. Carefully remove skillet from oven, and whisk in granulated sugar, fresh lemon juice, cornstarch, grated ginger, salt, and reserved ½ cup cooking water. Arrange potatoes in an even layer in sugar mixture.

4. On a lightly floured surface, roll out dough to a 12-inch square. Use a rectangular cutter to cut several dough pieces. Lay dough pieces, overlapping slightly, on top of sweet potatoes. Continue to cut and arrange pieces on top of sweet potatoes until Filling is fully covered.

5. Whisk egg with 1 tablespoon water in a small bowl. Brush dough with egg wash; sprinkle with coarse sugar. Bake in preheated oven until Filling is bubbly and thickened and crust is golden brown, 35 to 40 minutes. Serve with ice cream, if desired.

SWEET POTATO
COBBLER

Secrets to a Southern Thanksgiving

Make your crowd feel warm and welcome with
foolproof recipes designed to impress

Take It Outside

*The oven is full, and the kitchen is hot.
Let guests gather on a porch or patio
with self-serve drinks and snacks to
tide them over till the meal is ready.*

Pickapeppa Snack Mix

ACTIVE 15 MIN. - TOTAL 1 HOUR, 15 MIN.,
PLUS 30 MIN. COOLING
SERVES 12

Preheat oven to 250°F with racks in top
third and center of oven. Line two large
rimmed baking sheets with parchment
paper. Heat 1 (5-oz.) bottle **Pickapeppa
Sauce**, ½ cup **unsalted butter**, ½ cup
packed **light brown sugar**, 1½ tsp.
chili powder, 1½ tsp. **cayenne pepper**,
and 1¼ tsp. **kosher salt** in a small
saucepan over medium. Cook, stirring
occasionally, until butter is melted.
Remove from heat. Combine 5 cups
rice cereal squares (such as Chex),
3 cups **pretzels**, and 1½ cups **unsalted
peanuts** in a large bowl. Drizzle with
half of the butter mixture; gently toss
to coat. Add remaining butter mixture;
gently toss to coat. Arrange in a single
layer on prepared pans. Bake until
lightly browned and crisp, about 1 hour,
stirring every 15 minutes and rotating
pans halfway through bake time. Let
cool completely on baking sheets, about
30 minutes.

Mini Pimiento Cheese Balls

ACTIVE 25 MIN. - TOTAL 25 MIN.,
PLUS 1 HOUR CHILLING
MAKES 36

Process 2 cups **shredded sharp cheddar
cheese**, 1 cup softened **cream cheese**,
¼ tsp. **cayenne pepper**, ¼ tsp. **black
pepper**, ⅛ tsp. **kosher salt**, and ⅛ tsp.
garlic powder in a food processor
until combined, about 15 seconds. Add
1 drained (4-oz.) jar **diced pimientos**,
and pulse until evenly distributed and
slightly chopped, 6 to 8 pulses. Transfer
cheese mixture to a medium bowl,
and cover with plastic wrap. Chill at
least 1 hour or up to 24 hours. Sprinkle
1¼ cups finely chopped **toasted pecans**
and ¼ cup finely chopped **fresh chives**
on a large baking sheet in an even
layer. Scoop out cheese mixture using
a 2-teaspoon cookie scoop; roll in your
hands to create a ball. Roll cheese balls,
1 at a time, in pecan mixture to coat
evenly. This will yield about 36 mini
balls. Transfer to a platter; insert small
square crackers into cheese balls, if
desired. Serve with additional crackers.

Thanksgiving Punch

ACTIVE 10 MIN. - TOTAL 10 MIN.,
PLUS 1 HOUR CHILLING
SERVES 12

Heat 1 cup packed **light brown sugar**,
1 cup **water**, 3 (3-inch) **cinnamon
sticks**, and 4 **star anise** in a small
saucepan over medium-high. Cook,
stirring often, until sugar dissolves
and mixture comes to a simmer, about
5 minutes. Remove from heat; transfer
simple syrup and spices to a heatproof
container. Chill, uncovered, until cool,
about 1 hour. (Can be made 1 week in
advance; store in an airtight container

in refrigerator.) Combine 8 cups **chilled
apple cider**, 1 (750-milliliter) bottle of
chilled Champagne or **Prosecco**, 2 cups
bourbon, 1 cup **orange juice**, ½ cup **fresh
lemon juice**, and 1 cup of the spiced
simple syrup in a large drink dispenser
or punch bowl; stir to combine. (Serve
without bourbon or Champagne for a
nonalcoholic option.) Top with 10 thin
orange slices, 6 thin **apple slices**, and
1 cup **frozen cranberries**; add spices
from simple syrup. Serve over ice.

Okra in a Blanket

ACTIVE 20 MIN. - TOTAL 20 MIN.
MAKES 30

Whisk together ½ cup **mayonnaise**,
2 Tbsp. **Dijon mustard**, 4 tsp. **honey**,
1 tsp. chopped **fresh dill**, and ⅛ tsp.
kosher salt in a small bowl until well
combined. Line a baking sheet with
paper towels; place 30 **whole pickled
okra pods** (from 1 [64-oz.] jar) on baking
sheet to drain. Cut 4 thin slices of
country ham into ½-inch-wide strips.
Wrap 1 ham strip around each okra pod,
securing with a wooden pick. Transfer
wrapped okra to a large platter. Serve
with mustard sauce.

GET AHEAD
Make the punch's simple syrup a week
in advance and the Pickapeppa Snack
Mix three days ahead. Roll the Mini
Pimiento Cheese Balls in pecan mixture
the night before, and assemble Okra
in a Blanket appetizers the morning of
the gathering.

THANKSGIVING
PUNCH

PICKAPEPPA
SNACK MIX

MINI
PIMIENTO
CHEESE
BALLS

OKRA IN A
BLANKET

OVERNIGHT
GIBLET
GRAVY

BUTTER-BASTED
TURKEY

Tackle the Turkey

Let's be honest: The sides usually steal the spotlight. That will all change with this incredibly tender, crisp-skinned bird. The secret? Plenty of butter.

Butter-Basted Turkey

ACTIVE 45 MIN. - TOTAL 3 HOURS, 45 MIN.,
PLUS 30 MIN. RESTING
SERVES 10

1	(14- to 16-lb.) fresh or thawed, frozen whole turkey
2½	Tbsp. kosher salt
1	Tbsp. black pepper
1	large yellow onion, quartered
6	fresh rosemary sprigs
6	garlic cloves, crushed
3	fresh or dried bay leaves
1½	cups unsalted butter
2	cups dry white wine
	Cheesecloth

1. Preheat oven to 450°F with oven rack in lower third of oven; place a roasting rack in a large roasting pan. Remove giblets and neck from turkey to reserve for Overnight Giblet Gravy (recipe, below right); store giblets and neck in a zip-top plastic freezer bag in refrigerator for up to 3 days. Trim any excess fat and skin around neck and cavity, and reserve for another use or discard. Pat turkey dry with paper towels, including inside of cavity. Starting at neck end, loosen and lift skin from breast by inserting fingers and gently pushing between skin and meat. (Do not detach skin completely.) Season turkey on all sides with salt and pepper, including inside of cavity and underneath skin on breasts. Place onion, rosemary sprigs, garlic cloves, and bay leaves in cavity. Tie ends of legs together with kitchen twine, and tuck wing tips behind back. Place turkey on rack in prepared roasting pan, breast-side up, and set aside at room temperature while preparing basting mixture.
2. Add butter and white wine to a medium saucepan, and cook over medium, stirring occasionally, until butter has melted and mixture is warm, 5 to 7 minutes; remove saucepan from heat. Fold a 9- x 20-inch piece of cheesecloth in half twice so it is 4 layers thick. Submerge in butter mixture, allowing cheesecloth to absorb mixture. Remove cheesecloth, and

unfold until it is 2 layers thick. Place soaked cheesecloth on top of turkey to cover it entirely, and gently smooth out cheesecloth so it is in direct contact with turkey skin. Cover remaining butter mixture in saucepan to keep warm.
3. Bake turkey in preheated oven until cheesecloth appears dry, about 30 minutes. Carefully baste cheesecloth with some of the reserved butter mixture. Reduce oven temperature to 350°F, and bake 2 hours more, basting cheesecloth and any exposed areas of turkey with some of the reserved mixture every 30 minutes. (If all the mixture is used, baste with any juices that have accumulated in roasting pan.) Gently remove and discard cheesecloth, being careful not to tear the skin. Baste turkey, and bake until skin is deeply golden brown and a thermometer inserted into thickest portion of the breast registers 160°F, about 30 minutes.
4. Remove turkey from oven, and let rest at room temperature 30 minutes. (Internal temperature will continue to rise as turkey rests, reaching a minimum of 165°F.) Carve and serve.

Overnight Giblet Gravy

ACTIVE 30 MIN. - TOTAL 30 MIN., PLUS 8 HOURS
SLOW-COOKING
SERVES 16

1	(4½-oz.) pkg. fresh turkey giblets, reserved from 1 (14- to 16-lb.) fresh or thawed, frozen whole turkey
1	(5- to 6-oz.) turkey neck, reserved from 1 (14- to 16-lb.) fresh or thawed, frozen whole turkey
6	cups lower-sodium turkey or chicken broth
4	cups chopped yellow onions (from 2 large onions)
2	cups chopped celery (from 4 large stalks)
2	cups chopped, peeled carrots (from 2 large carrots)
½	cup unsalted butter
½	cup all-purpose flour
1	tsp. kosher salt, plus more to taste
1	tsp. black pepper, plus more to taste
¼	cup chopped fresh flat-leaf parsley
1	Tbsp. chopped fresh sage
2	tsp. chopped fresh thyme

1. Add turkey giblets, turkey neck, lower-sodium broth, yellow onions,

celery, and carrots to a 5- to 6-quart slow cooker. Cover and cook on LOW for 8 to 12 hours.
2. Gently remove turkey giblets and neck, and reserve for gravy. Carefully pour broth mixture in slow cooker through a fine-mesh strainer into a large bowl or pot to equal 6 cups broth. Discard solids, and set broth aside.
3. Melt butter in a large saucepan over medium heat. Add flour, and cook, whisking constantly, until butter mixture is well combined and turns golden brown, 3 to 4 minutes. Slowly and carefully add reserved broth to butter mixture in saucepan, whisking constantly to prevent lumps from forming. Bring broth mixture to a boil over medium heat; reduce heat to low. Simmer, whisking occasionally, until broth mixture has thickened enough to coat the back of a spoon, about 10 to 15 minutes.
4. While broth mixture simmers, pick meat from reserved turkey neck, and transfer meat to a cutting board, discarding bones. Cut away and discard any silver skin or tendons from gizzards and heart, if necessary. Roughly chop turkey neck meat and cooked giblets, and add to thickened gravy in saucepan; whisk in salt and pepper. Cook gravy over low, whisking occasionally, until hot, about 5 minutes. Whisk in chopped fresh parsley, sage, and thyme, and add more salt and pepper to taste. Keep gravy hot before serving it with turkey.

HOW MUCH TURKEY SHOULD YOU BUY?

The size of the bird not only depends on the number of people eating and how many side dishes will be served but also on how much extra meat you'd like to have. (Remember, cooked turkey lasts three to four days in the refrigerator and two to six months in the freezer.)

"I Love Leftovers!" Plan for about 2 pounds of turkey per person to ensure you'll have plenty of meat for post-Thanksgiving sandwiches, soups, and any other way you enjoy it.

"Extra Turkey? No, Thanks." If you're hosting a small gathering, serving a wide variety of side dishes, or don't want a lot of leftovers, aim to have around 1 to 1½ pounds of turkey per person.

Show Off the Sides

It's not Thanksgiving unless there are more dishes than folks around the table. Add to the bounty with a new recipe that everyone will demand at next year's feast.

Slow-Cooker Cornbread Dressing
ACTIVE 30 MIN. - TOTAL 30 MIN., PLUS 4 HOURS SLOW-COOKING

SERVES 10

- 9 oz. smoked sausage, such as kielbasa (Polish sausage), chopped (2 cups)
- 2 Tbsp. unsalted butter
- 1 large yellow onion, chopped (2 cups)
- 2 medium celery stalks, chopped (1 cup)
- 2 medium carrots, chopped (1 cup)
- 2 large shallots, chopped (½ cup)
- 8 cups crumbled cornbread
- 1 cup mayonnaise
- 1 cup sour cream
- ¼ cup chopped fresh flat-leaf parsley, plus more for garnish
- 2 Tbsp. chopped fresh sage leaves
- 2 Tbsp. chopped fresh thyme
- 2 large eggs, lightly beaten
- 1½ tsp. kosher salt
- ¾ tsp. black pepper
- 2 to 3 cups lower-sodium chicken stock, as needed
- 1½ cups chopped toasted pecans

1. Heat a large skillet over medium-high. Add sausage, and cook, stirring occasionally, until sausage is beginning to brown, about 5 minutes. Add butter, onion, celery, carrots, and shallots; cook, stirring often, until vegetables have softened, about 6 minutes. Transfer to a large bowl, and stir in cornbread.
2. Whisk together mayonnaise, sour cream, parsley, sage, thyme, eggs, salt, pepper, and 2 cups of the chicken stock in a medium bowl; stir in pecans. Pour over cornbread mixture; stir until cornbread absorbs most of the liquid. If mixture looks too dry, add up to 1 cup additional chicken stock, ¼ cup at a time, until moistened but not soupy.
3. Lightly coat a 6-quart slow cooker with cooking spray. Transfer dressing to prepared slow cooker. Drape a clean kitchen towel or several layers of paper towels over top to absorb excess moisture (towel should not touch dressing), and cover slow cooker.
4. Cook on LOW until dressing is firm to touch on top and the sides are golden brown, 4 to 4½ hours. Garnish with additional chopped parsley, and serve.

Perfect Make-Ahead Macaroni and Cheese
ACTIVE 20 MIN. - TOTAL 45 MIN., PLUS 12 HOURS CHILLING

SERVES 10

- 10 oz. uncooked elbow macaroni
- 4 Tbsp. unsalted butter, divided
- 3½ cups heavy whipping cream
- ⅛ tsp. ground nutmeg
- 2 cups shredded fontina cheese, divided
- 1½ cups shredded Monterey Jack cheese, divided
- 1¼ tsp. kosher salt, divided, plus more for salting water
- 1 tsp. black pepper, divided
- 5 white bread slices
- 2 Tbsp. chopped fresh flat-leaf parsley

1. Bring a large pot of salted water to a boil. Add pasta; cook 4 minutes. (Pasta will not be fully cooked.) Drain and spread on a rimmed baking sheet to cool 10 minutes.
2. Grease a 13- x 9-inch baking dish with 1 tablespoon of the butter. Return pasta to pot; stir in cream, nutmeg, 1 cup of the fontina, ¾ cup of the Monterey Jack, 1 teaspoon of the salt, and ¾ teaspoon of the pepper until well blended. Pour mixture into prepared baking dish; sprinkle evenly with remaining 1 cup fontina and ¾ cup Monterey Jack. Cover dish; refrigerate at least 12 hours or up to 24 hours.
3. When ready to bake, remove baking dish from refrigerator. Let stand 30 minutes while oven preheats to 400°F.
4. Meanwhile, place white bread in a food processor. Pulse until coarse crumbs form, 6 to 8 pulses. Microwave remaining 3 tablespoons butter in a medium microwavable bowl on HIGH until melted, about 30 seconds. Stir in breadcrumbs and remaining ¼ teaspoon each salt and pepper, and toss until breadcrumbs are evenly coated. Uncover baking dish, and sprinkle casserole evenly with breadcrumb mixture.
5. Bake in preheated oven until topping is golden brown, about 25 minutes. Sprinkle with chopped parsley.

Layered Squash Casserole
ACTIVE 40 MIN. - TOTAL 1 HOUR, 20 MIN.

SERVES 8

- 3 Tbsp. unsalted butter, divided, plus more for greasing baking dish
- 4 lb. mixed yellow squash and zucchini, cut into ¼-inch-thick rounds (about 15 cups)
- 2 large eggs, beaten
- 1½ cups sour cream
- ½ cup mayonnaise
- 1 Tbsp. chopped fresh thyme
- 1½ tsp. kosher salt
- 1 tsp. Dijon mustard
- ½ tsp. cayenne pepper
- ½ tsp. grated garlic (from 1 large clove)
- 1½ cups shredded white cheddar cheese
- 1½ cups bite-size white cheddar cheese crackers (such as Cheez-It), coarsely crushed
- 1½ tsp. hot sauce

1. Preheat oven to 350°F. Lightly grease a 3-quart oval baking dish with butter; set aside.
2. Melt 2 tablespoons of the butter in a large Dutch oven over medium-high. Add mixed squash; stir to coat in butter. Cover and cook, stirring occasionally, until squash is tender-crisp, 8 to 10 minutes. Transfer squash to a colander set over a bowl, and let stand 10 minutes. Gently press out excess water.
3. Stir together eggs, sour cream, mayonnaise, thyme, salt, Dijon, cayenne pepper, and garlic in a medium bowl. Spread 1¼ cups of the sour cream mixture evenly across bottom of prepared baking dish. Arrange squash slices on top of sour cream mixture in overlapping concentric circles, tucking cheddar cheese in between squash

Continued on page 275

SLOW-COOKER CORNBREAD DRESSING

LAYERED SQUASH CASSEROLE

PERFECT MAKE-AHEAD MACARONI AND CHEESE

SMOKY GREENS SOUFFLÉ (PAGE 275)

ROASTED VEGGIES YOUR WAY
Mix and match your favorite vegetables with three savory toppings.

ROASTED BROCCOLI WITH CHEESE STRAW CRUMBLES

ROASTED BRUSSELS SPROUTS WITH BACONY ALMONDS

ROASTED GREEN BEANS WITH CRISPY SHALLOTS AND MUSHROOMS

Continued from page 272

slices. Spread remaining 1 cup sour cream mixture over squash, allowing sour cream mixture to settle between squash slices. If necessary, use a fork to lift and separate squash slices to allow sour cream mixture to fall between slices.

4. Microwave remaining 1 tablespoon butter in a medium-size microwavable bowl on HIGH until melted, about 30 seconds. Add crackers and hot sauce to melted butter, and stir to combine. Sprinkle cracker mixture over casserole. Bake in preheated oven until sour cream mixture is set and crackers are lightly browned, 25 to 30 minutes. Let cool 10 minutes, and serve.

Smoky Greens Soufflé

(Photo, page 273)
ACTIVE 40 MIN. - TOTAL 1 HOUR, 15 MIN.
SERVES 6

- 1 (15-oz.) pkg. frozen chopped collard greens, thawed
  Unsalted butter, for greasing soufflé dish
- 3 Tbsp. grated Pecorino Romano cheese
- 4 thick-cut hickory-smoked bacon slices, chopped (1 cup packed)
- 3 Tbsp. all-purpose flour
- 1 cup whole milk
- ¾ cup shredded fontina cheese
- 4 large egg yolks
- 1¼ tsp. Creole seasoning
- 1 tsp. hot sauce, plus more for serving
- ½ tsp. grated garlic (from 1 clove)
- 7 large egg whites
- ½ tsp. cream of tartar

1. Preheat oven to 375°F. Place collards in a clean kitchen towel, and squeeze firmly over sink to remove as much liquid as possible; transfer to a cutting board. Finely chop greens, and transfer to a large bowl.

2. Grease a 2-quart soufflé dish evenly with butter. Sprinkle dish with Pecorino Romano cheese, and tilt to coat in an even layer; tap out excess. Place on a rimmed baking sheet.

3. Cook chopped bacon in a large saucepan over medium, stirring occasionally, until it's crisp and the fat has rendered, 8 to 10 minutes. Remove

from heat. Using a slotted spoon, add cooked bacon to greens in large bowl, reserving drippings in pan. Pour drippings into a small heatproof bowl. Wipe saucepan clean.

4. Add 2 tablespoons reserved drippings to saucepan, and place over medium heat. Whisk in flour, and cook, whisking constantly, 1 minute. Gradually add milk, whisking constantly, and bring to a simmer. Cook, whisking often, until milk mixture is very thick and smooth, about 2 minutes. Remove from heat, and whisk in fontina cheese until melted and smooth, about 30 seconds. Let cool slightly, about 5 minutes. Add egg yolks, 1 at a time, whisking to blend after each addition. Stir into collard greens mixture in large bowl along with Creole seasoning, hot sauce, and garlic.

5. Beat egg whites and cream of tartar with an electric mixer on medium-high speed until glossy and stiff peaks form, 3 to 4 minutes. Stir about one-third of egg white mixture into collard greens mixture until well incorporated. Gently fold in remaining egg white mixture until just incorporated. Spoon mixture into prepared dish. To encourage proper rising, use the tip of a paring knife to trace a circle (about ½ inch deep) 1 inch from sides of dish. Bake soufflé in preheated oven until puffed, top is browned, and a long skewer inserted into middle of soufflé comes out clean, 30 to 35 minutes. Serve immediately with hot sauce.

Choose-Your-Own Roasted Veggie

ACTIVE 20 MIN. - TOTAL 35 MIN.
SERVES 6

- 1½ lb. (1-inch) broccoli florets, halved Brussels sprouts, or trimmed green beans
- ¼ cup olive oil
- 1½ tsp. kosher salt
- ½ tsp. ground black pepper
  Bacony Almonds, Cheese Straw Crumbles, or Crispy Shallots and Mushrooms (recipes right)

Place an aluminum foil-lined baking sheet on middle rack in oven; preheat oven to 425°F. Place vegetables in a large bowl; toss with olive oil, salt, and pepper until fully coated. Once oven has preheated, carefully spread vegetables

evenly over hot baking sheet, using a rubber spatula and scraping remaining olive oil and seasonings from bowl over vegetables. Roast until browned and tender-crisp, 14 to 16 minutes, tossing halfway through. Transfer to a serving platter. Sprinkle with desired toppings, and serve.

Bacony Almonds

Place 6 slices chopped **thick-cut bacon** in a large skillet over medium; cook, stirring occasionally, until rendered and crispy, about 10 minutes. Remove to a paper towel-lined plate, reserving 1 Tbsp. drippings in skillet. Reduce heat to medium-low. Add ¾ cup **sliced almonds,** and cook, stirring often, until toasted, 2 to 3 minutes. Remove almonds from pan; toss with cooked bacon.

Cheese Straw Crumbles

Melt 2 Tbsp. **butter** in a large skillet over medium-high. Crumble 1½ cups **cheese straws** into skillet, and cook, stirring occasionally, until toasted, 2 to 3 minutes. Remove from heat, and stir in 1 tsp. **fresh thyme leaves.**

Crispy Shallots and Mushrooms

Heat ¼ cup **olive oil** in a large skillet over medium-high. Add 2 **shallots** (sliced into rings); cook, stirring, until browned and crispy, about 4 minutes. Remove shallots with a slotted spoon. Add 8 oz. sliced **wild mushrooms** to skillet; cook, undisturbed, 2 minutes. Stir and continue to cook, stirring occasionally, until browned and crispy, about 10 minutes. Remove mushrooms from pan; toss with shallots and ½ tsp. **flaky sea salt.**

Surprise Them!

Keep things interesting with a party trick or two. These clever spins on nostalgic favorites will delight people of all ages.

Layered Cranberry Salad

ACTIVE 50 MIN. - TOTAL 50 MIN.,
PLUS 6 HOURS CHILLING

SERVES 10

- 2 cups fresh whole cranberries, thawed if frozen
- 5 (¼-oz.) envelopes unflavored gelatin
- 6 cups cranberry juice cocktail, divided
- 1 cup granulated sugar
- 1 cup fresh orange juice (from 2 large or 3 medium oranges)
  Ice
- 1 (14-oz.) can sweetened condensed milk

1. Lightly spray a 10-cup Bundt pan with cooking spray; set aside. Place cranberries in refrigerator until ready to use. Whisk together gelatin and 1 cup of the cranberry juice in a medium bowl; set aside at room temperature.
2. Bring sugar, fresh orange juice, and remaining 5 cups cranberry juice to a simmer in a large saucepan over medium, stirring often. Remove from heat; whisk in gelatin mixture until dissolved. Set aside 3 cups cranberry-gelatin mixture.
3. Place remaining 4 cups cranberry-gelatin mixture in a medium bowl; place that over a large bowl filled with ice. Chill mixture, stirring often, until thickened, 30 to 45 minutes. Scrape and discard any foam from top. Gently fold in chilled cranberries until evenly distributed. Pour fruit mixture into prepared pan. Refrigerate, uncovered, until set, about 2 hours.
4. Meanwhile, stir together reserved 3 cups cranberry-gelatin mixture and sweetened condensed milk in a medium bowl; cover and let stand at room temperature while fruit layer chills. Slowly pour milk mixture over fruit layer, turning pan as you pour to create an even layer. Chill, uncovered, until firmly set, at least 4 hours or up to 48 hours.
5. To unmold, fill a large bowl with warm water. Carefully lower the Bundt pan into the water until the sides begin to loosen, 10 to 15 seconds. Lift the pan from the water and pat dry. Use your fingertips to gently coax the salad away from the edges of the pan. Place a serving plate on the pan. Firmly hold the pan and plate together and flip. Gently lift the pan away.

Pull-Apart Butter Roll Loaves

ACTIVE 35 MIN. - TOTAL 1 HOUR, 40 MIN.,
PLUS 1 HOUR, 15 MIN. RISING

MAKES 2 LOAVES

- 1⅓ cups warm whole milk (105°F to 110°F)
- 2 Tbsp. granulated sugar
- 2 (¼-oz.) pkg. active dry yeast (4½ tsp.)
- 6 cups all-purpose flour, divided, plus more for dusting
- ½ cup plus 2 Tbsp. unsalted butter, melted and divided
- 4 large eggs
- 1 Tbsp. kosher salt
- ½ cup unsalted butter, softened and divided
  Flaky sea salt, for garnish
  Fresh rosemary sprigs, for garnish

1. Whisk together warm milk, sugar, and yeast in a small bowl until well combined; let stand at room temperature until foamy, about 5 minutes.
2. Place yeast mixture and 2 cups of the flour in the bowl of a stand mixer fitted with the paddle attachment, and beat on low speed just until combined, about 20 seconds. Add ½ cup of the melted butter and 1 cup of the flour; continue beating on low speed until combined, about 30 seconds. With mixer on low, add eggs, 1 at a time, beating just until combined after each addition. Gradually add salt and remaining 3 cups flour, beating on low speed until a soft, sticky dough forms, about 2 minutes.
3. Place dough in a large bowl coated with cooking spray; lightly coat top of dough with cooking spray, and cover with plastic wrap. Let rise in a warm place (75°F) until doubled in size, 45 minutes to 1 hour. Place dough on floured work surface, and shape into a ball. Cover loosely with a clean kitchen towel, and let rest 10 minutes. Divide dough in half. Working with 1 half at a time, roll dough into a 20- x 12-inch rectangle (¼ inch thick). Spread ¼ cup of the softened butter in a thin layer over dough. Using a knife or pizza cutter, cut dough into 20 (4- x 3-inch) rectangles.
4. Preheat oven to 350°F. Spray 2 (8½- x 4½-inch) loaf pans with cooking spray. Prop 1 end of 1 prepared pan up to place it at an angle. Beginning at low end of prepared pan, place 1 dough rectangle, buttered side up, and repeat with remaining dough rectangles,

LAYERED CRANBERRY SALAD

buttered sides up. Repeat procedure with remaining dough, ¼ cup softened butter, and pan. Cover pans loosely with plastic wrap, and let rise in a warm place until doubled in size, about 30 minutes.

5. Bake both pans in preheated oven until golden brown, about 40 minutes, covering loosely with aluminum foil halfway through baking time to prevent overbrowning, if needed. Let cool in pans 10 minutes. Remove from pans, and brush with remaining 2 tablespoons melted butter; garnish with flaky sea salt and rosemary before serving.

New-School Pineapple Casserole

ACTIVE 25 MIN. - TOTAL 60 MIN.

SERVES 10

- 2 fresh pineapples, peeled and cored
- ¼ cup packed light brown sugar
- 3 Tbsp. cornstarch
- 3 Tbsp. fresh lemon juice (from 1 lemon)
- 1½ cups shredded aged white cheddar cheese, divided
- 1 (8-oz.) pkg. cream cheese, cut into small cubes
- 26 buttery crackers, coarsely crushed (about 1½ cups)
- 1 cup sliced almonds
- 1 Tbsp. chopped fresh rosemary leaves
- 3 Tbsp. unsalted butter, melted

1. Preheat oven to 350°F. Lightly grease a 13- x 9-inch baking dish with cooking spray. Halve pineapples lengthwise, and then slice crosswise into ½-inch-thick half-moons. Place slices on several layers of paper towels, and gently pat dry. Shingle slices lengthwise in 2 rows, curved sides up, in prepared baking dish.

2. Whisk together brown sugar, cornstarch, and lemon juice in a small bowl, and pour evenly over pineapple slices. Sprinkle evenly with ¾ cup of the cheddar; scatter cream cheese cubes evenly over surface.

3. Combine crackers, almonds, and rosemary in a medium bowl; drizzle with butter, and toss to coat. Stir in remaining ¾ cup cheddar, and sprinkle mixture evenly over casserole.

4. Bake in preheated oven until topping is golden brown and pineapple slices are tender, 30 to 35 minutes.

PULL-APART BUTTER ROLL LOAVES

NEW-SCHOOL PINEAPPLE CASSEROLE

End with a Bang

We dressed up the classic chess pie with holiday flavors. Our simple recipe can be made three different ways, whether you prefer apple, pumpkin, or pecan.

Apple Chess Pie

ACTIVE 20 MIN. - TOTAL 1 HOUR, 30 MIN.,
PLUS 2 HOURS, 30 MIN. COOLING

SERVES 8

All-Butter Pie Dough (recipe opposite)

2 cups granulated sugar

3 Tbsp. all-purpose flour, plus more for work surface

1 tsp. ground cinnamon

¼ tsp. kosher salt

3 large eggs, lightly beaten

¼ cup unsalted butter, melted

3 Tbsp. evaporated milk

½ tsp. grated lemon zest plus 1 Tbsp. fresh juice (from 1 lemon)

1 tsp. vanilla extract

2 medium Granny Smith apples, peeled and thinly sliced (3½ cups)

Powdered sugar, for garnish

Vanilla ice cream, for serving

1. Roll out All-Butter Pie Dough on a lightly floured work surface into a 12-inch round. Place in an ungreased 9-inch pie plate, pressing dough into bottom and sides of pie plate. Fold excess dough under edges; crimp as desired. Freeze 30 minutes. Preheat oven to 400°F, and remove pie plate from freezer while oven preheats. Line pastry with parchment paper; fill with pie weights or (see "Cooking School," page 284) dried beans. Bake 10 minutes. Remove parchment and weights. Prick bottom and sides of crust with a fork; return to oven, and bake 8 minutes. Let cool 30 minutes.

2. Whisk together granulated sugar, flour, cinnamon, and salt in a large bowl until combined. Add eggs, butter, milk, lemon zest, lemon juice, and vanilla, whisking until smooth.

3. Arrange apple slices in bottom of prepared piecrust. Pour egg mixture over apples.

4. Reduce oven to 350°F. Bake until center is set and barely jiggles, 55 to 60 minutes, covering edges with aluminum foil halfway through baking

time to prevent overbrowning, if needed. Let cool completely on a wire rack, about 2 hours. Garnish with powdered sugar, and serve with ice cream.

Chocolate-Pecan Chess Pie

ACTIVE 20 MIN. - TOTAL 1 HOUR, 30 MIN., PLUS 2 HOURS, 30 MIN. COOLING

SERVES 8

Prepare crust as directed in Step 1 of Apple Chess Pie. In Step 2, proceed as directed, decreasing sugar to 1½ cups and flour to 2 Tbsp., omitting cinnamon, adding 3 Tbsp. **cocoa powder,** increasing **evaporated milk** to ⅔ cup, and omitting lemon zest and lemon juice. In Step 3, replace apples with 1 cup **semisweet chocolate chips,** and pour egg mixture over chocolate chips. In Step 4, bake pie at 350°F for 45 minutes. Carefully remove pie from oven, and top evenly with 1½ cups **toasted pecan halves.** Return to oven, and bake until center is set and barely jiggles, about 10 minutes. Let cool as directed. Omit powdered sugar.

CHOCOLATE-PECAN CHESS PIE

Pumpkin Chess Pie

ACTIVE 20 MIN. - TOTAL 1 HOUR, 30 MIN.,
PLUS 2 HOURS, 30 MIN. COOLING

SERVES 8

Prepare crust as directed in Step 1 of
Apple Chess Pie. In Step 2, proceed
as directed, reducing flour to 2 Tbsp.,
replacing cinnamon with 1 tsp. **pumpkin
pie spice**, increasing **evaporated milk**
to ⅔ cup, and adding 1 cup **canned
pumpkin**. In Step 3, omit apples, and
pour egg mixture into prepared piecrust.
In Step 4, bake pie at 350°F until
center is set and barely jiggles, 50 to
55 minutes. Let cool as directed. Omit
powdered sugar and ice cream; serve
with **whipped cream**, and sprinkle with
additional **pumpkin pie spice.**

All-Butter Pie Dough

ACTIVE 10 MIN. - TOTAL 10 MIN.,
PLUS 30 MIN. CHILLING

MAKES 1 PIECRUST

- 1¼ cups all-purpose flour
- 1 Tbsp. granulated sugar
- ½ tsp. kosher salt
- ½ cup cold unsalted butter, cubed
- 3 to 4 Tbsp. ice water, as needed

1. Pulse flour, sugar, and salt in a food
processor until just combined, about
3 pulses. With processor running,
add cubed butter through food chute,
processing until some pea-size pieces
of butter remain, about 10 seconds. Add
water through food chute, 1 tablespoon
at a time as needed, pulsing until dough
just begins to clump together, about
10 pulses.

2. Transfer dough to a work surface,
and knead until it just holds together,
about 3 times. Shape into a disk. Wrap in
plastic wrap, and chill until firm, at least
30 minutes or up to 3 days.

PUMPKIN CHESS PIE

APPLE
CHESS PIE

Lightened-Up Leftovers

If you're sick of sandwiches, use up that turkey in this tasty seasonal salad

Turkey-and-Persimmon Salad

ACTIVE 15 MIN. · TOTAL 15 MIN.

SERVES 4

- 2 Tbsp. apple cider vinegar
- 2 tsp. honey
- 1 tsp. grated fresh ginger (from 1 [1-inch] piece)
- 1½ tsp. kosher salt
- ½ tsp. black pepper
- ¼ cup olive oil
- 1 lb. sliced or chopped cooked turkey breast (about 3 cups)
- 5 oz. mixed baby greens
- 2 medium-size fresh Fuyu persimmons, unpeeled and thinly sliced (about 1 cup)
- ½ cup thinly sliced fennel (from 1 small bulb), fronds reserved
- ½ cup thinly sliced celery (from 2 medium stalks)
- ½ cup loosely packed fresh flat-leaf parsley
- ½ cup pecans, toasted and roughly chopped

1. Whisk together vinegar, honey, ginger, salt, and pepper in a small bowl. Slowly drizzle in oil while whisking constantly until emulsified. Set dressing aside.

2. Combine turkey, greens, persimmons, fennel with fronds, celery, parsley, and pecans in a large bowl. Drizzle with ¼ cup of the dressing, and gently toss until coated. Serve immediately with remaining dressing.

CALORIES: **431** − CARBS: **14 G** − FAT: **26 G**

PICK A PERSIMMON
The Fuyu type is small and firm with a tomato-like appearance. The acorn-shape Hachiya is larger and completely soft when ripe.

Start Your Engine

Get the day going with a fantastic, protein-packed make-ahead breakfast

Cheesy Mushroom-Spinach Mini Frittatas

Beating the mixture with a fork (instead of a whisk) incorporates less air, giving the frittatas a lighter texture.

ACTIVE 20 MIN. · TOTAL 45 MIN.

MAKES 12

- 8 large eggs
- ¼ cup heavy whipping cream
- 1 oz. Parmesan cheese, grated (about ¼ cup)
- 2 tsp. Dijon mustard
- ¼ tsp. black pepper
- 1 tsp. kosher salt, divided
- 3 Tbsp. olive oil
- 5 oz. mixed fresh mushrooms (such as shiitake, baby portobello, and oyster), sliced
- 2 medium garlic cloves, finely chopped (2 tsp.)
- 1 tsp. finely chopped fresh thyme leaves
- ¼ tsp. crushed red pepper
- 3 cups fresh baby spinach (from 1 [5-oz.] pkg.)
- 3 oz. fontina cheese, grated (about ¾ cup)

1. Preheat oven to 350°F. Lightly coat a 12-cup muffin tray with cooking spray.
2. Place eggs, whipping cream, Parmesan, Dijon, black pepper, and ¾ teaspoon of the salt in a large bowl. Beat with a fork until combined (do not overbeat). Set egg mixture aside.
3. Heat oil in a large skillet over medium-high. Add mushrooms, and cook, undisturbed, until golden on bottom, 2 to 3 minutes. Stir mushrooms. Cook, stirring often, until golden on all sides, 3 to 4 minutes more. Stir in garlic, thyme, crushed red pepper, and remaining ¼ teaspoon salt. Cook, stirring constantly, until fragrant, about 1 minute. Remove from heat; stir in spinach until wilted.
4. Divide grated fontina evenly among prepared muffin wells (about 1 tablespoon per well). Spoon mushroom-spinach mixture evenly on top (about 2 tablespoons each), and ladle egg mixture evenly into wells, filling each about three-fourths full (about 3 tablespoons per well).
5. Bake in preheated oven until puffed and set, about 18 minutes. Cool in pan 5 minutes. (Frittatas will deflate as they cool.) Run a paring knife around edges to loosen and remove frittatas. Serve immediately, or (if making ahead) transfer to a wire rack to cool completely, about 20 minutes. Store in an airtight container in refrigerator up to 3 days or in freezer up to 3 months.
6. To reheat, place frittatas on a microwavable plate and microwave on MEDIUM (50% power) for 1 minute to 1 minute, 30 seconds (if refrigerated) or 2 minutes (if frozen). Serve immediately.

PAM'S BEST-EVER
PUMPKIN-PECAN
CHEESECAKE

One Sweet Legacy

For retired Test Kitchen professional Pam Lolley and countless others,
this incredible cheesecake is an absolute must

EVERY NOVEMBER, retired Test Kitchen professional Pam Lolley was faced with the same challenge: to invent yet another awe-inspiring dessert (or more) for this magazine. Pam, who joined our staff back in 2003, always went above and beyond, creating new recipes that became instant classics, like the Pumpkin Spice Magic Cake (a Bundt with a built-in layer of flan and a decadent caramel sauce). It bakes together in one pan, and we're still not quite sure how she pulled it off.

When Pam announced her retirement earlier this year, one of the first things we did (after drying our tears) was ask for her most cherished Thanksgiving dessert. After insisting that this question was like picking a favorite child, she gave in: Pumpkin-Pecan Cheesecake.

Published in 2011, it's a showstopping pumpkin cheesecake covered with a thin layer of rich sauce. "Lawd have mercy..." exclaimed the article that went with it. After it was taste-tested, Pam took home the leftovers (a perk of the job). "My youngest son just about ate the entire thing by himself," she remembers. "He told me—not asked me—that I had to make this for Thanksgiving from now on."

It's impossible to say how many holiday meals throughout the South have ended on a sweet note and how many happy memories have been made in the kitchen because of Pam. "I have laid out all my best ideas and recipes for Southern Living, the brand that holds my heart," she says. And we're all very thankful for that. –Lisa Cericola

Pam's Best-Ever Pumpkin-Pecan Cheesecake

ACTIVE 30 MIN. · TOTAL 3 HOURS, 20 MIN., PLUS 8 HOURS CHILLING

SERVES 12

CHEESECAKE

- 2 cups graham cracker crumbs (from 1 [13½-oz.] pkg.)
- ⅓ cup finely chopped pecans
- 5 Tbsp. unsalted butter, melted
- 3 Tbsp. light brown sugar
- 4 (8-oz.) pkg. cream cheese, softened
- 1 cup granulated sugar
- 1 tsp. vanilla extract
- 4 large eggs
- 1½ cups canned pumpkin (from 1 [15-oz.] can)
- 1½ Tbsp. fresh lemon juice (from 1 lemon)

TOPPING

- 1 cup packed light brown sugar
- ⅓ cup whipping cream
- ¼ cup unsalted butter
- ¼ tsp. kosher salt
- 1 cup powdered sugar, sifted
- 1 tsp. vanilla extract

ADDITIONAL INGREDIENT

Spiced Glazed Pecans (recipe follows)

1. Prepare the Cheesecake: Preheat oven to 325°F. Stir together graham cracker crumbs, pecans, melted butter, and brown sugar in a bowl until well blended. Press mixture into bottom and 1½ inches up sides of an ungreased 9-inch springform pan. Bake until lightly browned, 8 to 10 minutes. Remove from oven; set crust aside. Do not turn oven off.

2. Beat cream cheese, granulated sugar, and vanilla with a stand mixer fitted with a paddle attachment on medium speed until blended and smooth, about 2 minutes. Add eggs, 1 at a time, beating just until blended after each addition, stopping to scrape down sides as needed. Add pumpkin and lemon juice, beating until blended and no streaks remain, about 30 seconds. Pour batter into prepared crust. (Pan will be very full.)

3. Bake at 325°F until almost set, about 1 hour to 1 hour, 10 minutes. Turn oven off. Let Cheesecake stand in oven, with door closed, 15 minutes. Remove from oven, and gently run a knife around outer edge of Cheesecake to loosen from sides of pan. (Do not remove sides of pan.) Cool completely on a wire rack, about 1 hour. Cover; refrigerate at least 8 hours or up to 24 hours. Remove sides and bottom of pan, and transfer to a serving plate.

4. Prepare the Topping: Bring brown sugar, cream, butter, and salt to a boil in a 1-quart saucepan over medium, stirring often. Boil, stirring occasionally, 1 minute; remove from heat. Gradually whisk in powdered sugar and vanilla until smooth. Let stand 5 minutes, whisking occasionally.

5. Slowly pour Topping over top of chilled Cheesecake, spreading to within ¼ inch of edge. Garnish with Spiced Glazed Pecans. Refrigerate Cheesecake, uncovered, until Topping is set, about 20 minutes.

Spiced Glazed Pecans

ACTIVE 10 MIN. · TOTAL 25 MIN.

MAKES 1 CUP

Stir together ¼ cup **granulated sugar,** ¼ tsp. **ground cinnamon,** ¼ tsp. **ground ginger,** and ⅛ tsp. **ground cloves** in a heavy saucepan until combined. Stir in 1 cup coarsely chopped **pecans;** cook over medium, stirring constantly, until sugar melts and coats pecans, about 7 minutes. Spread on greased waxed paper; cool completely, 15 to 20 minutes. Store in an airtight container at room temperature up to 1 week.

How to Blind-Bake a Piecrust

Making pumpkin or pecan pie this season? Fall back on this classic technique to guarantee a gorgeous, flaky crust

STEP 1
Press dough into the bottom and up the sides of a pie plate. Trim the edges, and crimp as desired. Place pie plate in freezer for 30 minutes.

STEP 2
Line the dough with parchment paper. Fill with pie weights or dried beans to cover the bottom and almost all the way up the sides. Bake at 400°F for 10 minutes.

STEP 3
Remove parchment and weights, and pierce the bottom and sides of the crust with a fork 12 to 15 times. Return to oven, and bake 8 minutes.

STEP 4
Let crust cool before filling and baking as directed (see recipes, p. 278). Cover edges of crust with aluminum foil to prevent burning, if needed.

SMALL CHANGES, BIG RESULTS

Take your Thanksgiving recipes from good to great

FLUFFIER MASHED POTATOES
Don't peel the potatoes before boiling them; the skins keep them from absorbing too much water.

SMOOTHER PUMPKIN PIE
Blend canned puree or pie filling in the food processor for 1 minute.

PERFECTLY SEASONED DRESSING
Make homemade stock or use a low-sodium store-bought version to control the amount of salt.

SNAZZIER CASSEROLE
Swap the topping from canned fried onions to caramelized onions or leeks.

EVEN-SWEETER SWEET POTATOES
Before adding this veggie to pies and casseroles, roast it to enhance its natural flavor.

KICKED-UP CRANBERRIES
Add fresh orange juice and zest or grated ginger to jazz up any cranberry sauce, even the canned kind.

December

Power of the Pom

Packed with seeds bursting with ruby-red juice, pomegranates shine this time of year.
Add a punch to happy hour with these vibrant recipes

Pomegranate Margarita

ACTIVE 5 MIN. - TOTAL 5 MIN.
MAKES 2

Mix ¼ cup each **margarita salt** and **granulated sugar** on a small plate. Lightly coat rims of 2 margarita glasses evenly with 1 tsp. **simple syrup**; dip glasses in salt mixture to coat rims. In a cocktail shaker filled with **ice**, combine 3 oz. **pomegranate juice**; 2 oz. **silver tequila**; 1 oz. each **lime juice, orange liqueur**, and **pomegranate liqueur**; and 4 tsp. **simple syrup**. Shake until very cold and cocktail shaker is frosty. Fill margarita glasses with **ice**, and strain mixture into glasses. Garnish each with **pomegranate arils** and a **lime wheel**.

Baked Brie with Pomegranate and Pistachios

(Photo, page 5)
ACTIVE 20 MIN. - TOTAL 25 MIN.
SERVES 8

Preheat oven to 375°F. In a small saucepan, bring ½ cup **pomegranate juice**, ¼ cup **fresh orange juice**, and 2 Tbsp. **honey** to a boil over medium-high. Reduce heat to medium, and simmer, stirring occasionally, until reduced to ¼ cup, 15 to 20 minutes. Remove from heat; let cool. Place 1 (8-oz.) **Brie round** on a rimmed baking sheet lined with parchment paper. Bake until softened and thoroughly heated, 8 to 10 minutes. Combine ¼ cup each **chopped roasted, salted pistachios** and **pomegranate arils**, leaves of 3 **thyme sprigs**, and ½ tsp. **orange zest** in a small bowl. Transfer Brie to a serving plate; drizzle with 1 Tbsp. of the cooled pomegranate syrup. Top with pistachio mixture, ½ tsp. **flaky sea salt**, and 2 **thyme sprigs**. Drizzle with some of the remaining pomegranate syrup, reserving any leftover syrup for another use. Serve with **toasted baguette slices or crackers**.

POMEGRANATE
MARGARITA

A Tasteful Wreath

Surprise guests with an appetizer that's lighter than the usual
cheese board and doubles as a centerpiece

Stuffed-Pepper Wreath

ACTIVE 30 MIN. · TOTAL 30 MIN.
SERVES 8

- 1 (8-oz.) goat cheese log
- 1 oz. Parmesan cheese, grated (about ¼ cup)
- 2 tsp. extra-virgin olive oil
- 2 tsp. fresh orange juice (from 1 orange)
- ½ tsp. kosher salt
- ½ tsp. black pepper
- 1 garlic clove, grated (¼ tsp.)
- 2 (½-oz.) pkg. rosemary sprigs
- 2 (½-oz.) pkg. sage sprigs, leaves and thin stems only
- 1 (½-oz.) pkg. thyme sprigs, woody stems removed
- 2½ cups mild Peppadew peppers (about 32 peppers)
- ½ cup whole green olives
- 1 Tbsp. thinly sliced fresh chives

1. Place goat cheese, Parmesan, oil, orange juice, salt, black pepper, and garlic in a food processor; pulse until smooth, about 12 pulses, stopping to scrape down sides halfway through. Transfer goat cheese mixture to a small zip-top plastic bag or piping bag fitted with a decorative star tip. Snip a ½-inch tip off zip-top bag, if using.
2. Arrange herb sprigs in a circle around the perimeter of a large round platter. Pipe about 1½ teaspoons cheese mixture into each pepper. Arrange stuffed peppers, cheese sides up, on top of and around herb sprigs. Garnish with olives; sprinkle peppers with chives. Serve at room temperature, or refrigerate until ready to serve.

CALORIES: **148** – CARBS: **8 G** – FAT: **10 G**

PICK A PEPPER
If Peppadews aren't available, substitute jarred sweet or hot pickled cherry peppers.

CHRISTMAS CACTUS COCKTAILS

CHEESY CHORIZO-STUFFED CHILES

Mixing and Mingling

Get the party started with tasty bites paired with festive big-batch drinks

Cheesy Chorizo-Stuffed Chiles

ACTIVE 25 MIN. - TOTAL 35 MIN.
SERVES 8

- 8 oz. fresh Mexican chorizo sausage, casings removed
- 1½ cups preshredded Monterey Jack cheese (6 oz.)
- 4 oz. cream cheese, softened
- ¼ cup chopped fresh cilantro, plus more for garnish
- ¼ cup chopped scallions
- ¼ cup crushed tortilla chips (about 10 chips)
- 6 large red Fresno chiles, divided
- 5 large jalapeño chiles

1. Preheat oven to 375°F. Heat a medium skillet over medium-high. Add chorizo; cook, stirring often to crumble, until browned, 6 to 8 minutes. Transfer to a paper towel-lined plate to drain; pat with paper towels to remove as much grease as possible.
2. Stir together cooked chorizo, Monterey Jack cheese, cream cheese, cilantro, scallions, and chips in a medium bowl.
3. Finely chop 1 of the Fresno chiles; set aside for garnish. Cut jalapeño chiles and remaining 5 Fresno chiles in half lengthwise, keeping stems on, if possible. Remove ribs and seeds with a small spoon; discard. Place chile halves, cut sides up, on a parchment paper-lined baking sheet. Spoon 1 heaping tablespoon of the cheese mixture into each chile, mounding a bit in center.
4. Bake in preheated oven until cheese melts and is lightly browned, 10 to 12 minutes. Garnish with additional cilantro and reserved finely chopped Fresno chile.

Christmas Cactus Cocktails

ACTIVE 10 MIN. - TOTAL 10 MIN.
SERVES 8

Combine 1½ cups (12 oz.) **silver tequila**, ¾ cup loosely packed **fresh cilantro** leaves, 1 sliced medium **jalapeño** chile, ½ cup **fresh lemon juice**, and 4 teaspoons **chili-lime seasoning** (such as Tajín) in a pitcher; muddle using a wooden spoon handle. Stir in 2 cups bottled refrigerated **lemonade** and 2 cups bottled chilled **tomato-clam juice** (such as Clamato). Pour 2 tablespoons **lemon juice** on a small plate; place 1 tablespoon **chili-lime seasoning** in an even layer on a second small plate. Dip rims of 8 rocks glasses in lemon juice, then dip in chili-lime seasoning until coated. Fill glasses with **ice**; pour tequila mixture into prepared glasses. Garnish each with a **lemon wheel** and thin slice of **jalapeño chile** (if desired).

Smoked Salmon-Potato Chip Canapés

(Photo, page 290)

ACTIVE 20 MIN. - TOTAL 20 MIN.
SERVES 8

- ¼ cup crème fraîche
- 2 tsp. chopped drained capers
- 4 tsp. chopped fresh chives, divided
- 2 tsp. grated lemon zest (from 1 lemon), divided
- ¾ tsp. coarsely ground black pepper, divided
- 24 medium-size kettle-cooked potato chips (such as Cape Cod Original Sea Salt)
- 1 (4-oz.) pkg. smoked salmon
- 1 Tbsp. finely chopped red onion
- ¼ tsp. flaky sea salt

1. Stir together crème fraîche, capers, 2 teaspoons of the chives, 1 teaspoon of the lemon zest, and ½ teaspoon of the pepper in a small bowl.
2. Place chips in an even layer on a platter. Cut salmon evenly into 24 bite-size pieces; top each chip with 1 salmon piece. Dollop with crème fraîche mixture; sprinkle evenly with red onion, flaky sea salt, and remaining 2 teaspoons chives, 1 teaspoon lemon zest, and ¼ teaspoon pepper. Serve immediately.

Cranberry Mules

(Photo, page 290)

ACTIVE 5 MIN. - TOTAL 5 MIN.
SERVES 8

Stir together 3 cups chilled **cranberry juice cocktail**, 2 cups (16 oz.) **vodka**, 2 cups chilled **nonalcoholic ginger beer** (such as Fever-Tree or another spicy ginger beer), 1 cup (8 oz.) **ginger liqueur** (such as Domaine de Canton), and ½ cup **fresh lime juice** (from 4 limes) in a large pitcher. Serve in copper mule mugs filled with **ice**, and garnish with **lime wheels** and **fresh cranberries**.

Fig, Pecan, and Brie Bites

(Photo, page 291)

ACTIVE 25 MIN. - TOTAL 1 HOUR, 15 MIN.
SERVES 8

- 1 (8-oz.) triple-cream Brie cheese round
- 1 frozen puff pastry sheet (from 1 [17.3-oz.] pkg.), thawed All-purpose flour, for work surface
- ⅔ cup chopped glazed pecans (from 1 [5-oz.] pkg.)
- 1 tsp. olive oil
- 1 tsp. finely chopped fresh rosemary, plus more for garnish
- ½ tsp. kosher salt
- ½ tsp. coarsely ground black pepper
- ¼ cup fig preserves

1. Cut away rounded edges of Brie to create a square. Cut square lengthwise into 4 even strips, and cut crosswise into 6 even strips. You'll have 24 even pieces of cheese. Transfer to a plate, and chill until ready to use.
2. Roll puff pastry sheet into a 10- x 14-inch rectangle on a lightly floured surface. Cut pastry lengthwise into 4 even strips, and cut crosswise into 6 even strips to yield 24 (about 2½-inch) pieces. Press 1 pastry piece into each well of 2 (12-cup) miniature muffin trays coated with

Continued on page 290

CRANBERRY
MULES
(PAGE 289)

SMOKED SALMON-
POTATO CHIP
CANAPÉS (PAGE 289)

Continued from page 289

cooking spray. Place 1 Brie piece in each pastry cup. Chill 30 minutes.

3. Preheat oven to 400°F. Stir together glazed pecans, oil, rosemary, salt, and pepper in a medium bowl. Remove muffin trays from refrigerator, and divide pecan mixture evenly among pastry cups (1 heaping teaspoon each).

4. Bake in preheated oven until pastry is puffed and golden and cheese is melted, 15 to 18 minutes. Let cool in muffin trays on wire racks 5 minutes; use an offset spatula to gently remove pastry cups from muffin trays, and transfer to a platter. Top evenly with fig preserves (½ teaspoon each). Garnish with additional rosemary, and serve warm or at room temperature.

Snow Day Sangría

ACTIVE 25 MIN. - TOTAL 25 MIN., PLUS 30 MIN. COOLING AND 8 HOURS CHILLING
SERVES 8

Scrape 1 **vanilla bean pod,** halved lengthwise, with the back of a paring knife, and place scraped seeds and pod in a small saucepan. Use a vegetable peeler to remove wide strips of zest from 1 **lemon** and 1 **orange,** leaving as much white pith behind as possible, and add zest strips to saucepan. Squeeze zested lemon and **another lemon** to yield ¼ cup juice, and add lemon juice to saucepan. Stir in 1 cup water, ½ cup **granulated sugar,** 3 **whole star anise,** and 2 (3-inch) **cinnamon sticks.** Bring mixture to a simmer over medium heat, stirring occasionally until sugar dissolves. Simmer, stirring occasionally, 5 minutes. Remove from heat, and let cool to room temperature, about 30 minutes. Remove and discard lemon and orange zest and vanilla bean pod from cooled syrup. Thinly slice 2 **lemons,** 1 medium **Honeycrisp apple,** and 1 medium **red or green Anjou pear** crosswise. Place fruit in a large pitcher or punch bowl. Add 2 (750-milliliter) bottles **dry white wine** and cooled syrup. Cover and refrigerate at least 8 hours or up to 12 hours. Cut orange peel twists from 1 **orange.** Ladle cold sangría into 8 glasses. Garnish glasses with orange peel twists.

SNOW DAY
SANGRÍA

FIG, PECAN,
AND BRIE BITES
(PAGE 289)

Ham for the Holidays

Rethink the holiday classic with three easy, flavor-packed glazes

Glazed Spiral-Cut Ham

ACTIVE 30 MIN. - TOTAL 2 HOURS, 30 MIN.
SERVES 15

1   **(7- to 10-lb.) fully cooked bone-in spiral-cut half ham**
    Desired glaze (recipes follow)
    Whole and halved fresh figs, fresh thyme sprigs, halved small apples, fresh sage sprigs, fresh bay leaves, and orange wedges, for garnish (optional)

1. Preheat oven to 350°F with oven rack in lower third position. Let ham stand at room temperature 30 minutes.
2. Line a roasting pan with aluminum foil, and place a rack into prepared pan; pour 3 cups water into bottom of pan. Place ham on rack, cut side down.
3. Bake in preheated oven for 1 hour, 30 minutes, basting with pan drippings every 30 minutes, adding more water to roasting pan as needed if it evaporates.
4. Brush ham all over with half of desired glaze, and bake for an additional 15 minutes. Brush ham all over with remaining glaze, and bake until a thermometer inserted into thickest portion of ham registers 140°F, about 15 minutes. Remove from oven, and let stand 15 minutes. Transfer to a serving platter, and garnish based on desired glaze. Serve warm.

Fig-and-Thyme Glaze

Place 1 cup **fig preserves**, ¼ cup **apple cider vinegar**, ¼ cup **honey**, 1 Tbsp. **dried thyme,** and 1 tsp. **black pepper** in a medium saucepan. Bring to a simmer, whisking occasionally, over medium-high, and simmer until well combined, 2 to 3 minutes. Reduce heat to low, and simmer until thickened and reduced by half, about 20 minutes. Remove from heat.

Sage-and-Cider Glaze

Place ¾ cup **cane syrup**, ½ cup **spiced apple cider**, 1 Tbsp. **cracked pepper**, 1 Tbsp. **ground sage**, and 3 **fresh sage leaves** in a medium saucepan. Bring to a simmer, whisking occasionally, over medium-high, and simmer until well combined, 2 to 3 minutes. Reduce heat to low, and simmer until thickened and reduced by half, about 20 minutes. Remove from heat.

Ginger-Clove Glaze

Place ¾ cup **pure maple syrup**, ⅓ cup **nonalcoholic ginger beer**, ¼ cup **light brown sugar**, 1 Tbsp. **Dijon mustard**, 1 Tbsp. grated **fresh ginger**, 2 tsp. **whole cloves**, and 2 **fresh bay leaves** in a medium saucepan. Bring to a simmer, whisking occasionally, over medium-high, and simmer until well combined, 2 to 3 minutes. Reduce heat to low, and simmer until thickened and reduced by half, about 20 minutes. Remove from heat.

Slow-Cooker Ham Stock

Use a ham bone to make a rich base for soups, stews, and more.
ACTIVE 10 MIN. - TOTAL 10 MIN., PLUS 9 HOURS SLOW-COOKING AND 1 HOUR COOLING
MAKES ABOUT 6 CUPS

Place 1 (15-oz.) **ham bone**; 8 cups **water**; 2 medium **carrots**, chopped; 2 large **celery** stalks, chopped; 1 small **yellow onion**, quartered; 4 **garlic** cloves; 4 **thyme** sprigs; 2 **bay leaves**; and 2 tsp. black **peppercorns** in a slow cooker. Cover; cook on LOW, undisturbed, 9 to 10 hours. Skim fat from surface of stock; discard. Line a fine mesh strainer with cheesecloth; set over a large heatproof bowl. Remove and discard bone from stock. Carefully pour the stock through the strainer; discard solids. Season to taste with **kosher salt,** if desired. Place 4 to 6 ice cubes in stock; cool to room temperature, 1 to 2 hours. Transfer to an airtight container; store in refrigerator up to 5 days or in freezer up to 6 months.

Eyes on the Sides

Presenting the dishes everyone expects to see on the table, just a little fancied up

Roasted Green Beans with Spicy-Sweet Glazed Shallots

ACTIVE 25 MIN. - TOTAL 25 MIN.

SERVES 6

- 2 lb. fresh green beans, trimmed
- 8 medium shallots, halved lengthwise
- 3 Tbsp. extra-virgin olive oil
- 2¼ tsp. kosher salt, divided
- ½ tsp. black pepper
- ¾ cup red wine vinegar
- ¼ cup honey
- 2 Tbsp. golden raisins, chopped
- ½ tsp. crushed red pepper

1. Preheat oven to 450°F. Toss together green beans, shallots, oil, 2 teaspoons of the salt, and black pepper in a large bowl until evenly coated. Transfer to a large rimmed baking sheet.
2. Roast in preheated oven until green beans are tender, 15 to 18 minutes, stirring once halfway through bake time.
3. While beans and shallots roast, stir together vinegar, honey, raisins, red pepper, and remaining ¼ teaspoon salt in a medium saucepan. Bring to a boil over medium. Boil, stirring often, until syrupy and reduced to about ⅓ cup, 10 to 12 minutes. Remove from heat.
4. Transfer beans to a platter. Place shallots in honey mixture in saucepan, tossing to coat. Transfer glazed shallots to platter with beans. Drizzle with any remaining honey mixture.

Green Chile Spoon Bread

ACTIVE 35 MIN. - TOTAL 1 HOUR, 15 MIN.

SERVES 8

- ½ cup unsalted butter, softened, plus more for greasing
- 4 thick-cut bacon slices, chopped (about 1 cup)
- 1 large sweet onion, finely chopped (about 1¼ cups)
- 2 large poblano chiles, chopped (about 1⅓ cups)
- 3 cups whole milk
- 1 cup fine yellow cornmeal
- 2 tsp. granulated sugar
- 1½ tsp. kosher salt
- ¼ tsp. black pepper
- 1 tsp. baking powder
- 3 large eggs, separated
  Sliced scallions, for garnish

1. Preheat oven to 350°F. Grease a 9-inch square baking dish with butter; set aside.
2. Cook chopped bacon in a large skillet over medium-high, stirring often, until crisp, about 10 minutes. Transfer bacon to a paper towel-lined plate, reserving drippings in skillet. Add onion and poblanos to drippings in skillet; cook over medium-high, stirring often, until tender, about 5 minutes. Remove from heat. Set onion mixture aside for batter; reserve ⅓ cup onion mixture for topping.
3. Bring 2 cups of the milk to a boil in a medium saucepan over medium. Stir together cornmeal, sugar, salt, pepper, and remaining 1 cup milk in a small bowl. Gradually whisk cornmeal mixture into hot milk. Reduce heat to low, and simmer, stirring constantly, until thickened, 3 to 5 minutes.
4. Remove saucepan from heat, and sprinkle in baking powder. Add the ½ cup butter to saucepan, and stir until melted and combined. Beat egg yolks in a small bowl; stir in a small amount of hot cornmeal mixture. Add yolk mixture to pan, and stir well.

ROASTED GREEN BEANS WITH SPICY-SWEET GLAZED SHALLOTS

5. Beat egg whites with an electric mixer on high speed until stiff peaks form, about 3 minutes. Fold egg whites, bacon, and reserved onion mixture for batter into cornmeal mixture. Pour mixture into prepared baking dish. Top with reserved ⅓ cup onion mixture.
6. Bake in preheated oven until puffed and golden brown, 40 to 45 minutes. Let cool 10 minutes. Garnish with sliced scallions, and serve warm.

Smoky Creamed Greens
ACTIVE 45 MIN. - TOTAL 45 MIN.
SERVES 6

- **2** bunches fresh collard greens, stems removed
- **6** thick-cut bacon slices, chopped (about 1⅓ cups)
- **1** medium-size yellow onion, chopped (about 1½ cups)
- **2** Tbsp. all-purpose flour
- **2** cups heavy whipping cream
- **1½** cups lower-sodium chicken broth
- **1½** tsp. kosher salt, plus more for salting water
- **½** tsp. black pepper

1. Cut collard greens into bite-size pieces. Bring a large pot of salted water to a boil over high. Add collards, and cook, stirring occasionally, until bright green and just softened, 3 to 4 minutes. Drain and rinse with cold water. Squeeze to release any excess liquid.
2. Cook chopped bacon in a large skillet over medium-high, stirring often, until crisp, about 10 minutes. Transfer cooked bacon to a paper towel-lined plate. Reserve 2 tablespoons drippings in skillet.
3. Add yellow onion to skillet, and cook, stirring often, until tender, about 5 minutes. Stir in flour, and cook, stirring constantly, until toasted, about 1 minute. Gradually stir in cream and chicken broth. Bring to a boil over medium-high, stirring constantly. Stir in collards and half of the cooked bacon (about ⅓ cup), and reduce heat to medium-low. Simmer, stirring often, until collards are tender and liquid is reduced, about 15 minutes. Stir in salt and pepper. Top with remaining cooked bacon, and serve.

SMOKY CREAMED GREENS

GREEN CHILE SPOON BREAD

DELUXE BUTTERMILK
BISCUITS WITH SAGE
BROWN BUTTER

Deluxe Buttermilk Biscuits with Sage Brown Butter

ACTIVE 30 MIN. - TOTAL 1 HOUR, 55 MIN.

MAKES 16

1½ cups cold unsalted butter, divided

¼ cup fresh sage leaves (from 1 [½-oz.] pkg.)

3½ cups all-purpose flour, plus more for work surface

2 Tbsp. granulated sugar

1 Tbsp. baking powder

2 tsp. kosher salt

½ tsp. black pepper, plus more for sprinkling

½ tsp. baking soda

1 cup whole buttermilk

1 large egg, beaten

1. Heat 1 cup of the butter in a medium saucepan over medium until melted and bubbling, about 2 minutes. Add sage leaves, and cook, stirring occasionally, until sage is crispy, 2 to 3 minutes. Remove sage, and transfer to a paper towel-lined plate; set aside. Continue cooking butter over medium, stirring and swirling pan occasionally, until butter turns a medium-brown color and has a nutty aroma, about 6 minutes. Place butter in a small heatproof bowl; freeze until solid, about 1 hour. Cut solidified brown butter and remaining ½ cup butter into cubes. Place cubed butter in refrigerator until ready to use.

2. Preheat oven to 425°F. Line 2 large baking sheets with parchment paper.

3. Stir together all-purpose flour, granulated sugar, baking powder, kosher salt, black pepper, and baking soda in a large bowl. Using 2 forks or a pastry blender, cut in reserved butter cubes until mixture is crumbly. Stir in buttermilk until a shaggy dough forms.

4. Turn dough out onto a lightly floured work surface. Pat into a rectangle, and cut dough in half crosswise and then in half lengthwise into 4 equal, smaller rectangles. Stack rectangles evenly on top of each other, and pat down into a larger rectangle again. Repeat process 3 more times.

5. Pat or roll dough into an 8-inch square, about 1 inch thick (trim edges to straighten, if desired). Cut dough into 2-inch squares. Place biscuits 2 inches apart on prepared baking sheets. Freeze 10 minutes. Brush with beaten egg, and sprinkle with additional pepper.

SPIRALED SWEET POTATO GRATIN

6. Bake in preheated oven until golden brown, 12 to 15 minutes. Sprinkle biscuits evenly with fried sage. Serve warm or at room temperature.

Spiraled Sweet Potato Gratin

ACTIVE 35 MIN. - TOTAL 1 HOUR, 50 MIN.

SERVES 6

1 Tbsp. unsalted butter, softened

5 medium sweet potatoes, peeled

1½ cups heavy whipping cream

4 garlic cloves, crushed

1 Tbsp. fresh thyme leaves, plus more for garnish

¼ tsp. black pepper

3 tsp. kosher salt, divided

2 oz. Parmesan cheese, finely grated (about ½ cup)

1. Preheat oven to 350°F. Grease bottom of a 10-inch cast-iron skillet or baking dish with butter. Using a mandoline, thinly slice sweet potatoes (about 1/16 inch thick). (Alternatively, thinly slice sweet potatoes ⅛ inch thick using a chef's knife.) Place stacks of potato slices vertically on their sides in prepared pan, fanning slightly.

2. Bring cream, crushed garlic, thyme, pepper, and 2 teaspoons of the salt to a boil in a medium saucepan over medium. Reduce heat to medium-low; simmer, stirring often, until garlic is softened, about 15 minutes. Remove and discard garlic, if desired. Pour cream mixture over potatoes in skillet. Sprinkle with Parmesan cheese and remaining 1 teaspoon salt. Cover tightly with aluminum foil.

3. Bake in preheated oven until potatoes are tender and easily pierced with a knife, 50 to 55 minutes. Remove foil, and bake until top begins to brown, about 15 minutes. Remove from oven; let cool 10 minutes. Garnish with additional thyme leaves, and serve.

Pucker Up!

Tart and tangy cranberries take a starring role in these special-occasion desserts

Orange Chess Pie with Cranberry Gelée

Creating this layered dessert requires a little patience, but the combination of tart cranberry gelée and citrusy chess filling is worth the effort.

ACTIVE 35 MIN. - TOTAL 2 HOURS, 5 MIN., PLUS 2 HOURS COOLING AND 3 HOURS CHILLING

SERVES 8

CHESS PIE

- 1 (14.1-oz.) pkg. refrigerated piecrusts (such as Pillsbury)
- 1½ cups granulated sugar
- 1 Tbsp. all-purpose flour, plus more for work surface
- 1 Tbsp. plain yellow cornmeal
- ¼ tsp. kosher salt
- ¼ cup butter, melted
- 2 tsp. grated orange zest plus ⅓ cup fresh juice (from 1 large navel orange)
- 1 Tbsp. fresh lemon juice (from 1 lemon)
- 4 large eggs, lightly beaten

CRANBERRY GELÉE

- 1 (12-oz.) pkg. fresh cranberries
- ¼ cup fresh lemon juice (from 2 large lemons)
- ½ cup plus 1 Tbsp. granulated sugar, divided
- 2½ tsp. unflavored gelatin (from 1 [¼-oz.] envelope)
- 2 Tbsp. fresh orange juice (from 1 orange)

MASCARPONE WHIPPED CREAM

- 1 (8-oz.) container mascarpone cheese
- ¼ cup powdered sugar
- 2 tsp. vanilla extract
- 1 cup heavy whipping cream

ADDITIONAL INGREDIENT

Sparkling Cranberries (recipe follows), for garnish

1. Prepare Chess Pie: Preheat oven to 450°F. Unroll piecrusts; stack on a lightly floured surface. Roll stacked piecrusts into a 12-inch circle. Lightly grease a 9-inch pie plate with cooking spray, and fit piecrust into pie plate; fold edges under, and crimp. Prick bottom and sides of crust with a fork. Line with a piece of parchment, allowing ends to extend over edges of crust. Fill with pie weights. Bake 9 minutes; remove pie weights and parchment. Let cool on a wire rack 15 minutes. Reduce oven temperature to 350°F.

2. Meanwhile, whisk together sugar, flour, cornmeal, and salt in a large bowl. Whisk in melted butter, orange zest and juice, lemon juice, and eggs until thoroughly combined. Pour into prepared piecrust.

3. Bake at 350°F until center is set, 40 to 45 minutes, shielding edges with aluminum foil after 30 minutes to prevent excessive browning, if necessary. Let cool on a wire rack 2 hours. Cover and chill until cold, about 2 hours.

4. Meanwhile, prepare the Cranberry Gelée: Combine cranberries and 4 cups water in a saucepan; bring to a boil over medium-high. Cover, reduce heat to medium-low, and simmer until berries have popped, 15 to 20 minutes. Pour berry mixture through a fine mesh strainer into a small bowl, discarding berries. (Do not press on berries; you want liquid to remain as clear as possible.) Return strained cranberry juice to saucepan. Stir in lemon juice and ½ cup of the granulated sugar. Cook over medium-high, stirring constantly, until sugar has dissolved, about 3 minutes. (Cranberry juice mixture can be made up to 2 days ahead; cover and chill until ready to use.)

5. Stir together 1¼ cups cranberry juice mixture and remaining 1 tablespoon granulated sugar in a small saucepan. Sprinkle gelatin over mixture, and let stand 5 minutes. Cook over medium, stirring occasionally, just until mixture is steaming and gelatin dissolves, about 5 minutes. Remove from heat; let cool 20 minutes. Stir in orange juice.

6. Gently drizzle cranberry mixture evenly over top of chilled pie. Chill, covered, until gelée sets, about 1 hour.

7. Prepare Mascarpone Whipped Cream: Whisk together mascarpone cheese, powdered sugar, and vanilla in a large bowl just until blended. (Be careful not to overmix.) Beat heavy whipping cream with an electric mixer on medium speed until stiff peaks form, about 1½ minutes. Gently fold whipped cream into mascarpone mixture. Dollop on top of pie, and garnish with Sparkling Cranberries.

Sparkling Cranberries

ACTIVE 20 MIN. - TOTAL 20 MIN., PLUS 8 HOURS CHILLING AND 2 HOURS STANDING

MAKES 1 CUP

Cook ½ cup **pure maple syrup** in a small saucepan over medium-low until just hot, 1 to 2 minutes. (Don't let syrup get too hot, or cranberries will pop.) Remove from heat, and stir in 1 cup **fresh cranberries.** Cover and chill 8 to 24 hours. Place cranberries in a fine mesh strainer, and let drain 15 minutes. Gently toss 4 or 5 cranberries at a time in ½ cup **granulated or sparkling sugar** until completely coated. Place in a single layer on a parchment paper-lined baking sheet. Let stand at room temperature until completely dry, 2 to 3 hours.

CRANBERRY-CITRUS
PARFAITS (PAGE 304)

BROWN SUGAR-CRANBERRY
POUND CAKE WITH
CARAMEL FROSTING
(PAGE 304)

GINGERBREAD CAKE WITH
CRANBERRY-VANILLA
FROSTING (PAGE 304)

CRANBERRY-PEAR CRISP
(PAGE 305)

Cranberry-Citrus Parfaits

(Photo, page 300)

Cheesecake lovers take note: This recipe delivers all the flavor of your favorite dessert with none of the fuss. The cranberry compote provides a sweet-tart balance; it's also great for spooning over pound cake or yogurt for breakfast.

ACTIVE 20 MIN. - TOTAL 1 HOUR, 20 MIN., PLUS 4 HOURS CHILLING

SERVES 6

COMPOTE
- 1 cup fresh cranberries
- ½ cup granulated sugar
- 1 tsp. grated lemon zest plus 2 Tbsp. fresh juice (from 1 large lemon)
- 1 tsp. grated orange zest plus ¼ cup fresh juice (from 1 large orange)

LEMON TOPPING
- 1½ (8-oz.) pkg. cream cheese, softened
- 1 Tbsp. sour cream
- ½ cup granulated sugar
- 1 tsp. grated lemon zest plus 1 Tbsp. fresh juice (from 1 large lemon)
- 1 tsp. grated orange zest

ADDITIONAL INGREDIENT
- 1 (5.25-oz.) pkg. almond or ginger thin cookies, crushed (such as Anna's Swedish Thins)

1. Prepare the Compote: Combine cranberries, sugar, lemon zest and juice, orange zest and juice, and 2 tablespoons water in a small saucepan; bring to a boil over medium. Boil, stirring often, until cranberries burst and mixture thickens, 8 to 9 minutes. Let stand at room temperature 1 hour. Cover and chill at least 4 hours or up to overnight.

2. Prepare the Lemon Topping: Beat cream cheese and sour cream with an electric mixer on medium speed until smooth, about 1 minute. Add sugar, lemon zest and juice, and orange zest; beat until light and fluffy, about 2 minutes, stopping to scrape down sides as needed.

3. Assemble the parfaits: Spoon about 4½ tablespoons cookie crumbs into each of 6 (1-cup) glasses or ramekins; top each with about ⅓ cup Lemon Topping. Cover and chill until ready to serve. Just before serving, uncover and top each glass with about 2 tablespoons chilled Compote.

Brown Sugar-Cranberry Pound Cake with Caramel Frosting

(Photo, page 301)

ACTIVE 20 MIN. - TOTAL 1 HOUR, 30 MIN., PLUS 1 HOUR, 15 MIN. COOLING

SERVES 12

CAKE
- 2 cups butter, softened
- 2½ cups packed light brown sugar
- 6 large eggs
- 3 cups all-purpose flour
- 2 tsp. baking powder
- 1 tsp. ground cinnamon
- ¼ tsp. kosher salt
- ¼ tsp. baking soda
- 1 cup whole buttermilk
- 2 cups fresh cranberries, coarsely chopped
- 1 cup chopped toasted pecans
- 1 Tbsp. vanilla extract
- Baking spray

FROSTING
- 1 cup packed light brown sugar
- ½ cup butter
- ¼ cup whole milk
- 1 cup powdered sugar, sifted
- 1 tsp. vanilla extract

ADDITIONAL INGREDIENT
- 1 cup coarsely chopped toasted pecans

1. Prepare the Cake: Preheat oven to 325°F. Beat butter with a stand mixer fitted with a paddle attachment on medium speed until creamy, about 1 minute. Gradually add brown sugar, beating until light and fluffy, about 4 minutes, stopping to scrape down sides as needed. Add eggs, 1 at a time, beating until just blended after each addition.

2. Whisk together flour, baking powder, cinnamon, salt, and baking soda in a medium bowl. Add flour mixture to butter mixture alternately with buttermilk, beginning and ending with flour mixture. Beat on low speed just until blended after each addition. Using a rubber spatula, stir in cranberries, pecans, and vanilla until blended. Spoon batter into a 15-cup Bundt pan coated with baking spray.

3. Bake in preheated oven until a wooden pick inserted in center comes out clean, 1 hour, 10 minutes to 1 hour, 15 minutes. Let cool in pan on a wire rack 15 minutes; remove from pan to wire rack, and let cool completely, about 1 hour.

4. Prepare the Frosting: Bring brown sugar, butter, and milk to a boil in a saucepan over medium, whisking constantly; boil 1 minute. Remove from heat, and whisk in powdered sugar and vanilla until smooth. Stir gently until mixture begins to cool and thickens slightly, 3 to 5 minutes. Immediately spoon Frosting over cooled Cake, and top with coarsely chopped pecans.

Gingerbread Cake with Cranberry-Vanilla Frosting

(Photo, page 302)

ACTIVE 35 MIN. - TOTAL 1 HOUR, 35 MIN., PLUS 1 HOUR CHILLING

SERVES 12

CAKE LAYERS
- 1 cup butter, softened
- 2 cups packed light brown sugar
- 3 large eggs
- 1 tsp. vanilla extract
- 3 cups all-purpose flour
- 1 tsp. baking soda
- ½ tsp. baking powder
- ½ tsp. kosher salt
- ½ tsp. ground cinnamon
- ¼ tsp. ground cloves
- 1½ cups whole buttermilk
- ⅓ cup finely chopped crystallized ginger
- Baking spray

FROSTING
- 1½ cups fresh cranberries
- ⅓ cup granulated sugar
- 1 cup butter, softened
- 1 Tbsp. vanilla extract
- ¼ tsp. kosher salt
- 2 (16-oz.) pkg. powdered sugar
- 6 to 8 Tbsp. heavy whipping cream, divided
- Sparkling Cranberries (recipe page 299), for garnish

1. Prepare the Cake Layers: Preheat oven to 350°F. Beat butter with a stand mixer fitted with a paddle attachment on medium speed until creamy, about 1 minute. Gradually add brown sugar, and beat until light and fluffy, about 4 minutes. Add eggs, 1 at a time, beating just until blended after each addition. Stir in vanilla.

2. Whisk together flour, baking soda, baking powder, salt, cinnamon, and cloves in a medium bowl. Add flour mixture to brown sugar mixture alternately with buttermilk, beginning and ending with flour mixture. Beat on low speed just until blended after each addition. Gently stir in crystallized ginger. Spoon batter into 3 (8-inch) round baking pans coated with baking spray. Bake in preheated oven until a wooden pick inserted in center comes out clean, 25 to 30 minutes. Let cool in pans on wire racks 10 minutes. Remove from pans to wire racks, and let cool completely, about 1 hour.

3. While cakes bake and cool, prepare the Frosting: Combine cranberries, granulated sugar, and 2 tablespoons water in a small saucepan. Cook over medium, stirring often, until cranberries begin to pop and mixture is thickened, about 5 minutes. Remove from heat, and let cool 10 minutes. Place mixture in a food processor or blender, and process until smooth, 1 to 2 minutes. Transfer cranberry puree to a small bowl; cover and chill at least 1 hour or up to 5 days.

4. Beat butter, vanilla, salt, and ¼ cup of the chilled cranberry puree with a stand mixer fitted with a paddle attachment on medium speed until creamy, about 2 minutes, stopping to scrape down sides as needed. Gradually add powdered sugar alternately with 6 tablespoons heavy whipping cream, beating on low speed until blended and smooth after each addition. Beat in additional cream 1 tablespoon at a time, if needed, to reach desired consistency. Increase speed to medium, and beat until light and fluffy.

5. Assemble the cake: Spread frosting between Cake Layers and on top and sides of cake. Garnish with Sparkling Cranberries.

Cranberry-Pear Crisp

(Photo, page 303)

Anjou pears are available in red and green varieties. To test for ripeness, gently press near the stem with your thumb; if the pear flesh gives slightly, it's ready.

ACTIVE 15 MIN. - TOTAL 1 HOUR, 15 MIN., PLUS 1 HOUR COOLING

SERVES 8

- 1½ cups all-purpose flour
- ¾ cup packed light brown sugar
- ½ cup butter, melted
- ¼ tsp. kosher salt
- 1 cup coarsely chopped pecans
- 2 cups fresh cranberries, rinsed and drained
- 3 large firm-ripe Anjou pears, peeled and thinly sliced (about 2 lb.)
- 1 cup granulated sugar
- ¼ cup pure maple syrup
- 3 Tbsp. cornstarch
- 1 Tbsp. vanilla extract
- 1 tsp. ground cinnamon
  Vanilla or cinnamon ice cream (optional)

1. Preheat oven to 375°F. Stir together flour, brown sugar, melted butter, salt, and chopped pecans in a medium bowl until thoroughly combined. Chill until brown sugar mixture is firm enough to crumble into small pieces, about 10 minutes.

2. Meanwhile, combine cranberries, pears, granulated sugar, maple syrup, cornstarch, vanilla, and cinnamon in a large bowl; toss gently to thoroughly combine. Lightly grease a 9-inch square baking pan with cooking spray; spoon cranberry mixture into prepared pan. Sprinkle top with brown sugar mixture.

3. Bake in preheated oven until filling is bubbly and topping has browned, 45 to 50 minutes. Cover loosely with aluminum foil after 35 minutes to prevent excessive browning, if needed. Let cool on a wire rack for 1 hour. Serve warm with ice cream, if desired.

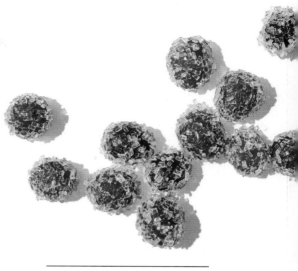

Berry Good Advice

Harvested in the fall, cranberries are usually at their peak in supermarkets from October through December, but they have a longer shelf life than most fruits. When purchasing, look for firm, brightly colored berries—softness does not equal ripeness. Store them in their original packaging in the refrigerator for about a month, or stock up and freeze them for up to one year. (Do not thaw before cooking.) Wash the fruit when you're ready to use it; then sort through it carefully, discarding berries that are soft or discolored.

Memories by the Dozen

For Birmingham chef Rob McDaniel, the sweetest gifts have always come tucked in a cookie tin

MY FAMILY WOULD USUALLY go to my grandmother Helen's house for Thanksgiving, and that's when the cookies started making their appearance. We'd typically have sugar cookies that day, but Nanny would have already started making other kinds in preparation for Christmas. She had a little credenza by the front door, and that, for whatever reason, was where she kept all of the cookies. I remember there being 10 to 15 decorative tins filled with different treats in there. She would bake everything from apricot thumbprints with pecans (my favorite) to millionaires, chocolate turtles, and cheese straws—just a huge array of stuff.

We ate those cookies almost every time my family got together in December. Whether my grandparents came to our house or we went to my sister's, there was always an assortment of sweets. They may have been condensed into two or three tins for easier transport, but they usually traveled with us.

At my own home when I was growing up, my mom—like her mother, Helen—baked cookies and stored them in tins. We kept ours in an antique icebox. I specifically recall my mom asking me what kind of cookie I wanted to make one Christmas, and I said the peppermint wreaths that were on the cover of the 1985 December issue of *Southern Living.* I vividly remember making a variety of treats that day—sitting around the kitchen table, playing with balls of red and green dough to form the wreaths, rolling out the butterfingers, and licking sugar cookie frosting from the mixer beaters.

Baking with my mom, the Sears Wish Book showing up, the crocheted angel on top of Nanny's tree—these were signs that Christmas was coming. I think, as you get older, you get caught up in the ins and outs of the holidays, like making sure all the gifts are bought. It's easy to get lost in that and forget the meaning of the season. But to me, the cookie tins always make me have that feeling, that sense of the Christmas spirit. They're so welcoming and comforting.

Last year, we started making cookies at home with our young daughters and my mom. I love the fact that they're baking with her just like I used to. I don't know if they'll remember it, but it means the world that we can continue the tradition. –Rob McDaniel

Sugar Cookies

ACTIVE 45 MIN. - TOTAL 1 HOUR, PLUS 2 HOURS CHILLING AND 3 HOURS STANDING
MAKES ABOUT 32 COOKIES

- 1½ cups powdered sugar
- 1 cup unsalted butter, softened
- 1 large egg
- 1 tsp. vanilla extract
- ½ tsp. almond extract
- 2½ cups all-purpose flour, plus more for work surface
- 1 tsp. baking soda
- 1 tsp. cream of tartar
- ½ tsp. kosher salt
- Glaze (recipe follows)
- Icing (recipe follows)

1. Beat sugar and butter in a large bowl with an electric mixer on medium-high speed until light and fluffy, 3 to 4 minutes. Add egg, vanilla, and almond extract, beating until combined, about 1 minute. Whisk together flour, baking soda, cream of tartar, and salt in a medium bowl. With mixer running on low speed, gradually add flour mixture to butter mixture, beating just until combined, about 1 minute, stopping to scrape down sides of bowl as needed. Divide dough in half; wrap each half in plastic wrap. Chill at least 2 hours or up to 24 hours.
2. Preheat oven to 375°F with racks in top and bottom positions. Line 2 large baking sheets with parchment paper.
3. Roll out each half of cold dough to ¼-inch thickness on a lightly floured work surface. Cut into desired shapes using 2½- to 3½-inch cookie cutters. Place about 2 inches apart on prepared baking sheets. Reroll dough scraps as needed.

4. Bake in preheated oven in 2 batches until cookies are lightly browned around edges, 7 to 8 minutes per batch, rotating baking sheets between top and bottom racks halfway through baking time. Let cool on baking sheets, about 1 hour.
5. Decorate using Glaze and Icing as desired. Let cookies stand until completely dry, about 2 hours. Store in an airtight container at room temperature for up to 5 days.

Glaze

ACTIVE 5 MIN. - TOTAL 5 MIN.
MAKES ½ CUP

- 1 cup powdered sugar
- 1 Tbsp. plus 1 tsp. whole milk
- 1 Tbsp. plus 1 tsp. light corn syrup
- Liquid or gel food coloring (assorted colors), optional

Whisk together sugar, milk, and corn syrup in a small bowl until smooth. If desired, divide glaze evenly into separate bowls, and stir in food coloring. Store in an airtight container in refrigerator for up to 5 days. Before using, bring to room temperature and stir.

Icing

ACTIVE 5 MIN. - TOTAL 5 MIN.
MAKES ABOUT 1¾ CUPS

- 1 (16-oz.) pkg. (about 3¾ cups) powdered sugar
- 1 Tbsp. unsalted butter, softened
- 1 tsp. vanilla extract
- 4 to 6 Tbsp. whole milk, as needed
- Liquid or gel food coloring (assorted colors), optional

Beat sugar, butter, and vanilla in a medium bowl with an electric mixer on high speed, adding milk as needed, until mixture is smooth and desired consistency, about 2 minutes. If desired, divide icing evenly into separate bowls and stir in food coloring. Store in an airtight container in refrigerator for up to 5 days. Before using, bring to room temperature and stir.

SUGAR
COOKIES

BUTTERFINGERS
(PAGE 312)

GINGERSNAPS
(PAGE 309)

MELT-AWAY
PEPPERMINT
WREATHS
(PAGE 310)

APRICOT
THUMBPRINTS

DIVINITY

CHERRY
WINKS

Apricot Thumbprints

ACTIVE 25 MIN. - TOTAL 1 HOUR, 5 MIN.
MAKES 20 COOKIES

- ½ cup vegetable shortening
- ½ cup granulated sugar
- 1 large egg, separated
- 1 tsp. vanilla extract
- 1 cup all-purpose flour, sifted
- ½ tsp. kosher salt
- 1 cup chopped pecans
- ⅓ cup apricot preserves

1. Preheat oven to 325°F with racks in top and bottom positions. Line 2 large baking sheets with parchment paper.
2. Beat shortening and sugar in a large bowl with an electric mixer on high speed until light and fluffy, 3 to 4 minutes. Add egg yolk and vanilla, and beat until just combined, about 1 minute. Reduce mixer speed to low; gradually add flour and salt, beating until combined, about 1 minute. Shape dough into 20 (1-tablespoon) balls.
3. Place pecans in a bowl. Whisk egg white in a small bowl until frothy. Dip dough balls in egg white; roll in chopped pecans to coat. Arrange 1½ inches apart on prepared baking sheets.
4. Bake in preheated oven 5 minutes. Remove from oven; using a clean thimble or the end of a wooden spoon, make a ½-inch-deep indentation in the center of each ball. Place a heaping ¾ teaspoon apricot preserves in center of each cookie.
5. Bake until lightly browned, 12 to 15 minutes, rotating baking sheets between top and bottom racks halfway through baking time. Let cool on baking sheets 5 minutes. Transfer to wire racks, and let cool completely, about 15 minutes.

Divinity

ACTIVE 25 MIN. - TOTAL 25 MIN.,
PLUS 1 HOUR STANDING
MAKES ABOUT 20 CANDIES

- 2 cups granulated sugar
- ½ cup light corn syrup
- ¼ tsp. kosher salt
- 2 large egg whites
- ⅛ tsp. cream of tartar
  Pecan halves

1. Line 2 large baking sheets with parchment paper. Stir together sugar, corn syrup, ½ cup water, and salt in a 1-quart saucepan; attach a candy thermometer to side of pan. Cook over medium-high, stirring often, until mixture begins to boil. Boil, undisturbed, until thermometer reaches 260°F (hard-ball stage), 7 to 10 minutes. Remove from heat.
2. Beat egg whites and cream of tartar with a stand mixer fitted with a whisk attachment on high speed until stiff peaks form, about 2 minutes. With mixer running on high speed, slowly pour hot sugar mixture into egg white mixture; beat until stiff peaks form and mixture loses its glossy sheen, 7 to 10 minutes.
3. Working quickly, drop by tablespoonfuls onto prepared baking sheets. Garnish with pecan halves. Let stand at room temperature until dry to the touch, about 1 hour. Store with wax paper or parchment paper between candies in an airtight container at room temperature for up to 1 week.

Cherry Winks

ACTIVE 30 MIN. - TOTAL 2 HOURS
MAKES 3½ DOZEN COOKIES

- ⅓ cup plus 42 red maraschino cherries (from 2 [16-oz.] jars), divided
- 2½ cups all-purpose flour
- 1 tsp. baking powder
- ½ tsp. baking soda
- ½ tsp. kosher salt
- 1 cup granulated sugar
- ¼ cup plus 2 Tbsp. vegetable shortening
- 6 Tbsp. unsalted butter, softened
- 2 large eggs
- 2 Tbsp. whole milk
- 1 tsp. vanilla extract
- 1 cup pecans, chopped
- 1 cup dried dates, chopped
- 3½ cups cornflakes cereal, crushed

1. Chop ⅓ cup of the cherries; set aside. Preheat oven to 375°F with racks in top and bottom positions. Line 2 large baking sheets with parchment paper. Sift together flour, baking powder, baking soda, and salt in a medium bowl. Set aside.
2. Beat sugar, shortening, and butter in a large bowl with an electric mixer on medium-high speed until light and fluffy, 3 to 4 minutes. Add eggs, 1 at a time, beating until well combined, about 1 minute. Add milk and vanilla; beat until combined, about 30 seconds. Reduce mixer speed to low. Gradually add flour mixture, beating until just combined, about 1 minute, stopping to scrape down sides of bowl as needed. Stir in pecans, dates, and the chopped cherries.
3. Place crushed cereal in a bowl; drop 1 heaping tablespoonful of dough into cereal, and roll until well coated. Shape into a ball. Place on prepared baking sheet. Press 1 whole cherry into top of ball. Repeat process with remaining dough, cereal, and cherries, arranging balls 2 inches apart on prepared baking sheets.
4. Bake in preheated oven in batches until cookies are light golden around the edges, 10 to 14 minutes per batch, rotating baking sheets between top and bottom racks halfway through baking time. Let cool on baking sheets about 5 minutes. Transfer to wire racks; let cool completely, about 15 minutes. Store in an airtight container at room temperature for up to 4 days.

Gingersnaps

(Photo, page 307)
ACTIVE 20 MIN. - TOTAL 45 MIN.
MAKES ABOUT 2 DOZEN COOKIES

- 1 cup packed light brown sugar
- ¾ cup unsalted butter, softened
- 1 large egg
- ¼ cup unsulphured molasses
- 2¼ cups all-purpose flour
- 2 tsp. baking soda
- 1 tsp. ground cinnamon
- 1 tsp. ground ginger
- ½ tsp. ground cloves
- ¼ tsp. kosher salt
- ½ cup sanding sugar

1. Preheat oven to 350°F with racks in top and bottom positions. Line 2 large baking sheets with parchment paper.
2. Beat brown sugar and butter in a large bowl with an electric mixer on high speed until light and fluffy, 3 to 4 minutes. Add egg, beating until just combined, about 1 minute. Add molasses; beat until combined, about 30 seconds, stopping to scrape down sides of bowl as needed.

Continued on page 310

Continued from page 309

3. Stir together flour, baking soda, cinnamon, ginger, cloves, and salt in a medium bowl until combined. With mixer running on low speed, gradually add flour mixture to butter mixture, beating until just combined, about 1 minute.

4. Place sanding sugar in a bowl. Scoop dough into 1½-tablespoon balls, and roll in sanding sugar. Place rolled balls 3 inches apart on prepared baking sheets.

5. Bake in preheated oven until cookies are lightly browned around edges, about 10 minutes, rotating baking sheets between top and bottom racks halfway through baking time. Let cool on baking sheets 5 minutes. Transfer cookies to wire racks, and let cool completely, about 10 minutes. Store in an airtight container at room temperature for up to 5 days.

Melt-Away Peppermint Wreaths

(Photo, page 307)
ACTIVE 30 MIN. - TOTAL 1 HOUR, 40 MIN.
MAKES ABOUT 28 COOKIES

1¼	cups unsalted butter, softened
¾	cup powdered sugar, sifted
2½	cups all-purpose flour
¼	tsp. kosher salt
¾	tsp. peppermint extract
	Red and green liquid or gel food coloring

1. Preheat oven to 375°F with racks in top and bottom positions. Line 2 large baking sheets with parchment paper.

2. Beat butter and sugar in a large bowl with an electric mixer on high speed until creamy and smooth, about 2 minutes. Reduce mixer speed to low; gradually add flour and salt, and beat until combined, about 1 minute. Stir in peppermint extract. Divide dough in half; place in separate bowls. Stir red food coloring into 1 dough half until desired shade is reached; stir green food coloring into remaining dough half until desired shade is reached.

3. Divide and shape dough into ½-teaspoon balls. Alternating colors, arrange 6 balls in a circle on prepared baking sheet, slightly touching. Press balls to flatten slightly so they stick together and form a wreath shape.

Repeat process with remaining dough balls to make about 28 wreath cookies total, spacing them about 2 inches apart on prepared baking sheets.

4. Bake in preheated oven in batches until cookie tops look dry, about 8 minutes per batch, rotating baking sheets between top and bottom racks halfway through baking time. Let cool on baking sheets 10 minutes. Transfer cookies to wire racks, and let cool completely, about 15 minutes. Store in an airtight container at room temperature for up to 5 days.

Millionaire Candies

ACTIVE 25 MIN. - TOTAL 55 MIN.
MAKES ABOUT 30 CANDIES

	Butter, for greasing pan
55	caramel candies (such as Kraft) (from 2 [11-oz.] pkg.)
1	Tbsp. whole milk
2	cups pecan pieces, toasted
	Pinch of kosher salt
2	cups milk chocolate melting wafers (such as Ghirardelli) (from 2 [10-oz.] pkg.)

1. Line 2 large baking sheets with parchment paper or wax paper; grease with butter.

2. Fill a medium saucepan with water to a depth of 1 inch; bring to a simmer over medium. Place a heatproof bowl over pan, making sure water does not touch bottom of bowl. Place caramels and milk in bowl; cook over medium, stirring often, until caramels are melted, about 12 minutes. Remove from heat; set pan aside. Stir in pecans and salt. Drop caramel mixture by tablespoonfuls onto prepared baking sheets. (You will have about 30 mounds.)

3. Return pan with water to a simmer over medium. Place a second heatproof bowl over pan, making sure water does not touch bottom of bowl. Place chocolate in bowl; cook, stirring occasionally, until melted, 3 to 5 minutes. Remove from heat. Spoon chocolate evenly over caramel mounds. Refrigerate until chocolate is just set, 10 to 15 minutes. Before serving, let come to room temperature, about 20 minutes. Store with wax paper or parchment paper between candy layers in an airtight container at room temperature for up to 2 weeks.

Pecan Kisses

ACTIVE 10 MIN. - TOTAL 1 HOUR, 25 MIN.
MAKES ABOUT 16 COOKIES

1	large egg white
¾	cup packed light brown sugar
½	tsp. vanilla extract
2	cups pecans, roughly chopped

1. Preheat oven to 250°F with racks in top and bottom positions. Line 2 large baking sheets with parchment paper.

2. Beat egg white in a large bowl with an electric mixer on high speed until soft peaks form, 1 to 2 minutes. Gradually add sugar and vanilla; beat until smooth, about 2 minutes. Fold in pecans. Drop mixture by 1½ tablespoonfuls about 1 inch apart onto prepared baking sheets.

3. Bake in preheated oven for 30 minutes, rotating baking sheets between top and bottom racks halfway through baking time. Turn off oven; leave cookies inside. Cool about 30 minutes. Remove from oven. Transfer cookies to a wire rack, and cool completely. Store in an airtight container at room temperature for up to 5 days.

Turtle Cookies

ACTIVE 30 MIN. - TOTAL 1 HOUR, 20 MIN.,
PLUS 1 HOUR CHILLING AND 2 HOURS STANDING
MAKES 2 DOZEN COOKIES

½	cup unsalted butter, softened
½	cup packed light brown sugar
1	large egg
1	large egg, separated
1	tsp. vanilla extract
1½	cups all-purpose flour
¼	tsp. baking soda
¼	tsp. kosher salt
2½	cups pecan halves (about 120)
	Turtle Cookie Frosting (recipe page 312)

1. Beat butter and brown sugar in a large bowl with an electric mixer on high speed until light and fluffy, 3 to 4 minutes. Reduce mixer speed to medium-high; add whole egg, egg yolk (reserve egg white), and vanilla, beating until just combined, about 1 minute. Stir together flour, baking soda, and salt in a medium bowl. With mixer on low speed, gradually add flour mixture to butter mixture, beating until just combined, about 1 minute, stopping to scrape down

Continued on page 312

MILLIONAIRE
CANDIES

PECAN KISSES

TURTLE
COOKIES

Continued from page 310

the sides of the bowl, if necessary. Cover; chill at least 1 hour.

2. Preheat oven to 350°F with racks in top and bottom positions. Line 2 large baking sheets with parchment paper.

3. Arrange pecan halves in groups of 5 on prepared baking sheets, in a star shape to resemble head and legs of a turtle.

4. Shape dough into 24 (1-tablespoon) balls. Whisk reserved egg white in a small bowl; dip bottom of each dough ball in egg white. Gently press each ball into a cluster of pecans to resemble a turtle's body.

5. Bake in preheated oven in batches until cookies are lightly browned around edges, 10 to 12 minutes per batch, rotating baking sheets between top and bottom racks halfway through baking time. Carefully transfer cookies to wire racks; let cool completely, about 15 minutes.

6. Spoon frosting evenly over the top of each cookie to resemble a turtle shell. Let cookies stand until completely dry, about 2 hours. Store in an airtight container with wax paper or parchment paper between cookie layers at room temperature for up to 5 days.

Turtle Cookie Frosting
ACTIVE 5 MIN. - TOTAL 5 MIN.
MAKES ABOUT 1 CUP

- 2 (1-oz.) semisweet chocolate baking squares
- ¼ cup brewed coffee
- 1 Tbsp. unsalted butter
- 1¾ cups powdered sugar, sifted

Place chocolate, coffee, and butter in a small saucepan. Cook over low, stirring constantly, until chocolate is melted, about 2 minutes. Remove from heat. Whisk in powdered sugar until smooth. Use immediately.

Butterfingers
(Photo, page 307)
ACTIVE 20 MIN. - TOTAL 1 HOUR, 40 MIN.
MAKES 30 COOKIES

- 1 cup unsalted butter, softened
- ¼ cup plus 2 Tbsp. powdered sugar, plus more for rolling
- 2 cups all-purpose flour
- 1 tsp. vanilla extract
- ¼ tsp. kosher salt
- 2 cups chopped pecans

1. Preheat oven to 250°F with racks in top and bottom positions. Line 2 large baking sheets with parchment paper.

2. Beat butter and sugar in a bowl with an electric mixer on high speed until creamy, about 2 minutes. Reduce mixer speed to low; gradually add flour, vanilla, and salt, and beat until just combined, about 2 minutes. Stir in pecans. Shape dough into 30 (1½-tablespoon) logs, each about 2½ to 3 inches long. Arrange 2 inches apart on prepared baking sheets.

3. Bake in preheated oven until bottoms are just browned, about 50 minutes, rotating baking sheets between top and bottom racks halfway through baking time. Cool slightly on baking sheets, about 10 minutes. Roll warm cookies in additional powdered sugar to coat. Cool completely on baking sheets, about 20 minutes. Store in an airtight container at room temperature for up to 4 days.

Cheese Straws
ACTIVE 25 MIN. - TOTAL 1 HOUR, 55 MIN.
MAKES ABOUT 21 DOZEN

- 1 lb. sharp cheddar cheese, shredded (about 4 cups)
- ½ cup unsalted butter, softened
- 2 cups all-purpose flour
- 1 tsp. kosher salt
- ½ tsp. paprika
- ½ tsp. cayenne pepper

1. Preheat oven to 350°F with racks in top and bottom positions. Line 2 large baking sheets with parchment paper. Beat cheese and butter in a large bowl with an electric mixer on medium-high speed until mixture is creamy, about 8 minutes. Reduce mixer speed to low. Gradually add flour, salt, paprika, and

cayenne pepper; beat until combined, about 1 minute.

2. Place some of the dough in a cookie press fitted with a ⅜-inch-wide star tip. Press out dough onto prepared baking sheets in strips running about the length of each baking sheet. Cut each strip into 2-inch pieces, and arrange ½ inch apart on baking sheets.

3. Bake cheese straws in preheated oven until firm and lightly browned, 10 to 12 minutes, rotating baking sheets between top and bottom racks halfway through baking time. Let cool completely on baking sheets, about 20 minutes.

4. Repeat Steps 2 and 3 in batches with remaining dough. Store cheese straws in an airtight container at room temperature for up to 4 days.

Candied Peanuts
ACTIVE 20 MIN. - TOTAL 50 MIN., PLUS 1 HOUR STANDING
MAKES ABOUT 6 CUPS

Preheat oven to 300°F. Line a large rimmed baking sheet with parchment paper. Place 2 cups **granulated sugar** and 1 cup **water** in a medium saucepan; cook over medium, stirring often, until sugar dissolves, about 2 minutes. Add 4 cups **raw blanched peanuts**, and cook, stirring often, until liquid evaporates and sugar crystallizes around peanuts, 14 to 16 minutes. Spread in an even layer on prepared baking sheet. Bake in preheated oven, stirring every 10 minutes, until peanuts are roasted and dry, about 30 minutes. Remove from oven; let cool completely on baking sheet, about 1 hour. Store in an airtight container at room temperature for up to 3 weeks.

CHEESE STRAWS

CANDIED PEANUTS

Layers of Love

For cookbook author Vallery Lomas, baking our annual December cover cake is a cherished family ritual—and even more so this year because she created the recipe

RED VELVET
DOBERGE CAKE WITH
CHEESECAKE CUSTARD
(PAGE 314)

IN MY FAMILY, Christmas officially starts at our mailbox. We have plenty of traditions–decorating the tree, singing carols around the piano–but the real sign that the season is here is when the December issue of *Southern Living* arrives.

When I was a kid growing up in Baton Rouge, it was a treat to come home, check the mail, and admire the spectacular cake on the cover. It was not a question of if my mother and I would make it but when. When I moved to the West Coast for college, those times in the kitchen during the holidays became all the more special. It was our chance to catch up and fill each other in on the happenings in our lives.

Of all the *Southern Living* December cakes we've baked over the years, there's one that stands out from the others: the Red Velvet-White Chocolate Cheesecake from 2013. My sisters looked on in awe as we prepared the two cheesecake layers and the three vibrant red cake layers and then assembled them into a towering dessert covered in white frosting.

When we sat down to enjoy dinner that year, the cake stood in the center of the table as a festive centerpiece. Things started as usual: "Please pass the candied yams." "Please pass the ham." Then, my older sister, Lucy, asked me to pass her the cake. The cake?! "I'm starting with cake," she said. It was so impressive she didn't want to wait until the end of the meal. So we all followed her lead, and a new tradition was born.

My Red Velvet Doberge Cake is an ode to that memorable dessert–but with a Louisiana accent. This recipe is a twist on a classic New Orleans cake, and uses my favorite red velvet recipe that I developed for my cookbook, *Life Is What You Bake It*. The Cheesecake Custard filling makes it insanely moist and adds a tangy note, and the white chocolate-based frosting is simply divine. Make it for your own celebration, but be warned: It may upstage the rest of the menu.

WHAT'S A DOBERGE CAKE?

Pronounced "DOUGH-bosh" by some, this cake originated in New Orleans and is based on the many-tiered Hungarian Dobos torte. It has at least six thin layers, alternating with custard or pudding filling. It's traditionally filled with both chocolate and lemon custard and then covered with icing—half brown and half yellow, indicating the flavors inside. Local bakeries offer different flavors for order—caramel, strawberry, even cookies and cream.

Red Velvet Doberge Cake with Cheesecake Custard

This striking cake is made of three components: the Cake Layers, the Cheesecake Custard filling, and the White Chocolate Frosting. We recommend breaking up the project—make the layers and the custard up to 3 days in advance. Prepare the frosting and assemble the cake the day you plan to serve it.

ACTIVE 1 HOUR, 30 MIN. - TOTAL 4 HOURS, 35 MIN., PLUS 12 HOURS DRYING

SERVES 16

CAKE LAYERS

	Baking spray with flour
3⅓	cups bleached cake flour
⅓	cup unsweetened cocoa powder
1¼	tsp. kosher salt
2	cups canola oil
2	cups granulated sugar
2	large eggs plus 1 large egg yolk, at room temperature
1	Tbsp. vanilla extract
1	tsp. red liquid food coloring or ½ tsp. red food coloring gel
1⅓	cups whole buttermilk
2	tsp. white vinegar
1½	tsp. baking soda

FILLING

	Cheesecake Custard (recipe follows)

WHITE CHOCOLATE FROSTING

1	lb. high-quality white chocolate bars (such as Lindt, from 4 [4.4-oz.] bars), finely chopped (about 2⅔ cups)
1⅓	cups powdered sugar
1¼	cups unsalted butter, softened
2	tsp. vanilla extract
⅛	tsp. kosher salt

1. Prepare the Cake Layers: Preheat oven to 350°F with rack in center position. Coat 3 (8-inch) round cake pans with baking spray (or coat with a thin layer of softened butter, and dust with flour).

2. Sift cake flour and cocoa into a large bowl; whisk in salt, and set aside.

3. Beat oil and sugar in a stand mixer fitted with a paddle attachment on medium-high speed until combined, about 20 seconds. Reduce mixer speed to medium, and add eggs and egg yolk, 1 at a time, beating until each is incorporated before adding the next, 1 minute total. Add vanilla and red food coloring; beat until combined.

4. Reduce mixer speed to low, and gradually add flour mixture to egg mixture, alternating with buttermilk, in 3 additions, beginning and ending with flour mixture. Use a spatula to scrape down sides and bottom of bowl as needed. (Batter will be very loose.)

5. Stir together vinegar and baking soda in a small bowl (it will fizz). Pour into cake batter; beat on medium speed until just combined, about 10 seconds. Stop mixer; use a rubber spatula to scrape down the sides of the bowl and thoroughly combine the batter. Immediately pour cake batter evenly into prepared cake pans (about 2 cups per pan).

6. Bake in preheated oven until a wooden pick inserted into centers of cakes comes out clean, 25 to 30 minutes. Cool in pans on a wire rack 10 minutes. Invert onto wire rack, and cool completely, about 1 hour. (Cooled cake may be wrapped in plastic wrap and stored at room temperature up to 3 days.)

7. Using a long serrated knife, cut each Cake Layer in half horizontally to make a total of 6 layers. (If the cake is crumbly when you attempt to cut it, wrap the layer in plastic, and freeze until chilled.) Evenly trim the cut side of each cake half to make flat and even, reserving trimmings to accumulate about 1 cup of crumbs. Wrap trimmed Cake Layers individually in plastic wrap, and set aside at room temperature until ready to use. Place crumbs in an even layer on a rimmed baking sheet, and let stand at room temperature, uncovered, until dry, about 12 hours.

8. Place 1 Cake Layer, cut side up, on a cake stand or platter. Using a small offset spatula, spread layer with ⅔ cup Cheesecake Custard, leaving a ½-inch border around edges. Top with a second layer, cut side up, and another ⅔ cup custard. Continue, alternating layers and custard, and ending with top Cake Layer, cut side down. Chill, uncovered, until filling is set, about 1 hour.

9. Meanwhile, prepare the White Chocolate Frosting: Place chocolate in a large glass heatproof bowl, and set aside. Fill a medium saucepan with water to a depth of 2 inches. Bring water to a boil over medium-high, then reduce the heat to a simmer over medium-low. Set the glass bowl on top of saucepan, making sure bottom of bowl doesn't touch water. Stir with a heatproof silicone spatula, carefully scraping bottom and sides of bowl, until chocolate has melted, 2 to 3 minutes. (Take care that the water does not boil, as this could scorch the chocolate.)

10. Remove bowl from saucepan; remove saucepan from heat. Stir melted chocolate with spatula until combined and smooth. Let stand at room temperature, stirring occasionally, until cooled to almost room temperature but still melted, and a thermometer registers 89°F to 90°F, 25 to 30 minutes.

11. Beat powdered sugar, butter, vanilla, and salt in a stand mixer fitted with a paddle attachment on high speed until smooth and fluffy, 2 to 3 minutes, stopping to scrape down sides of bowl as needed. Reduce mixer speed to low, and gradually add cooled white chocolate, beating until smooth, about 2 minutes. Set White Chocolate Frosting aside at room temperature until ready to use.

12. Using a bench scraper or large offset spatula, spread a thin layer of White Chocolate Frosting (about 1¼ cups) over top and sides of chilled cake as a crumb coat. Spread remaining (about 2½ cups) White Chocolate Frosting over top and sides of chilled cake.

13. Spoon ¾ cup White Chocolate Frosting into a piping bag fitted with a ¼-inch plain tip. Spread remaining (about 2 cups) White Chocolate Frosting over top and sides of chilled cake. Pipe small dollops of frosting around top edge of cake; sprinkle dollops with about 2 tablespoons of the dried cake crumbs. Place remaining dried cake crumbs around the bottom edge of cake, pressing lightly into cake to adhere, to create a collar about 1 inch tall.

14. The finished cake can stand at room temperature up to 4 hours, or be stored, uncovered, in refrigerator up to 6 hours. Let chilled cake stand at room temperature for 1 hour before slicing and serving.

Cheesecake Custard

ACTIVE 15 MIN. - TOTAL 15 MIN.
PLUS 2 HOURS CHILLING

MAKES ABOUT 3⅓ CUPS

- 3 large egg yolks plus 1 large egg, at room temperature
- 3 Tbsp. cornstarch
- ½ cup granulated sugar, divided
- 2 cups whole milk
- 1 tsp. vanilla extract
- ¼ tsp. kosher salt
- 1½ (8-oz.) pkg. cream cheese, softened and cut into 1-inch pieces

1. Whisk together egg yolks, egg, cornstarch, and ¼ cup of the sugar in a large heatproof bowl until lightened in color, 2 to 3 minutes.

2. Cook milk and remaining ¼ cup sugar in a medium saucepan over medium, whisking occasionally, until sugar dissolves and milk begins to boil, about 2 minutes. Remove from heat.

3. While constantly whisking egg mixture, slowly drizzle one-third of the hot milk mixture into egg mixture to temper. Slowly pour egg mixture back into milk mixture in pan, whisking milk mixture constantly. Whisk in vanilla and salt.

4. Return pan to stove; cook over medium-high, whisking bottom and inside edges of pan constantly, until thickened and starting to boil, about 4 minutes.

5. Once bubbles start to erupt on surface, cook, whisking constantly, until thick, about 2 minutes. Remove pan from heat. Pour mixture through a fine mesh strainer into a medium bowl; discard solids. Wipe pan clean. Return strained mixture to pan. Add cream cheese, stirring until melted and smooth. Transfer custard to a medium bowl. Place a piece of plastic wrap directly on surface of custard to prevent a film from forming. Chill until cold, at least 2 hours or up to 2 days.

Break Out the Crackers

The best celebratory treats start with a sleeve of saltines

SALTINE
PEPPERMINT
BARK

Saltine Peppermint Bark

ACTIVE 30 MIN. - TOTAL 35 MIN.,
PLUS 1 HOUR CHILLING
SERVES 24

- 50 saltine crackers (from 1 [16-oz.] pkg.)
- 2 (11-oz.) pkg. white chocolate chips (about 3⅓ cups)
- 2 (10-oz.) pkg. 65% cacao bittersweet chocolate chips (about 3⅓ cups)
- 12 peppermint candy canes or 30 hard peppermint candies
- ¾ tsp. peppermint extract
  Flaky sea salt

1. Line a 13- x 18-inch rimmed baking sheet with aluminum foil. Arrange crackers in a single layer on prepared baking sheet without overlapping; cut crackers to fit into any gaps as needed. Place white chocolate chips in a medium-size heatproof bowl; place bittersweet chocolate chips in a separate medium-size heatproof bowl. Place candy canes in a large heavy-duty zip-top plastic bag; seal bag. Use a rolling pin or meat mallet to crush candy into small pieces. Set aside.
2. Fill a medium saucepan with water to a depth of 1 inch. Bring to a simmer over medium-high; reduce heat to low so water is barely simmering. Place bowl of white chocolate chips over saucepan, making sure bottom of bowl does not touch water. Heat, stirring occasionally, until chips are melted and smooth, about 8 minutes. Remove bowl from heat; stir in peppermint extract.
3. Pour melted white chocolate evenly over crackers. Using the back of a spoon, spread in an even layer. Gently tap baking sheet on countertop to even out surface. Chill until starting to set, about 10 minutes.
4. Place bowl of bittersweet chocolate chips over simmering water, making sure bottom of bowl does not touch water. Heat, stirring occasionally, until chips are melted and smooth, about 5 minutes.
5. Remove bowl from heat; pour melted bittersweet chocolate over hardened white chocolate layer, spreading evenly. Gently tap baking sheet on countertop to even out surface. Let stand 5 minutes. Sprinkle with crushed candy and sea salt.

6. Chill, uncovered, until completely firm, at least 1 hour or up to 24 hours. Break bark into large (about 3-inch) pieces. Store in an airtight container in refrigerator up to 1 week.

Five-Alarm Firecrackers

(Photo, page 318)

ACTIVE 15 MIN. - TOTAL 2 HOURS
SERVES 8

- 1 cup olive oil
- ¼ cup hot sauce
- 1½ tsp. cayenne pepper
- 1 tsp. paprika
- 1 tsp. garlic powder
- 1 tsp. onion powder
- ½ tsp. black pepper
- ½ tsp. kosher salt
- 2 (4-oz.) sleeves saltine crackers (about 78 crackers total)

1. Place oil, hot sauce, cayenne, paprika, garlic powder, onion powder, black pepper, and salt in a large zip-top plastic bag. Press out excess air, and seal. Shake vigorously until mixture is combined. Add crackers to bag; reseal and gently shake to coat evenly in oil mixture.
2. Let crackers soak at room temperature at least 1 hour or up to overnight, shaking and turning over bag every 10 to 15 minutes.
3. Preheat oven to 300°F with racks in the upper third and lower third positions. Line 2 large rimmed baking sheets with aluminum foil, and place an ovenproof wire rack on top of each.
4. Remove crackers from oil mixture in bag; discard remaining oil mixture. Transfer crackers to prepared wire racks, arranging crackers in a single layer. Use your fingers or a pastry brush to break up any large clumps of seasoning on the tops of the crackers, which could burn in the oven. Bake in preheated oven until dry, crisp, and golden, 15 to 18 minutes, rotating baking sheets between top and bottom racks halfway through bake time.
5. Remove from oven. Let crackers cool on racks completely, about 30 minutes. Serve immediately, or store in an airtight container at room temperature up to 5 days.

Buttery Parmesan-Herb Mini Crackers

ACTIVE 10 MIN. - TOTAL 50 MIN.
SERVES 8

- 1 (11-oz.) pkg. mini saltine crackers (about 6½ cups)
- ½ cup unsalted butter
- 1 Tbsp. dried Italian seasoning
- 1 tsp. garlic powder
- ½ tsp. seasoned salt (such as Lawry's)
- 1 oz. Parmesan cheese, grated (about ¼ cup)

1. Preheat oven to 300°F. Line a large rimmed baking sheet with aluminum foil. Place mini crackers in a large heatproof bowl; set aside.
2. Melt butter in a small saucepan over medium-low. Stir in Italian seasoning, garlic powder, and seasoned salt. Cook, stirring often, until fragrant, about 30 seconds.
3. Pour butter mixture over crackers in bowl; toss well until crackers are evenly coated. Transfer crackers to prepared baking sheet (it's okay if they overlap).
4. Bake in preheated oven for 5 minutes. Remove from oven. Sprinkle crackers evenly with cheese, and toss well to coat. Return to oven, and bake until crackers are lightly golden and crisp, 6 to 8 minutes.
5. Toss crackers, and let cool completely on baking sheet, about 30 minutes. Serve immediately, or store in an airtight container at room temperature up to 3 days.

BUTTERY PARMESAN-HERB MINI CRACKERS

FIVE-ALARM
FIRECRACKERS
(PAGE 317)

Triple-Decker Toffee Bars

ACTIVE 35 MIN. - TOTAL 45 MIN,
PLUS 2 HOURS CHILLING
MAKES 25

48	saltine crackers (from 1 [16-oz.] pkg.), divided
¾	cup packed light brown sugar
½	cup unsalted butter
1	(14-oz.) can sweetened condensed milk
3	Tbsp. heavy whipping cream
2	Tbsp. light corn syrup
¼	tsp. kosher salt
½	tsp. vanilla extract
1	cup (6 oz.) milk chocolate chips (from 1 [11½-oz.] pkg.)
1	tsp. flaky sea salt

1. Line an 8-inch square baking pan with aluminum foil, leaving a 2-inch overhang on all sides. Generously coat foil with cooking spray. Arrange 16 of the crackers in a single layer on prepared pan. Set aside.

2. Cook sugar and butter in a saucepan over low, stirring often, until sugar is dissolved and butter is melted, about 5 minutes. Stir in condensed milk, cream, corn syrup, and salt. Increase heat to medium; bring to a simmer, stirring constantly. Simmer, stirring constantly, until mixture is thickened and darkened to a deep golden color, 6 to 8 minutes. Remove toffee mixture from heat; stir in vanilla.

3. Pour one-third of the toffee mixture (about ⅔ cup) over crackers in pan; using an offset spatula, gently spread into an even layer. Arrange 16 of the saltines evenly over toffee layer. Repeat layers with one-third toffee mixture and remaining 16 crackers. Finish with a layer of remaining toffee mixture on top. Let cool slightly, about 5 minutes.

4. Heat chocolate chips in a medium-size microwavable bowl on HIGH until melted, 1 to 2 minutes, stopping to stir every 30 seconds. Slowly pour melted chocolate over toffee; spread into an even layer. Let cool slightly, about 5 minutes. Sprinkle evenly with sea salt.

5. Transfer pan to refrigerator. Chill, uncovered, until set, about 2 hours.

6. Remove from refrigerator. Using foil overhang as handles, gently lift bars from pan and transfer to a cutting board. If desired, trim edges using a sharp knife. Slice into 25 (½-inch) square bars. Store in an airtight container in refrigerator up to 1 week.

TRIPLE-DECKER
TOFFEE BARS

NICE AND NEAT
When slicing the bars, warm the knife's blade under hot water, then wipe it dry.

Oh, Fudge!

First–time candy maker? This customizable recipe is your ticket to sweet success

Foolproof Brown Sugar Fudge

ACTIVE 25 MIN. - TOTAL 25 MIN.,
PLUS 2 HOURS COOLING
MAKES 64 (1-INCH) SQUARES

- 2 cups packed light brown sugar
- 1 (14-oz.) can sweetened condensed milk
- ½ cup whole milk
- 1 cup white chocolate chips
- ¼ cup butter, softened, cut into pieces
- 1 tsp. vanilla extract

1. Line an 8-inch square baking pan with parchment paper, leaving a 2-inch overhang on all sides. Lightly coat pan with cooking spray. Stir together sugar, sweetened condensed milk, and whole milk in a medium saucepan. Cook over medium–low, stirring constantly, until a candy thermometer registers 238°F, about 16 minutes. Transfer mixture to the bowl of a stand mixer fitted with a paddle attachment.
2. Add white chocolate, butter, and vanilla to stand mixer bowl; beat on low speed until melted, about 1 minute. Increase mixer speed to medium; beat until thickened and no longer shiny, 5 to 6 minutes. Pour into prepared pan; gently tap bottom of pan on counter until top is an even layer. Let cool, uncovered, at room temperature until firm, at least 2 hours or up to 12 hours. Remove from pan using parchment paper overhang as handles. Cut into 64 (1-inch) squares.

Bourbon-Pecan Brown Sugar Fudge

Prepare recipe as directed, substituting 2 Tbsp. **bourbon** for vanilla and adding 1 tsp. **pumpkin pie spice** to unbeaten white chocolate mixture. Halfway through beating mixture on medium, add ¾ cup **chopped toasted pecans.** Pour into pan; tap on counter as directed. Sprinkle with ¼ cup **chopped toasted pecans,** gently pressing to adhere. Let cool; cut as directed.

Coconut-Brown Sugar Fudge

Prepare recipe as directed, substituting 1 tsp. **coconut extract** for vanilla. Halfway through beating the white chocolate mixture on medium, add 1 cup **unsweetened shredded coconut.** Pour into pan; tap on counter as directed. Sprinkle with ½ cup **unsweetened shredded coconut,** gently pressing to adhere. Let cool; cut as directed.

Marbled Brown Sugar Fudge

Prepare recipe as directed, adding ½ cup **bittersweet chocolate chips** to the beaten and thickened white chocolate mixture. Let stand until chocolate is melted, about 1 minute. Fold gently until marbled. Pour into pan; tap on counter as directed. Sprinkle with 1 tsp. **flaky sea salt,** gently pressing to adhere. Let cool; cut as directed.

Three Keys to Fantastic Fudge

1. Line the Pan
A layer of lightly greased parchment paper (with an overhang on all sides) keeps the cooled fudge from sticking and helps you lift it from the pan with ease.

2. Make It Smooth
Stirring throughout the process helps dissolve the sugar and ensures that the fudge sets firmly enough to slice. (A mixer makes this job easier.)

3. Be Precise
Your grandma's soft-ball candy test is classic, but use a candy thermometer (an instant-read digital one is best!) for more consistent results every time.

FOOLPROOF BROWN SUGAR FUDGE

BOURBON-PECAN BROWN SUGAR FUDGE

COCONUT-BROWN SUGAR FUDGE

MARBLED BROWN SUGAR FUDGE

BLACK-EYED PEA SOUP
WITH HAM HOCKS

Lucky You

Start the New Year off right with a soul-satisfying black-eyed pea soup that can be tailored to your tastes

Black-Eyed Pea Soup with Ham Hocks

ACTIVE 30 MIN. - TOTAL 30 MIN., PLUS 4 HOURS SLOW-COOKING

SERVES 8

- 1 Tbsp. olive oil
- 2 cups chopped yellow onion (from 1 large onion)
- 3 garlic cloves, minced (1 Tbsp.)
- 1 tsp. ground cumin
- 2 lb. smoked ham hocks
- 1 lb. dried black-eyed peas
- 10 cups lower-sodium chicken broth
- 3 cups chopped stemmed collard greens (from 1 [8-oz.] bunch)
- ¾ cup chopped celery (from 3 small celery stalks)
- 2 dried bay leaves
- 1 (8½-oz.) pkg. precooked microwavable white rice
- 1½ Tbsp. fresh thyme leaves
- ¾ tsp. black pepper
- ½ tsp. kosher salt
- ¼ tsp. cayenne pepper

1. Heat olive oil in a large nonstick skillet over medium. Add onion; cook, stirring often, until translucent, but not brown, about 5 minutes. Add minced garlic and cumin; cook, stirring frequently, until garlic is fragrant, about 1 minute. Transfer mixture to a 6-quart slow cooker. Stir in ham hocks, black-eyed peas, chicken broth, collard greens, celery, and bay leaves. Cover and cook until ham hocks and peas are very tender, about 4 hours on HIGH or 7 to 8 hours on LOW.
2. Remove and discard bay leaves from soup. Use tongs to transfer ham hocks to a cutting board. Let stand until cool enough to handle, about 5 minutes. Remove and discard bones and skin; shred meat into bite-size pieces. Return shredded ham hocks to mixture in slow cooker, and stir to combine. Add rice; stir until heated through, about 1 minute. Mix in thyme, black pepper, salt, and cayenne. Serve hot.

BLACK-EYED PEA SOUP WITH TURKEY

VEGAN BLACK-EYED PEA SOUP

Healthy and Hearty

Two lightened-up soup spin-offs

Black-Eyed Pea Soup with Turkey

Prepare recipe as directed, replacing ham hocks with 2 lb. **smoked turkey wings** in Step 1. Stir in 2 Tbsp. **apple cider vinegar** with thyme, black pepper, salt, and cayenne at the end of Step 2.

Vegan Black-Eyed Pea Soup

Prepare recipe as directed, adding 1 Tbsp. **tomato paste** and 1½ tsp. **smoked paprika** to garlic in Step 1; also, replace ham hocks with 1½ cups chopped **carrots**, and replace chicken broth with **vegetable broth.** Increase salt amount to 1 tsp. at end of Step 2.

The Magic of Cornbread Dressing

Actress Lacey Chabert marks the season with her great-grandmother's treasured (and time-tested) recipe

LACEY CHABERT has made her family's cornbread dressing for so many years that she can bake it from memory. Finally getting it down on paper was a joint effort with her sister.

The recipe originated with her great-grandmother. "It was passed down from her to my grandmother, to my mom, to myself," says the Hallmark Channel actress. Chabert lived next door to her mother's mother, "Nanny," until she was 7 years old, and it was in Nanny's house in Purvis, Mississippi, where she first learned how to prepare this beloved dish.

"I have so many memories of growing up and being in the kitchen with my great-grandmother, my grandmother, and my mother. We made the same things every Thanksgiving and Christmas," says Chabert. "The smell of cornbread dressing mingling with sweet potato casserole and pecan pie brings me back to my childhood and all the warmth and excitement of the holidays."

It's fitting that the actress is big on the season: Chabert is widely regarded as the queen of Hallmark Christmas movies. Her newest title with the network, *Haul Out the Holly,* debuts this year.

While each winter seems to bring a new festive movie with it, Chabert's holiday menus have stayed the same, filled with tried-and-true recipes that her family has been making for decades. "To me, these dishes are perfect," she says. "I figure, why mess with them? I just follow the directions as well as I can."

For the actress, it's all about keeping a special recipe alive. "There's something about food and the memories of preparing it that is just so comforting, especially when you realize you've passed down a tradition for four generations," says Chabert. "It's something I really treasure."

Lacey's Cornbread Dressing

ACTIVE 30 MIN. · TOTAL 3 HOURS, 30 MIN.
SERVES 12

CORNBREAD
- 2 (8½-oz.) pkg. cornbread mix (such as Jiffy)

DRESSING
- 1 (3- to 4-lb.) whole chicken
- 2 tsp. black pepper
- ¼ cup poultry seasoning, divided
- ¼ cup onion powder, divided
- 3 Tbsp. garlic powder, divided
- 3 Tbsp. celery salt, divided
- ½ cup unsalted butter
- 1½ cups chopped celery (from 4 stalks)
- 1½ cups chopped yellow onion (from 1 medium onion)
- 1 cup chopped scallions (from 5 large scallions)
- 4 hard-cooked eggs, peeled and chopped
- 4 large eggs, lightly beaten
- 2 (10½-oz.) cans cream of chicken soup

1. Prepare the Cornbread: Prepare cornbread mix according to package directions (a day ahead is best). Let cool to room temperature, about 1 hour. Crumble into a large bowl, and set aside.
2. While Cornbread bakes, prepare the Dressing: Place whole chicken, pepper, and 2 tablespoons each of the poultry seasoning, onion powder, garlic powder, and celery salt in a large pot. Add water to pot until chicken is covered.
3. Bring to a boil over medium-high; reduce heat to medium. Simmer until chicken is cooked through and a thermometer inserted into thickest portion of thigh registers 165°F, about 30 minutes. Remove chicken from pot, reserving cooking liquid, and place chicken on a baking sheet. Let rest until cool enough to handle, about 30 minutes.
4. Remove and discard skin and bones from chicken meat. Chop meat into

¾-inch pieces to measure 2 cups; add to Cornbread. Reserve remaining meat for another use.
5. Melt butter in a large skillet over medium. Add celery, onion, and scallions to skillet; cook, stirring often, until soft, about 7 minutes.
6. Preheat oven to 375°F. Coat a 13- x 9-inch baking dish with cooking spray; set aside. Add cooked vegetables, hard-cooked eggs, beaten eggs, and soup to Cornbread mixture, stirring well to combine. Fold in remaining 2 tablespoons each poultry seasoning and onion powder and remaining 1 tablespoon each garlic powder and celery salt.
7. Stir reserved cooking liquid into Cornbread mixture until consistency resembles porridge, beginning with 2 cups liquid and adding ¼ cup more at a time as needed. Spoon mixture into prepared baking dish, and bake in preheated oven until golden brown and set, about 1 hour. (Cover with aluminum foil halfway through cook time if it begins to brown too quickly.) Let rest 15 minutes. Serve.

Rooting for Rutabagas

The underdog of the vegetable world deserves a spot on your table

RUTABAGAS ARE THE BIG DADDY of the turnip family. Starchy with an earthy, slightly sweet flavor, they are easy to grow and high yielding. They gained popularity in the 19th century, when they were valuable as animal food. Unlike many of the other items that could be used as fodder, rutabagas also tasted good to humans and eventually made their way to our tables. Sometimes known as swedes or Swedish turnips, they are likely a cross between turnips and wild cabbage and may have originated in Scandinavia or Russia in the Middle Ages.

I dote on rutabagas because I only had them once a year as a child, during the holidays. My mother would create a densely flavored puree of rutabaga fragrant with the sweet smoke of bacon. She'd mute some of the vegetable's strong taste with the addition of a white potato and a pinch of sugar.

That dish was bliss. I never expected to encounter this taste of a memory again. Then decades later, at the table of my adopted family in New Orleans, I peeked into a casserole dish and was astonished to see the familiar buff-color puree of my youth. I was doubly surprised because it was swirled with a contrasting orange sweet potato puree in a yin and yang of deliciousness. The flavors formed an elegant combination where the savory taste of the rutabaga played nicely off the honeyed sweet potato.

The fortuitous serving of the two reminded me of my love of rutabagas, and now I have them frequently during the cooler months rather than waiting for the yuletide season. They're lovely paired with sweet potatoes, but frankly I enjoy rutabagas too much to waste stomach space on other veggies at the same time. Follow the recipe below for a showy side dish to brighten up your sideboard, or skip the sweet potatoes and enjoy this underappreciated vegetable in its own right. –Jessica B. Harris

Rutabaga-Sweet Potato Swirl

ACTIVE 50 MIN. - TOTAL 1 HOUR, 50 MIN.
SERVES 12

- 5   large (4 lb. total) sweet potatoes, scrubbed
- 5   tsp. vegetable oil
- 6   bacon slices
- 1   (2-lb.) rutabaga, peeled and cut into 1-inch chunks
- 1   large (1-lb.) russet potato, peeled and cut into 1-inch chunks
- Pinch of granulated sugar
- 2   tsp. kosher salt, divided
- ½   tsp. black pepper, divided
- ½   cup unsalted butter, plus more for serving (optional)

1. Preheat oven to 400°F with rack in lowest position. Line a rimmed baking sheet with aluminum foil. Evenly pierce sweet potatoes 8 to 10 times using a paring knife. Rub each sweet potato with 1 teaspoon of the oil; place on baking sheet. Bake until skins look loose and sunken, 1 hour to 1 hour, 30 minutes.
2. Meanwhile, fry bacon in a large heavy saucepan over medium-high until bacon begins to brown and fat is rendered, 6 to 8 minutes (do not drain). Add rutabaga to saucepan; add enough water to cover rutabaga by 2 inches. Bring to a boil over high; reduce heat to medium, and cook, undisturbed, for 20 minutes. Add the russet potato, and cook until rutabaga and russet potato are very tender, about 20 minutes.

3. Drain rutabaga and russet potato, discarding bacon. Place rutabaga and russet potato in a food processor or food mill, and pulse until blended. Transfer to a medium bowl. Stir in sugar, 1 teaspoon of the salt, and ¼ teaspoon of the pepper; stir until combined.
4. Carefully remove and discard skins from warm sweet potatoes. Place flesh in a bowl; add butter and remaining 1 teaspoon salt and ¼ teaspoon pepper. Mash until smooth and creamy.
5. Spoon rutabaga mixture into 1 side of a large bowl; spoon sweet potato mixture into other side of the bowl. Draw a knife through mixtures to create a swirl pattern of orange and buff. Serve with additional butter, if desired. Serve immediately.

Mama's Latkes

A Tennessee family's passed–down recipe for potato pancakes is as precious as any antique

WHEN THE AIR OUTSIDE begins to nip and the neighborhood is adorned in twinkle lights and strands of garland, my childhood home fills with the smell of oil and crisping potatoes as my mother, Emily Angel Baer, transforms into the Latke Lady. I come from a very big family in Memphis, and we spend the eight days of Hanukkah celebrating with different groups of people each night. While these celebrations take place in various homes of cousins, aunts, uncles, or family friends, the one constant is my mama's potato latkes. No one makes them better.

Tradition is important in the Jewish religion. Many of the ways that we observe and celebrate holidays are not mandated in the Torah; rather, they are rituals that are passed down from generation to generation, like making latkes. We eat them on Hanukkah as a symbolic nod to the oil that should have lit the temple for only one day but instead lasted eight miraculous nights.

My family's latkes can be traced back decades to Russia. My great-grandmother, Tamara Tiba Malkin, made them with a version of the recipe shared below, and when my mother was a child, Tamara Tiba turned the responsibility over to her eldest daughters. My great-aunt Mary, whom I remember fondly as a real spitfire, passed the recipe on to my mother, who then shared it with me.

Mom cranks out about 250 delicious fried delights in advance every holiday season—yes, in advance. She has the perfect trick for making them taste like they were just pulled out of a hot pan.

When I asked Mom why hers are the best, I was hoping for some cooking tips or insight into our family's roots, but she answered in her typical witty fashion: "I don't put anything healthy in them. Some people like to use sweet potatoes or add some kind of strange vegetable into the mix to make them more nutritious, but I say, 'Rubbish to that.' "
–Rebecca Angel Baer

Mama's Potato Latkes
ACTIVE 1 HOUR, 45 MIN. · TOTAL 1 HOUR, 45 MIN.
MAKES 48

Ice water
5   large russet potatoes, scrubbed
¼   cup all-purpose flour
2   tsp. kosher salt
1¼ tsp. baking powder
1   large yellow onion, cut into 1-inch pieces (2 cups)
2   large eggs
2   Tbsp. fresh lemon juice (from 1 lemon)
Canola oil, for frying

1. Fill a large bowl with ice water. Peel potatoes, and cut into 1-inch pieces; as you work, place potatoes in the bowl of ice water. Drain, and blot dry using paper towels. Set aside.
2. Stir together flour, salt, and baking powder in a small bowl. Place half of the potatoes, half of the onion pieces, 1 egg, and half of the flour mixture in a food processor. Process until mixture forms a thick, smooth batter with no chunks remaining, about 30 seconds. Add 1 tablespoon of the lemon juice; process until combined to keep the batter from oxidizing and turning gray. Transfer batter to a large bowl, and place near stovetop. Repeat process with remaining potatoes, onion, egg, flour mixture, and 1 tablespoon lemon juice. Set aside.
3. Fill a large skillet with oil to a depth of about ⅓ inch (about 1½ cups); heat over medium-high until oil reaches about 325°F. Using a spoon, scoop 2 to 3 tablespoons of the batter, and carefully add to the hot oil, using the spoon to support the batter until it just starts to set, about 10 seconds. The oil is hot enough if the batter quickly sizzles. (If it's not hot enough at this point, continue heating oil.) Cook latke until golden brown around the edges, about 4 minutes. Using 2 spoons or a fish spatula, flip and cook until other side is golden brown, about 4 minutes. Transfer latke to a paper towel–lined baking sheet.
4. Working in batches of six, being careful not to overcrowd the skillet, repeat process until all the latke batter is used, stirring the batter in between batches and reducing the heat as needed. (If the oil becomes too hot, the latkes will fall apart.) If needed, add more oil between batches to maintain depth of ⅓ inch. To serve hot, place cooked latkes on a single layer on a baking sheet, and transfer to a 225°F oven to keep warm until ready to eat. To make ahead and freeze, follow to the steps below.

How to Freeze

Step One
Remove latkes from hot oil, and transfer to a makeshift 3-layer drying surface: newspaper topped with brown paper bags covered with paper towels. Allow excess oil to drain off. Let latkes cool completely, about 15 minutes.

- -

Step Two
Arrange cooled latkes in a single layer on a baking sheet lined with parchment paper. Freeze, uncovered, until firm, about 15 minutes.

- -

Step Three
Remove baking sheet from freezer. Transfer latkes to a gallon-size zip-top plastic freezer bag, being careful to keep them from sticking together or breaking apart by placing parchment paper between layers, with 2 to 3 layers total. Seal bag. Write the number of latkes on the outside, and gently place in freezer. Freeze up to 3 months.

- -

Step Four
To reheat, preheat oven as hot as possible, 450°F to 500°F. Place frozen latkes in a single layer on a baking sheet. Bake until hot, 5 to 10 minutes; keep an eye on them, as they can burn quickly. Serve immediately.

Making Spirits Bright

Charleston, South Carolina, mixologist Miguel Buencamino pours two cocktails suited for whatever is on your social calendar, from bubbly celebrations to fireside chats

"PEOPLE GET INTIMIDATED by cocktails because of the technique, but you can never overcook a drink," says Miguel Buencamino, a recipe developer and commercial photographer in Charleston, South Carolina. "You can't really mess it up. Say you added half an ounce of something instead of a quarter ounce–that just means you'll have to balance it out by adding more of the other ingredients, and now you'll have an extra cocktail to share with a friend." Buencamino, who learned to cook from his two Filipino grandmothers, originally launched *Holy City Handcraft* (@holycityhandcraft) as a cooking blog but realized over time that he–and his followers–were more interested in the drinks he was pouring than the dishes he was plating. The switch to spirits felt like a natural fit. "Making cocktails is like cooking," he says. "You try to find flavors that work together and the right ratio that makes those elements shine." Here, Buencamino shares how to capture the cheerful mood of the holidays in a cup.

SPICED APPLE SPRITZ

Spiced Apple Spritz
ACTIVE 5 MIN. - TOTAL 5 MIN.
SERVES 1

- 3   Tbsp. (1½ oz.) Jamaican rum (such as Appleton Estate)
- 1½   Tbsp. Spiced Demerara Syrup (recipe follows)
- 1   Tbsp. fresh lemon juice (from 1 lemon)
    Ice
- ⅓   cup chilled sparkling apple cider
    Optional garnishes: apple slice, cinnamon stick, or whole star anise

Place rum, Spiced Demerara Syrup, and lemon juice in a cocktail shaker filled with ice. Place lid on shaker; shake vigorously until chilled, about 15 seconds. Strain into a glass filled with ice. Top with sparkling apple cider. Garnish with apple, cinnamon stick, or star anise, if desired.

Spiced Demerara Syrup
ACTIVE 15 MIN. - TOTAL 45 MIN.
MAKES ABOUT 1 CUP
(ENOUGH FOR 10 COCKTAILS)

Bring 1 cup **demerara sugar**, ¾ cup **water**, ¼ cup apple cider, 1 (3-inch) **cinnamon stick**, 1 whole **star anise**, and 4 whole **cloves** to a simmer in a medium saucepan over medium-high, stirring occasionally. Simmer, stirring often, until mixture has reduced to about 1 cup, about 10 minutes. Remove from heat, and let cool 30 minutes. Pour through a fine mesh strainer into an airtight container or bottle; discard solids. Syrup may be stored in refrigerator up to 1 month.

Gingered Toddy
ACTIVE 5 MIN. - TOTAL 5 MIN.
SERVES 1

- 3   Tbsp. (1½ oz.) bourbon
- 1   Tbsp. Ginger-Honey Syrup (recipe follows)
- 1   Tbsp. fresh lemon juice (from 1 lemon)
- 4   dashes orange bitters
- ½   cup hot water
    Lemon peel twist
    Whole star anise

Stir together bourbon, Ginger-Honey Syrup, lemon juice, and bitters in a heatproof mug until combined. Stir in hot water until incorporated. Garnish with lemon peel and star anise.

Ginger-Honey Syrup
ACTIVE 10 MIN. - TOTAL 40 MIN.
MAKES ABOUT 1 CUP
(ENOUGH FOR 14 COCKTAILS)

Bring ½ cup water and ⅓ cup sliced unpeeled **fresh ginger** (from 1 [3-inch] piece) to a simmer in a medium saucepan over medium. Stir in ½ cup **honey** until combined, about 1 minute. Remove from heat; let cool 30 minutes. Pour through a fine mesh strainer into an airtight bottle or jar; discard solids. Store in refrigerator up to 1 month.

Citrus, Spice & Everything Nice

Rise and shine on Christmas morning with these deliciously scented make–ahead rolls

Spiced Orange Rolls
ACTIVE 25 MIN. - TOTAL 2 HOURS, 45 MIN.
SERVES 15

- 1 (¼-oz.) envelope active dry yeast
- ¼ cup warm water (about 110°F)
- 1¼ cups plus 1 tsp. granulated sugar, divided
- 3 large eggs, lightly beaten
- 1 cup whole milk
- 1¼ tsp. kosher salt
- 6 to 6⅓ cups bread flour, divided, plus more for work surface
- 1 cup unsalted butter, softened, divided
- ½ tsp. ground cinnamon
- ¾ cup orange marmalade, divided
- ½ cup powdered sugar
- 2 tsp. orange zest plus 1 Tbsp. fresh juice

1. Stir together yeast, warm water, and 1 teaspoon of the granulated sugar in bowl of a stand mixer fitted with a paddle attachment. Let stand until foamy, about 5 minutes. Add eggs, milk, salt, 1 cup of the granulated sugar, 2 cups of the flour, and ½ cup of the butter to yeast mixture in bowl. Beat on low speed just until smooth, about 1 minute. Replace paddle attachment with dough hook attachment. Add 3 cups of the flour to mixture; beat on medium speed until dough is smooth but still sticky, about 5 minutes.

2. Dust a work surface with 1 cup of the flour. Turn dough out onto floured surface. Knead until elastic and just a little tacky to the touch, incorporating flour from work surface into dough and adding up to ⅓ cup additional flour as needed if dough is too sticky. Transfer to a large bowl lightly coated with cooking spray, turning once to grease top. Cover and let rise in a warm place (80°F) until roughly doubled in size, about 1 hour.

3. Stir together cinnamon, ½ cup of the marmalade, and remaining ¼ cup granulated sugar and ½ cup butter in a small bowl until mostly smooth. Set aside.

MAKE IT AHEAD
Refrigerate the pan of unbaked rolls overnight. Omit the second rise, and let the rolls sit at room temperature for about an hour before baking.

4. Turn dough out onto a lightly floured work surface. Roll out to an 18- x 12-inch rectangle. Spread butter–marmalade mixture over surface, leaving a ½-inch border. Starting at 1 long end, roll up dough into a log. Cut crosswise into 15 pieces (about 1¼ inches thick each). Arrange rolls in a 13- x 9-inch baking pan lightly coated with cooking spray. Cover with plastic wrap; let rise in a warm place (80°F) until puffy and almost doubled in size, about 30 minutes.

5. Preheat oven to 350°F. Uncover rolls; gently brush with remaining ¼ cup marmalade. Bake until golden brown, about 30 minutes. Let cool in pan on a wire rack 15 minutes.

6. Whisk together powdered sugar and orange zest and juice in a small bowl until smooth; drizzle over rolls. Serve warm or at room temperature.

The Gift of Cake

Test Kitchen professional Ivy Odom shares the dessert that sparked a lifelong love of cooking

WHEN PEOPLE FIND OUT that I cook for a living, most immediately respond with, "What's your favorite thing to make?" Whenever I am prompted with this question, my mind is flooded with the memory of a cake from my childhood.

I was over at my friend Hannah's house to play, when her mama, Heather (Mrs. Heather to me), asked if I wanted to help gather eggs at a neighbor's house. I jumped at the chance. We collected six eggs—just enough for a pound cake, she said.

Mrs. Heather pulled out her big KitchenAid mixer and started creaming the butter, cream cheese, and sugar together while I cracked the eggs. She let me add them in, one at a time, and I couldn't hide my excitement as I watched the paddle carefully swirl the yellow yolks into the pale batter. We put the pan into a cold oven, which flabbergasted this novice baker. The smell of the caramelized crust filled the house, making those two hours the longest of my life. I barely got to have a slice before it was time to leave, but one bite of the warm, buttery cake was enough to change my life forever.

I came home begging my parents for a KitchenAid mixer of my own. They finally gave in when I turned 13. I remember hoisting the shiny pink appliance onto the counter for the first time with one recipe in mind—Mrs. Heather's pound cake.

In the years since, my mixer has moved with me seven times and made more cakes than I can remember. But even after graduating first in my class from culinary school and working in the Southern Living Test Kitchen for six years, the recipe my family and friends request most often—Mrs. Heather's—is the one my pink mixer knows by heart.

Ivy's Favorite Pound Cake

ACTIVE 20 MIN. - TOTAL 2 HOURS, 20 MIN., PLUS 2 HOURS COOLING
SERVES 18

   Baking spray with flour
3 cups granulated sugar
1½ cups butter, softened
1 (8-oz.) pkg. cream cheese, softened
6 large eggs
3 cups bleached cake flour
¼ tsp. kosher salt
2 tsp. bourbon
2 tsp. fresh lemon juice (from 1 lemon)
1 tsp. vanilla extract
½ tsp. almond extract

1. Coat a light-color 18-cup (10-inch) tube pan with baking spray. Set aside. Do not preheat oven.
2. Beat sugar and butter with a stand mixer fitted with a paddle attachment on medium-high speed until mixture is light and fluffy, about 3 minutes. Beat in cream cheese until smooth, about 30 seconds. Add eggs, 1 at a time, beating on low speed until just combined.
3. Add flour, 1 cup at a time, beating on low speed until blended after each addition and stopping to scrape down sides of bowl as needed, about 1 minute total. Beat in salt, bourbon, lemon juice, vanilla, and almond extract until smooth. Transfer batter to prepared pan, and smooth top.
4. Place on rack in lower third of a cold, unpreheated oven. Turn oven on to 300°F, and bake until a wooden pick inserted into center of the cake comes out clean, 1 hour, 50 minutes to 2 hours. Let cool in pan 30 minutes. Run an

offset spatula around edges of cake to loosen; remove from pan, and let cool completely on a wire rack, about 1 hour, 30 minutes.

Mini Loaf Variation

ACTIVE 20 MIN. - TOTAL 1 HOUR, 40 MIN., PLUS 1 HOUR, 5 MIN. COOLING
MAKES 3 (8½- x 4½-INCH) LOAVES

Prepare recipe as directed, dividing batter evenly among 3 (8½- x 4½-inch) loaf pans coated with baking spray (about 3 cups per pan). Place pans in a cold, unpreheated oven; bake at 300°F until a wooden pick inserted into the center of each loaf comes out clean, 1 hour, 20 minutes to 1 hour, 30 minutes. Let cool in pans 20 minutes. Run an offset spatula around edges of each loaf to loosen. Remove from pans, and let cool completely on wire racks, about 45 minutes.

BAKING SCHOOL

TIPS AND TRICKS FROM THE SOUTH'S MOST TRUSTED KITCHEN

Clever Baking Tools

Pull out these everyday household items to up your cookie game

POTATO MASHER

Give plain cookies an interesting texture by gently pressing the raw dough with a potato masher.

METAL BINDER CLIPS

If parchment paper is rolling up at the edges of your baking pan, keep it in place with all-metal binder clips.

BISCUIT CUTTER

A round or square cutter can slice through rolled-out dough just as well as a star or Christmas tree-shape one.

Southern Staple

Pearson Farm Pecans

You'll find some of the freshest pecans from Georgia-based Pearson Farm. The Elliot pecan has a small, round shape that's ideal for topping cookies and cakes. The Mammoth version is larger and a great choice for snack mixes, pie fillings, and side dishes. Here are a few of our favorite ways to use them:

■ Make a breading for chicken, pork, or fish.

■ Grind into pecan butter.

■ Chop finely, and press pieces into pie dough.

Inner Circle

Never have a dozen cookies turn into one misshapen mass again. **Silpat's Perfect Cookie Non-Stick Silicone Baking Mat** has two circular guides per cookie: one for the amount of dough and one to represent the size of the final product. Plus, there's no need to line or oil your baking sheet. $29 each (fits a 13" x 18" pan); *amazon.com*

Time to Test These Ingredients

Make sure baking powder is fresh by stirring a small amount into boiling water. It is still active if the mixture gets fizzy. To check baking soda, combine a small amount of boiling water with a little vinegar, and then add baking soda. You'll know it's fine to use if the mixture starts to bubble up.

COOKING SCHOOL

TIPS AND TRICKS FROM THE SOUTH'S MOST TRUSTED KITCHEN

Ring Around the Table
Make any gathering feel festive with these fun appetizer ideas

BUNDLES
Wrap green apple slices and arugula leaves in prosciutto; sprinkle with pomegranate seeds and black pepper.

SKEWERS
Arrange a bed of rosemary sprigs around a platter. Thread cherry tomatoes, sliced and folded salami, pimiento-stuffed green olives, and white cheddar cheese cubes onto bamboo skewers. Arrange on top of rosemary.

CROSTINI
Top toasted baguette slices with garlic-and-herb spreadable cheese (such as Boursin), and sprinkle with diced red and green bell peppers.

HOW TO CARVE A HAM

1. MAKE A FLAT BASE
Place the ham on a large cutting board. Using a carving knife, cut one or two slices off the bottom of the ham to create a steady base. Place the ham flat-side down on the cutting board.

2. CUT THIN SLICES
Make ¼-inch-thick vertical cuts running perpendicular to the bone, working from the narrow end toward the thicker end of the ham. You can use a carving fork to steady it as you slice.

3. REMOVE FROM THE BONE
Cut horizontally along the bone to release the slices. Transfer ham to a serving platter.

Our Favorite Casserole Recipes

There's nothing more comforting than a warm and bubbling casserole fresh from the oven, with the promise of satisfaction for both stomach and soul. This collection features casseroles for all kinds of occasions and situations. For brunch, consider One-Dish Blackberry French Toast (page 334). On a busy weeknight, toss together Crunchy Chicken Casserole (page 337). Company coming? Serve Baked Shrimp Risotto (page 345) with a green salad. And when you can't decide, any one of our fabulous mac and cheese recipes (page 335) is sure to deliver.

Breakfast & Brunch

Sausage-Hash Brown Breakfast Casserole

ACTIVE 25 MIN. - TOTAL 1 HR., 5 MIN.
SERVES 10

- 1 lb. mild ground pork sausage
- 1 lb. hot ground pork sausage
- 1 (30-oz.) pkg. frozen hash browns
- 1½ tsp. salt, divided
- ½ tsp. freshly ground black pepper
- 4 oz. Cheddar cheese, shredded (about 1 cup)
- 6 large eggs
- 2 cups milk

1. Preheat oven to 350°F. Cook mild and hot pork sausages in a large skillet over medium-high, stirring frequently, until sausage crumbles and is no longer pink, 6 to 8 minutes. Drain well.
2. Prepare hash browns according to package directions, using ½ tsp. of the salt and the pepper. Stir together hash browns, sausage, and cheese. Pour into a lightly greased 13- x 9-inch baking dish.
3. Whisk together eggs, milk, and remaining 1 teaspoon salt. Pour evenly over potato mixture.
4. Bake in preheated oven until golden brown, 35 to 40 minutes. Let stand 5 minutes before serving.

Bacon-Mushroom Frittata

ACTIVE 25 MIN. - TOTAL 25 MIN.
SERVES 6 TO 8

- 2 Tbsp. olive oil
- ½ cup sliced fresh mushrooms
- 1 garlic clove, minced
- ½ (6-oz.) pkg. baby spinach
- 1 (10-oz.) can diced tomatoes with green chiles, drained
- 3 bacon slices, cooked and crumbled
- ¼ tsp. salt
- ¼ tsp. freshly ground black pepper
- 12 large eggs, beaten
- ½ cup crumbled garlic-and-herb feta cheese

1. Preheat oven to 350°F. Heat oil in a 10-inch nonstick ovenproof skillet over medium-high. Cook mushrooms in hot oil until browned, 2 to 3 minutes. Add garlic, and cook 1 minute. Stir in spinach, and cook, stirring constantly, just until spinach begins to wilt, about 1 minute.
2. Add tomatoes and green chiles, bacon, salt, and pepper. Add eggs, and sprinkle with cheese. Cook 3 to 5 minutes, gently lifting edges of frittata with a spatula and tilting pan so uncooked portion flows underneath.
3. Bake in preheated oven until set and lightly browned, 12 to 15 minutes. Let stand 5 minutes before serving.

Creamy Egg Strata

ACTIVE 35 MIN. - TOTAL 10 HR., 10 MIN., INCLUDING CHILL TIME
SERVES 8 TO 10

- ½ (16-oz.) French bread loaf, cubed (about 4 to 5 cups)
- 6 Tbsp. butter, divided
- 8 oz. Swiss cheese, shredded (about 2 cups)
- 2 oz. Parmesan cheese, grated (about ½ cup)
- ⅓ cup chopped onion
- 1 tsp. minced garlic
- 3 Tbsp. all-purpose flour
- 1½ cups chicken broth
- ¾ cup dry white wine
- ½ tsp. salt
- ½ tsp. freshly ground black pepper
- ¼ tsp. ground nutmeg
- ½ cup sour cream
- 8 large eggs, lightly beaten
  Chopped fresh chives, for garnish

1. Place bread cubes in a well-greased 13- x 9-inch baking dish. Melt 3 tablespoons butter and drizzle over bread cubes. Sprinkle with Swiss and Parmesan cheeses.
2. Melt remaining 3 tablespoons butter in a medium saucepan over medium; add onion and garlic. Cook until tender, 2 to 3 minutes. Whisk in flour until smooth; cook, whisking constantly, until lightly browned, 2 to 3 minutes. Whisk in broth, wine, salt, pepper, and nutmeg until blended. Bring

Continued on page 332

Continued from page 331

mixture to a boil; reduce heat to medium-low, and simmer, stirring occasionally, until thickened, about 15 minutes. Remove from heat and stir in sour cream.

3. Gradually whisk about one-fourth of hot sour cream mixture into eggs; add egg mixture to remaining sour cream mixture, whisking constantly. Pour mixture over bread cubes and cheese in baking dish. Cover with plastic wrap, and chill 8 to 24 hours.

4. To bake, let strata stand at room temperature about 1 hour. Preheat oven to 350°F. Remove plastic wrap, and bake in preheated oven until set, about 30 minutes. Let stand 5 minutes before serving.

Grits-and-Greens Breakfast Bake

ACTIVE 20 MIN. - TOTAL 2 HR., 10 MIN., INCLUDING GREENS

SERVES 8

1	tsp. salt
1½	cups quick-cooking grits
4	oz. white Cheddar cheese, shredded (about 1 cup)
3	Tbsp. butter
½	cup half-and-half
¼	tsp. freshly ground black pepper
¼	tsp. cayenne pepper
10	large eggs, divided
3	cups Simple Collard Greens, drained (recipe follows)
	Chopped green onions and chopped pimientos, for garnish
	Hot sauce (optional)

1. Preheat oven to 375°F. Bring salt and 4 cups water to a boil in a large saucepan over medium-high; gradually whisk in grits. Reduce heat to medium, and cook, whisking often, until thickened, 5 to 7 minutes. Remove from heat, and stir in cheese and butter.

2. Whisk together half-and-half, black pepper, cayenne, and 2 of the eggs in a medium bowl. Stir half-and-half mixture into grits mixture. Stir in Simple Collard Greens. Pour mixture into a lightly greased 13- x 9-inch baking dish.

3. Bake in preheated oven until set, 25 to 30 minutes. Remove from oven.

4. Make 8 indentations in grits mixture with the back of a large spoon. Break remaining 8 eggs, 1 at a time, into each indentation. Bake until eggs are cooked to desired doneness, 12 to 14 minutes.

5. Let stand for 10 minutes. Garnish with chopped green onions and pimientos. Serve with hot sauce, if desired.

Simple Collard Greens

ACTIVE 10 MIN. - TOTAL 40 MIN.

MAKES 3 CUPS

2	Tbsp. olive oil
1	medium-size sweet onion, chopped (about 1 cup)
1	(16-oz.) pkg. fresh collard greens, washed, trimmed, and chopped
1½	tsp. salt

1. Heat oil in a large Dutch oven over medium. Cook onion in hot oil, stirring occasionally, until tender, about 10 minutes. Add collard greens, salt, and 3 cups water. Bring to a boil; reduce heat, and simmer until tender, about 30 minutes.

Ham-and-Cheese Croissant Casserole

ACTIVE 15 MIN. - TOTAL 9 HOURS, 15 MIN., INCLUDING CHILLING

SERVES 6

3	large croissants
1	(8-oz.) pkg. chopped cooked ham
1	(5-oz.) pkg. shredded Swiss cheese
6	large eggs
1	cup half-and-half
1	Tbsp. dry mustard
2	Tbsp. honey
½	tsp. salt
½	tsp. freshly ground black pepper
¼	tsp. ground nutmeg (optional)

1. Cut croissants in half lengthwise, and cut each half into 4 or 5 equal pieces. Place croissant pieces in a lightly greased 10-inch deep-dish pie plate. Top with ham and cheese.

2. Whisk together eggs, half-and-half, dry mustard, honey, salt, pepper, and, if desired, nutmeg in a large bowl.

3. Pour egg mixture over croissant mixture, pressing croissants down to submerge in egg mixture. Cover tightly with aluminum foil, and chill 8 to 24 hours.

4. Preheat oven to 325°F. Bake, covered, in preheated oven for 35 minutes. Uncover and bake until browned and set, 25 to 30 minutes. Let stand 10 minutes before serving.

Cheesy Sausage-and-Croissant Casserole

ACTIVE 20 MIN. - TOTAL 1 HOUR, 15 MIN., PLUS 8 HOURS CHILLING

SERVES 8 TO 10

1	lb. hot ground pork sausage
5	oz. Parmesan cheese, grated (about 1¼ cups)
1	tsp. kosher salt
6	green onions, sliced (about ¾ cup)
1	(13.22-oz.) pkg. mini croissants (about 24), torn
	Vegetable cooking spray
3	cups milk
1	cup heavy whipping cream
5	large eggs, lightly beaten
8	oz. Gruyère cheese, shredded (about 2 cups)

1. Cook sausage in a skillet over medium-high, stirring to crumble, 8 minutes. Toss together sausage, Parmesan, salt, green onions, and croissants; arrange in a 13- x 9-inch baking dish coated with cooking spray.

2. Whisk together milk, cream, and eggs; pour over sausage mixture. Cover and chill 8 hours.

3. Preheat oven to 350°F. Uncover casserole, and sprinkle with cheese. Bake in preheated oven until golden, about 45 minutes. Let stand 10 minutes before serving.

Sausage, Biscuit, and Gravy Bake

ACTIVE 15 MIN. - TOTAL 1 HOUR

SERVES 6 TO 8

2	tsp. vegetable oil
1	lb. ground pork sausage
5	Tbsp. butter
¼	cup all-purpose flour
3	cups milk
¾	tsp. salt
½	tsp. freshly ground black pepper
	Vegetable cooking spray
8	refrigerated jumbo biscuits
4	green onions, chopped (about ½ cup)
6	oz. sharp Cheddar cheese, shredded (about ¾ cup)

1. Preheat oven to 350°F. Heat oil in a large skillet over medium-high. Cook sausage in hot oil until crumbly and no longer pink, about 8 minutes; remove from skillet, and drain.

2. Melt butter in skillet; whisk in flour. Whisk constantly 1 minute. Gradually whisk in milk, salt, and pepper. Bring to a boil, whisking constantly; cook 2 minutes. Stir in sausage.

3. Grease an 11- x 7-inch baking dish with cooking spray; place dish on a baking sheet. Split biscuits in half lengthwise; place 8 halves in baking dish. Top with half of sausage mixture and ¼ cup of the green onions. Repeat layers. Sprinkle with cheese.

4. Bake in preheated oven until golden, about 40 minutes.

Mini Cheese Grits Casseroles

If you don't have 8-ounce ramekins, you can make this recipe in a 2-quart baking dish, but increase the baking time to about 50 to 55 minutes.

ACTIVE 15 MIN. - TOTAL 1 HOUR, 25 MIN., PLUS 8 HOURS CHILLING

SERVES 6

- 1½ cups uncooked quick-cooking grits
- 2 tsp. kosher salt, divided
- 1 cup half-and-half
- 1 tsp. dry mustard
- ¼ tsp. black pepper
- 2 large eggs
- 1 large egg yolk
- 12 oz. sharp Cheddar cheese, shredded (about 3 cups)
- 2 Tbsp. chopped fresh chives

1. Bring 4½ cups water to a boil in a medium saucepan over high. Add grits and 1 teaspoon of the salt. Reduce heat to medium-low, and cook, stirring occasionally, until grits are thickened and tender, about 5 minutes. Remove pan from heat; cover and let stand 5 minutes.

2. Meanwhile, whisk together half-and-half, dry mustard, pepper, eggs, egg yolk, and remaining 1 teaspoon salt. Stir in grits and cheese until cheese is melted. Divide mixture evenly among 6 (8-ounce) lightly greased ramekins. Cover and chill 8 hours or overnight.

3. Preheat oven to 350°F. Uncover ramekins, and place on a baking sheet; let stand at room temperature while oven preheats, 15 to 20 minutes. Bake in preheated oven until puffed and edges are set, 40 to 45 minutes. Let stand 10 minutes. Sprinkle with chives, and serve.

Mini Tomato-Herb Frittatas

Transferring the bottom baking sheet to the middle rack during the last few minutes of cooking time allows the top to brown slightly.

ACTIVE 15 MIN. - TOTAL 30 MIN.

SERVES 8

- 12 large eggs
- 1 cup half-and-half
- ½ tsp. kosher salt
- ¼ tsp. freshly ground black pepper
- 2 Tbsp. chopped fresh chives
- 1 Tbsp. chopped fresh parsley
- 1 tsp. chopped fresh oregano
- 1 pt. grape tomatoes, halved
- 6 oz. shredded Italian three-cheese blend (about 1½ cups)

1. Preheat oven to 450°F. Process eggs, half-and-half, salt, and pepper in a blender until blended. Stir together chives, parsley, and oregano in a small bowl. Place 8 lightly greased 4-inch (6-oz.) ramekins on 2 baking sheets; layer tomatoes, 1 cup of the cheese, and the chive mixture in ramekins. Pour egg mixture over top, and sprinkle with remaining ½ cup cheese.

2. Bake in preheated oven for 7 minutes, placing 1 baking sheet on middle oven rack and other on lower oven rack. Switch baking sheets, and bake until set, 7 to 8 minutes more. Remove top baking sheet from oven; transfer bottom sheet to middle rack, and bake until lightly browned, 1 to 2 minutes more.

King Ranch Breakfast Strata

ACTIVE 40 MIN. - TOTAL 2 HOURS, 45 MIN., PLUS 8 HOURS CHILLING

SERVES 8

- ½ (16-oz.) French bread loaf, cubed (about 4 cups)
- 8 (6-inch) fajita-size corn tortillas, cut into strips
- 2 cups shredded cooked chicken
- 10 oz. pepper Jack cheese, shredded (about 2½ cups), divided
- 3 Tbsp. butter
- 1 (14.5-oz.) can diced tomatoes, drained
- 1 medium-size yellow onion, chopped (about 1 cup)
- 1 celery stalk, chopped (about ½ cup)
- 1 (4-oz.) can diced green chiles, drained
- 2 garlic cloves, minced
- 1 bell pepper, chopped (about 1 cup)
- 1 tsp. kosher salt
- ¾ tsp. ground cumin
- ½ tsp. dried oregano
- 10 large eggs
- 1 (10¾-oz.) can condensed cream of mushroom soup
- 2½ cups milk, divided

1. Toss together bread cubes and tortilla strips, and arrange in a lightly greased 13- x 9-inch baking dish. Sprinkle with chicken and 2 cups of the cheese.

2. Melt butter in a medium saucepan over medium. Add tomatoes, onion, celery, green chiles, garlic, bell pepper, salt, cumin, and oregano, and cook, stirring often, until tender, 5 to 8 minutes. Remove from heat, and cool 10 minutes.

3. Whisk together eggs, soup, and 1½ cups of the milk in a large bowl. Pour over bread mixture. Sprinkle with cooled onion mixture. Cover with plastic wrap, and chill 8 to 24 hours.

4. Pour remaining 1 cup milk over strata; top with remaining ½ cup cheese. Let stand 45 minutes.

5. Preheat oven to 325°F. Bake in preheated oven until set, about 1 hour and 10 minutes. Let stand 5 minutes before serving.

Swiss Chicken Crêpes

ACTIVE 20 MIN. - TOTAL 1 HOUR, 5 MIN.

SERVES 4 TO 6

- 1 (12-oz.) jar roasted red bell peppers, drained
  Swiss Cheese Sauce (recipe follows)
- 3 cups finely chopped cooked chicken
- 1 (5-oz.) pkg. fresh baby spinach, chopped
- 4 oz. Swiss cheese, shredded (about 1 cup)
- ¼ cup chopped fresh basil
- 1 garlic clove, minced
- 1 tsp. seasoned pepper
- 8 egg roll wrappers
  Fresh basil leaves, for garnish

1. Preheat oven to 350°F. Process peppers in a blender until smooth, stopping to scrape down sides as needed. Pour into 4 lightly greased 7- x 4½-inch baking dishes.

Continued on page 334

Continued from page 333

2. Prepare Swiss Cheese Sauce. Stir together chicken, spinach, cheese, chopped basil, garlic, seasoned pepper, and 1 cup of the Swiss Cheese Sauce.
3. Divide chicken mixture among wrappers, spooning down centers; gently roll up. Place, seam sides down, over puréed red peppers. Top with remaining cheese sauce. Cover with aluminum foil.
4. Bake in preheated oven, covered, for 15 minutes or until thoroughly heated.

Swiss Cheese Sauce
ACTIVE 20 MIN. - TOTAL 20 MIN.
MAKES ABOUT 4 CUPS

- ⅓ cup dry vermouth
- 1 garlic clove, minced
- 3 cups half-and-half
- 3 Tbsp. cornstarch
- 1 tsp. kosher salt
- ½ tsp. freshly ground black pepper
- 8 oz. Swiss cheese, shredded (about 2 cups)

1. Bring vermouth and garlic to a boil in a large skillet over medium-high; reduce heat to medium-low, and simmer until vermouth is reduced to 1 tablespoon, 7 to 10 minutes.
2. Whisk together half-and-half and cornstarch. Whisk salt, pepper, and half-and-half mixture into vermouth mixture; bring to a boil over medium-high, whisking constantly. Boil, whisking constantly, until mixture is thickened, about 1 minute. Add cheese; reduce heat to low, and simmer, whisking constantly, until sauce is smooth, about 1 minute. Remove from heat, and use immediately.

Italian Brunch Casserole
ACTIVE 20 MIN. - TOTAL 1 HOUR, 20 MIN.,
PLUS 8 HOURS CHILLING
SERVES 8

- 1 (8-oz.) pkg. sweet Italian sausage
- 8 green onions, sliced (about 1 cup)
- 2 medium-size zucchini, diced (about 3 cups)
- 1 tsp. kosher salt
- ½ tsp. black pepper
- 1 (7-oz.) jar roasted red bell peppers, drained and chopped
- 1 (16-oz.) Italian bread loaf, cut into 1-inch cubes (about 8 cups)
- 8 oz. sharp Cheddar cheese, shredded (about 2 cups)
- 6 large eggs
- 1½ cups milk

1. Remove and discard casings from sausage. Cook sausage in a large skillet over medium-high, stirring until sausage crumbles and is no longer pink; drain. Return to skillet.
2. Add green onions, zucchini, salt, and black pepper to skillet. Cook until vegetables are tender, about 4 minutes. Stir in bell peppers. Drain and cool.
3. Spread 4 cups of the bread cubes in a lightly greased 13- x 9-inch baking dish. Top with half each of the sausage mixture and cheese. Repeat with remaining bread, sausage, and cheese.
4. Whisk together eggs and milk. Pour egg mixture over bread. Cover and chill 8 hours.
5. Preheat oven to 325°F. Bake in preheated oven, covered, until bubbly, about 1 hour.

Easy French Toast Casserole
ACTIVE 30 MIN. - TOTAL 55 MIN.,
PLUS 8 HOURS CHILLING
SERVES 6

- ⅔ cup firmly packed dark brown sugar
- 2 Tbsp. butter
- 2 Tbsp. dark corn syrup
  Vegetable cooking spray
- 2 large eggs
- 1 large egg white
- 1½ cups milk
- 1 tsp. vanilla extract
- ¼ tsp. salt
- 6 (1-inch-thick) French bread baguette slices
- 2 Tbsp. finely chopped toasted pecans
  Sliced strawberries and powdered sugar, for garnish

1. Combine brown sugar, butter, and corn syrup in a small, heavy saucepan. Cook over medium until bubbly and sugar dissolves, stirring constantly, 3 to 4 minutes. Pour sugar mixture into an 11- x 7-inch baking dish coated with cooking spray, spreading evenly over bottom of dish.

2. Whisk together eggs and egg white in a shallow dish or pie plate. Stir in milk, vanilla, and salt. Lightly press bread slices, 1 at a time, into egg mixture, coating both sides of bread, and arrange over brown sugar mixture. Pour any remaining egg mixture evenly over bread slices. Cover and chill 8 to 24 hours.
3. Preheat oven to 350°F. Bake, uncovered, in preheated oven until lightly browned, about 30 minutes.
4. To serve, place 1 toast piece on each of 6 plates. Sprinkle each with 1 teaspoon pecans. Garnish with strawberries and powdered sugar.

One-Dish Blackberry French Toast
ACTIVE 10 MIN. - TOTAL 45 MIN.,
PLUS 8 HOURS CHILLING
SERVES 8 TO 10

- 1 cup blackberry jam
  Vegetable cooking spray
- 1 (12-oz.) French bread loaf, cut into 1½-inch cubes
- 1 (8-oz.) pkg. ⅓-less-fat cream cheese, cut into 1-inch cubes
- 4 large eggs
- 2 cups half-and-half
- 1 tsp. ground cinnamon
- 1 tsp. vanilla extract
- ½ cup firmly packed brown sugar
  Maple syrup and whipped cream, for topping

1. Cook jam in a small saucepan over medium until melted, 1 to 2 minute and smooth, stirring once, 1 to 2 minutes.
2. Lightly grease a 13- x 9-inch baking dish with cooking spray. Place half of bread cubes in bottom of dish. Top with cream cheese cubes, and drizzle with melted jam. Top with remaining bread cubes.
3. Whisk together eggs, half-and-half, cinnamon, and vanilla. Pour over bread mixture. Sprinkle with brown sugar. Cover tightly, and chill 8 to 24 hours.
4. Preheat oven to 325°F. Bake in preheated oven, covered, 20 minutes. Uncover and bake until bread is golden brown and mixture is set, 10 to 15 minutes. Serve with toppings.

Cinnamon-Pecan Rolls

ACTIVE 45 MIN. - TOTAL 1 HOUR, 20 MIN.

MAKES 12 ROLLS

- 1 (16-oz.) pkg. hot roll mix
- ½ cup butter, softened
- 1 cup firmly packed light brown sugar
- 2 tsp. ground cinnamon
- 1 cup chopped toasted pecans
- 1 cup powdered sugar
- 2 Tbsp. milk
- 1 tsp. vanilla extract

1. Prepare hot roll dough according to package directions; let dough stand 5 minutes. Roll dough into a 15- x 10-inch rectangle; spread with softened butter. Stir together brown sugar and cinnamon; sprinkle over butter. Sprinkle pecans over brown sugar mixture. Starting at one long end, roll up tightly; cut into 12 slices. Place rolls, cut sides down, in a lightly greased 12-inch cast-iron skillet or 13- x 9-inch pan. Cover loosely with plastic wrap and a cloth towel; let rise in a warm place (85°F), free from drafts, until doubled in size, about 30 minutes.
2. Preheat oven to 350°F. Uncover rolls, and bake in preheated oven until center rolls are golden brown and done, 20 to 25 minutes.
3. Cool in pan on a wire rack 10 minutes. Stir together powdered sugar, milk, and vanilla; drizzle over rolls.

Mac & Cheese

Best-Ever Macaroni and Cheese

ACTIVE 25 MIN. - TOTAL 1 HOUR, 10 MIN.

SERVES 10

- 16 oz. uncooked large elbow macaroni, large shells, or cavatappi pasta
- 6 Tbsp. butter
- ⅓ cup grated yellow onion
- 2 tsp. dry mustard
- 1 tsp. kosher salt
- ¼ tsp. black pepper
- ⅛ tsp. freshly grated nutmeg
- ⅛ tsp. cayenne pepper
- 6 Tbsp. all-purpose flour
- 3½ cups milk
- 1¾ cups heavy whipping cream
- 2 tsp. Worcestershire sauce
- 4 oz. extra-sharp yellow Cheddar cheese, shredded (about 1 cup), plus 4 oz. diced (about 1 cup), divided
- 4 oz. sharp white Cheddar cheese, shredded (about 1 cup), plus 4 oz. diced (about 1 cup), divided

1. Preheat oven to 350°F. Cook pasta according to package directions.
2. Melt butter in a large saucepan over medium. Add onion, dry mustard, salt, black pepper, nutmeg, and cayenne; cook, stirring, 30 seconds. Add flour, and cook, stirring, until golden, about 2 minutes. Gradually whisk in milk and cream. Bring to a boil, whisking occasionally. Reduce heat to medium-low; simmer, whisking, until slightly thickened, about 5 minutes. Stir in Worcestershire sauce. Remove from heat; stir in ¾ cup each of shredded Cheddar cheeses until melted. (Reserve remaining ¼ cup each of shredded cheeses.) Stir in pasta and diced cheeses; pour into a lightly greased 13- x 9-inch baking dish.
3. Bake in preheated oven on a rimmed baking sheet until bubbly and golden, about 30 minutes. Remove from oven, and increase oven temperature to broil. Sprinkle with reserved shredded cheeses; broil 6 inches from heat until cheeses are melted and golden, about 2 minutes. Remove from oven; cool slightly on a wire rack, about 15 minutes.

Herbed Breadcrumb-Topped Macaroni and Cheese

Prepare as directed using entire amount of cheeses through Step 2. Stir together ½ cup **panko breadcrumbs**, 2 Tbsp. melted **salted butter**, 1 tsp. **chopped fresh sage**, and ½ tsp. each **chopped fresh thyme** and **rosemary**; sprinkle over casserole before baking. Bake until topping is golden brown. Omit broiling.

Four-Cheese Macaroni

ACTIVE 40 MIN. - TOTAL 1 HOUR, 15 MIN.

SERVES 8

- 12 oz. uncooked cavatappi pasta or macaroni
- ½ cup butter
- ½ cup all-purpose flour
- ½ tsp. cayenne pepper
- 3 cups milk
- 8 oz. white Cheddar cheese, shredded (about 2 cups)
- 4 oz. Monterey Jack cheese, shredded (about 1 cup)
- 4 oz. fontina cheese, shredded (about 1 cup)
- 4 oz. Asiago cheese, shredded (about 1 cup)
- 1½ cups soft, fresh breadcrumbs
- ½ cup chopped cooked bacon
- ½ cup chopped pecans
- 2 Tbsp. butter, melted

1. Preheat oven to 350°F. Cook pasta according to package directions.
2. Melt butter in a Dutch oven over low; whisk in flour and cayenne until smooth. Cook, whisking constantly, 1 minute. Gradually whisk in milk; cook over medium heat, whisking constantly, until thickened and bubbly, 6 to 7 minutes. Remove from heat.
3. Toss together Cheddar, Monterey Jack, fontina, and Asiago cheeses in a medium bowl; reserve 1½ cups of the cheese mixture. Add remaining cheese mixture and hot cooked pasta to sauce, tossing to coat. Spoon into a lightly greased 13- x 9-inch baking dish. Top with reserved 1½ cups cheese mixture.
4. Toss together breadcrumbs, bacon, pecans, and melted butter. Sprinkle over the top.
5. Bake in preheated oven until bubbly and golden brown, 35 to 40 minutes. Let stand 10 minutes before serving.

Dinner Mac and Cheese

ACTIVE 30 MIN. - TOTAL 1 HOUR

SERVES 8

- 16 oz. uncooked cellentani (corkscrew) pasta
- 3 Tbsp. butter
- ¼ cup all-purpose flour
- 4 cups milk
- 4 oz. sharp Cheddar cheese, shredded (about 1 cup)
- 1 (10-oz.) block sharp white Cheddar cheese, shredded
- 1 (3-oz.) pkg. cream cheese, softened
- ½ tsp. kosher salt
- 2 cups chopped cooked ham
- 2 cups coarsely chopped assorted roasted vegetables

Continued on page 336

Continued from page 335

1¼ cups crushed round buttery crackers

2 Tbsp. butter, melted

1. Preheat oven to 400°F. Cook pasta according to package directions.
2. Meanwhile, melt the 3 tablespoons butter in a Dutch oven over medium. Gradually whisk in flour; cook, whisking constantly, 1 minute. Gradually whisk in milk until smooth; cook, whisking constantly, until slightly thickened, 8 to 10 minutes. Whisk in 1 cup sharp Cheddar cheese, white Cheddar cheese, cream cheese, and salt until smooth. Remove from heat, and stir in ham, vegetables, and hot cooked pasta.
3. Spoon pasta mixture into a lightly greased 13- x 9-inch baking dish. Stir together cracker crumbs and 2 tablespoons melted butter; sprinkle over pasta.
4. Bake in preheated oven until golden and bubbly, 25 to 30 minutes. Let stand 5 minutes before serving.

King Ranch Chicken Mac and Cheese

ACTIVE 20 MIN. - TOTAL 45 MIN.
SERVES 6

8 oz. uncooked cellentani (corkscrew) pasta (from ½ [16-oz. pkg.])

2 Tbsp. butter

1 medium-size yellow onion, diced (about 1 cup)

1 green bell pepper, diced

1 (10-oz.) can diced tomatoes and green chiles

1 (8-oz.) pkg. pasteurized prepared cheese product, cubed

3 cups chopped cooked chicken

1 (10¾-oz.) can cream of chicken soup

½ cup sour cream

1 tsp. chili powder

½ tsp. ground cumin

Vegetable cooking spray

6 oz. Cheddar cheese, shredded (about 1½ cups)

1. Preheat oven to 350°F. Cook pasta according to package directions.
2. Meanwhile, melt butter in a large Dutch oven over medium-high. Add onion and bell pepper, and cook until tender, about 5 minutes. Stir in tomatoes and green chiles and prepared cheese product; cook, stirring constantly, until cheese melts, about 2 minutes. Stir in chicken, soup, sour cream, chili powder, cumin, and hot cooked pasta until blended. Lightly grease a 10-inch cast-iron skillet or an 11- x 7-inch baking dish with cooking spray. Spoon mixture into skillet; sprinkle with shredded Cheddar cheese.
3. Bake in preheated oven until bubbly, 25 to 30 minutes. Let stand 5 minutes before serving.

Baked Smokin' Macaroni and Cheese

ACTIVE 25 MIN. - TOTAL 1 HOUR
SERVES 8

16 oz. uncooked cellentani (corkscrew) pasta

3 Tbsp. butter, divided

¼ cup all-purpose flour

3 cups fat-free milk

1 (12-oz.) can fat-free evaporated milk

4 oz. smoked Gouda cheese, shredded (about 1 cup)

2 oz. 1.5% reduced-fat sharp Cheddar cheese, shredded (about ½ cup)

3 oz. fat-free cream cheese, softened

½ tsp. kosher salt

¼ tsp. cayenne pepper, divided

1 (8-oz.) pkg. chopped smoked ham

Vegetable cooking spray

1¼ cups cornflakes cereal, crushed

1. Preheat oven to 350°F. Cook pasta according to package directions.
2. Meanwhile, melt 2 tablespoons of the butter in a Dutch oven over medium. Gradually whisk in flour; cook, whisking constantly, 1 minute. Gradually whisk in milk and evaporated milk until smooth; cook, whisking constantly, until slightly thickened, 8 to 10 minutes. Whisk in Gouda cheese, Cheddar cheese, cream cheese, salt, and ⅛ teaspoon of the cayenne pepper until smooth. Remove Dutch oven from heat, and stir in chopped ham and cooked pasta.
3. Pour pasta mixture into a 13- x 9-inch baking dish coated with cooking spray. Melt the remaining 1 tablespoon butter. Stir together crushed cereal, melted butter, and remaining ⅛ teaspoon cayenne pepper; sprinkle over pasta mixture.
4. Bake in preheated oven until golden and bubbly, about 30 minutes. Let stand 5 minutes before serving.

Poultry

Oven Chicken Risotto

ACTIVE 20 MIN. - TOTAL 1 HOUR
SERVES 6

2 Tbsp. butter

2½ cups chicken broth

1 cup Arborio rice

½ small onion, diced

½ tsp. salt

2 cups chopped roasted or rotisserie chicken

8 oz. fresh mozzarella cheese, cut into ½-inch cubes

1 cup cherry or grape tomatoes, halved

¼ cup shredded fresh basil

1. Preheat oven to 400°F. Place butter in a 13- x 9-inch baking dish; bake until melted, about 5 minutes. Stir in broth, rice, onion, and salt.
2. Bake, covered, for 35 minutes. Remove from oven. Fluff rice with a fork. Stir in chicken, mozzarella, and tomatoes; sprinkle with shredded basil. Serve immediately.

Chicken and Wild Rice with Pecans

ACTIVE 45 MIN. - TOTAL 1 HOUR, 5 MIN.
SERVES 6

1 cup uncooked long-grain and wild rice mix

1 leek, sliced

2 Tbsp. unsalted butter

1 (16-oz.) pkg. fresh mushrooms, stemmed and quartered

½ cup dry white wine

4 cups shredded roasted or rotisserie chicken

1 cup sour cream

1 tsp. salt

½ tsp. freshly ground black pepper

2 oz. white Cheddar cheese, shredded (about ½ cup)

½ cup coarsely chopped pecans

Chopped fresh chives, for garnish

1. Cook wild rice blend according to package directions.
2. Meanwhile, remove and discard root ends and dark green tops of leek. Cut in half lengthwise, and rinse thoroughly

under cold running water to remove grit and sand. Thinly slice leek.

3. Preheat oven to 350°F. Melt butter in a large skillet over medium-low. Add leek, and cook until lightly browned, 6 to 7 minutes. Add mushrooms, and cook, stirring often, 15 minutes. Add wine, and bring to a simmer; cook 3 minutes.

4. Transfer cooked rice to a large bowl. Add leek mixture and stir until blended. Add chicken, sour cream, salt, and pepper, and stir until blended. Transfer to a lightly greased 11- x 7-inch baking dish. Top with cheese.

5. Bake in preheated oven for 10 minutes. Top with pecans; bake until pecans are toasted and casserole is bubbly, about 10 minutes more. Let stand 5 minutes before serving. Garnish with chives.

Chicken-and-Poppy Seed Casserole

ACTIVE 15 MIN. - TOTAL 1 HOUR, 15 MIN.
(INCLUDING SOUP)
SERVES 6

- 2½ cups Cream of Mushroom Soup (recipe follows)
- 5 cups chopped roasted or rotisserie chicken
- 1 (16-oz.) container sour cream
- 1 Tbsp. poppy seeds
- ¼ cup butter, melted
- 18 buttery round crackers, crushed

1. Preheat oven to 350°F. Stir together Cream of Mushroom Soup, chicken, sour cream, and poppy seeds. Spoon into a lightly greased 11- x 7-inch baking dish.

2. Stir together melted butter and crackers; sprinkle over casserole.

3. Bake in preheated oven until bubbly, 35 to 40 minutes. Let stand 5 minutes before serving.

Cream of Mushroom Soup

MAKES 2½ CUPS

- 3 cups chicken stock, divided
- 2 (¾-oz.) pkg. dried mixed mushrooms
- ¼ cup butter
- 1 medium shallot, chopped (about 3 Tbsp.)
- ½ (8-oz.) pkg. sliced cremini mushrooms
- 2 garlic cloves, minced
- ¼ cup Marsala or dry white wine

- ⅓ cup all-purpose flour
- 1 cup heavy whipping cream
- ⅓ tsp. salt
- ¼ tsp. freshly ground black pepper
  Chopped fresh parsley (optional)

1. Bring 2½ cups of the chicken stock to a boil in a medium saucepan. Add dried mushrooms; reduce heat to medium, and simmer 5 minutes. Remove from heat; let stand 20 minutes. Remove mushrooms with a slotted spoon; reserve soaked mushrooms for another use. Pour mushroom liquid through cheesecloth-lined wire-mesh strainer; reserve liquid.

2. Melt butter in a Dutch oven over medium. Add shallot, and cook until softened, about 3 minutes. Add fresh mushrooms; cook, stirring occasionally, until mushrooms are browned, about 4 minutes. Stir in garlic; cook 1 minute. Stir in wine; cook until liquid almost evaporates, about 2 minutes. Stir in flour; cook 1 minute. Gradually add mushroom liquid and remaining ½ cup chicken stock, whisking until blended. Stir in cream, salt, pepper, and parsley, if desired. Bring to a boil; reduce heat to medium-low, and simmer 20 minutes or until thickened to desired consistency.

Crunchy Chicken Casserole

Top with crushed potato chips just before baking so they don't become soggy.
ACTIVE 20 MIN. - TOTAL : 45 MIN.
SERVES 8

- 1 Tbsp. butter
- 1 medium-size yellow onion, chopped
- 1 (8.8-oz.) pouch ready-to-serve long grain rice
- 3 cups chopped cooked chicken
- 1½ cups frozen petite English peas
- 6 oz. sharp Cheddar cheese, shredded (about 1½ cups)
- 1 cup mayonnaise
- 1 (10¾-oz.) can cream of chicken soup
- 1 (8-oz.) can sliced water chestnuts, drained
- 1 (4-oz.) jar sliced pimientos, drained
- 3 cups coarsely crushed ridged potato chips

1. Preheat oven to 350°F. Melt butter in a skillet over medium. Add onion, and cook until tender, about 5 minutes.

2. Heat rice in microwave according to package directions. Combine cooked onion, rice, chicken, peas, cheese, mayonnaise, soup, water chestnuts, and pimientos in a large bowl; toss gently. Spoon mixture into a lightly greased 13- x 9-inch baking dish. Top with crushed potato chips.

3. Bake in preheated oven until bubbly, 20 to 25 minutes. Let stand 5 minutes before serving.

Loaded Chicken-Bacon Pot Pie

ACTIVE 40 MIN. - TOTAL 1 HOUR, 35 MIN.
SERVES 6

- 5 thick-cut bacon slices, diced
- 1 medium-size sweet onion, chopped (about 1 cup)
- 2 garlic cloves, chopped
- 1 medium carrot, chopped (about 1 cup)
- 1 (8-oz.) pkg. button mushrooms, halved
- ½ cup dry white wine
- ⅓ cup all-purpose flour
- 3 cups chicken broth
- ¾ cup whipping cream
- 1½ Tbsp. dry mustard
- 2 tsp. fresh thyme leaves
- 1 tsp. kosher salt
- ⅛ tsp. cayenne pepper
- 4 cups shredded deli-roasted chicken
- 1 cup frozen petite English peas
- ½ (17.3-oz.) pkg. frozen puff pastry, thawed and cut into strips (1 pastry sheet)
- 1 large egg, lightly beaten

1. Preheat oven to 400°F. Cook bacon in a Dutch oven over medium until crisp, 8 to 10 minutes. Drain on paper towels, reserving 3 tablespoons drippings.

2. Add onion to hot drippings, and cook 3 minutes. Add garlic, carrot, and mushrooms; cook 4 to 5 minutes or until carrot is crisp-tender. Remove from heat, and add wine. Return to heat; cook 2 minutes. Sprinkle with flour; cook, stirring constantly, 3 minutes. Whisk in broth; bring to a boil. Boil, whisking constantly, until thickened, 2 to 3 minutes. Stir in cream, mustard, thyme, salt, and cayenne pepper.

Continued on page 338

Continued from page 337

3. Remove from heat, and stir in chicken, peas, and bacon. Spoon mixture into a lightly greased 11- x 7-inch baking dish. Place pastry over hot filling, pressing edges to seal and trimming off excess. (Use scraps to cover any exposed filling, if necessary.) Whisk together egg and 1 tablespoon. water. Brush over pastry.

4. Bake in preheated oven on lower oven rack until browned and bubbly, 35 to 40 minutes. Let stand 15 minutes before serving.

Note: You can also make this recipe in 6 (12-oz.) ramekins. Cut pastry into circles; place over ramekins after filling. Bake as directed.

Classic Chicken Tetrazzini

ACTIVE 20 MIN. - TOTAL 55 MIN.
SERVES 8 TO 10

- 12 oz. uncooked vermicelli (from 1½ [8-oz.] pkg.)
- ½ cup butter
- ½ cup all-purpose flour
- 4 cups milk
- ½ cup dry white wine
- 2 Tbsp. chicken bouillon granules
- 1 tsp. seasoned pepper
- 8 oz. Parmesan cheese, grated (about 2 cups), divided
- 4 cups diced cooked chicken
- 1 (6-oz.) jar sliced mushrooms, drained
- ¾ cup slivered almonds

1. Preheat oven to 350°F. Cook pasta according to package directions.
2. Meanwhile, melt butter in a Dutch oven over low; whisk in flour until smooth. Cook 1 minute, whisking constantly. Gradually whisk in milk and wine; cook over medium, whisking constantly, until mixture is thickened and bubbly, 8 to 10 minutes. Whisk in bouillon granules, seasoned pepper, and 1 cup of the Parmesan.
3. Remove from heat; stir in chicken, mushrooms, and hot cooked pasta.
4. Spoon mixture into a lightly greased 13- x 9-inch baking dish; sprinkle with almonds and remaining 1 cup Parmesan.
5. Bake in preheated oven until bubbly, about 35 minutes.

Chicken Marsala Tetrazzini

ACTIVE 10 MIN. - TOTAL 45 MIN.
SERVES 6 TO 8

- 1 (8-oz.) pkg. uncooked vermicelli
- 2 Tbsp. butter
- 1 (8-oz.) pkg. sliced fresh mushrooms
- 3 oz. finely chopped prosciutto
- 3 cups chopped cooked chicken
- 1 cup frozen petite English peas
- 1 (10¾-oz.) can reduced-fat cream of mushroom soup
- 1 (10-oz.) container refrigerated light Alfredo sauce
- ½ cup chicken broth
- ¼ cup Marsala wine
- 4 oz. Parmesan cheese, grated (about 1 cup), divided

1. Preheat oven to 350°F. Cook pasta according to package directions. Meanwhile, melt butter in a large skillet over medium-high; add mushrooms and prosciutto, and cook 5 minutes.
2. Stir together mushroom mixture, chicken, peas, canned soup, Alfredo sauce, broth, Marsala, and ½ cup of the cheese; stir in pasta. Spoon mixture into a lightly greased 11- x 7-inch baking dish; sprinkle with remaining ½ cup cheese.
3. Bake in preheated oven until bubbly, about 35 minutes.

Pasta-Chicken-Broccoli Bake

ACTIVE 30 MIN. - TOTAL 1 HOUR, 15 MIN.
SERVES 6 TO 8

- ½ cup butter
- 1 small sweet onion, chopped (about ½ cup)
- 1 small red bell pepper, chopped (about ½ cup)
- 2 garlic cloves, minced
- ¼ cup all-purpose flour
- 3 cups chicken broth
- 1½ cups half-and-half
- ½ cup dry white wine
- 6 oz. Parmesan cheese, grated (about 1½ cups), divided
- ¼ tsp. kosher salt
- ¼ tsp. cayenne pepper
- 1 (20-oz.) pkg. refrigerated cheese-and-spinach tortellini
- 4 cups chopped fresh broccoli
- 4 cups chopped cooked chicken
- 15 round buttery crackers, crushed

- ½ cup chopped pecans
- 3 Tbsp. butter, melted

1. Preheat oven to 350°F. Melt the ½ cup butter in a Dutch oven over medium-high; add onion, bell pepper, and garlic, and cook until tender, 5 to 6 minutes.
2. Add flour, stirring until smooth. Cook, stirring constantly, 1 minute. Whisk in broth, half-and-half, and wine. Reduce heat to medium, and cook until thickened and bubbly, 6 to 8 minutes, stirring constantly.
3. Remove from heat; add 1 cup of the cheese, salt, and cayenne pepper, stirring until cheese melts. Stir in tortellini, broccoli, and chicken. Spoon into a lightly greased 13- x 9-inch baking dish.
4. Stir together the remaining ½ cup cheese, crushed crackers, pecans, and the 3 tablespoons butter. Sprinkle over casserole. Bake in preheated oven until bubbly, 40 to 45 minutes.

Mini Skillet Chicken Pot Pies

ACTIVE 30 MIN. - TOTAL 1 HOUR, 30 MIN.
SERVES 6 TO 8

- ⅓ cup plus 2 Tbsp. unsalted butter, divided
- ⅓ cup all-purpose flour
- 1½ cups chicken broth
- 1½ cups whole milk
- 1½ tsp. Creole seasoning
- 1 large sweet onion, diced (about 2 cups)
- 1 (8-oz.) pkg. sliced mushrooms
- 4 cups shredded rotisserie chicken
- 2 cups frozen cubed hash browns
- 1 cup matchstick-cut carrots
- 1 cup frozen petite English peas
- ⅓ cup chopped fresh flat-leaf parsley
- 1 (14.1-oz.) pkg. refrigerated piecrusts
- 1 large egg white

1. Preheat oven to 350°F. Lightly grease 8 (6-inch) cast-iron skillets or 1 (10-inch) cast-iron skillet.
2. Melt ⅓ cup of the butter in a large saucepan over medium; add flour, and cook, whisking constantly, 1 minute. Slowly whisk in chicken broth and milk; cook, whisking constantly, until thickened and bubbly, 6 to 7 minutes. Remove from heat, and stir in Creole seasoning.

3. Melt remaining 2 tablespoons butter in a large Dutch oven over medium-high; add onion and mushrooms, and cook, stirring often, until tender, about 10 minutes. Stir in chicken, hash browns, carrots, peas, parsley, and sauce.

4. If using mini skillets, cut piecrust to fit. If using one large skillet, place 1 piecrust in prepared skillet. Spread chicken mixture in piecrust(s); top with remaining piecrust(s). Whisk egg white until foamy; brush top of piecrust(s) with egg white. Cut 4 or 5 small slits in the top of the pie(s) to allow steam to escape.

5. Bake in preheated oven until golden brown and bubbly, 1 hour to 1 hour and 5 minutes.

Skillet Enchiladas Suizas

ACTIVE 15 MIN. - TOTAL 25 MIN.
SERVES 6

- 2 Tbsp. olive oil
- 1 medium-size yellow onion, chopped (about 1 cup)
- 3 garlic cloves, minced
- 1½ tsp. ground cumin
- 1 (14½-oz.) can diced tomatoes, drained
- 1¼ cups tomatillo salsa
- 4 cups shredded rotisserie chicken
- 1 cup Mexican crema or sour cream
- 6 (6-inch) corn tortillas, torn
- 8 oz. Monterey Jack cheese, shredded (about 2 cups), divided
- 1 small avocado, diced
  Coarsely chopped fresh cilantro

1. Preheat broiler to high. Heat oil in a medium-size cast-iron skillet over medium, swirling to coat. Add onion, and cook, stirring occasionally, until lightly browned, about 6 minutes. Add garlic and cumin; cook, stirring often, until fragrant, 1 to 2 minutes. Reduce heat to medium-low. Stir in tomatoes and salsa. Simmer over medium-low, stirring often, until slightly thickened, about 2 minutes.

2. Remove skillet from heat. Stir in chicken, crema, tortillas, and ½ cup of the cheese. Top evenly with remaining 1½ cups cheese.

3. Transfer skillet to oven, and broil until cheese is lightly browned, 8 to 10 minutes. Top with avocado and cilantro.

Top Your Own: Set out an assortment of flavorful fixings, such as thinly sliced radishes, crumbled Cotija cheese, pickled red onions, and pickled jalapeño slices.

Creamy Chicken Alfredo Casserole

ACTIVE 15 MIN. - TOTAL 50 MIN.
SERVES 4

- 1 (6-oz.) pkg. fresh baby spinach, chopped
- ⅓ cup refrigerated pesto sauce
- 1 (15-oz.) jar Alfredo sauce
- ¼ cup chicken broth
- 12 oz. uncooked penne pasta
- 2½ cups chopped rotisserie chicken
- 4 oz. low-moisture part-skim mozzarella cheese, shredded (about 1 cup)
- 2 Tbsp. thinly sliced fresh basil
- ¼ tsp. paprika

1. Preheat oven to 375°F. Cook pasta according to package directions.

2. Meanwhile, toss together spinach and pesto in a medium bowl.
r together Alfredo sauce and chicken broth in another bowl. Spread one-third of Alfredo mixture (about ½ cup) into a lightly greased 11- x 7-inch baking dish. Top with half of spinach mixture.

3. Stir together cooked pasta, chicken, and remaining Alfredo mixture; spoon half of chicken mixture over spinach mixture. Repeat layers once with remaining spinach mixture and chicken mixture.

4. Bake in preheated oven for 30 minutes. Remove from oven, and sprinkle with cheese. Return to oven, and bake until hot and bubbly, about 5 minutes. Top with basil and paprika.

Chicken Spaghetti Casserole

ACTIVE 1 HOUR - TOTAL 2 HOURS, 35 MIN.
SERVES 8

- 1 (4-lb.) whole chicken
- 4 Tbsp. kosher salt, plus more to taste
- 1 bay leaf
- 8 oz. uncooked spaghetti
- 3 Tbsp. butter
- 1 large yellow onion, chopped (about 2 cups)
- ½ medium-size green pepper, coarsely chopped (about ½ cup)

- 2 celery ribs, chopped
- 2 garlic cloves, minced
- 1 (10¾-oz.) can cream of mushroom soup
- 1 (28-oz.) can diced tomatoes, drained
- 1 tsp. Worcestershire sauce
- 4 drops hot sauce
- ⅛ tsp. freshly ground black pepper
  Vegetable cooking spray
- 4 oz. Cheddar cheese, shredded (about 1 cup)

1. Place chicken, 4 Tbsp. salt, bay leaf, and water to cover in a large Dutch oven. Bring to a boil over high. Cover and reduce heat to medium-low. Simmer 1 hour or until tender. Remove chicken, reserving broth in Dutch oven. Cool chicken, about 20 minutes. Discard bay leaf. Skin and bone chicken, and cut meat into pieces.

2. Preheat oven to 350°F. Remove and reserve ¼ cup chicken broth. Bring remaining broth in Dutch oven to a boil over high. Break spaghetti into thirds, and cook in broth until tender, 12 to 15 minutes; drain well, discarding broth. Return spaghetti to Dutch oven.

3. Melt butter in a skillet over medium-high. Add onion, green pepper, and celery, and cook 5 minutes or until tender; add to spaghetti. Stir together soup and reserved broth; stir into spaghetti. Stir in chicken, tomatoes, Worcestershire, hot sauce, and black pepper. Add salt to taste. Spoon mixture into a lightly greased 13- x 9-inch baking dish. Top with cheese.

4. Bake in preheated oven until bubbly, 15 to 20 minutes.

Chicken Pot Pie with Spring Vegetables

ACTIVE 20 MIN. - TOTAL 1 HOUR, 10 MIN.
SERVES 6

- ½ cup butter
- 1 large leek, thinly sliced (about 2 cups)
- 3 medium carrots, chopped (about 1 cup)
- ½ cup all-purpose flour, plus more for work surface
- 2 cups lower-sodium chicken broth
- 4 cups shredded rotisserie chicken
- 1 cup frozen petite English peas

Continued on page 340

Continued from page 339

¼ cup heavy whipping cream

2 tsp. finely chopped fresh thyme

1½ tsp. kosher salt

½ tsp. black pepper

1 large egg

1 (14.1-oz.) pkg. frozen piecrusts

1. Preheat oven to 400°F with rack in lower third of oven. Melt butter in a deep 10-inch ovenproof skillet over medium-high. Add leek and carrots. Cook, stirring often, until softened, about 6 minutes. Sprinkle with flour; cook, stirring constantly, 1 minute. Stir in broth; let mixture come to a simmer. Simmer, stirring constantly, until mixture thickens, 1 to 2 minutes. Stir in chicken, peas, cream, thyme, salt, and pepper. Remove from heat; let cool 10 minutes.

2. Whisk together egg and 1 tablespoon water in a small bowl. Roll each piecrust into a 16-inch circle on a lightly floured surface. Using a sharp knife or pizza cutter, cut piecrust into ¾-inch strips. Transfer chicken mixture to a casserole dish. Using the longest pastry strips, weave piecrust over chicken mixture to resemble a lattice. Discard any remaining crust. Lightly brush piecrust strips with egg mixture.

3. Place casserole on a rimmed baking sheet. Bake in preheated oven until top is browned and filling is bubbly, about 30 minutes. Let stand 10 minutes before serving.

Chicken-and-Biscuit Cobbler

ACTIVE 1 HOUR, 15 MIN. - TOTAL 1 HOUR, 45 MIN.
SERVES 8

3 Tbsp. butter

1 large carrot, sliced (about 1 cup)

1 medium-size onion, chopped (about 1½ cups)

2 (8-oz.) pkg. fresh mushrooms, quartered

2 garlic cloves, minced

½ cup dry white wine

⅓ cup all-purpose flour

3 cups chicken broth

¾ cup heavy whipping cream

1 Tbsp. white wine vinegar

3 Tbsp. sliced fresh chives

3 Tbsp. chopped fresh parsley

2 tsp. chopped fresh rosemary

2 tsp. chopped fresh thyme leaves

8 cups shredded cooked chicken

Kosher salt

Freshly ground black pepper

2½ cups self-rising flour

½ tsp. granulated sugar

1¼ cups chilled buttermilk

½ cup butter, melted

5 thick-cut slices bacon, cooked and chopped

Chopped fresh chives and parsley, for garnish

1. Preheat oven to 400°F. Melt the 3 tablespoons butter in a Dutch oven over medium-high. Add carrot and onion, and cook 5 minutes. Add mushrooms; cook until tender, about 5 minutes. Stir in garlic; cook 2 minutes. Add wine; cook 2 minutes. Sprinkle with ⅓ cup all-purpose flour, and cook, stirring constantly, 3 minutes. Slowly add broth, stirring constantly; bring mixture to a boil, stirring constantly, until thickened, about 2 minutes. Stir in cream, vinegar, chives, parsley, rosemary, and thyme. Stir in chicken, and season to taste with salt and pepper. Cover and remove from heat.

2. Whisk together flour and sugar in a medium bowl. Stir together buttermilk and ½ cup melted butter in a small bowl. Stir buttermilk mixture and bacon into flour mixture until dough pulls away from sides of bowl.

3. Return chicken mixture to medium-high heat; cook, stirring constantly, 2 minutes or until bubbly and hot. Spoon mixture into a buttered 3-quart ceramic or glass baking dish. Drop biscuit dough by level ¼ cupfuls, ½ inch apart, onto chicken mixture.

4. Bake in preheated oven until browned and bubbly, 30 to 35 minutes. Let stand 5 minutes before serving.

Chicken-and-Rice Bake

ACTIVE 15 MIN. - TOTAL 55 MIN.
SERVES 6

2 Tbsp. butter

1 (10-oz.) pkg. frozen chopped onions

2 (10-oz.) pkg. frozen steam-in-bag brown-and-wild rice with broccoli and carrots

3 cups chopped cooked chicken

1 (14-oz.) can chicken broth

1 (10¾-oz.) can cream of chicken soup with herbs

1 (8-oz.) container sour cream

1 (8-oz.) can diced water chestnuts, drained

¼ tsp. freshly ground black pepper

¾ cup sliced almonds

1. Preheat oven to 400°F. Melt butter in a large skillet over medium; add onions, and cook until tender, 6 to 8 minutes.

2. Stir together frozen rice, chicken, broth, soup, sour cream, water chestnuts, and pepper; stir in onions. Spoon mixture into a lightly greased 13- x 9-inch baking dish. Top with sliced almonds.

3. Bake in preheated oven until bubbly and almonds are lightly browned, 30 to 35 minutes. Let stand 10 minutes before serving.

Chicken-and-Wild Rice Skillet Casserole

ACTIVE 55 MIN. - TOTAL 1 HOUR, 40 MIN.
SERVES 4

1¼ tsp. kosher salt, divided

1 (6-oz.) pkg. uncooked wild rice

3 Tbsp. butter

⅓ cup all-purpose flour

1 cup milk

2½ cups chicken broth

1½ tsp. dry mustard

¾ tsp. freshly ground black pepper, divided

2 Tbsp. olive oil, divided

½ cup finely chopped country ham or bacon

1 medium-size yellow onion, chopped (about 1 cup)

1 large carrot, finely chopped (about ¾ cup)

1 (8-oz.) pkg. assorted fresh mushrooms, chopped

3 garlic cloves, finely chopped

2 Tbsp. dry sherry or white wine

4 boneless, skinless chicken breasts (about 1¼ lb.)

Fresh flat-leaf parsley and sliced almonds, for garnish

1. Bring ½ teaspoon of the kosher salt and 4 cups water to a boil in a 3-quart saucepan over high. Stir in rice, and return to a boil. Reduce heat to medium; cover and cook 30 minutes.

2. Meanwhile, melt butter in a heavy saucepan over low; whisk in flour until smooth. Cook, whisking constantly,

1 minute. Gradually whisk in milk, broth, and dry mustard. Increase heat to medium, and cook, whisking constantly, until mixture is thickened and bubbly, 3 to 4 minutes. Stir in ¼ teaspoon each of the salt and pepper.

3. Heat 1 tablespoon of the oil in a 12-inch cast-iron skillet over medium-high. Cook ham in hot oil, stirring occasionally, until beginning to brown, about 6 minutes. Stir in onion, carrot, and mushrooms. Cook, stirring occasionally, until onion is tender, about 6 minutes. Stir in garlic, and cook 1 minute. Add sherry, and cook, stirring constantly, until evaporated, about 1 minute. Remove mixture from skillet.

4. Preheat oven to 375°F. Sprinkle chicken with remaining ½ teaspoon each salt and pepper. Add remaining 1 tablespoon oil to skillet. Cook chicken until browned on both sides, about 8 minutes. Remove skillet from heat; transfer chicken to a plate.

5. Drain the rice. Stir together rice, ham mixture, and sauce in skillet. Place chicken on top of rice mixture.

6. Bake in preheated oven until bubbly and chicken is cooked through, about 30 minutes. Let stand 10 minutes before serving.

Chicken Tetrazzini with Prosciutto and Peas

ACTIVE 15 MIN. - TOTAL 50 MIN.
SERVES 6

- 2 tsp. vegetable oil
- 3 oz. finely chopped prosciutto
- 7 oz. uncooked vermicelli
- 3 cups chopped cooked chicken
- 4 oz. Parmesan cheese, grated (about 1 cup)
- 1 (10¾-oz.) can cream of mushroom soup
- 1 (10-oz.) container refrigerated Alfredo sauce
- 1 (4-oz.) can sliced mushrooms, drained
- ½ cup chicken broth
- ¼ cup dry white wine
- ¼ tsp. freshly ground black pepper
- 1 cup frozen petite English peas
- ½ cup slivered almonds

1. Preheat oven to 350°F. Heat oil in a small skillet over medium-high. Cook prosciutto in hot oil until crisp, 2 to 3 minutes.

2. Cook pasta according to package directions.

3. Meanwhile, stir together chicken, ½ cup of the cheese, the soup, Alfredo sauce, mushrooms, broth, wine, pepper, and peas. Spoon mixture into a lightly greased 11- x 7-inch baking dish. Sprinkle with almonds and remaining ½ cup cheese.

4. Bake in preheated oven until bubbly, about 35 minutes. Let stand 5 minutes before serving.

Pasta, Chicken, Broccoli Bake

ACTIVE 30 MIN. - TOTAL 1 HOUR, 15 MIN.
SERVES 6 TO 8

- ½ cup butter
- 1 small sweet onion, chopped (about ½ cup)
- 1 small red bell pepper, chopped (about ½ cup)
- 2 garlic cloves, minced
- ¼ cup all-purpose flour
- 3 cups chicken broth
- 1½ cups half-and-half
- ½ cup dry white wine
- 6 oz. Parmesan cheese, grated (about 1½ cups), divided
- ¼ tsp. kosher salt
- ¼ tsp. cayenne pepper
- 1 (20-oz.) pkg. refrigerated cheese-and-spinach tortellini
- 4 cups chopped fresh broccoli
- 4 cups chopped cooked chicken
- 15 round buttery crackers, crushed
- ½ cup chopped pecans
- 3 Tbsp. butter, melted

1. Preheat oven to 350°F. Melt ½ cup butter in a Dutch oven over medium-high; add onion, bell pepper, and garlic, and cook until tender, 5 to 6 minutes.
2. Add flour, and stir well. Cook, stirring constantly, 1 minute. Whisk in broth, half-and-half, and wine. Reduce heat to medium; cook, stirring constantly, until thickened and bubbly, 6 to 8 minutes.
3. Remove from heat; add 1 cup of the cheese, the salt, and cayenne, stirring until cheese melts. Stir in tortellini, broccoli, and chicken. Spoon into a lightly greased 13- x 9-inch baking dish.
4. Stir together the remaining ½ cup of the cheese, crushed crackers, pecans, and 3 tablespoons melted butter. Sprinkle over casserole. Bake in preheated oven until bubbly, 40 to 45 minutes.

Anytime Chicken and Dressing

You can either make or purchase cornbread that's to your liking for this recipe. We prefer cornbread that's not too sweet.
ACTIVE 25 MIN. - TOTAL 1 HOUR, 10 MIN.
SERVES 6

- ¼ cup butter
- 7 green onions, chopped (about 1 cup)
- 2 celery stalks, chopped (about 1 cup)
- 10 cornbread muffins, crumbled (about 3½ cups)
- ½ (16-oz.) pkg. herb-seasoned stuffing mix
- 5 cups chicken broth
- 1½ cups cooked chicken
- 2 large eggs, lightly beaten
- ½ tsp. poultry seasoning

1. Preheat oven to 350°F. Melt butter in a large skillet over medium; add green onions and celery, and cook until tender, about 5 minutes.
2. Combine crumbled cornbread, stuffing mix, broth, chicken, eggs, and poultry seasoning in a large bowl. Add cooked vegetables and stir well.
3. Spoon mixture into a lightly greased 13- x 9-inch baking dish. Bake in preheated oven, uncovered, until lightly browned, about 45 minutes.

Double-Crust Chicken Pot Pie

ACTIVE 30 MIN. - TOTAL 1 HOUR, 40 MIN.
SERVES 6 TO 8

- ½ cup butter
- 2 medium leeks, sliced
- ½ cup all-purpose flour
- 1 (14½-oz.) can chicken broth
- 3 cups chopped cooked chicken
- 1½ cups frozen cubed hash browns with onions and peppers
- 1 cup matchstick-cut carrots
- ⅓ cup chopped fresh flat-leaf parsley
- ½ tsp. kosher salt
- ½ tsp. freshly ground black pepper
- 1 (17.3-oz.) pkg. frozen puff pastry sheets, thawed
- 1 large egg

1. Preheat oven to 375°F. Melt butter in a large skillet over medium; add leeks, and cook 3 minutes. Sprinkle with flour; cook, stirring constantly, 3 minutes. Whisk in chicken broth; bring to a boil, whisking constantly. Remove from heat;

Continued on page 342

Continued from page 341

stir in chicken, hash browns, carrots, parsley, salt, and pepper.

2. Roll each pastry sheet into a 12- x 10-inch rectangle on a lightly floured surface. Fit 1 sheet into a 9-inch deep-dish pie plate; spoon chicken mixture into pastry. Place remaining pastry sheet over filling in opposite direction of bottom sheet; fold edges under, and press with tines of a fork, sealing to bottom crust. Whisk together egg and 1 tablespoon water, and brush over top of pie.

3. Bake in preheated oven on lower rack until browned, 55 to 60 minutes. Let stand 15 minutes before serving.

Chicken Enchilada Casserole

ACTIVE 30 MIN. - TOTAL 1 HOUR, 30 MIN.
SERVES 8 TO 10

- 2 Tbsp. canola oil
- 1 large sweet onion, diced (about 1½ cups)
- 2 large poblano peppers, seeded and diced (about 2 cups)
- 3 garlic cloves, minced
- 2 (10¾-oz.) cans cream of chicken soup
- 1 (8-oz.) container sour cream
- 2 (4½-oz.) cans chopped or diced green chiles
- 1 cup chicken broth
- 1 (1-oz.) envelope taco seasoning mix
- 18 (6-inch) corn tortillas, quartered
- 6 cups shredded cooked chicken
- 8 oz. extra-sharp Cheddar cheese, shredded (about 2 cups)
- 8 oz. pepper Jack cheese, shredded (about 2 cups)

1. Preheat oven to 350°F. Heat oil in a large skillet over medium-high. Cook onion and poblano peppers in hot oil until tender, about 5 minutes. Add garlic, and cook 1 minute. Stir in soup, sour cream, green chiles, chicken broth, and taco seasoning mix; remove from heat.
2. Spread 1 cup soup mixture in a lightly greased 13- x 9-inch baking dish. Arrange 24 tortilla quarters, slightly overlapping, over soup mixture; top with 3 cups chicken, ¾ cup each Cheddar and pepper Jack cheeses, and 1½ cups soup mixture. Repeat layers once. Top with remaining 24 tortilla quarters, soup mixture, and cheeses.

3. Bake in preheated oven until bubbly and golden, 45 to 50 minutes. Remove from oven to a wire rack, and let stand 15 minutes before serving.

Chicken-and-Wild Rice Casserole

ACTIVE 30 MIN. - TOTAL 1 HOUR, 15 MIN.
SERVES 10 TO 12

- 2 (6.2-oz.) boxes fast-cooking long-grain and wild rice mix
- ¼ cup butter
- 4 celery stalks, chopped (about 2 cups)
- 2 medium-size yellow onions, chopped (about 2 cups)
- 5 cups chopped cooked chicken
- 2 (10¾-oz.) cans cream of mushroom soup
- 2 (8-oz.) cans chopped water chestnuts, drained
- 1 (8-oz.) container sour cream
- 1 cup milk
- ½ tsp. kosher salt
- ½ tsp. freshly ground black pepper
- 16 oz. Cheddar cheese, shredded (about 4 cups), divided
- 2 cups soft, fresh breadcrumbs
- 1 (2¼-oz.) pkg. sliced almonds, toasted

1. Preheat oven to 350°F. Prepare rice according to package directions.
2. Meanwhile, melt butter in a large skillet over medium; add celery and onions. Cook until tender, about 10 minutes. Stir in chicken, soup, water chestnuts, sour cream, milk, salt, pepper, rice, and 3 cups of the cheese. Spoon mixture into a lightly greased 15- x 10-inch baking dish or 2 (11- x 7-inch) baking dishes. Top with breadcrumbs.
3. Bake in preheated oven for 35 minutes. Sprinkle with remaining 1 cup cheese, and top with almonds. Bake 5 minutes. Let stand 5 minutes before serving.

Cajun Chicken-and-Wild Rice Casserole

Omit salt and pepper. Reduce chicken to 2½ cups. Prepare as directed, cooking 1 lb. **andouille sausage**, chopped, and 1 **green bell pepper**, diced, with celery in Step 2. Stir 1 (15-oz.) can **black-eyed peas**, drained, and 1 tsp. **Cajun seasoning** into rice mixture. Proceed as directed.

Chicken-Mushroom-Sage Casserole

ACTIVE 1 HOUR - TOTAL 1 HOUR, 40 MIN.
SERVES 6

- ½ cup butter, divided
- 6 boneless, skinless chicken breasts
- 3 shallots, chopped
- 2 garlic cloves, minced
- 1 lb. assorted fresh mushrooms, coarsely chopped
- ¼ cup dry sherry
- 3 Tbsp. all-purpose flour
- 2 (14-oz.) cans chicken broth
- 1 (6-oz.) pkg. long-grain and wild rice mix
- 2 oz. Parmesan cheese, grated (about ½ cup)
- 2 Tbsp. chopped fresh flat-leaf parsley
- 1 Tbsp. chopped fresh sage
- ½ tsp. kosher salt
- ½ tsp. black pepper
  Vegetable cooking spray
- ½ cup sliced almonds, toasted

1. Preheat oven to 375°F. Melt 1 tablespoon of the butter in a large skillet over medium-high; add half the chicken, and cook 3 minutes or until browned; turn and cook 1 minute. Transfer to a plate. (Chicken will not be cooked completely.) Repeat with another 1 tablespoon butter and remaining chicken. Wipe skillet clean.
2. Melt 2 tablespoons of the butter in skillet over medium-high. Add shallots, and cook until translucent, about 3 minutes. Add garlic, and cook 30 seconds. Add mushrooms; cook, stirring often, until tender, 4 to 5 minutes. Stir in sherry, and cook, stirring often, 1 minute.
3. Melt remaining ¼ cup butter in a large saucepan over medium-high. Whisk in flour; cook, whisking constantly, 1 minute. Gradually whisk in broth. Bring to a boil, whisking constantly, and cook, whisking constantly, until slightly thickened, 1 to 2 minutes. Remove from heat; add rice (reserve flavor packet for another use), cheese, parsley, sage, salt, pepper, and shallot mixture. Lightly grease a 13- x 9-inch baking dish with cooking spray. Spoon mixture into dish. Top with chicken.
4. Bake in preheated oven until a meat thermometer inserted in the thickest portion of the chicken registers 165°F, 30 to 35 minutes. Remove from oven, and let stand 10 minutes. Sprinkle with almonds.

King Ranch Chicken

ACTIVE 1 HOUR · TOTAL 1 HOUR, 40 MIN.
SERVES 12

- 6 Tbsp. butter
- 1 large yellow onion, chopped (about 1½ cups)
- 1 large red bell pepper, chopped (about 1 cup)
- 2 medium poblano peppers, chopped (about 2 cups)
- 1 jalapeño pepper, seeded and chopped
- 2 garlic cloves, chopped
- 1 Tbsp. chili powder
- 1 Tbsp. ground cumin
- 1 tsp. kosher salt
- ½ tsp. freshly ground black pepper
- ¼ cup all-purpose flour
- 1¾ cups reduced-sodium chicken broth
- 1 (10-oz.) can diced tomatoes with green chiles, drained
- 1½ cups sour cream
- 5 cups coarsely chopped smoked chicken (about 2 lb.)
- 1 cup loosely packed fresh cilantro leaves, chopped
- 8 oz. Monterey Jack cheese, shredded (about 2 cups)
- 8 oz. sharp Cheddar cheese, shredded (about 2 cups)
- 18 (8-inch) soft taco-size corn tortillas
- ¼ cup canola oil
  Vegetable cooking spray

1. Preheat oven to 375°F. Melt butter in a large skillet over medium-high. Add onion, bell pepper, poblano peppers, and jalapeño pepper; cook, stirring occasionally, until softened and lightly browned, 8 to 10 minutes. Stir in garlic, chili powder, cumin, salt, and black pepper; cook, stirring occasionally, 1 minute.
2. Sprinkle flour over vegetable mixture, and cook, stirring constantly, 1 minute. Whisk in broth, and increase heat to high. Bring to a boil, stirring constantly. Boil, stirring occasionally, until thickened, 1 to 2 minutes. Remove from heat. Stir in tomatoes and sour cream.
3. Stir together chicken and cilantro in a large bowl; stir in vegetable mixture. Combine Monterey Jack and Cheddar cheeses in a small bowl.
4. Heat a large cast-iron skillet over high. Lightly brush each tortilla on both sides with canola oil. Cook tortillas,

in batches, in hot skillet until lightly browned and crisp, 1 to 2 minutes on each side.
5. Line bottom of a lightly greased (with cooking spray) 13- x 9-inch baking dish with 6 tortillas, overlapping slightly, to cover bottom of dish. Top with half the chicken mixture and one-third of cheese. Repeat layers once. Top with remaining tortillas and cheese. Lightly coat a sheet of aluminum foil with cooking spray, and cover baking dish.
6. Bake in preheated oven for 20 minutes. Uncover and bake until bubbly and lightly browned on top, about 10 minutes. Let stand 10 minutes before serving.

Creamy Chicken and Bacon with Herbed Puff Pastry

ACTIVE 45 MIN. · TOTAL 45 MIN.
SERVES 4

- 4 boneless, skinless chicken breasts (about 1½ lb.)
- 3 cups chicken broth
- 1 tsp. kosher salt, divided
- ½ (17.3-oz.) pkg. frozen puff pastry sheets (1 sheet), thawed
- 1 large egg, lightly beaten
- 12 fresh parsley leaves
- ¼ tsp. black pepper
- 2 (6-oz.) pkg. steam-in-bag fresh English peas or 3 cups frozen English peas
- 4 bacon slices
- 3 Tbsp. salted butter
- 1 medium Vidalia or other sweet onion, chopped (about 1 cup)
- 1 large celery stalk, cut diagonally into ¼-inch slices (about ½ cup)
- ¼ cup all-purpose flour
- ½ cup heavy whipping cream
- 2 oz. fontina cheese, shredded (about ½ cup)

1. Preheat oven to 400°F. Place chicken, broth, and ½ teaspoon of the salt in a large saucepan; bring to a boil over high. Reduce heat to medium-low; cover and cook until chicken is cooked through, about 15 minutes. Remove from heat, and let stand about 20 minutes. Remove chicken from stock, reserving 2½ cups of the stock. Coarsely shred chicken.
2. Meanwhile, place puff pastry sheet on a baking sheet lined with parchment paper. Cut pastry sheet into 4 squares;

separate squares. Brush squares lightly with egg; top each square with 3 parsley leaves, pressing gently to adhere. Sprinkle with pepper. Bake on oven rack in bottom third of preheated oven until dough is puffed and golden brown, 12 to 14 minutes.
3. Cook peas according to package directions; keep warm.
4. Cook bacon in a large skillet over medium-high until crisp, about 6 minutes. Remove bacon to a paper towel-lined plate, reserving drippings in skillet; crumble bacon. Add butter to hot drippings in skillet, and cook over medium until butter melts, about 1 minute. Add onion and celery; cook, stirring often, until onion is tender and celery is tender-crisp, about 8 minutes. Add flour, and cook, stirring constantly, about 1 minute. Stir in cream and reserved 2½ cups stock; bring to a simmer, stirring often. Stir in peas, cheese, chicken, bacon, and remaining ½ teaspoon salt; reduce heat to medium-low, and cook until mixture is thickened and thoroughly heated, about 10 minutes.
5. Divide mixture among 4 shallow bowls, and top each with a puff pastry square. Serve immediately.

Creamy Tex-Mex Cornbread Bake

ACTIVE 20 MIN. · TOTAL 45 MIN.
SERVES 6

- 2 lb. ground turkey
- 1 cup sliced green onions
- 1 (10¾ -oz.) can cream of mushroom soup
- 1 cup milk
- 1 (4-oz.) can chopped green chiles
- 4 oz. pepper Jack cheese, shredded, divided (about 1 cup)
- ¼ cup chopped fresh cilantro or parsley
  Salt and freshly ground black pepper
  Vegetable cooking spray
- 1 (6-oz.) pkg. buttermilk cornbread mix
- 3 Tbsp. chopped fresh cilantro

1. Preheat oven to 400°F. Cook ground turkey in a large skillet over medium, stirring often, until meat crumbles and is no longer pink, about 5 minutes. Add green onions, and cook 2 minutes.

Continued on page 344

Continued from page 343

2. Stir in soup, milk, and green chiles. Bring to a low boil, and remove from heat. Stir in ¾ of the cup cheese and the ¼ cup cilantro. Season to taste with salt and black pepper. Pour turkey mixture into a 2-quart baking dish coated with cooking spray.

3. Stir together cornbread mix, ¾ cup water, the 3 tablespoons cilantro, and remaining ¼ cup cheese. Pour cornbread mixture over turkey mixture in baking dish.

4. Bake in preheated oven until golden, 20 to 25 minutes. Let stand 5 minutes before serving.

Mini Turkey Pot Pies with Dressing Tops

ACTIVE 1 HOUR · TOTAL 3 HOURS, 15 MIN.

SERVES 8

CRUST

3¾ cups all-purpose flour, plus more for work surface

1½ tsp. sea salt

1½ cups cold unsalted butter, cut into cubes

1 cup cold whole buttermilk

FILLING

6 Tbsp. unsalted butter, divided

½ cup all-purpose flour

2 cups chicken broth

1¾ cups whole milk

1½ tsp. sea salt

¾ tsp. freshly cracked black pepper

1 small yellow onion, finely chopped (about ½ cup)

2 garlic cloves, minced

4 small carrots, peeled and thinly sliced (about 1½ cups)

1½ cups sliced fresh green beans

1 cup frozen English peas

1 Tbsp. chopped fresh thyme leaves

1 Tbsp. chopped fresh sage leaves

2 lb. cooked turkey breast, chopped

TOPPING

½ cup unsalted butter

2 (6-oz.) pkg. stuffing mix

EQUIPMENT

8 (6-inch) cast-iron skillets

1. Prepare the Crust: Whisk together flour and salt in a medium bowl. Add cold cubed butter, and use your fingers to quickly work butter into flour mixture. (Some butter pieces will be the size of oat flakes, and some will be the size of peas.) Create a well in flour mixture, and pour in cold buttermilk. Use a fork to bring dough together, moistening all flour bits. Dump dough mixture onto a lightly floured work surface. Dough will be moist and shaggy. Divide dough in 2 pieces, and gently knead each piece into a disk. Wrap each disk in plastic wrap, and chill 1 hour.

2. Meanwhile, prepare the Filling: Melt 4 tablespoons of the butter in a large saucepan over medium. Whisk in flour, and cook, whisking constantly, about 1 minute. (Mixture will be very thick.) Reduce heat to low; gradually add chicken broth, whisking constantly until no flour bits remain. Whisk in milk. Increase heat to medium-low; cook, whisking often, until mixture is consistency of thick pudding, about 20 minutes. Remove from heat, and whisk in salt and pepper.

3. Melt remaining 2 tablespoons butter in a large skillet over medium. Add onion; cook, stirring constantly, until translucent, about 3 minutes. Add garlic; cook, stirring constantly, 1 minute. Add carrots and green beans; cook, stirring occasionally, 5 minutes. (Vegetables will not be cooked through.) Stir in peas, thyme, and sage; cook 1 minute. Remove from heat, and stir in turkey. Stir turkey-vegetable mixture into stock mixture in saucepan; cool slightly, about 5 minutes.

4. Prepare the Topping: Bring 3 cups water and the butter to a boil in a large saucepan over medium, stirring occasionally to melt butter. Add stuffing mix, and gently stir to combine. Cover and remove from heat. Let stand 10 minutes.

5. Remove 1 pie dough disk from refrigerator. Unwrap and roll dough into a ¼-inch-thick round on a lightly floured surface. Cut an 8-inch circle from a piece of parchment paper. Use parchment round as a guide to cut eight 8-inch rounds from piecrust using a sharp knife. Fit 1 piecrust round in bottom and up sides of each skillet. Repeat with remaining dough disk, rerolling scraps as needed, until all 8 skillets are lined.

6. Preheat oven to 375°F, and place racks in lower and upper third of oven. Spoon about 1½ cups filling into each crust; cover with about ¾ cup topping. Bake in preheated oven until crust is golden brown and filling is lightly bubbling, 45 to 50 minutes, rotating skillets halfway through baking. Remove from oven, and let stand 20 minutes before serving.

Seafood

New Tuna Casserole

ACTIVE 35 MIN. · TOTAL 1 HOUR, 30 MIN.

SERVES 8

16 oz. uncooked ziti pasta

2 medium leeks, sliced

18 oz. haricots verts (French green beans), cut into 1-inch pieces

6 Tbsp. butter, divided

2 (4-oz.) pkg. gourmet mushroom blend

¼ cup all-purpose flour

3 cups heavy whipping cream

1 cup vegetable broth

8 oz. sharp white Cheddar cheese, shredded (about 2 cups)

1½ oz. Parmesan cheese, grated (about 6 Tbsp.), divided

¾ tsp. kosher salt

½ tsp. freshly ground black pepper

1 (12-oz.) can solid white tuna in spring water, drained

2 Tbsp. chopped fresh chives

1 Tbsp. chopped fresh tarragon or parsley

¼ cup crushed potato chips

¼ cup panko breadcrumbs

2 Tbsp. butter, melted

Sliced fresh chives, for garnish

1. Preheat oven to 350°F. Cook pasta according to package directions.

2. Remove and discard root ends and dark green tops of leeks. Cut in half lengthwise, and rinse thoroughly under cold running water to remove grit and sand. Thinly slice leeks.

3. Meanwhile, cook green beans in enough boiling salted water to cover 30 seconds to 1 minute or until crisp-tender; drain. Plunge into ice water to stop the cooking process; drain.

4. Melt 2 tablespoons of the butter in a large skillet over medium-high. Add leeks, and cook 2 minutes; add mushrooms, and cook until lightly browned, about 5 minutes. Transfer leek mixture to a small bowl. Wipe skillet clean.

5. Melt remaining 4 tablespoons butter in skillet over medium; whisk in flour, and cook, whisking constantly, 2 minutes. Gradually whisk in cream and broth. Bring mixture to a boil, stirring often. Reduce heat to medium-low; gradually whisk in Cheddar cheese and 4 tablespoons of the Parmesan until smooth. Stir in salt and pepper.

6. Stir cheese mixture into pasta. Stir in tuna, chives, tarragon, green beans, and leek mixture; transfer to a lightly greased 13- x 9-inch baking dish.

7. Stir together potato chips, breadcrumbs, the 2 tablespoons melted butter, and remaining 2 tablespoons Parmesan in a small bowl; sprinkle over pasta mixture.

8. Bake in preheated oven until bubbly, 35 to 40 minutes. Let stand 5 minutes before serving.

Baked Shrimp Risotto

ACTIVE 15 MIN. - TOTAL 55 MIN.

SERVES 4

- ⅓ cup butter
- 4 garlic cloves, minced
- 1 cup Arborio rice
- 4 cups chicken broth
- 1 lb. large shrimp, peeled and deveined
- 2 tsp. fresh thyme leaves
- ¼ tsp. salt
- ¼ tsp. freshly ground black pepper
- 2 oz. Parmesan cheese, grated (about ½ cup)

1. Preheat oven to 375°F. Melt butter in a large ovenproof Dutch oven over medium-high. Add garlic, and cook 1 minute. Add rice, and cook, stirring often, until rice is toasted, about 2 minutes. Stir in chicken broth and bring to a boil. Cover and bake in preheated oven until liquid is almost absorbed, about 25 minutes.

2. Remove from oven. Stir in shrimp; cover and bake 5 minutes more. Remove from oven, and let stand, covered, 10 minutes.

3. Uncover and stir in thyme, salt, and pepper. Sprinkle with cheese and serve.

Creamy Seafood Pot Pie

ACTIVE 25 MIN. - TOTAL 45 MIN.

SERVES 4 TO 6

- ½ cup butter
- 1 sweet potato, peeled and cubed
- 2 small leeks, chopped
- 1 cup chopped celery
- 1 Tbsp. chopped fresh thyme
- 3 garlic cloves, minced
- ½ cup all-purpose flour
- 4 cups milk
- 1½ lb. cod or halibut filet, cut into 2-inch cubes
- 1½ cups trimmed and halved green beans or haricots verts (French green beans), blanched
- 1½ tsp. salt
- ½ tsp. freshly ground black pepper
- 1 (17.3-oz.) pkg. frozen puff pastry sheets (2 sheets), thawed
- 1 large egg yolk

1. Preheat oven to 400°F. Melt butter in a large Dutch oven over medium-high. Cook potato, leeks, and celery until tender, about 10 minutes. Add thyme and garlic; cook 1 minute. Sprinkle flour over vegetables and cook, stirring constantly, 3 minutes. Whisk in milk; bring to a boil. Reduce heat to low, and simmer until potato is almost tender, 2 to 3 minutes. Add cod, green beans, salt, and pepper; return mixture to a simmer. Remove from heat. (Fish will be undercooked.) Ladle filling into 4 to 6 individual ovenproof soup crocks.

2. Roll out pastry on a lightly floured surface until smooth. Cut pastry into circles, cutting the circles 1 inch larger than the mouth of the soup crocks. Whisk together egg yolk and 1 tablespoon water; brush underside of pastry edges to seal. Brush tops with egg wash. Place crocks on baking sheet.

3. Bake in preheated oven until pastry is golden brown, 14 to 16 minutes. Let stand 5 minutes before serving.

Shrimp Casserole

ACTIVE 15 MIN. - TOTAL 1 HOUR

SERVES 6

- 1 cup uncooked long-grain rice
- ¼ cup butter
- 2 lb. medium shrimp, peeled and deveined

- 1 (10-oz.) pkg. frozen diced onion, red and green bell peppers, and celery
- 4 garlic cloves, minced
- 1 (10¾-oz.) can cream of shrimp soup
- 1 (10-oz.) container refrigerated Alfredo sauce
- ⅓ cup dry white wine or chicken broth
- ½ tsp. Cajun seasoning
- ¼ tsp. cayenne pepper
- 3 oz. Parmesan cheese, grated (about ¾ cup), divided

1. Preheat oven to 400°F. Bring 2 cups water to a boil; stir in rice, and cover. Reduce heat, and simmer 20 minutes or until water is absorbed and rice is tender.

2. Meanwhile, melt butter in a large skillet over medium-high. Add shrimp, frozen diced vegetables, and garlic; cook just until shrimp turn pink, 4 to 5 minutes. Stir in soup, Alfredo sauce, wine, Cajun seasoning, cayenne pepper, cooked rice, and ½ cup of the cheese. Spoon into a lightly greased 11- x 7-inch baking dish. Sprinkle with remaining ¼ cup Parmesan.

3. Bake in preheated oven until bubbly, 25 to 30 minutes. Let stand 5 minutes.

Cajun Shrimp Casserole

ACTIVE 30 MIN. - TOTAL 1 HOUR, 5 MIN.

SERVES 6

- 2 lb. large shrimp, peeled and deveined
- ¼ cup butter
- 1 small red onion, chopped (about ½ cup)*
- 1 small red bell pepper chopped (about ½ cup)*
- 1 small yellow bell pepper, chopped (about ½ cup)*
- 1 small green bell pepper, chopped (about ½ cup)*
- 4 garlic cloves, minced
- 2 cups fresh or frozen sliced okra
- 1 Tbsp. fresh lemon juice
- 1½ tsp. kosher salt
- 3 cups cooked long-grain rice
- 1 (10¾-oz.) can cream of shrimp soup**
- ½ cup dry white wine
- 1 Tbsp. soy sauce

Continued on page 346

Continued from page 345

½ tsp. cayenne pepper

1 oz. Parmesan cheese, grated (about ¼ cup)

1. Preheat oven to 350°F. Melt butter in a large skillet over medium-high. Add onion and chopped bell peppers, and cook until tender, about 7 minutes. Add garlic, and cook 1 minute. Stir in okra, lemon juice, and salt; cook 5 minutes. Add shrimp, and cook 3 minutes or until shrimp turn pink. Stir in rice, soup, wine, soy sauce, and cayenne until blended. Pour into a lightly greased 11- x 7-inch baking dish.

2. Sprinkle with Parmesan cheese. Bake in preheated oven until bubbly and cheese is lightly browned, 15 to 20 minutes.

* 1 (10-oz.) pkg. frozen chopped onions and peppers may be substituted for fresh onion and bell peppers.

** 1 (10¾-oz.) can cream of mushroom soup may be substituted for cream of shrimp soup.

Shrimp and Grits Casserole

ACTIVE 25 MIN. - TOTAL 1 HOUR
SERVES 6

2 cups whole milk

2¼ cups heavy whipping cream, divided

1 cup uncooked quick-cooking grits

¼ cup butter

1 large egg, lightly beaten

8 oz. sharp Cheddar cheese, shredded (about 2 cups)

1½ tsp. kosher salt, divided

5 thick-cut bacon slices, chopped

1 small red onion, finely chopped (about ½ cup)

1 small red bell pepper, finely chopped (about ½ cup)

2 garlic cloves, minced

⅓ cup all-purpose flour

1 lb. medium shrimp, peeled and deveined

½ cup dry white wine

1 cup chicken broth

1 Tbsp. chopped fresh flat-leaf parsley

2 tsp. chopped fresh thyme leaves

½ tsp. black pepper

⅛ tsp. cayenne pepper

¼ cup sliced scallions

1. Preheat oven to 350°F. Coat an 11- x 7-inch baking dish with cooking spray. Bring milk and 2 cups of the heavy cream to a boil in a medium saucepan over medium-high. Stir in grits and butter; let mixture return to a boil, whisking often. Reduce heat to medium; cook, whisking constantly, until grits are tender, 5 to 7 minutes. Remove from heat; stir in egg, cheese, and 1 teaspoon of the salt. Spoon mixture into prepared baking dish. Cover; bake in preheated oven until mixture is set, 35 to 40 minutes.

2. Meanwhile, cook bacon in a large saucepan over medium-high, stirring occasionally, until crisp, about 8 minutes. Drain on paper towels, reserving 3 tablespoons drippings in pan. Add onion and bell pepper to pan. Cook over medium-high, stirring often, until softened, about 3 minutes. Add garlic; cook, stirring constantly, 30 seconds. Add flour; cook, stirring constantly, 1 minute. Add shrimp; cook, stirring constantly, until shrimp are pink, about 3 minutes. Add wine; cook, stirring constantly, until thickened, about 2 minutes. Stir in broth, parsley, thyme, black pepper, cayenne pepper, and remaining ¼ cup heavy cream and ½ teaspoon salt.

3. Spoon shrimp mixture over baked grits casserole using a slotted spoon; sprinkle with scallions and cooked bacon. Pour shrimp gravy from pan into a serving bowl; serve alongside casserole.

Beef & Pork

Shepherd's Pie

ACTIVE 40 MIN. - TOTAL 1 HR., 20 MIN., INCLUDING MASHED POTATOES
(SERVES 8)

1½ lb. ground beef

1 medium-size onion, chopped (about 1 cup)

½ (8-oz.) pkg. fresh mushrooms, sliced

1 garlic clove, minced

1 cup frozen English peas, thawed

4 tsp. beef bouillon granules

½ tsp. salt

½ tsp. dried thyme

¼ tsp. freshly ground black pepper

1 Tbsp. all-purpose flour

1 (14½-oz.) can stewed tomatoes

1 bay leaf

2 Tbsp. red wine vinegar

Cheese-and-Carrot Mashed Potatoes (recipe follows)

1. Preheat oven to 400°F. Brown ground beef in a large nonstick skillet over medium-high, stirring often, until meat crumbles and is no longer pink, about 10 minutes. Remove ground beef from skillet using a slotted spoon, reserving 2 tablespoons drippings in skillet. Reduce heat to medium.

2. Cook onion, mushrooms, and garlic in hot drippings until tender, 10 to 11 minutes. Stir in ground beef, peas, bouillon, salt, thyme, and pepper. Sprinkle flour over meat mixture. Increase heat to medium-high, and cook, stirring constantly, 1 minute. Stir in tomatoes, bay leaf, and vinegar, breaking up large tomato pieces with a spoon. Reduce heat to medium; cook, stirring often, until slightly thickened, about 3 minutes. Remove bay leaf.

3. Transfer mixture to a lightly greased 3-quart baking dish. Spoon Cheese-and-Carrot Mashed Potatoes evenly over meat mixture, smoothing with back of spoon.

4. Bake in preheated oven until thoroughly heated through, about 15 minutes. Let stand 5 minutes before serving.

Cheese-and-Carrot Mashed Potatoes

ACTIVE 20 MIN. - TOTAL 30 MIN.
SERVES 8

1 (1-lb.) pkg. baby carrots

1 Tbsp. butter

1 (22-oz.) pkg. frozen mashed potatoes

2½ cups milk

4 oz. Cheddar cheese, shredded (about 1 cup)

1 Tbsp. fresh thyme leaves

1 tsp. salt

¼ tsp. freshly ground black pepper

1. Place carrots and ¼ cup water in a large microwave-safe bowl. Cover

tightly with plastic wrap; fold back a small edge to allow steam to escape. Microwave on HIGH 8 to 10 minutes or until carrots are tender. Drain.
2. Stir in butter. Coarsely mash carrots with a potato masher.
3. Prepare potatoes according to package directions, using the 2½ cups milk. Stir in cheese, thyme, salt, pepper, and carrot mixture until well blended.

Baked Linguine with Meat Sauce

ACTIVE 30 MIN. - TOTAL 1 HOUR
SERVES 8

- 2 lb. lean ground beef
- 2 garlic cloves, minced
- 1 (28-oz.) can crushed tomatoes
- 1 (8-oz.) can tomato sauce
- 1 (6-oz.) can tomato paste
- 2 tsp. sugar
- 1 tsp. salt
- 8 oz. uncooked linguine
- 1 (16-oz.) container sour cream
- 1 (8-oz.) pkg. cream cheese, softened
- 1 bunch green onions, chopped
- 8 oz. sharp Cheddar cheese, shredded (about 2 cups)

1. Preheat oven to 350°F. Brown ground beef and garlic in a Dutch oven over medium-high, stirring often, until meat crumbles and is no longer pink. Stir in tomatoes, tomato sauce, tomato paste, sugar, and salt. Simmer for 30 minutes.
2. Cook pasta according to package directions; drain. Place in a lightly greased 13- x 9-inch baking dish.
3. Stir together sour cream, cream cheese, and green onions. Spread over pasta. Top with meat sauce.
4. Bake in preheated oven until thoroughly heated through, 20 to 25 minutes. Sprinkle with Cheddar cheese, and bake 5 more minutes or until cheese melts. Let stand 5 minutes before serving.

Homestyle Ground Beef Casserole

ACTIVE 25 MIN. - TOTAL 1 HOUR, 20 MIN.
SERVES 6

- 1 lb. ground beef
- 1 (14½-oz.) can diced tomatoes with basil, garlic, and oregano, undrained

---

- 1 (10-oz.) can diced tomatoes and green chiles, undrained
- 1 (6-oz.) can tomato paste
- 1 tsp. salt
- ½ tsp. dried Italian seasoning
- ¼ tsp. black pepper
- 3 cups uncooked medium egg noodles
- 5 green onions, chopped (about ¾ cup)
- 1 (8-oz.) container sour cream
- 1 (3-oz.) pkg. cream cheese, softened
- 4 oz. sharp Cheddar cheese, shredded (about 1 cup)
- 4 oz. Parmesan cheese, grated (about 1 cup)
- 4 oz. mozzarella cheese, shredded (about 1 cup)

1. Brown ground beef in a large skillet over medium, stirring constantly, until meat crumbles and is no longer pink, 5 to 8 minutes; drain. Stir in both cans of tomatoes, tomato paste, salt, Italian seasoning, and pepper. Bring to a boil; reduce heat, and simmer, uncovered, 5 minutes. Remove from heat; set aside.
2. Preheat oven to 350°F. Cook egg noodles according to package directions. Stir together hot cooked noodles, green onions, sour cream, and cream cheese until blended; spoon mixture into a lightly greased 13- x 9-inch baking dish. Top with beef mixture; sprinkle with Cheddar cheese, Parmesan cheese, and mozzarella cheese in order listed.
3. Bake in preheated oven, covered, for 35 minutes. Uncover and bake 5 minute more. Let stand 10 to 15 minutes before serving.

Taco Beef-Noodle Bake

ACTIVE 25 MIN. - TOTAL 55 MIN.
SERVES 6

- 1 lb. ground beef
- 1 small yellow onion, chopped (about ½ cup)
- 1 (15-oz.) can tomato sauce
- 1 (1¼-oz.) pkg. taco seasoning mix
- 10 oz. uncooked medium egg noodles
- 2 cups small-curd cottage cheese
- ¼ cup sour cream
- 1 Tbsp. all-purpose flour
- 2 tsp. beef bouillon granules
- 2 green onions, chopped (about ¼ cup)
- 4 oz. mozzarella cheese, shredded (about 1 cup)

---

1. Preheat oven to 350°F. Cook ground beef and onion in a large skillet over medium-high until meat is browned, stirring often, 5 to 8 minutes; drain. Add tomato sauce, ½ cup water, and taco seasoning mix; bring to a boil. Reduce heat, and simmer 10 minutes.
2. Cook noodles according to package directions; drain. Combine noodles, cottage cheese, sour cream, flour, bouillon granules, and green onions in a large bowl; mix well. Spoon noodle mixture into a greased 2½-quart casserole. Top with meat mixture.
3. Bake in preheated oven for 25 minutes; sprinkle with mozzarella, and bake until cheese melts, about 5 minutes more. Let stand 10 minutes before serving.

Meatball Pasta Bake

ACTIVE 30 MIN. - TOTAL 1 HOUR, 10 MIN.
SERVES 8 TO 10

- 16 oz. uncooked penne pasta
- 2 Tbsp. olive oil
- 1 small sweet onion, chopped (about 1 cup)
- 1 medium-size fennel bulb, thinly sliced (optional)
- 3 garlic cloves, minced
- 1 tsp. fennel seeds
- 2 (24-oz.) jars marinara sauce
- 2 (14-oz.) pkg. frozen beef meatballs, thawed
- 1 cup fresh orange juice
- ¾ cup chicken broth
- 1 tsp. firmly packed orange zest
- 1 medium-size red bell pepper, chopped
- ½ tsp. kosher salt, plus more to taste
- 1 cup torn fresh basil
- 1½ (8-oz.) pkg. fresh mozzarella cheese slices
  Fresh basil leaves, for garnish

1. Preheat oven to 350°F. Cook pasta according to package directions.
2. Heat oil in a Dutch oven over medium. Cook onion and, if desired, fennel until tender, 8 to 10 minutes. Add garlic and fennel seeds, and cook 1 minute. Stir in marinara sauce, meatballs, orange juice, chicken broth, orange zest, bell pepper, and ½ teaspoon salt; increase heat to medium-high, and bring to a boil. Reduce heat to medium-low; cover and

Continued on page 348

Continued from page 347

simmer 10 minutes. Remove from heat, and stir in torn basil, cooked pasta, and salt to taste. Transfer to a lightly greased 13- x 9-inch baking dish. Place dish on an aluminum foil-lined baking sheet. Top with cheese.
3. Bake in preheated oven until bubbly, about 25 minutes.

Beefy Baked Ravioli

ACTIVE 30 MIN. - TOTAL 35 MIN.
SERVES 6

- 1 lb. lean ground beef
- 1 Tbsp. olive oil
- 1 medium-size red onion, thinly sliced (about 3 cups)
- 3 garlic cloves, minced
- 1 (28-oz.) can crushed tomatoes
- 1 cup chicken broth
- 1 tsp. dried Italian seasoning
- 1 tsp. kosher salt
- ¼ tsp. black pepper
- 1 (20-oz.) pkg. refrigerated four-cheese ravioli
- 1 (5-oz.) pkg. baby spinach
- 4 oz. low-moisture part-skim mozzarella, shredded (about 1 cup)
- 2 oz. Parmesan cheese, grated (about ½ cup)
- ¼ cup torn fresh basil leaves

1. Preheat oven to broil with rack 9 inches from heat. Cook beef in a 12-inch cast-iron skillet over medium-high, stirring often, until browned, 8 to 10 minutes. Remove beef; drain and set aside. Wipe skillet clean.
2. Heat oil in skillet over medium-high; add onion, and cook, stirring occasionally, until tender, 8 to 10 minutes. Add garlic to skillet; cook, stirring constantly, until fragrant, about 1 minute. Stir in crushed tomatoes, broth, Italian seasoning, salt, pepper, and ravioli. Bring to a boil; reduce heat to medium. Cover and simmer until ravioli are tender, about 8 minutes. Uncover and return cooked beef to skillet. Stir in half of spinach, and cook just until wilted. Repeat with remaining spinach. Top with mozzarella and Parmesan.
3. Broil in preheated oven until cheese is melted and golden, about 6 minutes. Remove from oven, and top with basil. Let stand 5 minutes before serving.

Saucy Sausage Manicotti

ACTIVE 30 MIN. - TOTAL 1 HR., 20 MIN.
SERVES 7

- 8 oz. uncooked manicotti shells
- 1 (16-oz.) pkg. Italian sausage, casings removed
- 1 large onion, chopped
- 9 garlic cloves, minced, divided
- 1 (26-oz.) jar seven-herb tomato pasta sauce
- 1 (8-oz.) container chive-and-onion cream cheese
- 24 oz. mozzarella cheese, shredded (about 6 cups), divided
- 3 oz. Parmesan cheese, grated (about ¾ cup)
- 1 (15-oz.) container ricotta cheese
- ¾ tsp. freshly ground black pepper

1. Preheat oven to 350°F. Cook manicotti according to package directions.
2. Cook sausage, onion, and half of the garlic in a large Dutch oven over medium-high until sausage crumbles and is no longer pink, about 6 minutes. Stir in pasta sauce; bring to a boil. Remove from heat.
3. Combine cream cheese, 4 cups of the mozzarella, the Parmesan, ricotta, pepper, and remaining garlic in a large bowl, stirring until blended.
4. Spoon 1 cup sauce mixture into a lightly greased 13- x 9-inch baking dish. Cut a slit down the length of each cooked manicotti shell. Spoon cheese mixture evenly into noodles, gently pressing cut sides together. Arrange stuffed pasta over sauce in dish, seam sides down. Spoon remaining sauce over stuffed pasta. Sprinkle with remaining 2 cups mozzarella cheese.
5. Bake, covered, in preheated oven until bubbly, about 50 minutes. Let stand 5 minutes before serving.

Cheese-Crusted Pizza Pot Pies

ACTIVE 30 MIN. - TOTAL 55 MIN.
SERVES 4

- 1 (12-oz.) pkg. pork sausage links, casings removed, or ¾ lb. ground beef
- ⅔ cup chopped onion
- ⅔ cup finely chopped carrots
- ½ cup chopped green bell pepper
- 3 garlic cloves, finely chopped
- 1¼ cups marinara sauce
- ⅔ cup sliced pepperoni
- ⅓ cup chopped pimiento-stuffed green olives
- 4 oz. shredded Italian cheese blend (1 cup)
  Vegetable cooking spray
- 1 (11-oz.) can refrigerated thin pizza crust dough
- 1 large egg, lightly beaten
- 8 slices part-skim mozzarella cheese

1. Preheat oven to 450°F. Cook sausage, onion, carrots, bell pepper, and garlic in a 12-inch skillet over medium, stirring occasionally, until sausage crumbles and is no longer pink, 10 to 12 minutes; drain. Stir in marinara sauce, pepperoni, and olives. Simmer until thickened, about 5 minutes. Remove from heat; stir in cheese blend.
2. Coat bottoms, sides, and rims of 4 (10-oz.) ramekins with cooking spray. Spoon meat mixture into dishes. Place on a large rimmed baking sheet.
3. Unroll dough on large cutting board. Cut in half lengthwise, then cut in half crosswise. Place 1 dough piece over meat mixture in each dish, overlapping rim. Brush with egg. Top each pot pie with 2 slices cheese, overlapping slightly. Bake in preheated oven until crust is golden brown, 16 to 20 minutes. Let stand 5 minutes before serving.

Baked Ziti with Sausage

Pancetta is the same thing as bacon without the smoke. Find it in the deli case of most supermarkets. Consider trying San Marzano tomatoes in place of regular crushed tomatoes in the sauce.

ACTIVE 30 MIN. - TOTAL 55 MIN.
SERVES 8

- 12 oz. uncooked ziti pasta
- 4 oz. pancetta or bacon, diced
- 1 large onion, chopped (about 2 cups)
- 3 garlic cloves, chopped
- 1 (1-lb.) pkg. ground Italian sausage
- 1 cup dry red wine
- 1 (28-oz.) can crushed tomatoes
- ½ cup firmly packed torn fresh basil
- ½ tsp. kosher salt
- ½ tsp. crushed red pepper
- 1 cup ricotta cheese
- 1 (8-oz.) pkg. shredded mozzarella cheese, divided
  Vegetable cooking spray
- 2 oz. Parmesan cheese, grated (½ cup)

1. Preheat oven to 350°F. Cook ziti according to package directions for al dente.
2. Meanwhile, cook pancetta in a large skillet over medium-high 3 minutes. Add onion and garlic, and cook 3 minutes or until onion is tender. Add sausage, and cook 5 minutes or until meat is no longer pink. Add wine, and cook 3 minutes. Stir in tomatoes, basil, salt, and crushed red pepper. Reduce heat to low; cook, stirring occasionally, 3 minutes.
3. Stir ricotta and 1 cup of the mozzarella into hot cooked pasta. Lightly grease a 13- x 9-inch baking dish with cooking spray. Transfer pasta mixture to prepared dish, and top with sausage mixture. Sprinkle with Parmesan and remaining 1 cup mozzarella.
4. Bake in preheated oven until bubbly, 25 to 30 minutes.

Pizza Casserole Deluxe
ACTIVE 40 MIN. - TOTAL 1 HOUR, 15 MIN.
SERVES 10

- 1 Tbsp. olive oil
- 1 (1-lb.) pkg. ground mild Italian sausage
- 2 garlic cloves, minced
- 1 (26-oz.) jar marinara sauce
- 1 tsp. kosher salt, divided
- ½ medium-size red onion, chopped
- ½ medium-size red bell pepper, chopped
- ½ medium-size green bell pepper, chopped
- ½ (8-oz.) pkg. sliced baby portobello mushrooms
- 1 cup sliced black olives
- ½ cup pepperoni slices, chopped
- 16 oz. uncooked rigatoni pasta
- 3 Tbsp. butter
- 3 Tbsp. all-purpose flour
- 3 cups half-and-half
- 8 oz. fresh mozzarella cheese, shredded (about 2 cups)
- 2 oz. Parmesan cheese, grated (about ½ cup)
- ½ tsp. freshly ground black pepper
- 1 (8-oz.) pkg. shredded mozzarella cheese
- 8 to 10 pepperoni slices

1. Preheat oven to 350°F. Heat oil in a large skillet over medium-high. Cook sausage and garlic in hot oil until sausage crumbles and is no longer pink,

5 to 7 minutes. Remove with a slotted spoon, reserving drippings in skillet. Drain sausage mixture on paper towels, and transfer to a medium bowl. Stir marinara sauce and ½ teaspoon of the salt into sausage mixture.
2. Cook onion, bell peppers, and mushrooms in drippings in skillet until tender, about 5 minutes; stir in olives and chopped pepperoni. Set aside, reserving ¼ cup onion mixture.
3. Cook pasta according to package directions in a large Dutch oven.
4. Melt butter in a heavy saucepan over low; whisk in flour until smooth. Cook, whisking constantly, 1 minute. Gradually whisk in half-and-half; cook over medium, whisking constantly, until mixture is thickened and bubbly, 7 to 10 minutes. Stir in fresh mozzarella, Parmesan, pepper, and remaining ½ teaspoon salt. Pour sauce over cooked pasta in Dutch oven, stirring to coat. Stir in onion mixture.
5. Transfer pasta mixture to a lightly greased 13- x 9-inch baking dish, and top with sausage mixture, packaged mozzarella cheese, reserved ¼ cup onion mixture, and pepperoni slices.
6. Bake in preheated oven until cheese is melted and lightly browned, about 30 minutes. Let stand 5 minutes before serving.

Ham-and-Vegetable Cobbler
ACTIVE 30 MIN. - TOTAL 1 HOUR, 20 MIN.
SERVES 6

- ¼ cup butter
- ¼ cup all-purpose flour
- 3½ cups milk
- ½ tsp. dried thyme
- 1 tsp. chicken bouillon granules
- 2 cups diced cooked ham
- 1 (10-oz.) pkg. frozen sweet peas and mushrooms
- 1 cup frozen crinkle-cut carrots
- 1 (14.1-oz.) pkg. refrigerated piecrusts (2 crusts)

1. Preheat oven to 450°F. Melt butter in a large saucepan over medium. Gradually whisk in flour, and cook, whisking constantly, 1 minute. Add milk, thyme, and bouillon. Cook, stirring constantly, until thickened and bubbly, 6 to 8 minutes. Stir in ham, peas and mushrooms, and carrots; cook until mixture is thoroughly heated through,

4 to 5 minutes. Spoon into a lightly greased 11- x 7-inch baking dish.
2. Unroll each piecrust on a lightly floured surface. Cut piecrusts into 1¼-inch-wide strips. Arrange strips in a lattice design over ham mixture.
3. Bake in preheated oven until crust is browned and filling is bubbly, about 40 minutes. Let stand 5 minutes before serving.

Ham-and-Greens Pot Pie with Cornbread Crust
ACTIVE 35 MIN. - TOTAL 1 HOUR
SERVES 8 TO 10

FILLING
- 2 Tbsp. vegetable oil
- 4 cups chopped cooked ham
- 3 Tbsp. all-purpose flour
- 3 cups chicken broth
- 1 (14-oz.) pkg. frozen diced onion, bell pepper, and celery mix
- 1 (16-oz.) pkg. frozen chopped collard greens
- 1 (15.8-oz.) can black-eyed peas, drained and rinsed
- ½ tsp. crushed red pepper
  Vegetable cooking spray

CRUST
- 1½ cups self-rising white cornmeal
- ½ cup all-purpose flour
- 1 tsp. sugar
- 2 large eggs, lightly beaten
- 1½ cups buttermilk

1. Prepare the Filling: Preheat oven to 425°F. Heat oil in a Dutch oven over medium-high. Cook ham in hot oil until lightly browned, about 5 minutes. Add flour to Dutch oven, and cook, stirring constantly, 1 minute. Gradually add chicken broth, and cook, stirring constantly, until broth begins to thicken, about 3 minutes.
2. Bring mixture to a boil, and add onion, bell pepper, and celery mix and collard greens; return to a boil, and cook, stirring often, 15 minutes.
3. Stir in black-eyed peas and crushed red pepper; spoon hot mixture into a lightly greased 13- x 9-inch baking dish.
4. Prepare the Crust: Stir together cornmeal, flour, and sugar in a large bowl, and make a well in the center of mixture. Add eggs and buttermilk,

Continued on page 350

Continued from page 349

stirring just until dry ingredients are moistened. Pour batter evenly over hot filling mixture.

5. Bake in preheated oven until crust is golden brown and set, 20 to 25 minutes. Let stand 5 minutes before serving.

Pulled Pork Enchilada Casserole

We also love this with smoky shredded barbecue brisket or chicken in place of the pork, or try small cooked, peeled shrimp.
ACTIVE 30 MIN. · TOTAL 1 HOUR, 30 MIN.
SERVES 8 TO 10

- 2 Tbsp. canola oil
- 1 large sweet onion, diced (about 1½ cups)
- 2 large poblano peppers, seeded and diced (about 2 cups)
- 3 garlic cloves, minced
- 2 (10¾-oz.) cans cream of chicken soup
- 1 (8-oz.) container sour cream
- 2 (4½-oz.) cans chopped or diced green chiles
- 1 cup chicken broth
- 1 (1-oz.) envelope taco seasoning mix
- 18 (6-inch) corn tortillas, quartered
- 6 cups shredded pulled pork
- 8 oz. extra-sharp Cheddar cheese, shredded (about 2 cups)
- 8 oz. pepper Jack cheese, shredded (about 2 cups)

1. Preheat oven to 350°F. Heat oil in a large skillet over medium-high. Cook onion and poblanos until tender, about 5 minutes. Add garlic and cook 1 minute. Stir in soup, sour cream, green chiles, chicken broth, and taco seasoning; remove from heat.
2. Spread 1 cup soup mixture in a lightly greased 13- x 9-inch baking dish. Arrange 24 tortilla quarters, slightly overlapping, over soup mixture; top with 3 cups pulled pork, ¾ cup each Cheddar and pepper Jack cheeses, and 1½ cups soup mixture. Repeat layers once. Top with remaining 24 tortilla quarters, soup mixture, and cheeses.
3. Bake in preheated oven until bubbly and golden, 45 to 50 minutes. Remove from oven to a wire rack, and let stand 15 minutes before serving.

Reunion Pea Casserole
ACTIVE 35 MIN. · TOTAL 1 HOUR, 35 MIN.
SERVES 12

- 1 lb. mild Italian sausage, casings removed
- 2 (16-oz.) cans black-eyed peas, drained
- 1 (4-oz.) can chopped green chiles, drained
- 1 tsp. garlic powder
- ¼ tsp. ground cumin
- ¼ tsp. dried oregano
- ½ tsp. black pepper
- ½ tsp. kosher salt
- 2 Tbsp. unsalted butter
- 2 medium yellow squash, sliced (about 2 cups)
- 2 medium zucchini, sliced (about 2 cups)
- 1 small onion, chopped (about ½ cup)
- 4 large eggs, well beaten
- 8 oz. mozzarella cheese, shredded (about 2 cups)
- 8 oz. Cheddar cheese, shredded (about 2 cups)
- 2 (8-oz.) cans refrigerated crescent rolls

1. Preheat oven to 350°F. Cook sausage in a large skillet over medium, stirring to crumble, until browned, about 8 minutes. Drain sausage well. Transfer sausage to a large bowl, and stir in peas, chiles, garlic powder, cumin, oregano, pepper, and salt.
2. Melt butter in the same skillet over medium, and add squash, zucchini, and onion. Cook, stirring occasionally, until softened, about 8 to 10 minutes; drain well. Cool 5 minutes. Stir together eggs and cheeses in a separate bowl; fold in squash mixture.
3. Separate crescent roll dough into 2 long rectangles; pinch dough seams together. Place dough in a lightly greased 13- x 9-inch baking dish; press dough on bottom and up sides to form crust, using a knife to cut away excess dough. Bake in preheated oven until crust begins to set, about 10 minutes.
4. Remove from oven, and layer sausage-pea mixture over crust; top with squash mixture. Return to oven, and bake until casserole is set, 25 to 30 minutes. Let stand 15 minutes before serving.

Smoked-Pork-Stuffed Shells
ACTIVE 20 MIN. · TOTAL 1 HOUR, 10 MIN.
(IF FREEZING, ADD 24 HOURS THAWING AND 20 MIN. BAKING)
SERVES 6

- 24 uncooked jumbo pasta shells
- 1 lb. chopped smoked pork
- 10 oz. ricotta cheese (about 1¼ cups)
- ¾ cup panko breadcrumbs
- 3 large garlic cloves, minced
- 1 tsp. kosher salt
- ½ tsp. black pepper
- ¼ tsp. crushed red pepper
- 8 oz. mozzarella cheese, shredded (about 2 cups), divided
- ¼ cup plus 2 Tbsp. chopped fresh flat-leaf parsley, divided
- 1 (24-oz.) jar marinara sauce
- ¾ cup bottled barbecue sauce

1. Preheat oven to 375°F. Cook pasta in according to package directions. Drain and transfer to a baking sheet. Cool 15 minutes.
2. Meanwhile, stir together pork, ricotta cheese, breadcrumbs, garlic, salt, black pepper, red pepper, 1 cup of the mozzarella, and ¼ cup of the parsley in a large bowl. Stir together marinara and barbecue sauces in a separate bowl. Spread 1¾ cups of the marinara mixture in the bottom of a 13- x 9-inch baking dish.
3. Fill each cooled shell with 2 heaping tablespoons pork mixture, and arrange in prepared baking dish. Pour remaining 2 cups marinara mixture over shells.
4. Sprinkle shells with remaining 1 cup mozzarella. Cover with aluminum foil. Bake in preheated oven until heated through, 20 to 25 minutes. Uncover; bake until bubbly, about 20 minutes more. Sprinkle with remaining 2 tablespoons parsley.

Tomato, Cheddar, and Bacon Pie

For best results, seed the tomatoes and drain the slices before baking.
ACTIVE 45 MIN. · TOTAL 3 HOURS
SERVES 6 TO 8

CRUST
- 2¼ cups self-rising soft-wheat flour
- 1 cup cold butter, cut up
- 8 bacon slices, cooked and chopped
- ¾ cup sour cream

FILLING

- 2¾ lb. assorted large tomatoes, divided
- 2 tsp. kosher salt, divided
- 6 oz. extra-sharp Cheddar cheese, shredded (about 1½ cups)
- 2 oz. Parmigiano-Reggiano cheese, grated (about ½ cup)
- ½ cup mayonnaise
- 1 large egg, lightly beaten
- 2 Tbsp. fresh dill sprigs
- 1 Tbsp. chopped fresh chives
- 1 Tbsp. chopped fresh flat-leaf parsley
- 1 Tbsp. apple cider vinegar
- 1 green onion, thinly sliced (about 2 Tbsp.)
- 2 tsp. sugar
- ¼ tsp. freshly ground black pepper
- 1½ Tbsp. plain yellow cornmeal

1. Prepare the Crust: Place flour in bowl of a heavy-duty electric stand mixer; cut in cold butter with a pastry blender or fork until mixture resembles small peas. Chill 10 minutes.
2. Add bacon to flour mixture; beat on low speed just until combined. Gradually add sour cream, ¼ cup at a time, beating just until blended after each addition.
3. Spoon mixture onto a heavily floured surface; sprinkle lightly with flour, and knead 3 or 4 times, adding more flour as needed. Roll in a 13-inch round. Gently place dough in a 9-inch fluted tart pan with 2-inch sides and removable bottom. Press dough into pan; trim off excess dough along edges. Chill 30 minutes.
4. Meanwhile, prepare the Filling: Cut 2 pounds of the tomatoes into ¼-inch-thick slices, and remove seeds. Place tomatoes in a single layer on paper towels; sprinkle with 1 teaspoon of the salt. Let stand 30 minutes.
5. Preheat oven to 425°F. Stir together Cheddar cheese, Parmigiano-Reggiano, mayonnaise, egg, dill, chives, parsley, vinegar, green onion, sugar, pepper, and remaining 1 teaspoon salt in a large bowl until combined.
6. Pat tomato slices dry with a paper towel. Sprinkle cornmeal over bottom of crust. Lightly spread ½ cup cheese mixture onto crust; layer with half of tomato slices in slightly overlapping rows. Spread with ½ cup cheese mixture. Repeat layers, using remaining

tomato slices and cheese mixture. Cut remaining ¾ lb. tomatoes into ¼-inch-thick slices, and arrange on top of pie.
7. Bake in preheated oven 40 to 45 minutes, shielding edges with foil during last 20 minutes to prevent excessive browning. Let stand 1 to 2 hours before serving.

Vegetarian & Sides

Zucchini-and-Spinach Lasagna

ACTIVE 15 MIN · TOTAL 55 MIN.
SERVES 4

- 1 (8-oz.) container whipped chive-and-onion cream cheese
- 1 (15-oz.) container ricotta cheese
- ⅓ cup chopped fresh basil
- 1 tsp. kosher salt
- 5 medium zucchini, thinly sliced (about 2½ lb.)
- 2 Tbsp. olive oil
- 1 (10-oz.) pkg. fresh spinach
- 2 garlic cloves, pressed
- 6 no-boil lasagna noodles
- 1 (7-oz.) pkg. shredded mozzarella cheese

  Fresh basil leaves, for garnish (optional)

1. Preheat oven to 425°F. Stir together cream cheese, ricotta cheese, chopped , and salt in a bowl.
2. Heat oil in a large skillet over medium-high. Cook zucchini in hot oil in a large skillet over medium-high until lightly browned, 3 to 4 minutes. Add spinach; gently toss until wilted. Add garlic; cook 1 minute.
3. Spoon one-third of the vegetable mixture into a lightly greased 9-inch square baking dish; top with 2 noodles and one-third of ricotta mixture. Repeat twice. Sprinkle with mozzarella.
4. Bake in preheated oven, covered with lightly greased aluminum foil, until bubbly and noodles are tender, 25 to 30 minutes. Uncover and bake until golden, 5 to 10 minutes. Let stand 10 minutes before serving. Garnish with basil leaves, if desired.

Eggplant Parmesan Lasagna

To reduce bitterness and make the eggplant slices firmer (not mushy), sprinkle both sides with salt, then place on paper towels for 10 minutes to rid of excess moisture. Pat dry before seasoning with salt and pepper in Step 2.
ACTIVE 1 HOUR, 10 MIN. · TOTAL 2 HOURS, 35 MIN.
SERVES 8 TO 10

- 2 (26-oz.) jars tomato, garlic, and onion pasta sauce
- ¼ cup chopped fresh basil
- ½ tsp. crushed red pepper
- ½ cup heavy whipping cream
- 4 oz. Parmesan cheese, grated (about 1 cup)
- 1 large eggplant (about 1½ lb.)
- ½ tsp. salt
- ¼ tsp. freshly ground black pepper
- 1 cup all-purpose flour
- 3 large eggs, lightly beaten
- 6 Tbsp. olive oil
- 6 lasagna noodles, cooked and drained
- 1 (15-oz.) container low-fat ricotta cheese
- 8 oz. mozzarella cheese, shredded (about 2 cups)

  Fresh basil leaves, for garnish

1. Preheat oven to 350°F. Heat pasta sauce, basil, and crushed red pepper in a large saucepan over medium-low for 30 minutes. Remove from heat; stir in cream and Parmesan cheese. Set aside.
2. Peel eggplant, and cut crosswise into ¼-inch thick slices. Sprinkle slices evenly with salt and black pepper. Set up a dredging station: Place flour in a shallow bowl or plate. Stir together eggs and 3 tablespoons water in a separate shallow bowl. Dredge eggplant slices in flour; dip into egg mixture, and dredge again in flour, shaking off excess.
3. Heat 1½ tablespoons of the olive oil in a large nonstick skillet over medium-high. Cook eggplant, in batches, in hot oil until golden brown and slightly softened, about 4 minutes each side. Drain on paper towels. Repeat with remaining oil and eggplant, wiping skillet clean after each batch, if necessary.
4. Layer 3 lasagna noodles lengthwise in a lightly greased 13- x 9-inch baking dish. Top with one-third tomato sauce mixture and half of eggplant. Dollop

Continued on page 352

Continued from page 351

half of ricotta cheese on eggplant; top with half of mozzarella. Repeat layers with remaining noodles, one-third sauce mixture, remaining eggplant, and remaining ricotta. Top with remaining one-third sauce mixture and mozzarella cheese.

5. Bake in preheated oven until golden brown, 35 to 40 minutes. Let stand 20 minutes before serving.

Sweet Potato, Cauliflower, and Greens Casserole

ACTIVE 55 MIN. - TOTAL 1 HOUR, 45 MIN.
SERVES 6 TO 8

- 1 head cauliflower (1½ to 2 lb.), cut into small florets
- 1 (8-oz.) pkg. cremini mushrooms, stemmed and halved
- 6 Tbsp. olive oil, divided
- 1 tsp. ground cumin, divided
- 1 tsp. kosher salt, divided, plus more to taste
- ¼ tsp. freshly ground black pepper, divided, plus more to taste
- 3 large sweet potatoes (2½ to 3 lb.), peeled and cut into ¼-inch-thick slices
- 2 garlic cloves, minced
- 4 cups chopped fresh kale, collards, or mustard greens
- 2 tsp. red wine vinegar
- 1 (14-oz.) can butter beans, drained and rinsed (optional)
  Easy Cheese Sauce (recipe follows)
- ½ cup panko breadcrumbs
- 1 Tbsp. chopped fresh cilantro
- 1 tsp. extra-virgin olive oil

1. Preheat oven to 475°F. Toss together cauliflower, mushrooms, 2½ tablespoons of the oil, ½ teaspoon of the cumin, ½ teaspoon of the salt, and ⅛ teaspoon of the pepper in a medium bowl. Spread cauliflower mixture in a single layer on a rimmed baking sheet.
2. Toss together sweet potatoes, 2½ tablespoons oil, and remaining ½ teaspoon cumin, ½ teaspoon salt, and ⅛ teaspoon pepper. Spread in a single layer on another rimmed baking sheet.
3. Bake potatoes and cauliflower in preheated oven until browned and just tender, 10 to 12 minutes, turning once. Cool on wire racks 10 minutes.

4. Reduce oven temperature to 375°F. Heat remaining 1 tablespoon oil in a large skillet over medium-high. Add garlic; cook, stirring often, 1 minute. Add kale; cook, stirring occasionally, until tender, about 10 minutes. Add salt and pepper to taste; stir in vinegar.
5. Layer half each of sweet potatoes, cauliflower mixture, beans (if desired), kale, and 1½ cups Easy Cheese Sauce in a lightly greased 13- x 9-inch baking dish. Repeat layers once. Top with remaining ½ cup cheese sauce. Stir together panko, cilantro, and extra-virgin olive oil, and sprinkle crumb mixture over casserole.
6. Bake in preheated oven until thoroughly heated, bubbly, and golden brown, 20 to 25 minutes. Let stand 5 minutes before serving.

Easy Cheese Sauce

ACTIVE 25 MIN. - TOTAL 25 MIN.
MAKES 3½ CUPS

- ⅓ cup dry vermouth or dry sherry
- 1 garlic clove, minced
- 3 cups half-and-half
- 3 Tbsp. cornstarch
- 1 tsp. kosher salt
- ½ tsp. freshly ground black pepper
- 8 oz. pepper Jack cheese, shredded (about 2 cups)

1. Bring vermouth and garlic to a boil in a large skillet over medium-high; reduce heat to medium-low, and simmer until vermouth is reduced to 1 tablespoon, 7 to 10 minutes.
2. Whisk together half-and-half and cornstarch. Whisk half-and-half mixture, salt, and pepper into vermouth mixture; bring to a boil over medium-high, whisking constantly. Boil, whisking constantly, until mixture is thickened, about 1 minute. Add cheese. Reduce heat to low, and simmer, whisking constantly, until cheese is melted and sauce is smooth, about 1 minute. Remove from heat, and use immediately.

Old-Fashioned Tomato Pie

Don't skip salting the tomatoes. This step rids them of excess juice so the pie won't get soggy.

ACTIVE 50 MIN. - TOTAL 3 HOURS, 25 MIN.
SERVES 6 TO 8

PIECRUST
- 1¼ cups all-purpose flour
- ¼ cup cold vegetable shortening, cut into pieces
- ¼ cup cold unsalted butter, cut into pieces
- ½ tsp. fine sea salt
- 3 to 4 Tbsp. ice-cold water

FILLING
- 2¼ lb. assorted heirloom tomatoes, thinly sliced
- 1¼ tsp. kosher salt, divided
- 1 small sweet onion, chopped (about 1 cup)
- 1¼ tsp. freshly ground black pepper, divided
- 1 Tbsp. canola oil
- ½ cup assorted chopped fresh herbs (such as chives, parsley, and basil)
- 2 oz. Gruyère cheese, grated (about ½ cup)
- 2 oz. Parmigiano-Reggiano cheese, grated (about ½ cup)
- ¼ cup mayonnaise

1. Prepare the Piecrust: Process flour, shortening, butter, and salt in a food processor until mixture resembles coarse meal. With processor running, gradually add 3 tablespoons ice-cold water, 1 tablespoon at a time, and process until dough forms a ball and leaves sides of bowl, adding up to 1 tablespoon more water, if necessary. Shape dough into a disk, and wrap in plastic wrap. Chill 30 minutes.
2. Unwrap dough, and place on a lightly floured surface; sprinkle lightly with flour. Roll dough to ⅛-inch thickness.
3. Preheat oven to 425°F. Press dough into a 9-inch pie plate. Trim dough 1 inch larger than diameter of pie plate; fold overhanging dough under itself along rim of pie plate. Chill 30 minutes or until firm.
4. Line piecrust with aluminum foil; fill with pie weights or dried beans. Place on an aluminum foil-lined baking sheet.
5. Bake in preheated oven for 20 minutes. Remove weights and foil. Bake 5 minutes or until browned. Cool completely on baking sheet on a wire

rack (about 30 minutes). Reduce oven temperature to 350°F.

6. Prepare the Filling: Place tomatoes in a single layer on paper towels; sprinkle with 1 teaspoon of the salt. Let stand 10 minutes.

7. Meanwhile, cook onion and ¼ teaspoon each salt and pepper in hot oil in a skillet over medium until onion is tender, about 3 minutes.

8. Pat tomatoes dry with a paper towel. Layer tomatoes, onion, and herbs in prepared crust, seasoning each layer with some of the remaining 1 teaspoon pepper. Stir together cheeses and mayonnaise; spread over pie.

9. Bake for 30 minutes or until lightly browned, shielding edges with foil to prevent excessive browning. Serve hot, warm, or at room temperature.

Farro-and-Wild Mushroom Casserole

ACTIVE 25 MIN. - TOTAL 1 HOUR, 10 MIN.
SERVES 8 TO 10

- 1 cup uncooked pearled farro
- ½ lb. Swiss chard with stems
- 3 Tbsp. extra-virgin olive oil
- 8 oz. shiitake mushrooms, stemmed and sliced (about 3¼ cups)
- 8 oz. cremini mushrooms, sliced (about 3¼ cups)
- 1 tsp. kosher salt
- 1 large carrot, peeled and diced (about 1½ cups)
- ½ large yellow onion, diced (about 1½ cups)
- 1½ cups mushroom broth (such as Pacific), divided
- ¼ cup dry white wine
- 4 Tbsp. butter, divided
- 3 Tbsp. all-purpose flour
- 4 oz. Parmesan cheese, grated (about 1 cup)
- ½ cup panko breadcrumbs
- ¼ cup chopped fresh flat-leaf parsley

1. Preheat oven to 400°F. Bring 2 cups water and the farro to a boil in a saucepan over high. Reduce heat to low; simmer until tender, 20 minutes. Drain and set aside.

2. Finely chop the chard stems to equal 2 cups. Roughly chop the leaves to equal 3½ cups. Heat oil in a large ovenproof skillet over medium–high. Add all mushrooms and the salt; cook, stirring occasionally, until browned, about

8 minutes. Add carrot, onion, and chard stems; cook, stirring often, until tender, about 5 minutes. Add chard leaves and ¼ cup of the broth; cover. Cook until wilted, 3 to 4 minutes.

3. Uncover skillet; add wine, stirring to loosen browned bits from the bottom. Simmer until the liquid has evaporated, about 1 minute. Stir in 3 tablespoons of the butter; cook until melted. Sprinkle flour over the mixture, stirring constantly. Gradually add remaining 1¼ cups mushroom broth, ½ cup at a time, stirring to incorporate. Bring mixture to a simmer, and cook, stirring often, until thickened, about 2 minutes. Remove from heat, and stir in cheese and cooked farro.

4. Melt remaining 1 tablespoon butter, and toss with panko; sprinkle mixture over farro in skillet. Transfer to preheated oven, and bake until edges are bubbly, about 30 minutes. Remove and sprinkle with parsley. Let stand 10 minutes before serving.

French Onion Soup Casserole

ACTIVE 1 HOUR, 20 MIN. - TOTAL 1 HOUR, 50 MIN.
SERVES 6

- ¼ cup unsalted butter
- 5 medium-size Vidalia onions, thinly sliced (about 3 lb.)
- 2 tsp. kosher salt
- ½ tsp. black pepper
- 3 fresh thyme sprigs
- 2 fresh flat-leaf parsley sprigs
- 2 bay leaves
- 1 (16-oz.) baguette, thinly sliced
- ⅓ cup all-purpose flour
- 3 cups reduced-sodium beef broth
- ½ cup dry sherry
- 8 oz. Gruyère cheese, shredded (about 2 cups)
- 1 tsp. fresh thyme leaves

1. Melt butter in a Dutch oven over medium–low; add onions, salt, pepper, thyme and parsley sprigs, and bay leaves; cook, stirring often, until onions are golden brown, about 1 hour.

2. Meanwhile, preheat oven to 350°F. Arrange baguette slices in a single layer on a baking sheet. Bake in preheated oven until lightly toasted, about 12 minutes. Set aside.

3. Remove and discard thyme and parsley sprigs and bay leaves from onion mixture. Add flour, and cook,

stirring constantly, 2 minutes. Add broth and sherry; bring to a boil over high. Boil, stirring constantly, until slightly thickened, 2 to 3 minutes.

4. Layer half of the toasted baguette slices in a 13- x 9-inch baking dish. Spoon onion mixture evenly over bread. Top evenly with remaining baguette slices. Sprinkle with cheese; cover with aluminum foil. Bake for 30 minutes. Increase heat to broil. Remove foil; broil until cheese is bubbly, about 3 minutes. Sprinkle with fresh thyme leaves.

Caramelized Onion Mashed Potato Bake

To caramelize onions, cook thinly sliced yellow or sweet onions in a mix of oil and butter over medium-low heat for about 45 minutes. When they are a deep golden-brown and almost jammy, deglaze the pan with water, broth, or dry white wine to loosen all the yummy browned bits and goodness.

ACTIVE 25 MIN. - TOTAL 55 MIN.
SERVES 6 TO 8

- 4 lb. russet potatoes, peeled and cut into 2-inch pieces
- 3 tsp. salt, divided
- 1¼ cups buttermilk, warmed
- ½ cup milk, warmed
- ¼ cup butter, melted
- ½ tsp. freshly ground black pepper
- 5 oz. Gruyère cheese, shredded (1¼ cups)
- 1 cup chopped caramelized onions
- 2 Tbsp. chopped fresh parsley

1. Preheat oven to 350°F. Bring potatoes, 2 teaspoons of the salt, and water to cover to a boil in a large Dutch oven over medium–high. Cook until tender, about 20 minutes; drain. Return potatoes to Dutch oven, reduce heat to low, and cook, stirring occasionally, until potatoes are dry, 3 to 5 minutes.

2. Mash potatoes with a potato masher to desired consistency. Stir in buttermilk, milk, butter, pepper, and remaining 1 teaspoon salt, stirring just until blended.

3. Stir in cheese, caramelized onions, and parsley, and spoon the mixture into a lightly greased 2½-quart baking dish or 8 (10-ounce) ramekins. Bake in preheated oven until potatoes are lightly golden brown on top, about 35 minutes.

Two-Potato Gratin

ACTIVE 45 MIN. - TOTAL 1 HOUR, 45 MIN.
SERVES 10 TO 12

- ¼ cup butter, divided
- 2 shallots, diced
- 2 cups heavy whipping cream
- 2 Tbsp. chopped fresh parsley
- 1 Tbsp. chopped fresh chives
- 1 tsp. kosher salt
- ½ tsp. ground white pepper
- ⅛ tsp. freshly grated nutmeg
- 1½ lb. Yukon gold potatoes
- 1½ lb. sweet potatoes
- 2 cups milk
- Softened butter, for greasing baking dish
- 6 oz. Gruyère cheese, shredded (about 1½ cups)
- 1 oz. Parmesan cheese, grated (about ¼ cup)

1. Preheat oven to 375°F. Heat 3 tablespoons of the butter in a saucepan over medium. Cook shallots in hot butter 2 minutes. Stir in cream, parsley, chives, salt, white pepper, and nutmeg. Cook 2 minutes. Remove from heat; cool 15 minutes.
2. Meanwhile, peel and thinly slice Yukon gold and sweet potatoes. Combine all sliced potatoes and milk in a large microwave-safe bowl. Cover with plastic wrap, and microwave on HIGH 5 minutes. Uncover and gently stir mixture. Re-cover and microwave 5 minutes more. Drain mixture, discarding milk.
3. Grease a 13- x 9-inch baking dish with softened butter. Layer one-third of the potatoes in the dish; top with one-third of cream mixture, and sprinkle with ½ cup of the Gruyère cheese. Repeat layers twice, and top with Parmesan. Cut remaining 1 tablespoon butter into small pieces, and dot over top. Cover with aluminum foil.
4. Bake in preheated oven for 30 minutes. Uncover and bake until browned, about 20 minutes more. Let stand 10 minutes before serving.

Cheddar Cheese Grits Casserole

ACTIVE 10 MIN. - TOTAL 50 MIN.
SERVES 6

- 4 cups milk
- ½ cup butter
- 1 cup quick-cooking grits
- 1 large egg, lightly beaten
- 8 oz. sharp Cheddar cheese, shredded (2 cups)
- 1 tsp. salt
- ½ tsp. freshly ground black pepper
- 1 oz. Parmesan cheese, grated (about ¼ cup)

1. Preheat oven to 350°F. Bring milk just to a boil in a large saucepan over medium-high; gradually whisk in butter and grits. Reduce heat, and simmer, whisking constantly, until grits are done, 5 to 7 minutes. Remove from heat.
2. Stir in egg, Cheddar cheese, salt, and pepper. Pour into a lightly greased 11- x 7-inch baking dish. Sprinkle with Parmesan cheese.
3. Bake, covered, in preheated oven until mixture is set, 35 to 40 minutes.

Savory Corn Pudding

ACTIVE 25 MIN. - TOTAL 1 HOUR, 10 MIN.
SERVES 12

- 3 Tbsp. all-purpose flour
- 2 Tbsp. granulated sugar
- 2 tsp. baking powder
- 2 tsp. kosher salt
- 6 large eggs
- 2 cups heavy whipping cream
- ½ cup butter, melted and cooled
- 2 Tbsp. canola oil
- 6 cups fresh corn kernels (from 8 ears)
- 1 small sweet onion, chopped (about ½ cup)
- 2 Tbsp. chopped fresh thyme, divided

1. Preheat oven to 350°F. Stir together flour, sugar, baking powder, and salt in a small bowl until blended. Whisk together eggs, cream, and melted butter in a medium bowl until blended.
2. Heat canola oil in a large skillet over medium-high. Add corn and onion, and cook, stirring often, until onion is softened, about 5 minutes. Stir in 1 tablespoon of the thyme. Remove from heat, and let cool slightly, about 5 minutes. Stir flour mixture and corn mixture into egg mixture. Spoon into a 13- x 9-inch (3-quart) baking dish, and bake in preheated oven until set and golden brown, about 40 minutes. Let stand 5 minutes before serving. Sprinkle with remaining 1 tablespoon thyme.

Green Chile-Corn Pudding

Omit chopped fresh thyme. Prepare recipe as directed, cooking 1 cup seeded, chopped **poblano chile** (from 1 medium chile) with corn and onion in Step 2. Stir 1 (8-oz.) pkg. **shredded Mexican cheese blend** (2 cups); 1 (5-oz.) can **mild diced green chiles**, drained; and ¼ cup chopped **fresh cilantro** into corn mixture before baking. Garnish with additional torn cilantro.

Three Cheese-Corn Pudding

Omit chopped fresh thyme. Prepare recipe as directed, stirring 3 oz. each shredded **white Cheddar, sharp yellow Cheddar**, and **Parmesan cheeses** (about ¾ cup each) and ¼ cup chopped **fresh flat-leaf parsley** into cooled corn mixture in Step 2. Bake casserole as directed.

Grandma Gwen's Beans

ACTIVE 45 MIN. - TOTAL 2 HOURS, 5 MIN.
SERVES 10

- 1 lb. bacon
- 4 medium-size yellow onions, sliced (about 4 cups)
- ½ cup firmly packed light brown sugar
- ½ cup apple cider vinegar
- 1 tsp. kosher salt
- 1 tsp. dry mustard
- ½ tsp. garlic powder
- 2 (16-oz.) cans butter beans, drained and rinsed
- 1 (15-oz.) can lima beans, drained and rinsed
- 1 (16-oz.) can kidney beans, drained and rinsed
- 1 (28-oz.) can baked beans

1. Preheat oven to 350°F. Cook bacon, in batches, in a large skillet over medium-high until crisp, 8 to 10 minutes. Remove bacon, and drain on paper towels, reserving desired amount of drippings in skillet. (We reserved about 3 tablespoons.) Crumble bacon.
2. Cook onions in hot drippings over medium until tender, 8 to 10 minutes. Add brown sugar, vinegar, salt, dry mustard, and garlic powder. Cover and cook 20 minutes.
3. Combine butter beans, lima beans, kidney beans, baked beans, and onion mixture in a 13- x 9-inch baking dish.
4. Bake in preheated oven for 1 hour.

Baking at High Altitudes

Liquids boil at lower temperatures (below 212°F) and moisture evaporates more quickly at high altitudes. Both of these factors significantly impact the quality of baked goods. Also, leavening gases (air, carbon dioxide, water vapor) expand faster. If you live at 3,000 feet or below, first try a recipe as is. Sometimes few, if any, changes are needed. But the higher you go, the more you'll have to adjust your ingredients and cooking times.

A Few Overall Tips

- Use shiny new baking pans. This seems to help mixtures rise, especially cake batters.
- Use butter, flour, and parchment paper to prep your baking pans for nonstick cooking. At high altitudes, baked goods tend to stick more to pans.
- Be exact in your measurements (once you've figured out what they should be). This is always important in baking, but especially so when you're up so high. Tiny variations in ingredients make a bigger difference at high altitudes than at sea level.
- Boost flavor. Seasonings and extracts tend to be more muted at higher altitudes, so increase them slightly.
- Have patience. You may have to bake your favorite sea-level recipe a few times, making slight adjustments each time, until it's worked out to suit your particular altitude.

Ingredient/Temperature Adjustments

CHANGE	AT 3,000 FEET	AT 5,000 FEET	AT 7,000 FEET
Baking powder or baking soda	Reduce each tsp. called for by up to 1/8 tsp.	Reduce each tsp. called for by 1/8 to 1/4 tsp.	Reduce each tsp. called for by 1/4 to 1/2 tsp.
Sugar	Reduce each cup called for by up to 1 Tbsp.	Reduce each cup called for by up to 2 Tbsp.	Reduce each cup called for by 2 to 3 Tbsp.
Liquid	Increase each cup called for by up to 2 Tbsp.	Increase each cup called for by 2 to 4 Tbsp.	Increase each cup called for by to 3 to 4 Tbsp.
Oven temperature	Increase 3°F to 5°F	Increase 15°F	Increase 21°F to 25°F

Metric Equivalents

The recipes that appear in this cookbook use the standard United States method for measuring liquid and dry or solid ingredients (teaspoons, tablespoons, and cups). The information on this chart is provided to help cooks outside the U.S. successfully use these recipes. All equivalents are approximate.

METRIC EQUIVALENTS FOR DIFFERENT TYPES OF INGREDIENTS

A standard cup measure of a dry or solid ingredient will vary in weight depending on the type of ingredient. A standard cup of liquid is the same volume for any type of liquid. Use the following chart when converting standard cup measures to grams (weight) or milliliters (volume).

Standard Cup	Fine Powder (ex. flour)	Grain (ex. rice)	Granular (ex. sugar)	Liquid Solids (ex. butter)	Liquid (ex. milk)
1	140 g	150 g	190 g	200 g	240 ml
¾	105 g	113 g	143 g	150 g	180 ml
⅔	93 g	100 g	125 g	133 g	160 ml
½	70 g	75 g	95 g	100 g	120 ml
⅓	47 g	50 g	63 g	67 g	80 ml
¼	35 g	38 g	48 g	50 g	60 ml
⅛	18 g	19 g	24 g	25 g	30 ml

USEFUL EQUIVALENTS FOR LIQUID INGREDIENTS BY VOLUME

¼ tsp.					=	1 ml
½ tsp.					=	2 ml
1 tsp.					=	5 ml
3 tsp.	=	1 Tbsp.		= ½ fl oz.	=	15 ml
		2 Tbsp.	= ⅛ cup	= 1 fl oz.	=	30 ml
		4 Tbsp.	= ¼ cup	= 2 fl oz.	=	60 ml
		5⅓ Tbsp.	= ⅓ cup	= 3 fl oz.	=	80 ml
		8 Tbsp.	= ½ cup	= 4 fl oz.	=	120 ml
		10⅔ Tbsp.	= ⅔ cup	= 5 fl oz.	=	160 ml
		12 Tbsp.	= ¾ cup	= 6 fl oz.	=	180 ml
		16 Tbsp.	= 1 cup	= 8 fl oz.	=	240 ml
		1 pt.	= 2 cups	= 16 fl oz.	=	480 ml
		1 qt.	= 4 cups	= 32 fl oz.	=	960 ml
				33 fl oz.	=	1000 ml = 1 l

USEFUL EQUIVALENTS FOR DRY INGREDIENTS BY WEIGHT

(To convert ounces to grams, multiply the number of ounces by 30.)

1 oz.	=	1/16 lb.	=	30 g
4 oz.	=	¼ lb.	=	120 g
8 oz.	=	½ lb.	=	240 g
12 oz.	=	¾ lb.	=	360 g
16 oz.	=	1 lb.	=	480 g

USEFUL EQUIVALENTS FOR LENGTH

(To convert inches to centimeters, multiply the number of inches by 2.5.)

1 in.				=	2.5 cm
6 in.	= ½ ft.			=	15 cm
12 in.	= 1 ft.			=	30 cm
36 in.	= 3 ft.	=	1 yd.	=	90 cm

USEFUL EQUIVALENTS FOR COOKING/OVEN TEMPERATURES

	Fahrenheit	Celsius	Gas Mark
Freeze Water	32°F	0°C	
Room Temperature	68°F	20°C	
Boil Water	212°F	100°C	
Bake	325°F	160°C	3
	350°F	180°C	4
	375°F	190°C	5
	400°F	200°C	6
	425°F	220°C	7
	450°F	230°C	8
Broil			Grill

Recipe Title Index

This index alphabetically lists every recipe by exact title

General Recipe Index

This index lists every recipe by food category and/or major ingredient.

DOTDASH MEREDITH CONSUMER MARKETING
Director, Direct Marketing-Books: Daniel Fagan
Marketing Operations Manager: Max Daily
Assistant Marketing Manager: Kylie Dazzo
Marketing Coordinator: Elizabeth Moore
Content Manager: Julie Doll
Senior Production Manager: Liza Ward

WATERBURY PUBLICATIONS, INC.
Editorial Director: Lisa Kingsley
Creative Director: Ken Carlson
Associate Design Director: Doug Samuelson
Contributing Copy Editor: Andrea Cooley
Contributing Proofreader: Carrie Truesdell
Contributing Indexer: Mary Williams

Recipe Developers and Testers: Dotdash Meredith Food Studios

Library of Congress Control Number: 2022933890

ISBN: 978-1-4197-6388-5

First Edition 2022
Printed in the United States of America
10 9 8 7 6 5 4 3 2 1
Call 1-800-826-4707 for more information.

Distributed in 2022 by Abrams, an imprint of ABRAMS.
Abrams® is a registered trademark of Harry N. Abrams, Inc.

ABRAMS The Art of Books
195 Broadway, New York, NY 10007
abramsbooks.com

Pictured on front cover:
Red Velvet Doberge Cake with Cheesecake Custard, page 314